A Guide to the 18th century Land Records in the Irish
Registry of Deeds

Corstown – MMXII

ISBN: 978-0-9556812-9-5
© Brian Nugent, Corstown, Oldcastle, Co. Meath, 2012-3.

CONTENTS

INTRODUCTION......6

CHAPTERS
  1. Irish 18th century Units and Land Divisions......21

  2. Legal Terms used in the Deeds......39

  3. The Historian and the Registry......53

  4. The Horizontal Problem......72

  5. The Vertical Problem......84

  6. Penal Laws......116

  7. Irish Economy and Prices in the 18th century......138

  8. Case Study of a Family History using the ROD and other sources......174

APPENDICES
  A. The Registry of Deeds Act......275
  B. A sample original Deed and its corresponding Memorial 296
  C. The Penal Laws, a 1703 speech and later account......303
  D. Folklore, a poem as an example of the use of......332
  E. 1867 debate: Registry of Deeds v. the Land Registry......355
  F. Mr Dillon's Invention of a Mechanical Index......396
  G. Hugh Maguire, Kedagh Geoghegan and Robert Nugent. 457
  H. ROD Note taking Template......511
  I. Images of the Registry......517

PREFACE

In a nutshell the Registry of Deeds is the great white hope of the over worked Irish historian of the 18th century. He is over worked because the fundamental and large collections of documents relating to that century, including for example Grand Jury papers, Irish held state papers pre c.1790 and Consistory wills, all went up in smoke in 1922 leaving the historian to chase the scraps that had been miscellaneously copied by historians or published before that date or remained in private hands.

While the effects of this destruction can sometimes be exaggerated nonetheless the presence of a completely intact collection of deeds from across Ireland from 1708 on is pretty priceless in the context of all the other gaps and omissions in the surviving papers from that century. Therefore the ROD is of very great importance but has lacked an easily accessible guide, except for some pioneering work by Margaret Falley in the 1950s, despite its significance. That is the gap this writer hopes to fill, to provide a readable guide particularly to the 18th century papers because it is with respect to that century that the other records are so lacking.

The reader should not be put off by the size of this book, it is in fact not strictly necessary to read all of it in order to understand the Registry and 18th century Irish land deeds. In particular the busy reader could skip all the appendices except the last two, H and I, and all of chapter 8 with the exception of the last section of that chapter. This obviously begs the question of why they are in the book in that event? I admit that much of Appendices D and G are a pretty blatant attempt to add colour to an otherwise potentially dry subject matter, chapter 8 I think might interest readers who would like a real world example of a family history that transcends the 17th and early 18th century gap, even if it mostly draws on other sources rather than the ROD, and if the curious reader would like to plough through all the other appendices I think such a person would emerge quite an expert on the ROD, and indeed on the competing Land Registry system in Ireland, even if that level of detail is not strictly needed.

In modern times the Registry of Deeds is indeed growing in importance especially among genealogists and one brave soul has even drawn up a volunteer program to list as many genealogical details from the ROD as possible: Nick Reddan, who has set up his scheme at:
http://freepages.genealogy.rootsweb.ancestry.com/~registryofdeeds/index.html .

One technical note must be made here. The Irish Registry of Deeds contains no deeds, as such, or at least very few, for the 18th century, only *memorials* of deeds, and this is described in the introduction. But throughout this book, along with many other commentators, I often use the word 'deeds' when it is in fact the memorials that I am referring to.

I would like to particularly thank the staff of the Registry of Deeds in Dublin for their help over the years (although this book is not in any sense an official publication of theirs) and also the following institutions for their assistance in compiling this book and other researches:
Public Record Office Northern Ireland, National Library of Ireland, National Archives of Ireland, Royal Irish Academy, UCD Library, Meath, Cavan, Westmeath and Louth County Libraries, and Gilbert Library Pearse St. Dublin. I would also like to thank the many others, both libraries and individuals, that have assisted me in this research both with books and folklore particularly in the Meath, Cavan, Westmeath and Longford areas.

Many thanks also to my parents and extended family, and to the Meath History Workshop (including Dr Danny Cusack, Joe Mooney, Brian Thornton, Dr Brian Casey, Micháel Ó Conlúin and Dr Peter Connell) for their expert knowledge on Irish estate and other land records.

INTRODUCTION

> "It has been conducted so as to secure public confidence, and any instances of errors or omissions in the certificates on the searches issued from that office whereby any individual purchaser or creditor has sustained loss or injury are unknown to us either personally or as matters of repute."
> – The Incorporated Law Society referring to the Irish Registry of Deeds in 1863 [1]

Origin of the Registry of Deeds

While some other countries have similar systems, like the Scottish *Register of Saisines*, the only counterpart to the Irish Registry of Deeds are a number of small offices in two counties in England, which are, along with their dates of creation:

Bedford Level 1663-1920 (This is in the Fens part of Eastern England where the *Bedford Level Corporation* kept Registry of Deeds style registers for those dates, now housed in the Cambridgeshire Archives in Cambridge.),

West Riding of Yorkshire, 1704-1970,

East Riding of Yorkshire (including Hull), 1708-1976,

Middlesex (most of London excluding the 'City'), 1709-1940,

North Riding of Yorkshire, 1736-1970.[2]

The Irish one, which was founded in 1708, was set up under very much the same model as these but it also seems that the powers that be in Ireland at the time were particularly interested in a registry for the purposes of policing the land transactions of Catholics as part of the Penal Laws. What the real origin of these registries is cannot be determined with great precision but it seems that, apart from the Penal Law issue, two phenomenon could be looked upon as the origin of the Registry of Deeds system in Yorkshire and then Ireland and Middlesex:

Firstly there always was a push to create a central registry for land transactions, partly no doubt to assist taxation by the centralised state, partly to assist lenders in securing their investment, and partly because some people genuinely felt that dealing in land was too complicated and cumbersome under the old system of title deeds held only by the landowner. It is said that as long ago as the 27th year of Henry VIII's reign that the state was always hoping to roll out a centralised registry – the 'great design' of the Statute of Enrolments –[3] but it had never come to pass for various political and legal reasons, as stated here for example:

> "In the middle ages, English landowners saw the need for some incontrovertible official record of land dealings and in 1536 the first bill to register land was sent to Parliament but the bill was rejected. During the next 300 years, at least 25 land bills were introduced in Parliament but were never passed." [4]

Then it seems that as you get into the late 17th century some writers swayed public opinion to get more behind this idea. Sir William Betham, a famous Irish genealogist, describing the ROD in the early 19th century claimed, for example, that it came about from pressure generated from the writings of people like Sir Matthew Hale ("...but a tract of Sir Matthew Hale, seems to have produced the English Acts of 2nd and 5th of Anne, from which ours are chiefly copied, perhaps with improved precision." (2nd Report of the *Irish Record Commission*, p.23.)). He was an influential judge in the mid 17th century who wrote the following on how such a registry should work:

> "There must be enrolled at least so much of the deed, or evidence that concerns, <u>first</u>, the parties, grantor and grantee, <u>secondly</u>, The things granted, <u>thirdly</u> the estate granted. <u>Fourthly</u> all those parts of the deed, or evidence, that have any influence upon the estate: as rent reserved, Conditions, Powers of Revocation, of Alteration, of Leasing, the Trust etc and those other things that have an influence upon the Estate; and without all this done and truly done, the Purchaser or Lender, in as much in the dark as before and cheated under the Credit of a public office erected to prevent it." [5]

Secondly, its also possible that these writers were influenced by the practice that was already current in America of using a Registry of Deeds type system. It of course suited the new colonies to register, in a public building in the county town, all the land parcels that were being allocated out for the first time. Its a lot easier to set up a registry at the beginning like this – as Sir Robert Torrens also found in Australia in the mid-19th century – and its value in helping to settle disputes must have been obvious to all. Its interesting too that these American Registry of Deeds offices seem to have started the practice of using large parchment volumes, too large to lose or get stolen easily, and to number the deeds according to their places in these manuscript volumes. Since this became the practice in the Irish and Yorkshire RODs later the suspicion is that, surprisingly, we have an example here of the UK and Ireland copying US administrative practices of the late 17th and early 18th century, the opposite to the usual case, of course, for that period.

The legislation that set up the Irish ROD was a very close copy of that which was used to set up the RODs in Yorkshire and Middlesex but it didn't evolve in the same way. A comparative study was done on these deeds and it showed that the English registries tended to only register brief memorials that included the bare minimum facts required under the legislation (i.e. the names of the lands, dates of the transactions, names and addresses of the parties and witnesses etc) but revealing very little of the thrust of the underlying deed. The Irish registry on the otherhand evolved in such a way that many memorials – which we will come to in a minute –, the vast majority, will describe the salient facts of the underlying deed and hence are of great value to the historian who now lacks the original deeds:

> "The Irish memorials are much more detailed than those in England. There was no legislative reason for this, for the clauses in the various acts which specified the details to be contained in memorials were identical." [6]

It seems then that the Irish Registry of Deeds stands alone as giving us such a great picture of land transfers over the course of the 18th century and right up today.

Steps needed to Register a Deed

With no further ado we will now describe exactly how the system operated in the 18th century and indeed, with some changes, still operates today. Taking each stage in turn:

1. Obviously we have the underlying land transaction that takes place. The pattern of Irish land transactions remained very similar throughout the 16th and 17th centuries and up to the 18th. One difference, that may be mentioned in passing, is that the Irish Tudor transactions tend to heavily use a trust system known as a feoff, or a 'use', which meant that technically a lot of Irish land was held by trustees, 'feoffees', who then managed trusts for the benefit, the 'use', of the person who really owned the land. By the time you get to the 18th century this trustee like system is much less in evidence but does come in somewhat with some of the marriage settlements later on in the century.

In any case to get us on our way we may make up a fictional land transaction. James Plunkett, the owner of 100 acres in Kilskyre Co. Meath, concludes a bargain in 1734, we will say, with John Reilly of Ballinlough whereby Plunkett leases to Reilly those 100 acres for 30 years at a yearly rent of £50. They then draw up the usual document that was in use all the way through from deepest antiquity, an indented deed. They will write the agreement in duplicate on a single sheet of parchment, its in duplicate because they write one text of the deal on the top of the parchment and the same text they will right at the bottom of it. Then they cut the parchment across in the middle, forming a jagged line. Then each of the two sections will be formally signed, sealed and dated by the two parties and also by, probably two, independent witnesses.

2. Now the question arises is do these two parties want to get the deed registered? The original act setting up the Registry of Deeds (ROD) did talk about deeds that were not registered being null and void, which obviously compelled landowners to register

their deeds, but in fact a number of court cases in the early 18th century determined that it wasn't compulsory. (For a description of the legal precedents that effectively nullified the concept that deeds *must* be registered in the ROD you should consult Robert Molesworth, *An essay upon the law regarding registration* (Dublin, 1838)). So James Plunkett and John Reilly may or may not decide to register their deed, and it has been determined that only approximately 13% of Irish deeds of the period were registered in the ROD.[7]

3. Nonetheless, unsurprisingly perhaps (!), we will assume they register it. The procedure then is that probably a solicitor, or a 'conveyancer' to use 18th century parlance, will prepare a 'memorial' of the deed based on various criteria outlined in the act setting up the ROD. (Incidentally you can read this act in Appendix A infra and Appendix B gives you a real example of a deed and its corresponding memorial.) This 'memorial' is basically a summary of the deed, its a document that hopes to capture all the essentials of the deed but without the huge amount of legalese that you get in original Irish land deeds.

That is the idea but actually the act is quite specific is setting out various pieces of information that must be included in the memorial (as pointed out above, again the names, addresses and occupations of the parties and witnesses, and the exact lands transacted and the monies that are transferred) and it really depends on the solicitor as to whether or not the memorial ends up as a good summary of the contents or not. So to clarify again, because this might not be perfectly clear, as far as the ROD is concerned the memorial must contain all those facts specified in the Act, and they will not agree to register a memorial that doesn't contain those facts that are in the deed and are specified in the Act, but whether or not the memorial is genuinely informative about the nature of the transaction really comes down to the solicitor and the parties making the deed, for this kind of descriptive information the ROD has no opinion as to whether it should be included or not in the memorial.[8] Hence in practice the memorials come in all shapes and sizes, some not very informative, some maybe as long and as informative as the deed itself or even longer as the memorial in Appendix B is, but it will always contain these statutory requirements that the act, and therefore the ROD, insist on. An example of the kind of fact in the deed that is not mentioned in legislation, and hence is not always in the memorial, would be the names of the 'three lives' – which is described in more detail later on in this book – on a lease. The vast majority of memorials of deeds of three life leases will name those three lives but its not a legal requirement so actually some don't name them.[9]

Another point to bear in mind is that the memorial is very much a legal document and in court will suffice as proof of the existence of a deed and the transaction contained therein. Hence the memorial will be signed and witnessed, just like the deed, and one of those witnesses to the memorial will also have signed the original deed and hence can swear as to the existence of the original deed. In fact as the century wore on the ROD memorials frequently became quasi title deeds in the sense that they could be used instead of those deeds if they became lost through fire or theft etc:

> "In England the known and accepted gauge of unencumbered ownership is the possession of the title deeds, but in Ireland the known and accepted gauge is the clear negative search at the Registry."[10]

To clarify what title deeds actually are, in case the reader is confused on the subject: These are supposed to be a succession of leases or wills or settlements that cascade down the years from a time when the crown might have given the lands away, via Letters Patent for example, to the present and which will show how the bearer of the deeds came to own the land. In the Irish context if you wish to see examples of these kind of title deeds you can see a lot of them in the catalogue of the deeds in the possession of the Irish Land Commission, housed in the National Library of Ireland. But many of these became lost or stolen in Ireland and so it evolved that a memorial registered in the ROD, along with a negative search of the lands in the ROD, will suffice in lieu of title deeds. By 'negative search' we mean that there is no other entry in the ROD which, if you like, contradicts the original ROD memorial that states that you, or whoever, own the land. At any rate these memorials became very important and were used extensively in Irish courts to prove ownership over land.

4. The solicitor will have left place on the memorial for the signature of the Registrar or whoever will register the memorial for him in the ROD. So the solicitor or his clerk will now travel to the ROD, located in Dublin Castle for much of the 18th century, and seek to get it registered. He will present the memorial that he has prepared and the original deed and the ROD will then determine if the memorial meets the legal requirements as regards recording properly a given set of facts that are in the deed. If they agree to register it they will swear the witnesses to the memorial, that it is an accurate memorial etc, and will give the memorial a number.

5. The next step is that the ROD will transcribe, copy, the full text of the memorial into large parchment volumes called transcript books, books that are available for public inspection to this day. (Actually the staff have nicknamed them tombstones, because they are so heavy and contain 'memorials'!) They will then note the volume number of the book they have transcribed it into, the page in that volume and the number of the memorial and they will write those three numbers down onto the back of the original deed that they still have in their possession. They will then send back the original deed to the solicitor and will file away the original memorial in the vaults under the ROD.

6. After that we get the indexing. The ROD will immediately seek to include the deed into a names index of the grantors of all the deeds whose memorials are registered in the ROD. Although, as far as I am aware, the grantees of leases are never indexed as such nonetheless many deeds will have multiple parties mentioned in them and the ROD will generally err on the side of indexing all of those parties, which could be three or four for each deed but might just be one. This Names Index, which the public can inspect, was kept up quickly and up to date but there is also a Lands Index. Here the ROD drew up an index divided up into

counties and then into the first letter of each townland, which allows you to search for memorials via the lands mentioned in them. This however proved very time consuming so it appears that the Lands Index was usually a little bit in arrears while the Names Index was always up to date i.e. the Names Index, or one version of it at any rate, might have been indexed up to each day but the Lands Index was probably not updated until a few months, at least, had elapsed. This is the basic picture but the indexing in reality was a little more complex than that, you have 'consolidated indexes' which were draw up at intervals such as every five years etc. The indexes of course will work on the three numbers that are mentioned earlier, it refers to the memorials via the book and page number of the transcript books with the last number being the number of the memorial.

And that is it as far as the historian now is concerned. Those transcript books and indexes are now available for you to see if you go to the Registry of Deeds in Dublin today and a great treasure trove of history they are too. The original memorials, incidentally, are still contained in those vaults and to inspect them you have to pay a fee of 20 euro and the ROD will send you a copy of it.

The Three documents prepared for each deed in the 18th century, and four post 1833

To clarify then there are three documents involved in this chain (and I include below another type of document which arose in the ROD post 1833) and to aid the conscientious historian it might help to clarify exactly what type of information is available in each:

a) *The original deed.* For the 18th century you will probably work under the assumption that the underlying original deed is now lost, although there are some in the main research libraries in Ireland and further afield such as the National Library, the National Archives and the Public Record Office Northern Ireland.

Most of the time the memorial will probably contain nearly all the relevant historical data that the original deed had, although this in truth is not so easy to be precise about because we have lost so many of these original deeds. But two things will strike you as being present in the originals which are not in the memorials:

– The signatures and seals of the parties to the deed. Obviously a manuscript copy of the deed cannot accurately copy out the signatures which is a pity because sometimes you can trace people through their signatures, as indeed you can sometimes with seals.

– Maps that are affixed to these original deeds describing the lands that are traded therein. Although most deeds don't have those maps, many nonetheless do, very roughly you could say 1 in every 15, and of course that would be of great interest to an historian. The presence of these maps is usually mentioned by the memorial but, unfortunately, the large transcript volumes of memorials never contain any maps nor are they contained in the original memorials held in the vaults. It seems you will normally have to try and track down the original deeds themselves, if they are in existence, if you want to see these maps.

b) The *original memorial* which was prepared by the solicitor for the parties and which is now in the vaults of the ROD. Although these are in existence they are not normally easily accessible, except by paying that fee as described. The large transcript books contain an exact, although there can be some errors on occasion, full copy of the text in these original memorials and so there is usually no need to check the originals. However there maybe a few issues here:

– The question of errors in the transcription, which is not a big issue most of the time. It probably isn't worth your while trying to see the original in the off chance that there is some error in the copy in the transcript books.

– Gaps in the transcript books that may be filled by looking at the originals. We are not talking here about gaps in the memorial itself as you read it, they are normally in good condition and the full text of a memorial is there if any of it is there. We are also not referring here to gaps in the transcript volumes themselves, they have stood the test of time very well and generally there are no missing pages etc. What isn't unheard of though is a reference to a memorial in the indexes which doesn't seem to have made it at all into the transcript books, in otherwords you cannot find the memorial although you are absolutely sure of your book-volume-memorial number. It seems possible that it might be worthwhile trying to see if the original memorial in some of these cases is there, although you will need to be confident of your reading of the indexes because for the novice user it is much more likely that you have taken the numbers down wrong from the index! (As a general rule there tends to be more errors in the page numbers of the volumes than in the other numbers, especially towards the end of the 18th century, so you should always see if you can find the memorial by using the memorial number alone, which are transcribed in sequence into the volumes, if you cannot find it the normal way.)

– The same issue arises as above with respect to signatures and seals. Again the manuscript copy of the memorial in the transcript books cannot reproduce the exact signature of course and yet it could be interesting to see the signature sometimes. To clarify, what we are talking about here are signatures that are in the memorial, i.e. the witnesses to the memorial, not, necessarily, the witnesses to the deed itself because for that we would need the original deed not the original memorial. One example where it could be useful to see the signature, it seems to this observer, is in respect to the Dublin addresses. Its very frustrating the number of people who only describe themselves in the deeds as 'Pat Murphy, Dublin City' so it would be interesting to track the signatures, if you could, to figure out if it is the same 'Pat Murphy, Dublin City' that you may have read in another memorial.

The same goes for seals, it may help to identify people like the above Pat Murphy but the seals are not likely to be as helpful as the signatures. The reason for this is that many, the vast majority probably, of seals used, especially as we get into the later 18th and early 19th century, will be standard and common non identifying seals. There might be exceptions to that though where looking at the seal could be useful.

c) The *copy of the memorial* which is contained in the large transcript books in the ROD. This is the document that you are probably going to be working on and is available for public inspection if you go into the ROD and is incidentally also available in some large research libraries as a set of microfilms. A catalogue of some of these microfilms was prepared by Margaret Falley and contained in her book, *Irish and Scotch-Irish ancestral research* (Evanston, Illinois, 1962), i, p.51-106.

d) For the sake of completion I will add here the '*abstract*' which began to be compiled in the ROD in the early 19th century and which therefore is not available for the 18th century deeds. The idea behind this was that the ROD themselves would look over the memorials and draw up a small, maybe just a few lines, abstract of the memorial which would help future users to grasp the essentials of the document without needing to see the full memorial. It also uses helpful headings like 'marriage settlement' which can help you to zone in on the document you want quite quickly, and they are also contained in handy small volumes easily consulted, unlike the very large transcript books.

These are therefore the three or four documents, with their different quirks, that you need to think of in the context of the ROD. Of course in practice for the vast majority of uses it isn't going to be worth your while chasing up any document other than the publicly available transcript, for the 18th century, trying to trace seals or signatures would in nearly all cases not be worth the trouble, or expense, involved.

Old Handwriting of the Deeds

One obvious point should however be uppermost in an introduction to the Irish Registry of Deeds for the 18th century and that is that it is very much an original handwritten archive for that century, which means that you need to have some knowledge of reading 18th century documents to have any hope of understanding these records. This is not beyond anybody though, with a bit of practice. Some obvious things you need to know include:

– In this century an *'s'* is sometimes written like an 'f' but without the cross stroke in the middle, and this will be true of printed books as well. It might even look a little like a slash running vertically down the line of text, a bit like a large, but not capital, 'l'.

– The *numbers* look the same as modern times but watch out for the '8', sometimes it can appear like a modern printed zero with a diagonal dash through the centre, a little bit like this: Ø.

– *Abbreviations* are very common in these deeds and a few points will help you here. The normal rule is that if a cross stroke appears above a word (this stroke will seem a bit like an Irish 'fada' but perfectly horizontal) then it means that there are letters missing inside the word, i.e. letters that are left out in the abbreviation. So for example if you read the word 'als' and there was a horizontal stroke over it, which might in this case cross the 'l', then it means there are letters missing that you should guess and in this case we can assume it means 'alias', having left out the 'ia'.

Yes that is exactly what you do, you just guess the letters that are missing, whatever word would seem to fit the context is probably the right word. Which means of course that a knowledge of 18th century terminology, including legal terminology, is pretty essential although you should be able to pick it up as time goes on.

More common than the stroke across the top of the word is the idea of writing letters in superscript at the end of the word that has been abbreviated. So for example consider the modern 'M^r' Murphy or 'M^{rs}' Smith, written like that with the 'r' and 'rs' super scripted. Well when you read that of course you will guess it means Mister and Missus, i.e. you will guess the missing letters in 'M^r' to be 'iste'. That is what a lot of the words in the ROD look like. For example you will get "Ja^s Murphy" and you can guess that to mean 'James Murphy' etc etc. When you realise that all you have to do is fill out the abbreviation you shouldn't find it too difficult, remember they aren't going to abbreviate townland names or surnames because the ROD will always wish to be properly accurate. Also the handwriting itself is large and in good condition in these parchment volumes, its not the rushed micro handwriting that you sometimes get for the 19th century. The Lands Index is sometimes more of a challenge depending on how cramped it is. There are so many 'Bally..." type townlands that they seemed to cram the words into the edge of the volume on occasion!

– *Punctuation* is not common and also the words themselves frequently will run into one another, you can find it difficult to find the space between words but you will get better at it after a while.

– '*Ditto*' is usually abbreviated to 'do' and means that the word directly above this one in the text is to be substituted for the 'ditto'.

– 'see fur.', 'see further', and 'alp. bef.', 'alphabetted before', are also abbreviations used.

– There are a few phrases or words of *Latin* used, like 'liber' for 'book', but not as much as would cause any real trouble I don't think. Irish, by the way, is strictly never seen in any of the deeds despite such a large proportion of the population speaking it in the 18th century.

As well as the handwriting you will need to know the different units, land and money etc, used throughout the records and also some grasp of the legal terms, and these issues are teased out in the next two chapters.

Footnotes
1. Joseph Maguire, *Land Transfer, Registration of Deeds and Title*, read 17th Feb 1922 and published in the *Journal of the Statistical and Social Inquiry Society of Ireland*, vol XIV, p.161.

2. You can see here that the Yorkshire system was very like the Irish one:
"From 1708 to 1884 a memorial (abbreviated copy) of the original deed was written on vellum or parchment under the hand or seal of one of the grantors or grantees or devisees. It was then attested by two witnesses, one of whom was a witness to the execution of the deed. The memorial and the original deed were both taken to the Registrar or his deputy and proved upon oath. Date, time and

details of registration were endorsed on the original deed before it was returned. The memorial was then retained and its details copied into paper registers.

The amount of information in each memorial was carefully specified. The precise date of the original deed or will, the names of all parties and witnesses, and their abode, and details of the property involved were to be recorded."

One difference though is that the Yorkshire registry used letters for volume names whereas from the beginning the Irish registry always used the three numbers: volume, page and memorial number.

("Yorkshire East Riding Registry of Deeds" founded in 1708 at http://www.eyfhs.org.uk/content/resources/treasurehouse/register_of_deeds.pdf .)

In the index to the published London *House of Commons Journals* of the 18th century are listed 'Petitions for Bills for the Public Registry of all Deeds, Conveyances' etc...and mentions:

"Derbyshire, Dropped after the first reading;

Northumberland, Not brought in;

Surrey, Dropped after third reading;

Yorkshire, North Riding of, Negative to bringing it up."

This shows how the drive to set up RODs in England petered out with the exceptions only of Yorkshire and Middlesex.

3. Sir Matthew Hale, *A Treatise Showing how Useful, safe, reasonable and beneficial, the inrolling and registering of all conveyances of lands, may be to the inhabitants of this kingdom, by a person of great learning and judgement* (London, 1694), p.15.

4. http://www.alanmann.com/class/files/Yorkshire%20Registry%20of%20Deeds.htm .

5. Sir Matthew Hale, *A Treatise Showing how Useful, safe, reasonable and beneficial, the inrolling and registering of all conveyances of lands, may be to the inhabitants of this kingdom, by a person of great learning and judgement* (London, 1694), p.7.

6. Peter Roebuck, *The Irish Registry of Deeds: A Comparative Study*, published in, *Irish Historical Studies*, vol.18 no.69 (March 1972), p.61 and 66.

7. Judith Eccles Wright, *Estate Records*, in, *Ancestry Magazine*, Jan-Feb 1996, p.19.

8. Examples of what seem to be memorials which contain, maybe accidentally, the full text of the underlying deed can be seen at: 1776 314-30-209125 and 1791 448-199-286951.

9. For example the names of the lives in this deed are referred to in the

memorial only as "therein mentioned" in the deed, so now we will probably never know what the lives were: 1787 389-219-256045.

10. P.P. Phair, *Guide to the Registry of Deeds*, Analecta Hibernica (1966) no.23, p.261.

A few other important points that my predecessor in writing about the Irish ROD makes:

Under the Act leases under 21 years, "with possession", were not to be registered but in practice were (p.260).

A few abstract books for 1708-1717 were compiled after the 1833 act and are now placed in the vault behind the enquiry room (p.262).

The Location of the ROD:
1708-1805, firstly a private house and then the Lower Castle Yard of Dublin Castle,
1805-1831, Inns Quay near the Four Courts,
1831- , present location (p.260).

CHAPTER 1
Irish 18th century Units and Land Divisions

Territorial Irish Land Divisions

The normal land divisions of Ireland are very distinctive and almost as true for today as much as they were in the 18th century, and these are in ascending order of size:

Townland
Of course there are some differences in townlands between the great 17th century surveys (Civil and Down) and the Ordnance Survey, Griffith's, and Tithe Applotment lists of the early and mid 19th centuries but the overall pattern remained remarkably the same.

There are however a lot of miscellaneous names for land that are not official townland names in either of those two lists and these names occur a lot in the deeds. Sometimes they are old Irish names for places that for some reason never made it into the maps of Petty etc e.g. if you study the 1609 maps for Cavan you can see a lot of placenames that are not carried over into the 17th century surveys but are nonetheless still in use in the 18th century, as can be seen in the old Catholic Registers and these Memorials e.g. 'Rootagh' and 'Legawoge' which are in the environs of Barcony in the extreme south of Co Cavan but are not official townland names. Sometimes these are new 'fancy' names that were given to patches of land in the 18th century, e.g. 'Bobsgrove' or 'Mountprospect', some of which in turn died out before the Ordnance Survey arrived, such as Hawksfield, an 18th century name for Baltrasna in Co.Meath, and some of which made it into the modern townland names, like 'Mountprospect'. Where the latter occurs it obviously gives rise to the question of what original name is being supplanted by the new 18th century one. Luckily these Memorials, and even the Lands Index itself, are generally quite informative on the subject and will frequently say something like 'Bobsgrove otherwise Farrenconnell' to assist the reader.

Civil Parish

Not quite the same as the current religious parishes, they are usually smaller units which can be easily seen in the Civil Survey and then in the 19th century records. Sometimes the Memorials specify the Parish but not nearly as frequently as they do the Barony.

Barony

For some reason this is the standard territorial division – alongwith the County – recognised by the Registry of Deeds in the 18th century. Most of the lands mentioned will state which Barony they are in and the early Lands Indexes will also list the Barony name beside the placename. (Gradually, post 1750, the Lands Index becomes less exact that way.)

County

Virtually all the lands mentioned in the deeds will state which county they are in and of course, similar to the Baronies, the County structure in Ireland is almost the same now as it was in the 18th century. Remember though that 'King's County' is modern day Offaly and 'Queen's County' is Laois.

Province

Obviously Leinster, Ulster, Connaught and Munster, which are sometimes referred to in the Deeds.

Some other territorial placenames are mentioned as well which do not have a distinct place in the above structure. Manors, which are very old Mediaeval placenames, are sometimes referred to, often in the deeds registered by surviving members of the old Norman aristocracy. Old Plunkett deeds for example refer to the 'Manor of Carrick' and the 'Manor of Munterconnaught' in South Cavan and these areas are hard to place in the normal Civil Parish / Barony structure although the Books of Survey and Distribution will sometimes indicate the extent of these Manors. A phrase 'the lands of', e.g. 'the lands of Rathaspick' etc, can sometimes be used to indicate some townlands, or parts of townlands, that normally go together and have been a distinct estate for a particular family for some time. This though is just an informal distinction and again is not something that can be traced easily in the established Civil Parish / Barony structure but might be identified by going back over old deeds transacted by the same family.

Then there are a number of different land divisions that emerged in the 19th century. In particular in 1838 came the Poor Law Union, an area that surrounded a workhouse for the relief of the poor and which demarcated the area where the local taxes were raised to pay for the workhouse. It is this area that Griffith's Valuation mapped and surveyed to determine the rates to be paid on the land to the individual Poor Law Unions. These areas generally 'doughnut' – as it were – the town where the workhouse was located and do not respect at all the old Barony or even County structures, but do respect the townland boundaries. In order to facilitate the electing of guardians to the Poor Law Unions the latter areas were subdivided into District Electoral Divisions (DEDs) which are the essential units used in modern Irish elections but again are poor reflections of the 18th century land structures.

The late John Broderick drew up a very useful online database of all Irish townlands which you can search here: http://www.seanruad.com/ . A successful search for a townland will return information as to what Civil Parish, Barony, County and Poor Law Union the townland is in.

Normal Irish Land Area Units

In standard English area measurements – known in Ireland as 'statute' measure – you have:
- 1 perch = 16.5 X 16.5 square feet
- 1 rood = 40 perches
- 1 acre = 4 roods

These are written in a similar way to pounds/shilling/pence in the form e.g. 'in Ballytullagh 12 acres 6 roods and 10 perches', or using 'a', 'r' and 'p' for the respective terms.

However in Ireland the standard measurements are:

1 perch = 21 X 21 square feet
1 rood = 40 perches
1 acre = 4 roods

Hence there is 70,560 square feet in an Irish, or 'plantation', acre, while there is 43,560 in an English, or 'statute', acre. Officially then we can write the acreage as:

1 English/Statute Acre = 0.617347 Irish/Plantation Acre
1 Acre Irish/Plantation = 1.619835 English/Statute Acre

This difference also extended to longitudinal, not just area, land measures so "the Irish perch or pole is 7 yards, and that of England only 5½." Hence we are told, by a traveller in 1775, that "11 Irish miles are exactly equal to 14 English".

But in fact acreage could be more complicated again, this is a quote from Capt Thomas Larcom of the Ordnance Survey writing in 1846:

> "The acres were by estimation only, and differed considerably. The origin of this measure (the acre) would lead me far beyond the present subject; but, for example, there were in times comparatively recent, the "large acre" and the "small acre", with no fixed ratio between them; and even now the acre differs: the Cunningham acre [this acre, used only in East Ulster, is a different measurement again with 1 Acre Cunningham = 1.291322 Statute]; the plantation [i.e. 'Irish'] and statute acre. The areas of the Ordnance Survey are all in statute acres." [1]

This kind of confusion, or flexibility, in actual land area corresponding to the acreage must be allowed for at all times e.g. one part of the lands of Russagh in Co Westmeath was always known as 'the twelve acres' but when surveyed c.1771 it was found to contain 43 acres.[2]

Sometimes the Memorials will specifically mention the 'profitable' and 'unprofitable' acreage which is a reference to the distinction made in the Books of Survey and Distribution which detail the land confiscations of the Cromwellian Period. Typically the new English Protestant owner only took possession of the 'profitable' land which is some cases meant that the original Irish

Catholic owner had retained ownership of the bogs and mountains etc.

Archaic Irish Land Units

The various other official English land units, like furlongs or square miles, are not very common at all in these deeds but archaic, and sometimes regional, Irish land measures are in fact quite frequently met with. Larcom himself drew up this list:

10 acres	= 1 Gneeve;
2 Gneeves	= 1 Sessiagh;
3 Sessiaghs	= 1 Tate or Ballyboe;
2 Ballyboes	= 1 Ploughland, Seisreagh or Carrow [i.e. a 'quarter'];
4 Ploughlands	= 1 Ballybetagh, or Townland;
30 Ballybetaghs	= Triocha Céad or Barony. [3]

Quarter or 'Carrow'

Some of these land distinctions are pretty rare in the deeds – except of course as townland names – but a 'quarter' is often mentioned, which is the English translation of the Irish 'Ceathramhadh' meaning a quarter of a townland, as described here by Patrick Weston Joyce in *Irish Names of Places* (Dublin, 1869) vol1, p.245-246:

> "Ceathramhadh [carhoo or carrow] signifies a quarter, from ceathair [cahir] four. The old townlands or ballybetaghs, were very often divided into quarters, each of which was commonly designated by this word ceathramhadh, which, in the present names generally takes one of the two forms carrow, and carhoo; the former being the more usual, but the latter occurring very often in Cork and Kerry. Carrow forms or begins the names of more than 700 townlands, and Carhoo of about 30; and another form, Carrive, occurs in some of the northern counties.
>
> The four quarters into which the townland was

divided were generally distinguished from one another by adjectives descriptive of size, position, shape, or quality of the land, or by suffixing the names of the occupiers. Thus, there are more than 60 modern townlands called Carrowkeel, Ceathramhadh-cael, narrow quarter; Carrowgarriff and Carrowgarve, rough (garbh) quarter, is the name of sixteen; there are 25 called Carrowbane and Carrowbaun, white quarter; 24 called Carrowbeg, little quarter; and more than 60 called Carrowmore, great quarter. Lecarrow, halfquarter, gives name to about 60 townlands, the greater number of them in Connaught."

Cartron

Joyce also describes the 'cartron', again a common term met in these deeds and which, confusingly, also means a quarter although it has a different etymology (but probably it just derives from the Normans translating the Gaelic 'carrow' into Norman French):

"Cartron signifies a quarter, and is derived through the French quarteron from the mediaeval Lat. quarteronus; it was in very common use in Connaught as well as in Longford, Westmeath, and King's County; and it was applied to a parcel of land varying in amount from 60 to 160 acres."

Poll, Pottle and Gallon

With respect to these terms which seem to be unique to Cavan, or at least rare elsewhere, there is this reference from the contemporary documents of the Ulster Plantation:

"The County of Cavan, commonly called O'Reylie's Country, is divided into Small Precincts [Parcels] of Land called Polls, every Poll containing 24 Acres by the Survey; whereof there are found in this County 1,620, which doth make 40,500 Acres. These Polls after the Division formerly used, will make 32 Proportions, viz., of the least 20, of the middle 7, and of the greatest 5; and every of these proportions may be a parish, with Glebes and tithes to the Incumbent as in Tyrone." [4]

Further clarification was provided by Dr Reeves, in the long quote given below, and he also drew attention to the peculiar etymology of these words:

"The *Tate* or *Tathe* of Fermanagh and Monaghan, together with the *Poll*, the *Gallon*, the *Pottle*, and the *Pint* of Cavan, are all English terms, introduced by some unknown influence. To find names of liquid measure applied to land is strange; and still more so when it is remembered that they are English, and in such an un-English quarter as East Breffny. They had all become naturalised long before 1600, for we find, soon after that date, townland names into which these words enter in combination with Irish terms of qualification." [5]

Personally I think the origin of this in Cavan could be the amount of land that produces a given quantity of cow's milk, i.e. a gallon or pint, etc. I say that because at least part of the ancient tithes of Cavan were specified as a given rate per milch cow. (The tithes of course are ancient monies due to the church, the Established, Church of Ireland, Church after the Reformation. They actually can have very peculiar and ancient origins, for example the tithes of Cavan seem to be partially based on ancient dues owed to the monastery of Fore, and in fact they are property rights which may have gone to some aristocratic families after the Reformation, not necessarily to the church at all. Most of the tithes of Cavan throughout the post-Plantation 17th century, and into the 19th century, were actually paid to the frequently Catholic Earls of Westmeath, much to the chagrin of the Church of Ireland Bishops of Kilmore!)

Tate

Meanwhile with respect to Fermanagh the 1608 surveyors also clarify the local land measurement:

"The County of Fermanagh, commonly called MacGwyer's Country is divided into small Precincts called Tathes, every Tathe containing by estimation 30 acres, or thereabouts, as it is found by the Survey, and doth contain 1,070 Tathes, or 33,437.5 acres, besides 46 islands, some of greater and some of lesser quantity; but what number of acres the said islands do contain is not setdown in the survey, because the country did not present the same." [6]

We are again indebted to Dr Reeves for some further details on this:

"Monaghan and Fermanagh, two contiguous counties, which have the lowest average, thereby denoting the minutest sub-division, were found at the close of the sixteenth century to consist of a certain number of ballybetaghs [townlands], each of which contained four quarters, and each quarter four tates – that is, in each ballybetagh 16 tates – a name peculiar to these two territories, the patrimonies respectively of MacMahon and Maguire. The tate was estimated at 60 acres native, and a sixteenth, instead of the more usual twelfth, was the unit; and this, continuing in local use, afterwards came to be stereotyped in these parts as a townland in the Ordnance Survey." [7]

Ploughland, Carucate, Carewe, Balliboes, Martland and others

This long quote from Dr Reeves will have to suffice for some of the other, of the numerous, archaic Irish land units. It might seem reading this that there is a lot of contradiction in the various units across the different counties but this may be more apparent than real. The real difference is that the surveyors of the various counties treated the separate divisions differently: in some cases the old Irish ballybetagh becomes the townland leaving the 'quarters' as just that, a quarter of the townland. In other cases the surveyors made townlands out of the 'quarters', hence it confuses the older land measurement. Also don't forget that our idea of a static universal area based land measure is not what we are referring to here. It is probably mostly based on the agricultural value of the land in ancient times. Hence a given area, say 200 acres, of good Meath land may be worth, agriculturally, a whole mountain of Mayo bogland, so in the Irish units you will have a townland made of each, which in area size will mean that the Meath townland is much smaller than the Mayo one.

"The Tate was estimated at sixty acres, and a sixteenth was the unit; and this came to be distinguished as a townland.

In Cavan the first division was the ballibet, identical with the ballybetagh of other parts; of this the proximate species was the poll or pole, sixteen of which constituted the ballybet. Each poll contained two gallons, each gallon two pottles, descending even to a subdivision called pints.

In Down the prevailing denomination was the ballyboe or cowland, sometimes called the carewe, from the Latin *carucata* or plowland, which has been estimated at sixty acres; three of these formed the quarterland, and twelve the ballybetagh; sometimes a smaller division was in use called the sessiagh.

In Antrim the townland, latinized *villa* and *villata*, was the prevailing denomination at the commencement of the seventeenth century: the higher division was, as in Down, the quarterland, that is, the conventional quarter of the ancient ballybetagh. Here as elsewhere the original name of the quarterland was often lost, while the specific ones were retained, or the generic name was given in exchange to a principal component part. In Antrim we have still the traditional aggregation in the "four towns" of Ahoghill, the "eight towns" of Muckamore, and the "sixteen towns" of Antrim.

The divisions in Donegal were ballybetaghs, descending to quarters, ballyboes, and sessiaghs, of which the ballyboe, with the occasional sessiaghs, was the denomination which eventually merged in the general townland.

In Londonderry it was found by inquisition that thirteen ballyboes were equivalent to the ballybetagh. In Armagh the prevailing denomination was the "ballyboe or town," which contained three sessiaghs; in several instances we meet with proportions of ten ballyboes in this county, which were estimated at 1,000 acres, that is 100 acres, with their appurtenances, to the ballyboe.

In Tyrone as in Armagh, the ballyboe or townland was the prevailing denomination, and contained three "sheshawghes" or sessiaghs; it had besides a compound denomination called *tullagh*, consisting of a ballyboe and a sessiagh, that is, a townland and a third.

The popular division of Longford was the cartron, which was estimated at from 60 to 160 acres; four of these made a quarter or ploughland. The cartron is represented by the modern "townland."

In Louth the carucate or carewe, of which 120, sometimes 60 acres, were the prevailing contents.

Meath had the plowland, and under it the carucate and townland.

In the direction of Cavan we find the poll.

Westmeath had the cartron and carucate. An inquisition finds three carucates to consist of 360 acres, or 120 acres each. We also meet "a half carucate," otherwise a "half plowland."

The county of Dublin was considerably subdivided. The prevailing denomination was the plowland or townland.

Kildare was similarly distributed.

Wicklow had villae, villatae, hamlets, lands, and cowlands, or ballyboes.

The divisions of Carlow were mart-lands or beef-lands, and fractional parts, also penny-lands; the half and quarter mart-lands are now represented by the townlands.

Thus, too, in Wexford besides quarters, carucates, and plowlands, we find an inquisition which sets out the barony of Ballaghkene as containing thirteen mart-lands.

In Kilkenny, also, we find the carucate and mart-land; it had besides a denomination called capelllands, three of which made a plowland, and a subdivision called a horse's-bed or horseman's-bed, containing twenty or thirty acres.

King's County [Offaly] had the carucate and cartron.

The English of Waterford reckoned by plowlands; the native Irish by mart-lands and the subdenomination, horsemen's-beds.

Tipperary had capell-lands of about 400 acres, English measure, each capell-land containing four quarter-meers. Limerick reckoned by quarters, each divisible into four quarter-meers; it had also a subdenomination called a gnieve.

In Cork we find the plowland Latinized carucata, and the gneeve a subdenomination. In Kerry the divisions were quarters and plowlands as one to three, each plowland estimated at 120 acres. In Connaught the prevailing distribution was into townlands of vague import; quarters, the fourth part of the former; cartron, the fourth of a quarter; gneeve, the sixth of a quarter. The cartron was computed at thirty native acres." [8]

Dates

Most European countries used the Gregorian Calendar during the 18th century but Britain and Ireland, and the former's empire, reverted to that calendar only in 1752. Officially then there are two things you need to note about dates prior to 1752, as well as the simple fact that continental dates were different to British and Irish ones from 1582-1752:

a) An Act of Parliament was passed which decreed that at midnight on Wednesday the 2nd of September 1752 the following day was to be known as Thursday the 14th of September 1752. Dates which refer to the pre 1752 era and are not adjusted for this change are known as Old Style (OS) dates and those which have been adjusted are known as New Style (NS). Unless you are trying to calculate the exact date of some astronomical event the chances are you don't need to worry about this too much and it is not normal to bother adjusting these dates. But some deeds that occur just around the changeover in 1752 do sometimes specify that the date is New Style or Old Style.

b) Also the Act specified that the 31st of December 1751 was to be followed by the 1st of January 1752. This might not seem an earth shattering piece of data except that prior to that date the New Year changed over during the night between the 24th and 25th days of March which gives you Lady Day, the Feast of the Annunciation of the Blessed Virgin on the 25th, as the old New Year's day. Unlike the other change this one can make a difference that historians need to be aware of. It is quite common that if the date on the original document is prior to 1752 and falls between the 1st of January and the 24th of March inclusive, then historians sometimes will silently adjust the date forward one year. So hence you can read a deed that writes "13th February 1721" and some historians will write that as "13th February 1722", silently adjusting the year, or, as is quite common, an historian might write it as "13th February 1721/22" to show that they have adjusted the date. Its also quite common for historians to just leave the date exactly as seen in the original document – as this writer does – but then also to write a note to that effect somewhere in the preface to their work in case it causes confusion.

Although not related to this changeover it is of course also the case that Acts passed during the 18th century in Ireland will be dated by the regal year of the reigning British monarch rather than

by our normal AD dating system. Here is a handy website where you can input say '3rd year of George III' and it will tell you it is '1729':
http://people.albion.edu/imacinnes/calendar//Regnal_Years.html . The dates on the deeds themselves are AD dates but of course sometimes they might refer to these regal dates, for various reasons, inside the deed.

Units of Money

The old English units for money are of course used throughout these deeds and they are obviously pounds, shillings and pence, sometimes abbreviated as £, s and d (note that a penny is not marked with a 'p', the 'd' actually derives from the Greek drachma). There was 12 pence (d) in a shilling and 20 shillings (s) in a pound (£) which in turn means that there was 240 pence in a pound.

However since the successful Irish devaluation of 1460 the normal Irish policy was always to have a separate and usually lower currency rate with England and this fruitful difference, to Ireland anyway!, lasted, in some shape or form, until 1826. So that from 1701 until the abolition of the Irish currency at the beginning of 1826 the Irish pound was pegged to sterling at the rate of 13 pence Irish = 1 British shilling (since the British shilling was also worth 12 British pence this meant that the Irish devaluation was such that 13 Irish pence = 12 British pence) and it followed that 13 Irish pounds = 12 pound sterling. Therefore, according to Richard Twiss, a traveller in Ireland in the late 18th century, "thus a guinea is 1l. [that last letter is an 'L' which is also used sometimes as an abbreviation for a pound] 2s. 9d Irish at par." [9] From 1783 the Bank of Ireland issued banknotes in either Irish pounds or guineas, the latter at that rate. As well as these banknotes, coins were in circulation in both copper, silver and gold:

Copper
farthing = a quarter of a penny

half penny

Irish copper half pennies and farthings were minted and circulated in Ireland in the 18th century, including an issue of both types of coins struck in Ireland by William Wood from 1722-24. The latter issue of course evoked the ire of Dean Swift and is probably more famous now in his writings than in Irish economic history!

Silver

penny

threepence, or 'thruppence'.

sixpence, known also as the tanner or half shilling. (Known in Irish as 'reul', from the Spanish 'real', presumably reflecting the fact that the Bank of Ireland tried to import the 'real' into Ireland c.1800 to address coin shortages.)

shilling = 12 pence (traditionally but note the Irish exchange rate referred to above.)

half crown = 2 shillings and six pence

crown = 5 shillings

Gold

guinea introduced in 1663 and originally worth 1 pound (i.e. 20 shillings), then fluctuated with the price of gold but in 1717 was officially pegged at 21 shillings. This is still the worth of a guinea (its no longer struck but still referred to e.g. in the sale of horses), that is 1 pound 1 shilling or 1.05 pounds post decimalization.

moidore, or 'moyder' or 'moydore', was a Portuguese gold coin that they traded in Ireland frequently in the 18th century.

Actually Ireland tended to use a lot of continental European currencies, reflecting the 'Wild Geese' diaspora who were in Europe at this time of course, and even natively produced local currencies. For example the aforementioned Richard Twiss informs us that:

> "The brass coins of the Isle of Man are current all along this coast [Co. Louth]. The beggars here are not extortionate in their demands, most of them offering a bad half penny, which they call *a rap*,

and soliciting for a good one in exchange." [10]

And as regards local currencies:

"In these parts [the road between Antrim and Ballymoney] I found many copper coins current, which were struck by tradesmen; on one of them was inscribed,

"I promise to pay the bearer two pence on demand, John Mac Cully, 1761;"

and on the reverse the representation of a beer cask, with the words,

"Brewer, 2 P." [11]

But in fact a lot of Irish land transactions, all the way from the 16th century, tended to specify that the currency used should be 'sterling' which obviously means that in those cases the British currency valuation should be used.

Footnotes
1. The quote on perches and yards is from Patrick Kelly, *The Universal Cambist and Commercial Instructor: Being a full and accurate treatise on the exchanges, coins, weights, and measures, of all trading nations and their colonies.* (London, 1835), p.195) and the 1775 traveller was Richard Twiss, in, *A Tour in Ireland in 1775* (London, 1776), p.52.
This quote is from:
http://www.clarelibrary.ie/eolas/coclare/history/territorial_divisions/units_land_measurement.htm .

The great Cavan historian Philip O'Connell addressed this question of the land divisions here:
"In mediaeval times the prevailing land denomination in Co. Cavan was the *Poll,* a unit which is mentioned frequently in the various *Inquisitions*; in Monaghan, Fermanagh, and elsewhere, it was called the *Tate.* The Poll was a unit of variable extent depending on the nature and fertility of the soil; hence it was not a fixed standard. In the *State Papers* of 1610 the Poll is defined as a unit of 25 acres. An earlier document of 1571 specifies it as containing 30 acres arable with 20 acres pasture and mountain. In 1601 another authority sets it down as equivalent to 60 acres arable. The unprofitable land, bog, wood, marsh, mountain, etc., was included with the arable land, but was definitely excluded for survey purposes. Different surveyors might not be unanimous in their opinions as to what constituted arable, or unarable, land. Everything would depend on the particular locality. In Co. Cavan, according to *Rawlinson MS.* [A.237, a survey of Cavan of 1608], a Poll was a parcel of 24 acres of *arable* land, and this may be accepted as its definition in the 1609 *Inquisition*.

In the *King's Project* for the Plantation of Ulster, reprinted in Harris' *Hibernica* (p. 117), a Poll is defined as 24 acres which agrees, substantially, with the estimate given in *Rawlinson*.

In Co. Fermanagh the *Tate* contained 30 acres: in Co. Armagh it was reckoned as 100. The Poll, or Tate, was commonly known as the Ballyboe – baile bó, i.e. cow land; it was supposed to be able to support about twenty cows. The Ballyboe enters largely into our placenames. Sixteen Ballyboes comprised the Ballybet – baile biatais i.e. the townland of the victualler. The Ballybet was the principal land unit within the *Tuath* or *Tricha Céd*, the "Cantred" or "District." The *Tricha Céd* usually comprised thirty Ballybets. According to the calculations of Dr. Reeves the extent of a Ballybet would have been about 1000 acres (Reeves and Hardinge, *Memoir on MSS. Mapped Townland Surveys in Ireland*, Trans. Royal Irish Academy, Vol. XXIV). But this estimate is based on the assumption that the measurements were absolute, including both arable and unarable land. We know that this was not the case and that the unarable land was not included for the purpose of survey, a fact which invalidate the conclusions of Dr. Reeves.

Poll, Tate, and Ballyboe, are synonymous terms, but the acreage was in every case dependent on local factors and varied with the circumstances in the particular county. Owing to the exclusion of the unprofitable land from the surveys it is now scarcely possible, with any degree of certainty, to equate these ancient land measures with those of the present day. In certain districts where there was an absence of waste and unprofitable lands approximate relations may be established. It is generally recognised that at the time of the Plantation of Ulster the variable extent of the Poll, and the rather arbitrary method of its determination, was duly taken advantage of by the unscrupulous Commissioners and purposely complicated in the interests of the Planters who had obtained grants of lands in Ulster. The adoption of the so-called "Irish Plantation Measure" – which still survives in Co. Cavan – at a somewhat later period and for the same purpose is a familiar fact of history.

The Poll and its sub-divisions, the Gallon, Pottle and Pint, enter largely into the placenames of Co. Cavan. The following inter-relations have been established :
1 Poll = 2 *Gallons* = 4 *Pottles* = 8 *Pints*.
The opening paragraph of the 1609 *Inquisition* specifies clearly the relations existing between these ancient land measures. The Pint, however, does not enter so frequently into placenames as do the larger divisions; as "point," it forms a few terminations.

In 1699 the *Carvagh,* which consisted of, approximately, 35 acres, was adopted as the unit of taxation in Co. Cavan. The whole County was estimated to contain 8,000 Carvaghs, averaging 1,000 per Barony for 8 Baronies – Loughtee being regarded as two, Upper and Lower. Tullyhaw was reckoned as 551½ Carvaghs; Loughtee Lower, 924½; Loughtee Upper, 1,776½;

Tullyhunco, 701½; Clanmahon, 916½; Clankee, 874; Tullaghgarvey, 1,498; Castlerahan, 757½. The mode of applotting the Carvaghs was determined by Act of Parliament, and the system was an intricate one. The Carvagh system was, as far as I have been able to ascertain, peculiar to Co. Cavan, where it survived until the beginning of the 19th century. But the Carvagh was a taxation unit rather than a unit of measurement. The word "carvagh," signifying a share, still survives in the popular idioms of Cavan speech, also in some townland names."
(Philip O'Connell, *The Cavan Inquisition of 1609*, in *Briefne Antiquarian Society Journal*, 1931-33, Vol III No. 3, p.364-5, available at: http://www.cavanlibrary.ie/file/Local-Studies/Library-Scanned-Docs/Breifny-Antiquarian-Society-Journal-1931-33-Vol-III-No-III.pdf .)

Another reference to this comes to us from J H Andrews:
"Examples of this quasi-equality [in land units] were the sessiagh or carucate, which supposedly contained enough land for one ploughteam; the knight's fee, or the ballybetagh, which could support a specified number of fighting men; the ballybo, colp or martland, which could feed a specified number of livestock; and the gallon or pottle, which could ripen a certain quantity of seed corn."
(J H Andrews, *Plantation Acres* (Belfast, 1985), p.8.)

Notice that O'Connell assumes that the large perch measurement in the Irish Acre came about only at the time of the plantation but in fact it seems to have a much earlier origin as J H Andrews notes here:
"As early as 1584 the 21 foot perch is described as 'Irish measure'."
(J H Andrews, *Plantation Acres* (Belfast, 1985), p.17.)

Incidentally on the question of the Ballybet (Baile Biadhtach) itself we have this insight from Robert Walker, who wrote about local placenames under the pseudonym *An Scolaire Bocht* in the Anglo-Celt in 1921:
"[the Ballybet] was the amount of land set apart for the public victualler, who was to keep open house for travellers in return. The extent of land so set apart varied with the nature of the country – the bogs, streams etc., being thrown in."
(*An Scolaire Bocht* articles in Cavan County Library, p.10)

2. 304-35-200032.

3. http://www.clarelibrary.ie/eolas/coclare/history/territorial_divisions/units_land_measurement.htm .

4. Rev George Hill, *The Fall of Irish Chiefs and Clans* (Kansas City, 2004), p.112.

5. *Proceedings of the Royal Irish Academy* vol vii, p.477, 489.

6. George Hill, *The Fall of Irish Chiefs and Clans* (Kansas City, 2004), p.106-107.
As regards the question of liquid units in Cavan, this is from a printed House of Lords Appeal case, Thomas Earl of Westmeath versus Revd John Madden Dean of Kilmore, on the subject of the tithes in that county:
"According to custom established soon after the said Inquisition [of the 29th December 1609], there had been constantly paid by the inhabitants of all the said rectories, for milch cows newly calved 9d and for Cows giving milk, not lately calved, called strappers, 4 1/2d as the full rate or value of the whole tithe thereof."
(PRONI D3835/B/4/2/15.)

7. *Proceedings of the Royal Irish Academy* vol vii, p.476.

8. Dr Reeves, *Townland Distribution of Ireland*, in *Proceedings of the Royal Irish Academy* vol vii, quoted in James Morrin, *Calendar of the Patent and Close Rolls in Chancery in Ireland, 1514-1575* (Dublin, 1862) vol ii, p.lvi.

9. Richard Twiss, *A Tour in Ireland in 1775* (London, 1776), p.52.

10. Ibid p.73.

11. Ibid p.82.

CHAPTER 2
Legal Terms used in the Deeds

Needless to say these 18th century deeds are legal documents and some familiarity with the legal terms used in Irish land law might be of some service.

Fine – A *fine*, in the context of land transactions, usually means a payment that is due to the owner of land because the tenant has breached some clause in the lease, by alienating the land to some third party for example. So for example if a person leased land under a lease of three lives and one of the lives had died, the tenant could negotiate with the landlord to add on another life to the lease and would agree to pay a *fine* to allow this to happen. Also in the case of legalistic old deeds a *fine* could relate to old payments due to the Crown because land had been sold or leased contrary to some clause in the ownership of land through *Knight's fee,* or indeed it could refer to monies due to the Crown because the land was transacted by a sale without going through the process of a *Lease and Release*.

Quit Rent – A large proportion of the land of Ireland was confiscated under the Cromwellian confiscations of the mid 17th century, the land being given to allies of Cromwell as can be read in records of this transaction known as the *Books of Survey and Distribution*. As part of this the government imposed a high rent on the new owners of the land called a *Quit Rent*. By the time of the mid 18th century this rent was really only a nominal figure, approximately equivalent to a ground rent in modern times. The question of who should pay this tax arises in the deeds, should it be the owner of the land or the tenant? Usually this is quite explicitly stated in the entry in the Registry of Deeds, where it might specify that the tenant must pay all taxes or fines due on the land "the Quit Rent only excepted" since the original owner of the land often wanted to pay this small sum himself, because it helped to prove his ownership of the land. Incidentally the original registers of the 18th century Quit Rent Office, and their copy of the Books of Books of Survey and Distribution, are still in existence and can be seen in the National Archives in Dublin. They continued this rent through at least part of the 19th century as one book written in 1844 notes: "In Ireland Quit Rents continue to be paid to the crown at the present day." [1]

Toties Quoties and *Bishop's Leases* – 'As often as the thing shall happen'. This was a clause often included in leases that a lessor immediately from a Bishop makes with his subtenants in turn and simply means that their lease will be renewed as often as the first lessor's lease is renewed by the Bishop. Various later Acts addressed this issue and they were subsequently converted into perpetual leases.

Statutes Staple – In the thirteenth century the government allowed certain ports to trade 'staple' goods with foreign merchants and at the same time set up a method of securing debts to assist that trade. This evolved into a kind of banking system where debtors or creditors could borrow or lend money on the 'staple', primarily in Dublin. Its possible that it was used particularly by Catholics at this time because with so many restrictions on their right to hold and purchase land they tended to secure marriage settlements, for example, by monies invested this way. Some of the registers for the Dublin staple survive for the 17th century and are published in a database attached to Jane H Ohlmeyer and Éamonn Ó Ciardha, *Irish statute staple books, 1596-1687* (Dublin, 1998), which can be consulted for further details on this.

Chief Rent – A fee which is very analogous to our current *ground rent*. In the 18th century it is usually a very small nominal sum due to some ancient proprietor of the land.

Fee Simple – This is a description of the type of landholding a person had, it means that the land was held properly and exclusively by the owner of the fee simple, in other words it was a good and solid ownership of the land.

Fee Tail – Any references to the *Fee Tail*, or to the *Tail* or to the *Entail*, refer to a different type of land ownership whereby the owner only has the lands for life with the land legally reverting to his 'heirs male', or whatever was normally written at the end of the original deeds whereby a person received the land, on that person's death. For example, Alexander Plunkett, the owner of 100 acres in Ballymagash, states that his title comes from say the will or the marriage settlement of his father. But in that will it might say that Alexander gets the land with succession going to "the heirs male of his body, lawfully begotten", hence Alexander himself cannot sell or alienate the property out of the family, effectively he only has a life interest in the estate.

Remainder – This follows on from the *Tail* in the original land deeds. For example, following on from our fictional Alexander Plunkett above, his original deeds – i.e. his father's will etc – might have added to the part where it says "the heirs male of his body, lawfully begotten" by including some phrase like "and in default of such heirs, remainder to the heirs male of John Plunkett of Ardmaghbeg, and in default of same to the heirs male of Phillip Plunkett of Dunsoghly" etc. What the original writer of that deed is saying is that if Alexander Plunkett ends up with no male heirs then the heir of John Plunkett gets the estate – of course this means that John Plunkett will be a close relative, but not a descendant, of Alexander – and if not him then the male heir of Phillip Plunkett etc. This is the *Remainder* and is actually very interesting to read if you get a chance to peruse an old 17th or 18th century will or settlement because it can obviously show the relationships of the different families. Unfortunately the summary of the deed contained in the *Memorials* in the Registry of Deeds do not normally go into the complexity of the full *Remainder* list, unlike some of the original deeds.

Recovery or *Common Recovery* –[2] The *Tail* and the *Remainder*, however, created a lot of problems for our permanently penniless Irish landed proprietor of the 18th century. Typically he needed to borrow money, or promise to give his future son-in-law a good estate as a dowry, and he couldn't easily do this if he only had a life interest in the lands. For example how could his creditors feel confident in the security of the land he was mortgaging to them if they couldn't then sell the land off if he doesn't pay his debts? Any future owner of that land would not have a proper title, because the land could not be sold off out of the family due to the *Tail* and the *Remainder*. Hence we have this archaic, very strange legal fixit known as a *Common Recovery*. If a proprietor was prepared to go through the legal expense of *suffering* a *recovery* then the land would revert back to the proprietor as a full *fee simple*, in otherwords he could then sell or give away his estate – to his future son-in-law for example – because he would now own it outright. You might ask how can that just happen like that, well it simply evolved over the centuries as one way for landed proprietors to get around these problems, it is in fact a bizarre fictional legal proceeding.

In England it seems that fictional names were used for the bizarre court case involved in a *recovery* – in the same sense that John Doe is a fictional name for an unnamed corpse in a Coroner's Court – but in Ireland they seem to use real people as part of the legal case and will name them in the Registry of Deed entry that mentions the *recovery*.

Another peculiarity in Ireland is that Catholic land owners will sometimes use a fake *Protestant discoverer* – a person that emerges under the Penal Laws against the Catholics – in order to break the *entail* and the *remainder*, saving them the expense of a *recovery*. Obviously what they are doing here is getting some Protestant friend of theirs to claim ownership of their lands – on the grounds that the owners were Catholic who had breached the laws against taking out long leases and he was the Protestant who first *discovered* this and hence is entitled to the lands under the Penal Laws – and then getting this Protestant to secretly pass the lands back to the original owners, now with all previous *tails* and *remainders* destroyed. (The full text of a sample deed and memorial given in appendix B is probably an example of this.)

Its also the case that sometimes when a mortgage is granted the landowner borrowing the money will promise to take out a *recovery* sometime in the near future, and will mention this in the deed. The same is sometimes true of marriage settlements, because again the family of the future son-in-law would like to be sure that the father of the bride really and properly owns the estate in question, and can therefore pass it on to the groom's family, especially in the case of heiresses of course.

A 1781 deed involving the Earl of Westmeath and James Glascock of Dublin esq mentions the common recovery, stating that Glascock will get land:

> "to the intent to make him tenant to freehold of the said lands and premises for the purpose of suffering one or more common recovery or recoveries which are by the said deed covenanted and agreed to be suffered by the said parties, in which recoveries the said William Glascock [also of Dublin] to be plaintiff or demandent, the said James Glascock tenant, and the said Thomas Earl of Westmeath and George Frederick Nugent, commonly called the Baron of Delvin, vouchees, which recoveries when suffered and executed are thereby declared to enure to the use of the said Thomas Earl of Westmeath for life and after his decease for the use and behoof of the said George Frederick Nugent."

The Glascocks are just dragged into this proceeding as nominal players in the complicated legal twists of the recovery process.[3]

While there was no real need to suffer a recovery if there was no remainder nonetheless it seems some lawyers hoped to generate a bit of business this way. That's the impression you get reading this letter to the family of Clonlost Co Westmeath from their lawyer dated to the 3rd of January 1681 (and notice how he seems to regard the new year as starting in January rather than Lady Day):

> "There is no absolute need of a Recovery in this case, because there is no Remainder but what is now vested in Robert Swift [of Carlingford, Co. Louth]. But I fancy you will be always be afraid that you want it, and it is usual to conveyances personally purchased [?, last two words unclear in the manuscript] to have a Recovery, and therefore I would advise you to have one. Thus wishing you a

good new year
I subscribe
Your faithful servant
Godwin Swift." [4]

Lease and Release –[5] This phrase is another ancient legal fiction. What happened is that under the Statute of Enrolment of 1536 all land bargains and sales, but not all types of leases, had to be centrally registered in London. This was much to the chagrin of the landed proprietors so they got around it by a nominal *lease* of land, of the type that didn't have to be registered, to a prospective buyer, and then on the next day, or shortly after, a *release* to that tenant of further rights to that land. This transfer of land rights together added up to a very effective transfer of the land but used legal forms that did not have to be registered in London. Hence this type of land transaction became the accepted form of leasing and selling land from the late 16th century until the 1840s. The vast majority of leases and sales of land in the 18th century Irish Registry of Deeds are in this form. This also accounts for the fact that these deeds are usually dated to two separate dates e.g. the deed will be transacted on the "18th and 19th of August 1745", because the nominal *lease* is dated to the 18th and the *release* to the 19th.

These legal technical niceties are not usually important to the historian though, for all practical purposes the phrase *lease and release* just means lease, and the type of lease or sale that it actually is will be revealed by the details of the deed not by the title i.e. a *lease or release* could refer to the outright sale of land, not just to a lease, in the same way that *bargain and sale* could refer to a lease of land and not actually to an outright sale of land. You have to ignore these old legal phrases and just read the details of the land transaction. Also bear in mind that outright sales of land are not common at all in these 18th century deeds, you will find that the original proprietors will always try to hold onto some rights over their land.

Indenture – The ancient procedure adopted in creating land deeds traditionally went something like this: The two parties agreed on the wording of the deed and it was then written twice, an identical set of words written underneath the first text, on one, large, sheet of parchment. Then when it was all signed and sealed, i.e. two sets of seals and signatures, one underneath each of the two texts, then the parchment was cut across in the middle, separating the two texts and so giving you two copies of the deed. The interesting mediaeval security system, as it were, that they used was that they left the tear shape of the parchment intact as a kind of jagged edge. Hence if you wanted to check if a given deed was a genuine copy of another one what you did was check the pattern of the jagged edges and see do they fit, if it did then the two copies had been at one time a single piece of parchment and therefore one was a genuine copy of the other. They called these type of deeds *indentured* deeds after that characteristic jagged or 'indented' edge shape (which for the 18th century look like large smooth edged zig zags on the top of the parchment) which you can still see clearly on the original deeds.

Deed Poll – A *deed poll* is then the opposite type to an *indented deed* or an *indenture*. One of the meanings of 'poll' was to 'shear', or clip to a straight line as it were, and so these deeds had no jagged edges because they only involved one party and hence did not need the second copy. An example of a deed that had only one party would be a deed where a person changes their name, for example, and this is still a well known use of deed polls. While not completely unheard of nonetheless deed polls are not at all common in the ROD, nearly all the deeds you will see are indentured deeds.

Bargain and Sale – This phraseology is very common in the deeds but in practice it is of very little use in understanding these documents. The crucial point to understand is that it does not necessarily mean that the land is actually being sold off as opposed to being leased, they will use this phraseology in both cases. In order to figure out if it is an outright sale – which is rare for the 18th century – you should just read the details of the deed. For example if it talks about a lease being given for a large consideration of money up front with no, or only a nominal, annual rent and 'renewable forever', or maybe with three lives also renewable forever, that might indicate, at least for all practical purposes, an outright sale of land. Technically the *Bargain and Sale* type transaction was the one that needed to be centrally registered from 1535 on and hence it needed the *Lease and Release* type of deed to remove that 1535 obligation.

Occupation – This word is also used a lot in reference to the deeds where, for example, it might talk about lands in the 'actual occupation of' so and so. Like the *bargain and sale* this is another word you have to be careful of. It means that the person is in real possession of some kind of lease, or ownership, of the land in question but it does not follow at all that the person actually physically lives on the land, which otherwise you might have assumed from those words. In order to determine that, i.e. who in reality is living and farming on the land, you often need to do quite a lot of in depth study of the land in question. One simple trick though is to take careful note of the addresses of the parties, obviously if Frank Plunkett, for example, gives his address as Ballykillroe in a deed that refers to that townland then obviously we can be sure he actually lives there but otherwise we cannot make such assumptions at all.

Assignment – If our fictional Alexander Plunkett leased lands for 30 years to Frank Pallas, for example, and then Pallas transferred all his rights under the lease, for a fee probably, to Oliver Tuite then technically what Pallas is doing is *assigning* his rights to Tuite. If, on the otherhand, Pallas retained some of the original rights that he held from Plunkett, for example if he gives Tuite a 10 year lease while he holds onto the last 20 years of the original 30 year lease, then he is just *leasing* the lands to Tuite rather than *assigning* them. It is only when he transfers all his rights do we say that he *assigns* the lease over.

In practice the busy historian can just understand *assignment* as meaning almost the same as *lease*.

Set – Again, in practice, this just means to lease. Hence, in the above scenario, instead of saying that Plunkett *leases* lands to

Pallas you could just say that he *set* the lands to Pallas.

Dower or *thirds* – This is the phrase used to describe property a widow inherited on the death of her husband. She was usually given on her husband's death, under the terms of her marriage settlement, a life interest, at least, in a third of the property of her husband and hence the phrase the 'thirds'. This word is obviously related to the word 'dowry' but that latter word never occurs in the 18th century deeds. These '*dower* lands' were sometimes fenced off on the ground and can lead to new land divisions as a result.

Also it must not be forgotten that these deeds were used widely in court cases and this is often mentioned in the entries in the ROD, hence giving rise to the frequent mention of normal Irish, and English Common Law, legal terms. For example legal practices like writs of *scire facias,* or *fieri facias,*[6] will sometimes be mentioned and also land might need to be sold off under the terms of a judicial judgement and you can get a memorial listed to that effect, which is useful for dating these judgements and clarifying the parties but not for details of the cases because these ROD references tend to be quite brief.

Footnotes
1. George Lewis Smyth, *Ireland: historical and statistical* (London, 1844) vol 1, p.428. He also tells us that:
"Much curious information respecting them and the rebellions of the years 1641 and 1688 to which they are more directly referable, is to be found in Howard's History of the Irish Exchequer and in the Fourth Report of the Irish Revenue Commissioners, 1812. According to Howard they produced for the year ending Lady Day, 1773, £64,152 19s 5 1/4d. In the year ending March 31, 1801, they amounted according to a return of the House of Commons (266, Sess 1834,) to £60, 613 17s. In the year 1826, they rose to £93,938 5s 3 1/2d. In 1835 they realised (Return 222, Sess. 1842) £83,350 14s 8d, and stood on the 5th of January, 1846 (Return 696, Sess. 1846), at £66,955 5s 1d."

2. The background to the *Common Recovery* is described in more detail here:
"For these reasons all classes in the community, except the great landowners, who in the uncertainty of civil wars desired the protection of their estates from forfeiture for treason, pressed for alterations in the Statute.[i] "The same was

attempted and endeavoured to be remedied at divers Parliaments, and divers Bills were exhibited accordingly, but they were always on one pretence or other rejected. For the Lords and Commons, knowing that their estates tail were not to be forfeited for felony or treason, as their estates of inheritance were before the Act de Donis...and finding that they were not answerable for the debts and incumbrances of their ancestors, nor did the sales alienations and leases of their ancestors bind them for the lands which were entailed to their ancestors, they always rejected such bills." [ii]

The remedy for this national evil, maintained by that class of the community having power in legislation for their own interests, came from the Law Courts, and is generally associated with the oddly named *Taltarum's Case*,[iii] decided by the judges in 1472. The process by which judicial ingenuity evaded in the interests of the community a statute passed in the interests of a class was that of a Common Recovery, or fictitious suit brought by a plaintiff in collusion against the tenant-in-tail who wished to alienate his land. This process had already been used by the clergy to evade the Statutes of Mortmain; and its use for that purpose had been restrained by special Statute.[iv] It was now brought into play for other purposes.

It is not very material to discuss whether *Taltarum's Case* was the "leading case" to establish the efficacy of common recoveries to bar estates tail, or whether their virtue for that purpose had been earlier recognized.[v] Coke says in *Mildmay's Case* that "about 1472 the judges, on consultation had amongst themselves, resolved that an estate tail might be docked and barred by a Common Recovery",[vi] while in *Mary Portington's Case*, he says that this method of barring an Estate Tail was "not newly invented in 1472, but oftentimes affirmed before;" [vii] citing a number of black-letter authorities and concluding that "these resolutions and opinions of law produced the judgment in 1472, which was not of any new invention, but proved and approved by the resolution of the sages of the law at all times after the Act *De Donis* until 1472. And the judges of the law then perceiving what contention and mischiefs had crept into the quiet of the law by these fettered inheritances, on consideration of the said act and of former expositions thereof by the sages of the law gave judgment that in such case the estate tail should be barred."

Taltarum's Case itself does not expressly decide on the validity of a Common Recovery, for while the plaintiff pleads a common recovery suffered by defendant's ancestor, defendant admits it, and sets up a previous estate tail in his ancestor, which alone, he says, was defeated by the common recovery suffered, and the Court agree with him: but it is assumed by both parties and by the Court itself that the Common Recovery in which T. Taltarum is concerned is effectual in barring some estate tail in the ancestor.

The procedure of a Common Recovery was based on the doctrine of Warranty, by which the heirs to an entailed estate were barred by the alienation of their ancestor, if they obtained from him Assets, or lands of equal value to those alienated. This proviso was satisfied if they had a right to lands of equal value, though the right might be valueless. The tenant-in-tail, therefore, who wished to alienate arranged that a fictitious suit should be brought against him for the lands: this he met, not by an assertion of his own title, but by calling upon a person whom he alleged to have granted to him the lands in question to warrant or defend the grant he had made. The alleged grantor appeared and acknowledged that he was bound to warrant, but then disappeared and failed to warrant. Whereupon the fictitious plaintiff had judgment against the tenant-in-tail for the lands which he claimed, and the tenant-in-tail had judgment over against the fictitious grantor who had so basely failed to defend his grant. This judgment over, or right to recover lands of equal value from the defaulter, served as Assets to the heir of the tenant-in-tail, who was therefore barred. And Lord Coke expressly rests his defence of Common Recoveries on this "intended recompense," [viii] and lays down, "that the judgment given in such case for the tenant-in-tail to have in value is a bar to the estate tail, although no recompense be had." [ix] For of course the heirs never did recover lands of the value they had lost: the defaulting warrantor was a man of straw, who had no lands to lose, and was indeed in later times, when the comedy was in full working order, the Crier of the Court of Common Pleas, who passed the Law Terms in failing to warrant for the consideration of fourpence per failure.

It is hardly necessary to set out in detail the technicalities of the Common Recovery, either at the time of *Taltarum's Case*, or as ultimately developed by the needs of conveyancing. The proceedings were based on an elaborate series of fictions, and were complicated and expensive in the highest degree; slight slips in them might prove fatal to the title to the land, and it was impossible to find any satisfactory justification for the numerous stages of the procedure, or reasonable explanation of its existence, other than a historical statement of its origin. The Real Property Commissioners in their first Report [x] speak of "the whole mass of technical law relating to common recoveries," as "a mere excrescence on the main body of our laws;" and claim to have shown both their "inaptitude for the purpose for which they (Common Recoveries) have been applied, and the shifts and contrivances to which ingenuity has been obliged to resort in order to render them subservient to those purposes." Previous legal authorities indeed rarely, if ever, even attempted to explain the reason of a Common Recovery, but contented themselves with upholding it. "None ought to be heard," says Coke, "in dispute against the legal pillars of common assurances of lands and inheritances." [xi] In a case which he mentions, "Hoord [sic] an utter barrister of counsel with the plaintiff" (who was barred by a Common Recovery) "rashly and with great ill will inveighed against common recoveries, not knowing the reason and foundation of them, who was with great gravity and some sharpness reproved by Sir J. Dyer, C. J., who said he was not worthy to be of the profession of the law, who durst speak against Common Recoveries, which were the sinews of assurances of inheritances and founded upon great reason and authority", but, adds Coke, "non omnis capit hoc verbum." In short, the procedure in Common Recoveries, invented to evade a Statute, complicated from time to time with provisions against all manner of technical difficulties, became an elaborate and technical formality, whose parts had survived their uses, whose elaboration was only productive of expense, and whose technicality abounded in deadly traps for any but the most skilled and careful lawyers. It had degenerated from a fiction which at its best was cumbrous to a juggle which had hardly the merits of solemnity.

Whatever may have been the law before *Taltarum's Case*, there is no doubt that, after 1472, the way of evading Estates Tail by Common Recoveries was in constant use; and that in consequence the restraints on alienation, and the limited line of succession, imposed by the Statute *de Donis*, were gone. The class legislation of Parliament was defeated by the national legislation of the judges, at the cost of the introduction into Real Property Law of a fiction which, like Frankenstein's monster, became too powerful for its authors.

...

"*Levying a Fine*",
[Another method of breaking the entail but not as much used as the recovery.]
As the system of Common Recoveries as bars to Estates Tail had been definitely established in 1472, the recognition in 1540 of the efficacy of fines for the same purpose was only of secondary importance. There were however two classes of cases in which the use of a fine instead of a common recovery was advisable. If the tenant-in-tail had also a reversion or remainder in fee, there was no one who need be barred but his privies or heirs, and this could be effected by a fine without the necessity of resorting to a common recovery. Secondly, where a remainderman in tail desired to bar the entail, but the person having the freehold in possession refused to play his part in a common recovery, a fine was the only method open to the remainderman though it would only bar and bind his own issue."

Footnotes
i. Reeves, ii. 341. Godbolt's *Reports*, p.303.

ii. *Mildmay's Case*. 6 Co. Rep. 40.

iii. Y. B. 12 Edw. IV. 19. Digby, *R. P.* 3rd. ed. p.211. Taltarum is not a party to the case, but had been the plaintiff in the common recovery alleged, so his 'immortality' is an usurpation and not of right.

iv. V. *supra*, p.65.

v. See Pollock, p. 83, note. Reeves, iii. 18, where Mr Reeves and Mr Finlason entirely disagree as to the effect of *Taltarum's Case*.

vi. 6 Rep. 40.

vii. 10 Rep. 37.

viii. *Mildmay's Case*, 6 Rep. 40.

ix. Mary *Portington's Case*, 10 Rep.

x. pp. 30, 31.

xi. *Mary Portington's Case*, 10 Rep. 40.
(Thomas Edward Scrutton, *Land in Fetters* (Cambridge, 1886), p.73-76, 78-79.)

3. 1781 349-122-233231. Another reference to both a common recovery and the levying of a fine comes from Co. Cavan and the lands of Bobsgrove in 1792, whereby the owners:
"did also at the same time levy and acknowledge unto the said Samuel Adams [of Dublin esq] two other several fines surconcesserat of the town and lands of Upper Castletown and Ardnegross Co. Westmeath and Lismecanegan and Barcony in the Co. of Cavan which said deed witnessed that the fines and recoveries so levied and suffered and the term of 100 years created thereby were to be enure to the use and behoof of the said John James Maxwell [this is the family of the Earls of Farnham] and Wogan Browne [of Co. Kildare esq]" (1792 451-517-290525).

4. PRONI D2620/2

5. This quote, from the Land Registry in the UK, sets out the historical background:
"Originally in English law the only way to transfer freehold land was by livery of seisin, that is the public transfer of the land by the vendor to the purchaser, this usually involved handing over a piece of turf in the presence of witnesses. This form of conveyance was not abolished until 1925, but lost favour after the Statute of Uses (1535) allowed conveyance by deed. But the legislators did not want to allow secret conveyancing, so the Statute of Enrolments of the same year made it compulsory to enrol deeds of bargain and sale with the keeper of the rolls of the county, or in one of the courts at Westminster. This act can be seen as the ancestor of the Land Registration Acts.
"But the invention of lawyers was at length too much for the precautions of Parliament". The Statute of Enrolments, saying nothing of estates less than freehold, was simply avoided by a new deed called a "lease and release", and thus the act had the wholly unintended result of making it even easier to transfer land without publicity. A situation that was not, in fact, finally resolved until 1990."
(http://www.landreg.gov.uk/assets/library/documents/bhist-lr.pdf)

We are told by Fabian Phillips, in his treatise on capiases and outlawries, that "the conveyance by lease and release was first contrived by Sir Francis More, at the request of Lord Norris, that his relations might not know what settlement he had." This was:

Sir Francis Moore, of East Ilsley, Berkshire, a lawyer, MP, author of 'Cases collected and reported', in 1614 was made Serjeant at Law and died on the 20th of November 1621.
(An example of what must have been his very early design of a 'lease and release' can be seen in the Danny Archives at the East Sussex Record Office, consisting of a 'lease' of 21 April 1597 at DAN/1126/fo.137v. and a corresponding 'release' a day later, 22 April 1597, at DAN/1126/fo.138r and v., catalogued at: http://www.nationalarchives.gov.uk/a2a/records.aspx?cat=179-danny&cid=-1#-1 .)

As regards Norris we have: Henry Norris (1525-1601), a scion of an old Berkshire family, was appointed ambassador to France in 1566 and raised to the House of Lords as the first Baron Norreys of Rycote in 1572. His will was dated 24th September 1589. And also:
Francis Norris (1582-1624), 2nd Baron of Rycote, succeeded his grandfather Henry in the title in 1601 when he was aged 19. Created 1st Earl of Berkshire in 1621. He committed suicide with a crossbow in 1624 and Sir Francis Moore took out probate on his will.

6. One such writ was served by the High Sheriff of Westmeath in 1758 in a dispute between Patrick Keating and Patrick Coffee over the land of Coolatore (1758 198-58-131078).

CHAPTER 3
The Historian and the Registry

Well what can we expect from the Registry of Deeds memorials from the point of view of the historian? Quite a lot in fact, as we can see if we break it down into a few specialist areas in history:

Genealogist

For the 'Ascendancy' families particularly, the ROD is *the* source for 18th century family history I would suggest. Remember for these families you are talking about an elite who are operating in a relatively small country and in the ROD there are a huge number of deeds. We are told that for the first two decades of the Registry some 35,000 Memorials were registered, by the 1760s 135,000, more that a quarter of a million by 1790, it had passed half a million by the 1820s and now the ROD has some five million memorials.[1] So the odds of any given family of the Ascendancy being mentioned somehow in the 18th century deeds is enormous. Also the chances of a non Ascendancy name being mentioned is also not poor at all, it would be a mistake just to assume that the name you are looking for is necessarily too poor, or too Catholic, to get mentioned in these deeds for that time. Catholics certainly are trading in land at this time and also don't forget that the pattern of landholding for a given family is not necessarily the same for the mid 19th century as it is for the early 18th. In other words a poor family on 4 acres of land in 1820 might, for all you know, have owned 200 acres in 1720 and consequently would be mentioned in the deeds.

Well what exactly can the genealogist expect from the Registry and how does he/she go about doing research there? The obvious first step is to look up the name you are tracking in the names index for the 18th century and this is a very obvious and worthwhile step if the name is a rare one, as is always the case in genealogy you can get very bogged down in numerous entries if the name is a common one. The names index will give you the book-page-number that allows you to look up the entry in the large transcript books and it will also give you the date, to one year or sometimes to a short group of years, and the Christian name and title of the grantor of the lease and the surname for the grantee (although the latter is not indexed as such). If you don't find the exact name you are looking for you might nonetheless find it worthwhile to search under other entries for that family or under cousins or other relatives of that family. This is because in many cases deeds will be witnessed by close relatives, and sometimes by friends or legal representatives, and it can be interesting to see if your target witnessed any of these deeds.

If that approach is not to your liking, maybe because the name is too common, and if you do know the townland where the family lived or farmed, then the Lands Index is your next port of call. This is an index that goes by the townland name broken down by county and sometimes by barony (for roughly the first four decades of the 18th century it lists the barony, for the second half it only sometimes lists it). So if you wish to find Ballymackeehola for Co Mayo you search out the two lands indexes for Mayo for the 18th century, one for roughly the first four decades of the century and the other for the rest of it, and look under 'B' (it doesn't list the entry in more detailed fashion than just the first letter of the name). If you find an entry it will tell you the parish it is in, rarely but sometimes, the barony, again sometimes but all the time for the early decades, and the grantor and grantee of the lands by surname or title, and the aforementioned book-page- and number. The exact date is not given, you only have the general years covered by the two indexes, but also the index might list 'aliases' for the lands in question, especially the different spellings of the townland, and it might refer to another part of the index where the land is also mentioned by writing something like 'see further', or its Latin equivalent, in the margin. An entry then might look something like this:

"Ballymackeehola als [abbreviation of 'alias'] Ballymacahola....Tirawley [Barony]....Dillon to Bligh lib.[meaning 'liber', the Latin for book] 23 p.34 No.365789, Bligh et al. [meaning 'et alios', 'and others', i.e. there are other parties to the deed giving the land to Hughes, watch out for 'and others' or 'and another' in the names index which obviously means the same thing] to Hughes et ux. ['et uxor' meaning 'and wife', also a party to the transaction in receiving the land] lib.36 pag.567 no.365801; Hughes to Murphy lib.67 p.498 no.366789."

In your notes I would suggest you should take down all this entry, even if you are only interested in Murphy it still can be helpful to see how the same patch of land was passed from Dillon to Bligh earlier. Then you might like to fill in a copy of the suggested template, printed in this book in appendix H, for every entry you see in the index (i.e. you can fill out the townland name, the book-page-number and the surnames of the parties on the form from the index itself) and then go to the transcript books and read the actual memorial corresponding to those numbers for the given book-page-number.

Before going further it should be mentioned that there are quite a few pitfalls in reading these indexes, it does actually take some time before you are used to their quirks and are certain of your entries. But two problems in particular will always catch the unwary:

– The Names Index for the 18th century changes its pattern for approximately 1786-93. Before that time the pattern is that if you pick up an index for say 1754-1764 then it will list at one point in the index all the entries for Murphy, for example, that occur between those dates. In otherwords its a consolidated index between those dates. Then if you pick up an index of the other type, for say 1790-1793, you will find Murphy listed in four different places in the index, a separate entry for 1792, another entry later on for 1793 etc. In otherwords its not consolidated, its separate for each year, and if you didn't realise that and thought it was the same as the other type you would miss many entries because on opening the book you would probably find the Murphy entries for 1792, say, and assume that you had read all the possible entries for 1790-3.

– The Lands Index has a separate part at the back of each county book listing entries for some of the towns in each county.

Hence if you looked up Kells in the County Meath Lands Index under 'K' in the main part you would actually miss most of the entries, you need to look at the back to see what towns are listed separately. The same is true incidentally of Dublin city which is listed separately to Dublin county.

Ultimately though which index you go for depends a lot on what information you have to start with. Again if the surname you are searching is too common, or you feel that the name you are looking for is likely only to be mentioned in passing in a deed (e.g. the person might be mentioned when land is being described in the deed, i.e. it could be that the land will be described as 'adjoining the farm of John Smith' etc, or the person might be named as a witness only and hence not indexed) then obviously the Lands Index might be more to your liking. Another point can also be made then that it would be much better if you knew for sure what townland the family were associated with before doing your research in the ROD so you can go straight to the Lands Index. But some similar considerations occur with that index. The Lands Index is the older of the two (because most of the 18th century names index was rewritten in approximately 1800) and hence more difficult to read and also ease of using it will depend on the degree to which your placename starts with 'B' or 'C' or some similar common letter. Since the index is not subdivided better than just the first letter then you can appreciate just how many 'B' townland names there are for a given Irish county! Therefore if it started with a rarer first letter it will probably end up a lot easier to look up. Then its just a question of reading and taking down those notes – onto a photocopy of the template I suggest, one for each memorial – for each of the entries for the given townland which might work out at, say, 30 deeds for the 18th century.

When you are reading the memorials, having got your entries from either of the indexes, its really up to you what you decide to take down in those notes but I would suggest that you could be guided by the categories and notes you see listed on the template infra. You will probably like to find a marriage settlement for your target but I would suggest that any series of dates, names and their corresponding addresses are always going to be of interest to the genealogist. Remember that is one of the requirements of the registration process for the deed, it must list the full names and addresses and occupations of the parties and witnesses to the deed. In this, for the genealogist, there is really one piece of good news and one of bad. The bad news is that anybody who lives in Dublin city will just write down exactly that as their address, Dublin city, which is hardly very exact in identifying people.

The good news is that the occupations that are listed are, I would suggest, one of the jewels of the ROD. It would be very difficult to find out otherwise that a given person is a vintner or milliner etc, because, with the exception of Thom's directory for Dublin city, we do not really have sufficient records for the 18th century to find out this. In fact there are all kinds of interesting occupations listed, for example: James Walter of Dublin in 1778 was a "sheer grinder",[2] Patrick Walsh in Dublin in 1794 was a "Quill merchant",[3] and John Sheridan of Mary's Lane in Dublin was a "man cook".[4] When Revd J B Burgess was researching the Roscommon side of Athlone in 1944 he made extensive use of the ROD for the period 1708-1850, from which he compiled a large typescript book of entries (currently in the Aidan Heavey Library in Athlone) and from that he indexed the following occupations listed in the ROD:

Accountant – John Gaynor,
Ale-drapers – (6 of them),
Apothecaries – (9 of them),
Architect – John Gibson,
Armourer – Henry McDonagh,
Attorneys,
Auctioneer – James Tighe,
Baker – Pat Ryan (only one of them),
Boat Builder – James Curly,
Brazier – William Robinson,
Brewers,
Builder – Robert Walker,
Carpenters, Chandlers,
Chapman – John Sweeney,

Cooper – Dan Keeley,
Cordwainer – (13 of them),
Cutler – John Parsons,
Dealer – Thomas Healy,
Distillers, Doctor,
Engineer – Michael Monks,
Farriers,
Feltmaker – Thomas Acton,
Flour Merchant – Pat Bracken,
Gardener – John Smith,
Gauger [sic] – Andrew Rutledge,
Glaziers, Glovers, Grocers, Hatters, Hosiers, Innkeepers,
Joiner – Edwin Thomas,
Justices,
Labourer – God[win?] Brocas (only one),
Land Surveyors,
Leather Cutter – Michael English,
Malsters, Masons,
Nailers – Thomas Burchell and Henry Murray,
Peruke Maker – Saquill [sic] Kidd,
Plumber – William Sproule,
Printer – Dan Daly,
Publicans, Schoolmasters, Saddlers, Shopkeepers,
Shop Assistant – William Gaynor,
Skinner and Glover – Hugh Brogan,
Smiths, Millers, Notary Publics (lawyers),
Stationer – James Potts,
Staymakers – William Jordan and Michael McCleland,
Surgeons, Tailors,
Tanner – James Coates,
Upholsterer – Fe. Naghten and Laugh[?],
Victuallers, Vintners, Watchmakers,
Weaver – Edward Hall,
Writing Clerks,
Writing Master – James Gallagher,
Yeomen.

 Unfortunately though most names listed will just specify under occupation 'gent[leman]' or 'esq[uire]' and with respect to these all you need to know is that 'esquire' is somewhat higher up on the scale of poshness that 'gentleman'.

Local Historian

Needless to say this party has much to sink his teeth into in these deeds. Possibly one of the most important and simplest problem the local historian faces is trying to locate all the different placenames that are not marked in the Ordnance Survey or Down Survey maps. The ROD is very helpful here, even the indexes will sometimes list the 'aliases' for given lands and certainly the memorials themselves abound in clear and accurate information as regards what other names given lands are sometimes called.

Sometimes the local historian can get lucky and the deeds can mention facts from a long time before the deed was written. For example when Viscount Clare was passing a lease of the lands of the Abbey of Multyfarnham (which was in two parts separated by the River Gore, one part lately held by Nicholas Tuite deceased and the other by Francis Nangle) to John, the Earl of Upper Ossory, in 1776, he grounded his title to the lands on an old 1696 lease from Nicholas Gaynor, formerly of Black Castle Co. Westmeath esq, to Clare's grandfather.[5] Any historian studying Lurgan in Co Armagh will be delighted to read one deed, from 1722 and registered in July 1728, that lists virtually all the different trades and tradesmen in the town as part of a large land transaction.[6]

By no means infrequently you can also trip across famous people in these deeds, as my predecessor in writing a *Guide to the Registry of Deeds*, P.P. Phair, outlines here:

"Countless references to well-known people, as a few examples, taken at random, will indicate:
Henry Grattan 350-112-234256,...
Wolfe Tone 487-496-314272...
Robert Emmett 489-261-309133...
Dean Swift 33-49-19613...
William Penn, son of the founder of Pennsylvania,

20-465-10930."

Then some miscellaneous local features or facts could get mentioned which will be exciting if they can be matched with particular evidence on the ground. One 1756 deed from Westmeath, for example, describes the proper dimensions for a new road to be built across the lands of Druganstown, Barony of Delvin, i.e. from the ditch of Prentinstown and Clonin through Druganstown to the road from Moortown to Clonin. Ditches of 6 feet deep were to be dug either side of the road, and the soil from them put on the road which was to be 12 feet across.[7] Land in Multyfarnham Co Westmeath being leased to Dudly Bradstreet of Granard on the 1st of August 1752 included a "parcel of land on which the walls of a large house now stands commonly called the Meadow land", and also included some land in Ballindura which the lessor "showed this day to the said Dudley Bradsheet." [8] In general the rule is that urban lands, particularly Dublin city, will very frequently provide explicit on the ground dimensions of property, of enormous help to the local historian, while for rural properties it is much rarer. As a rough estimate you can rely on receiving that kind of information about 2/3rds of the time for urban areas and maybe 1/15th of the time for rural areas.

There can be other titbits that can catch the eye of the local historian, for example the deeds might mention rights over land that are also being dealt in, rights that have nothing to do with farming as such, including:

– *turbary rights*, the right to cut turf, are very commonly mentioned and are usually quite important in rural Ireland.

When land was transferred in 1780 in Westmeath the new owner received the right to cut turf in the same place that the original owner did then, and

> "the undertenants of Derrymore aforesaid should be obliged to assist with six horses, cars, and leaders, each man in drawing home his the said"

original owner's turf, along with four men each day in cutting the same or ten shillings in lieu thereof.[9]

Thomas Seale, a shoemaker of Ballimore in Co Westmeath, leased out the Millhouses in the Barony of Moygoish and these came with the right to cut turf "on that part of the Bog of Russagh whereon Patrick Curly and Daniel Maugher generally cut their turf".[10]

– *fishing*, which is sometimes mentioned. When land in Killminin in Co Waterford was leased out in 1740 the original owner reserved the right to "draw a net or nets on the sea water of the premises at such seasons and times as the said" owner "shall think proper".[11]

– right to dig *lime*, as limestone stones – which will be burnt in a limekiln – or as soft clay known as marl. The lime of course is then spread on the land to increase its fertility. An example can be seen in the previous deed from Killminin which goes on to talk about the right to

> "dig, raise and cut limestones on the premises for his and their own use only, and to carry the same away with men and horses and carriages at all seasonable time through the common roads on the said demised premises."

When Patrick Reilly of Mullychoran [Mullahoran] Co Cavan took up a 999 year lease on 177 acres in that townland in 1785, along with the fair of Killgolagh he received the right to

> "raise marl in the bog of Lisnetinnure and to carry away same at all times they or any of them should want it to manure said lands".[12]

– right to hunt for *rabbits*.

When the mansion house of Pallas in Galway was leased out to Richard Gorges, of Kilbrew Co Meath, in 1733 the deed mentioned the castle, the pigeon houses, courts, turrets, and also allowed the new owner

> "full and free liberty to catch, kill, and carry away, and make use of, as many rabbits by ferrets, haynets, pursenets, or any other way or means, in the burrows or conny warren of Pallas." [13]

This is the 18th century house of Pallas near Tynagh Co. Galway, and the tower house beside it. The old house was completely destroyed in 1945 as you can read here in a newspaper clipping of the time:

"Public auction of Important Demolition Material, ...150 interior and exterior doors, about 150 mahogany and other windows, presses, copper cylinder, gilt mirrors, library shelving, marble mantle pieces, various sizes...to be sold Monday next 23rd July [1945]."

(*Irish Independent,* 27th July 1945, p.5, and many thanks also to the Kelly family of Tynagh for their kind help on this.)

– right to hold *fairs*, is quite frequently mentioned and no doubt carried with it the right to some tax on the people using the fair.

Richard Archer of Pallas bought in 1737 the duties of the fair or "patrons" [patterns] of Kilcorban, which were kept yearly on the lands of Oltroctean in the half barony of Leitrim in Co Galway.

When the land on which the fair of Kilgolagh was sited, near Finea in Co. Cavan, was traded in 1785 attached to the deed was the necessity to provide the following facilities:

> "a proper field or park by way of fair green on said lands, for cattle to stand on to be bought and sold on the fair day, and also for leave and liberty to erect tents or booths on said park or field on the days preceding said fairs to sell liquors and malt." [14]

– *law courts*. Although quite rare but where it occurs is of great interest to the local historian, is the mention of the right to hold courts on the land. Or indeed it might be mentioned in the deed that the tenant was obliged to bring any cases he had in such and such a local court.

In a lease of 1728 from John Nugent to Miles Kernan the latter was obliged to "do suit at the Manor of Coolamber as shall be required". This local court was run by John Nugent as the owner of Coolamber, which is a castle on the border of Westmeath and Longford.

– *mineral rights*. Of course this would be a major issue in many countries, the right to mine on the land, but in fact its very rare to come across explicit or detailed mention of that in these deeds although it is sometimes mentioned. In 1718 Walter Nugent of Carpenterstown Co. Westmeath gave a lease for lives to Robert Fitzsimons of Turin Co. Westmeath, of the lands of the same Turin, in which he specifically excluded any minerals on the land, including coal, from the lease.[15]

– *right to cut wood*. This was an important enough subject, frequently the higher landlord would reserve those rights over land to himself and would not like the tenant cutting down any trees. He might also specify that the tenant was to plant trees, or hedgerows, on the land as a condition of the lease.

When lands at Killinebeg Co Westmeath, "lately held by Bryan Sheereny", were leased to John Cunningham of Ballymore Co Westmeath in 1765 the lessee was also to receive "as much timber as would fully roof four houses fit for farmers to live in".[16]

Social Historian

Certainly there is a lot of social history to be met with in the deeds, probably the best source for this are some of the

– *Marriage Settlements*. These are effectively agreements on the rearranging of estates at the time of a marriage of the heir or heiresses to that estate, usually, and often throw up interesting social details. Remember there is no heading or statement that says 'marriage settlement' in the deed in the ROD but as you read such a deed it will talk about a groom and bride about to get married, or recently married, and any such deed we call a marriage settlement. They are one of the glories of the ROD, they can be really interesting and there are a lot of them, maybe about 1/5 of all deeds would be marriage settlements, very roughly. Even where they don't provide any new social history they can be nonetheless useful for clarifying the extent of a family's estates. The point is that because of the huge confusion caused by the multiple layers of leases – referred to in the 'vertical problem' chapter – it can be difficult when reading most deeds to get a handle on what exactly is the extent of a given family's estate. But for the marriage settlements the other party, the other family they are marrying into, will often require clarity as to the extent of an estate so frequently we will get a genuine list of leases or lands that a person holds in the marriage settlement deed as opposed to the other types.

As regards gossipy social history we have for example in 1719 in Dublin a marriage settlement that was arranged for Elizabeth the widow of Francis Power, who was marrying again, where she specified that her husband was not to have any rights over these named possessions of hers:

> "a gold watch, three diamond rings, a large bible, a common prayer book, all sorts of house linen a large quantity, two feather beds, two white quilts, a large looking glass, a Dutch table, chany [china?] of several sorts, a large clock, two scrotors [?], one large chest, a tea table, a tea equipage in plate, a side board in plate worth £150, my own picture, my uncle's picture, Frank Power's picture, my uncle's coat of arms, a pair of kettles, some pewter, a brass kettle, my own wearing clothes, etc." [17]

This elaborate list may reflect the fact that the trustees of the new marriage settlement were two 'councellors at law', Henry Singleton and Henry Coddington. In 1756 a marriage settlement in Dublin was rehashed and the terms changed to that originally agreed. Easter Cooke, otherwise Walsh otherwise Reilly (i.e. she was originally Reilly and had married Walsh before Cooke), the widow and acting executrix of the estate of her late husband James Cooke, a woollen draper of Dublin, found herself in straightened circumstances and couldn't pay the full marriage portion due to her son-in-law. What happened was that her son Ambrose Cooke, who died at age nineteen, had got ill and the expenses paid on doctors had used up all her husband's money, as she explains: "said Ambrose was sickly from the age of fifteen years until the time of his death" and the money was spent "seeing physicians and paying for medicines" for him. Her son-in-law, who married her daughter Lucy on the 22 December 1755, was prepared to take less money and this was registered by the deed.[18] This example of newly straightened circumstances being mentioned in the deeds in the context of a rearranged marriage settlement also occurs in 1799 with the O'Reilly family of Baltrasna Co. Meath. They had to rearrange the marriage settlement of their daughter-in-law Henrietta, reducing her jointure – a word for what is later called a dowry – because:

"it appeareth in the progress of said marriage treaty that the estate and property of said Thomas O'Reilly and James O'Reilly was so circumstanced as to render a charge of the annual sum of £400, proposed and agreed to be charged and secured to Henrietta for her life a jointure in case she survives said James O'Reilly, precarious and uncertain".[19]

– *Wills* of course are good sources of social history in any era and the original acts setting up the ROD envisaged that they would be commonly registered there. This though did not happen and wills remain very uncommon in the ROD, maybe about 1 in every 200 or so, and hence many people would look upon the marriage settlement as the ROD's equivalent of a will. The wills that are there were published by the Irish Manuscripts Commission, or rather abstracts of them, in three volumes: P. Beryl Eustace, *Registry of Deeds Dublin, Abstract of Wills, 1708–1832* (Dublin, 1954-84) vols i-iii which should be consulted for further details on the types of wills registered.

Since its not just deeds that relate to land that are registered in the ROD some social history can emerge in the miscellaneous nature of the other type of transactions. For example a 1768 deed resulted from an "Act of Vestry" by the "Church Wardens of the Parish of St Werburgh" in Dublin.[20]

– *Arbitration Agreements*. One common kind of 'miscellaneous deed' was the registering of an agreement between parties who settled their differences outside of court. These can be quite interesting because the parties might decide to provide details of the settled dispute which would otherwise not be found anywhere in the surviving papers of the 18th century. One example of a dispute resolved without going to court and then registered in the ROD comes from the Earls of Westmeath in 1753 which resulted in a huge complicated Memorial (c. seven pages) being registered detailing the settling of their differences with the Dysert family.[21] Another example of a potential dispute that was settled before it went to the courts comes from Offaly in

1743. Mary Leycester, the daughter of John Leycester deceased, owned lands at Gurken, 100 acres, and some lands in Killisheel, Curraghmore, and Kilcormack now called Frankfort in Co Offaly, among others. She married Daniel Egan of Ballyeighter in Co Tipperary and had a son John, her son and heir. Daniel died and she married secondly Pierce Nugent of Tihilly and had Luke, Pierce, and Thomas Herbert [in the original text they left out the 'Herbert' but we are told that before they signed "the word Herbert being first interlined in several places"], in that order, and other sons. Luke, Pierce and the other sons are long since dead without issue and now Mary and her husband Pierce are also dead. John Egan, as the heir of her mother, now claimed all the lands and Thomas Herbert unfortunately could not find the family settlement under which he inherited the lands. Hence in order to avoid the proceeds of going to law, Egan and Nugent agree to sell the farm and split the proceeds between themselves and they register all this in the memorial in the ROD.[22] Finally we read that when a father passed ownership of half of his demesne at Cloncullen Co Longford in 1797 to his son he couldn't decide which half to give him, so, in accordance with a letter that the father sent to the son, it went to arbitration locally to John O'Brien esq and the Revd James Ahmuty and we read all about this in an arbitration settlement registered in the ROD.[23]

Economic Historian

In theory the ROD should be one of the best sources in existence for Irish economic history of the 18th century, particularly allowing for the fact of the huge number of deeds registered and the scrupulous recording of the financial transactions therein. Surely there is no other repository currently in existence which could come close to that level of historical data, bearing in mind the great losses of Irish historical documents for the 18th century.

But in practice there are lot of caveats that the historian should be aware of here. The deeds contain such a hugely interlocking structure of leases (the 'vertical' issue discussed later) that the financial details contained in one or two deeds on their own cannot be trusted as giving us any solid economic statistics. Meaning: if you read, for example, that Joe Bloggs leases 30 acres of land for 10 years at £5 a year to John Smith, it doesn't necessarily follow that the land is worth anything like this £5 a year. You mightn't know what leases are above or below that in the leasing structure, for example Joe Bloggs might have to pay a rent to the landlord above him, and hence he is silently allowing for that in the figure he charges Smith, and Smith might be letting out the land again to some tenant below him and since you don't know what he intends to let it out for then you don't know how much Smith really hopes to make per acre. This is the reality in fact for virtually all these deeds, you cannot be certain about the real economic figures unless you do quite a bit of in depth research or you are lucky enough to read some very simple deed where you are sure there are no hidden 'middlemen' to consider.

Another caveat is that the economic activity we are referring to for the vast amount of deeds in the ROD in the 18th century is of course farming. But the details of farming, as such, are hardly ever mentioned in the ROD entries for some reason, doubtless its a sure sign that the people dealing in all these deeds were not the people who usually had to physically till the soil! So for example references to cattle, numbers or breeds of, or sheep or crops are well nigh completely absent from these deeds, surprisingly you will not read anything about this in the ROD. Therefore, as you can see, the economic data that is in the ROD is more limited than you might realise. As regards agriculture the only clues you can get will be from some placenames, clearly references to the 'sheep fold', or 'bull field', and of course the 'deer park' will tell their own story.

That said of course its not a complete washout with other trades possibly being easier to track than farming. For example the economics of builders and developers in Dublin city could be followed easily enough, because there might be an entry showing their purchase of land and then later various entries showing their sale of the finished houses, bearing in mind that these Dublin city entries very often elaborately describe the physical location of the houses. (They can even describe squares of houses that are about to be built, which is great for a local historian of course, e.g. a 1771 Dublin Memorial mentions a "piece of ground situate on the North Side of new intended square to be laid out and to be called Merrion Square".[24]) Another interesting trade in the ROD are millers because the patch of land they are on are often again elaborately described in the ROD entries. That of course refers to mills turned by water but amazingly the other type is also mentioned, although very very rarely: a windmill was rented out at Gortnysillagh, Galway, in 1732, to John Burke of Reaghan in Galway, plus liberty to transport, via horses, corn or meal to the mill through the lands of Gortnysillagh.[25] Even publicans can be seen at work in these deeds, for example a 'taphouse' in Castlepollard was transferred in 1768 to a merchant of that town called Edward Sweeney, including "the underpart or passage between the malthouse and still house." [26] A brewer in Kells Co. Meath selling his still to a local merchant in 1760 mentions the "copper kieve and underbank".[27]

And of course the miscellaneous, non land, type deeds mentioned above can also yield their economic secrets e.g. a partnership of two woolen drapers in Dublin was agreed and registered in 1770.[28] Incidentally for the 19th century its always possible that you could find deeds relating to the railways, maybe with interesting lists of shareholders etc.

Another fruitful source of economic and indeed social history can be provided by the sometimes miscellaneous nature of the rents that are charged. Of course its usually money that is mentioned as the price of rent but not always, sometimes you get the strangest things listed as customs that are usually paid with the rent or in lieu of rent. (By the way a peppercorn is often listed as rent in these deeds but that is definitely to be read as meaning that no rent is due, a peppercorn in practice means that the rent is nominal, i.e. the rent is really nothing. An example of this is where the rent for some land on Arran Quay in Dublin in 1749 was listed as "one peppercorn only".[29]) Some curious examples of this are: in 1768 a land transaction involving a plot of land on the north side of James St in Dublin included as part of the rent "a loaf of double remined [meaning 'refined', presumably] sugar, weighing at least 10 pounds at Christmas yearly".[30] Rent of some land in Coolamber Manor included "one fat hog" or a moyder or a moydore in lieu thereof, plus "two fat hens".[31]

So the historical value of the records in the ROD is really very great, its a positive treasure trove for the genealogist and local historian, at least, of the 18th century. But, there is always a 'but'!, there are traps here for the unwary. In particular there are two issues that need further teasing out:

a) firstly the question of identifying the different patches of land within townlands, bearing in mind that there are no maps in the ROD, 'a horizontal problem'; and

b) being conscious of the confusing overlapping lease structure that you get for Irish land of the 18th century, a 'vertical problem'.

This then will occupy the reader for the next two chapters.

Footnotes
1. Séan J Murphy, *A Most Valuable Storehouse of History*, in, *History Ireland*, vol 17 no.1 (Jan-Feb 2009), p.24.

2. 1778 321-335-266582.

3. 1794 488-386-311390.

4. 1796 502-203-324386.

5. 1776 370-214-247956.

6. 1722 40-7-23814.

7. 1756 180-134-119853. The Phair reference is from Analecta Hibernica (1966) no.23, p.264.

8. 1752 159-159-106368.

9. 1780 342-305-230133.

10. 1760 205-327-136305.

11. 1740 102-278-70740.

12. 1785 373-386-248779.

13. 1733 72-499-51715.

14. 1737 89-376-63988 and the Kilgolagh reference is from 1785 373-386-24877.

15. The Coolamber reference: 1728 55-460-37793, and the Turin reference: 1718 21-463-12140.

16. 1765 242-567-158344.

17. 1719 76-316-54596.

18. 1756 193-131-137249.

19. 1799 520-480-341357.

20. 1768 258-313-171618.

21. 1753 180-117-119782.

22. 1743 110-246-76946.

23. 1797 494-462-333848.

24. 1771 289-172-190198.

25. 1732 78-295-55788.

26. 1768 283-610-187582.

27. 1760 207-140-136415.

28. 1770 281-562-188156.

29. 1749 136-246-91238.

30. 1768 257-492-169516.

31. 1742 175-166-116597.

CHAPTER 4

The Horizontal Problem

The horizontal problem is easy to envisage. Imagine if you are looking across a gate at a townland horizontally stretched out in front of you on the horizon. The problem is that even if you have all the various records from the Registry of Deeds in front of you, how do you know which reference refers to which part of the townland you are looking at? Remember there are no maps corresponding to the 18th century entries in the ROD and while the townland is the smallest unit mentioned nonetheless many of the entries refer to specific parts within the given townland. Hence when you read of some landlord dealing in land in Ballybough, or wherever, it doesn't necessarily – although sometimes it does – mean that the landlord had *all* of the townland of Ballybough, probably it only refers to a certain part of it. But which part of it? is the question we ask ourselves here.

There is in fact no quick answer to this question. The basic policy is to try to link the land reference back to the mid 17th century Down Survey maps, going backwards in time, and to the early 19th century Ordnance Survey maps, going forwards in history. For that purpose it might help then to be clear on what those former maps actually contain:

17th century maps and surveys.

The date that dominates the 17th century maps is 1641 when the Catholic Irish – allegedly – rebelled against British rule and consequently suffered a huge land confiscation. This provided the pretext for Cromwell in the 1650s to conduct a number of surveys of the land to determine which land was to be confiscated and disposed of. In particular we have three surveys that you need to have cognizance of:

a) The **Civil Survey**. This was a written – not mapped – survey of the landholdings of Ireland as it existed in 1640. The procedure was that the government commissioned juries to be held in the various districts around Ireland and these juries came up with a list of land divisions – townlands, parishes and baronies – and listed who owned what land in these districts in 1640, i.e. just before the rebellion.

b) The **Down Survey**.[1] Then a great mapping survey was conducted across Ireland under the supervision of William Petty whose results became known as the 'Down Survey'. These are maps and come in various sizes but particularly we have Baronial Maps (to recap, a Barony again is a large land area covering, very approximately, about a fifth of a county) and Parish Maps (i.e. Civil Parishes, which in turn might contain, again very roughly, 10 townlands or thereabouts). Obviously then the Parish Maps in particular can be quite helpful in identifying the particular patch of land you are interested in.

c) The **Books of Survey and Distribution**.[2] These books – and there are various sets of them, including the set used by the Quit Rent Office which is available in the National Archives in Dublin – give you the final distribution of the land that resulted from the Cromwellian confiscations. It lists who owned the land in 1640 – taking the data from the Civil Survey of course, and its usually a Catholic landowner at that date – and then it lists who got the land as a result of the confiscations – normally giving the land to a Protestant. The latter landowner forms then the natural beginning to your searches in the 18th century deeds, hopefully you can trace a given patch of land back to the proprietor who got the land in the Books of Survey and Distribution.

There are a lot of caveats that should be borne in mind here though. The crucial point is that the Parish Maps of the Down Survey do not show you the internal subdivision made as a result of the confiscations. To explain this lets take a simple entry in the Books of Survey and Distribution for Westmeath:

Proprietors in 1640	Denominations of land	Acres Unprofitable	Lands Profitable	Acres Disposed Under the Acts	To whom disposed
James Tuite	Loghgare Begg		136-2-16	053-2-16	Duke of York
				055-0-0	John Buckland
				019-3-35	William Henman
		139-0-0[3]			

The last entry, of 'acres unprofitable', includes some of

73

Masetowne and remember this part is explicitly marked in the Down Survey maps so you can see the 'unprofitable acres' clearly. You would expect to find – although it is not always like this – that if the Tuites are dealing in land in Loghgare Begg after this then the lands that they are referring to are these unprofitable acres which you now have an exact map for.

That then is the good news, the bad news is that there is no contemporary mapping that can tell you what part of Loghgare begg went to the Duke of York (the future James II of Boyne fame) and what part to John Buckland etc. The Down Survey maps are then of particular interest only in identifying the 'unprofitable acres' – bogs and mountains etc – in the different townlands, you will need another plan to mark out the three internal divisions that occurred in Loghgare begg in the mid 17th century. These unprofitable acres incidentally were usually kept by the original Catholic proprietors and hence the accurate folklore that the Catholics were pushed into the bogs and mountains etc.

The other big caveat in using the 17th century surveys is that the real picture is not as neat as described here. The truth is that you have a number of different surveys and plantations – and hence maps – at different times for different parts of Ireland and therefore it can be a bit unclear trying to piece the situation together for your given patch of land. For example the Strafford Survey (1635-7) is often seen as a substitute for the Civil Survey for Mayo and the Ulster Plantation of 1609 was obviously very important and did indeed generate some interesting maps for the six counties affected (Cavan, Donegal, Fermanagh, Armagh, Derry and Tyrone, for the other three counties of Monaghan, Down and Antrim there were various other plantations of an earlier date). Note as well that for some counties we have a type of census for the 1650s, for which see Séamus Pender, *A Census of Ireland, circa 1659* (Dublin, 1939). Other caveats include the fact that the Down Survey maps sometimes have blank areas, often where Protestant proprietors already owned the land in 1640 and hence land that didn't need to be surveyed because it wasn't to be confiscated (an example of this can be seen in the Baronial Map for the Barony of Clanmahon in Co. Cavan). Also the final distribution of some lands was disputed and is even sometimes listed differently across the different Books of Survey and Distribution, although these differences are often quite minor.

Nonetheless getting a clear picture of the land holdings for the 17th century is certainly quite achievable and can be helpful in trying to solve this 'horizontal problem' for the 18th century deeds.

19th century maps and surveys.

The other way to go about it then is to move forward in history and try and match the land holding listed in the 18th century deeds to the patches of land mapped for us by the Ordnance Survey in the 19th century.

As you get into the 1830s you hit upon the great mapping done by the Ordnance Survey which can of course be a great help in clarifying the exact lands in question. One helpful thing to note, for example, is that in the early Ordnance Survey maps the exact extent of estates and desmesnes are marked out specially. Hence if you are researching a given 'big house' and accompanying estate it is perfectly straight forward to see the exact extent of the estate from the early OS maps. We also have a number of important surveys for that time as well and these can be helpful in clarifying specific patches of land:

a) The **Tithe Applotment Books**, resulting from the Composition Act of 1823 by which the tithes were paid through the landlord rather than directly to the Established Church, were compiled c.1830. They list who has to pay tithes – a kind of tax normally paid to the Church of Ireland – and were compiled by the local gentry rather than by some centralised body. For our purposes it can be quite interesting to see the acreage attached to a given landowner within a townland in these books which are housed in the National Archives in Dublin.

b) The **Griffith's Valuation**, made necessary by the Tenement Act of 1842, was compiled during the 1840s and 50s. This survey was printed and lists the local rates due to be paid to the new Poor Law Unions which ran the local, newly built, workhouses. It is a great source for the period and, crucially, in the Valuation Office in Dublin there is a set of Ordnance Survey maps which are linked directly to the landholdings listed by Griffith. This then is exactly what we are looking for to help us with our 'horizontal problem' because by these means we can see the exact location of the land parcels within the townland, for the 1840s at any rate.

c) There are lot more miscellaneous surveys available as you go into the 19th century depending on the land you are researching, including stray extracts from the 1821 census, especially for parts of Cavan and Meath, and rentals from the Landed Estates Court and Encumbered Estates Court for the immediate post Famine period (for both these sets of records you should again check with the National Archives in Dublin).

To clarify again, what you are trying to do, in seeking to identify the exact location within a townland of the lands mentioned in the 18th century deeds in the ROD, is to match that land back to the 17th century surveys – which is particularly helpful if the land was listed there as 'unprofitable' – and forwards to Griffith's Valuation which, in conjunction with the aforementioned marked OS maps, will give you the exact location of the lands on a map. As you work on your research there are a few specific things which might help you to achieve this objective:

i) Of course you will watch carefully the various *surnames of the proprietors* all the way from the Down Survey to Griffith and hopefully you can make the link that way. Hence obviously if some Robert Buckland, for example, was dealing in land in Loghgare begg in the mid 18th century then we could assume that it was the same patch that his Buckland ancestor received under the Cromwellian confiscations of the 17th century. Then in turn if you can continue to follow that land through the various owners that you can trace in the ROD up to the Griffith Valuation then you have the exact layout of the lands. For this reason when doing your research take careful note of any previous transactions of the land that are mentioned in the ROD. As a hypothetical example, in a deed referring to the Vicars family in Ballygarth in 1750 it might make mention of an earlier deed of 1710 involving the Beresfords, or whoever, and that then will of course be the same part of the townland and might make your quest to match the land back to the Down Survey that bit easier. Hence always take down any such references.

ii) Always take *careful note of the exact acreage*. This simple trick can be extremely helpful in tracking the specific land parcels within townlands. Hence, referring back again to the Westmeath example in the Books of Survey and Distribution listed earlier, if we found a land deed referring to 55 acres in Loghgare begg we will know immediately that it is the old Buckland parcel that they are referring to. The listed acreage doesn't change much throughout this time but if it does then the ROD deeds will usually alert you to it. It is quite common for a mid 18th century deed to state explicitly that land X was previously reckoned as 30 acres and now via a new survey by Y – the surveyor is nearly always named – it is thought to contain 35 acres 2 roods and 6 perches, or whatever. Otherwise you will find that the ROD deeds will just continue to use the acreage values listed in the Books of Survey and Distribution and this is then pricelessly helpful in keeping track of specific parts of townlands across the 18th century.

iii) While quite rare for rural lands, although common for urban ones, nonetheless *sometimes the actual ROD deed will tell you precisely where the lands are in the townland*. It might go into detail stating that this particular patch is west of the road leading from Castlepollard to Finea, and North of the branch of the Inny river crossing the townland, or whatever. These directions can be extremely helpful of course and even at a rate of only 1 in 30 rural deeds, or thereabouts, that give us that kind of information it can still be quite valuable at solving our 'horizontal problem'. 18th century ROD deeds for urban areas, particularly Dublin City Centre, will frequently go into exhaustative detail establishing exactly where a given parcel of land is located, including the exact distance from a main road etc and needless to say it makes the urban historian's job not a little easier.

iv) *18th century maps*. While no national mapping survey of Ireland was completed in the 18th century nonetheless there are quite a few local maps which were prepared:

– by improving landlords or proprietors who were preparing to sell estates;

– as a prelude to some land transactions and attached to some original land deeds of the time (not in the copies of the memorials in the transcript books in the ROD alas!) as are often mentioned in the ROD entries. There are many original deeds, some with these small maps attached, in the National Archives in Dublin, the National Library and the Public Record Office Northern Ireland.

– by some publishers of printed books of the time, particularly by George Taylor and Andrew Skinner in *Taylor and Skinner's maps of the roads of Ireland* (Dublin, 1778). These are relatively uninformative roadmaps but they can be quite useful sometimes and many of these maps are online here helpfully: http://failteromhat.com/Gallery/Taylor-Skinner-Road-Map-of-Ireland-1777 .

As well as the well known Taylor and Skinner you have some old Irish maps in these printed books: Herman Moll, *A Set of Twenty New and Correct Maps of Ireland* (London, 1728), Emanuel Bowen, *An Accurate Map of Ireland* (London, 1754), and Bernard Scale, *An Hibernian atlas* (London, 1776).

Also you might like to look for some maps that were produced for the use of the Grand Juries – County Councils – around Ireland in the 18th century and up to the Ordnance Survey years. Some of these maps include:

Kildare (by John Noble and James Keenan 1752),
Down (John Ridge 1755),
Dublin (John Rocque 1760),
Armagh (John Rocque 1760),
Wicklow (Jacob Neville 1760),
Louth (Taylor and Skinner 1777),
Clare (Henry Pelham 1779),
Antrim (James Lendrick 1780),
Kildare again (Alex Taylor 1783),
Clare (Henry Pelham 1787),
Monaghan (William McCrea 1790-93),
Derry (Henecy and Fitzpatrick 1795),
Carlow (published by William Allen in Dublin in 1798),
Kerry (Henry Pelham c.1800),
Donegal (William McCrea 1801),
Laois (Daniel Cahill 1805),

Fermanagh (the grand jury appointed William McCrea and Gabriel Montgomery to do a map of the county in 1807 but it seems only Montgomery's survey of Lough Erne was carried out),
Westmeath (William Larkin 1808),
Kilkenny (15 maps 1809-19, see Andrew Lewis, *The Grand Jury maps of County Kilkenny*, published in the *Old Kilkenny Review* (2010), p.91-95.),
Offaly (William Larkin 1809),
Wexford (Valentine Gill 1811),
Cork (Neville Bath 1811),
Longford (William Faden 1813),
Tyrone (William McCrea and George Knox 1813),
Meath (William Larkin 1817),
Roscommon (William Edgeworth and Richard Griffith 1817),
Waterford (William Larkin 1818),
Galway (William Larkin 1819),
Sligo (William Larkin 1819),
Leitrim (William Larkin 1819),
Dublin (William Duncan 1821),
Limerick (James Coffey 1825), and
Mayo (William Bald 1830).

Another source of pre Ordnance Survey maps are those drawn up by the 'Commissioners for Bogs in Ireland.' They published a lot of detailed high quality maps of various bogs in Ireland in the c.1810 period and are worth looking up if the area you are interested in is in a large bogland district. These maps were printed alongwith the reports of the commissioners and you can tell the general locations they surveyed from some of these titles:
Richard Lovell Edgeworth, *A map of the Bogs ... in the Western Division of district no. 7, situate in the county of Longford* (1811);
Richard Lovell Edgeworth, *A map of the Bogs ... in the Eastern Division of District no. 7, situate in the counties of Longford and Westmeath* (1811);
Richard Lovell Edgeworth, *A map of part of District No. 15, containing the Bogs on the West of the River Shannon, situate in the county of Roscommon* (1813);
Thomas Colbourne, *A map of the Bogs in the west part of the county of Clare* (1811);

James Alexander Jones, *Map of part of the counties of Meath and Wesmeath [sic], containing part of the Bogs in district no. four* (1811);

Richard Griffith, *Map of Geashill Bog [Co. Offaly], on which are laid down the whole of the proposed drains for the improvement of the Bog* (1811);

Richard Griffith, *Map of the mountainous and uncultivated parts of the counties of Dublin and Wicklow* (1812);

Richard Griffith, *Map of part of the Bogs Belonging to the District of the River Suck situated in the Counties of Galway and Roscommon* (1812);

Thomas Townsend, *A map of the Bogs in the western side of district no. 6, situate in Westmeath and King's counties* (1811);

Thomas Townsend, *A map of the Bogs on the eastern side of district no. 6, situate in the counties of Westmeath and Longford* (1811);

Thomas Townsend, *Lough Neagh district* (1813);

Alexander Nimmo, *Iveragh in the county of Kerry* (1811);

Alexander Nimmo, *The Bogs on the rivers Laure and Lower Maine, in Kerry* (1812);

Alexander Nimmo, *Bogs of Slievelvaghar in the countries of Kerry and Cork* (1812);

Alexander Nimmo, *Bogs on the river Cashen &c. in the North of Kerry* (1812);

Alexander Nimmo, *Bogs on the River Kenmare in Kerry* (1812);

Alexander Nimmo, *Bogs on the Upper Maine &c. in Kerry* (1812);

David Aher, *The Bogs of district no. 8, situated in the counties of Tipperary, Kilkenny & Queens County* (1811);

David Aher, *Map of the Bogs of District No. 12 in the Queens County* (1812);

William Bald, *Map of the Bogs lying in the South West part of the county of Mayo, whose waters discharge themselves into Clew Bay, Killery Harbour & Lough Mask* (London, 1812).

A few other 18th century county maps are printed in some published books of the period, for example in the following books by Charles Smith, a Dungarvan apothecary:

The antient and present state of the county of Down (Dublin,

1744),
The antient and present state of the county and city of Waterford (Dublin, 1746),
The antient and present state of the county and city of Cork (Dublin, 1750),
The antient and present state of the county of Kerry (Dublin, 1756).

For Dublin there are countless old maps, for example in this printed book: John Rutty, *An Essay Towards a Natural History of the County of Dublin* (Dublin, 1772).

For the Ordnance Survey you have the old 6 inch to a mile maps (1829-42) and the 25 inch to a mile (1887-1913) maps online here: http://maps.osi.ie . You can even flick between these two sets of maps, while retaining the precise location, to see clearly what had been built in the latter half of the 19th century.

It is completely hit and miss as to whether you can find these maps for the land you are researching but it is always worth checking out the above repositories to see if such a map exists.

v) *Folklore*, is another important source in solving this 'horizontal problem'. Its possible that if you simply visit that townland in Ireland – just watch out for the dogs! – and ask the locals what part was owned by what family they might be able to tell you, so solving your problem without any exhausting research.

By these means then it should be possible to zone in on the exact part of a given townland that is referred to in the 18th century deeds in the ROD.

At the time of this book going to press we now find that both sets of maps and surveys discussed here, that is the Down Survey maps and the Books of Survey and Distribution of c.1650-1660 and the 1840s Griffith Valuation and accompanying O.S. maps, with the specific land parcels marked in, are now completely online. The former is available at http://downsurvey.tcd.ie and the latter at http://www.askaboutireland.ie/griffith-valuation/ . So in fact its now perfectly feasible to arm yourself with those maps and surveys for your given townland before you begin your ROD research and of considerable help it is quite likely to be.

Footnotes
1. Down Survey Parish Maps are available for most counties, e.g. some of the maps are among the National Library Manuscripts:

Ms 712-713	Cork	M/F Pos 7382
Ms 714	Dublin	M/F Pos 7382
Ms 715	Meath	M/F Pos 7382
Ms 716	Offaly	M/F Pos 7383
Ms 717	Leitrim	M/F Pos 7383
Ms 718	Limerick	M/F Pos 7383
Ms 719	Longford	M/F Pos 7383
Ms 720	Laois and Kilkenny	M/F Pos 7383
Ms 721	Tipperary	M/F Pos 7384
Ms 722	Waterford	M/F Pos 7384
Ms 723-724	Westmeath	M/F Pos 7384
Ms 725	Wexford	M/F Pos 7384
Ms 726	Wicklow and Carlow	M/F Pos 7385

Also among the maps in the NLI there are photostat copies of maps at:

16-K-11	Antrim 1
16-K-12	Antrim 2
16-K-13	Donegal and Derry 3 (1-63)
16-K-14	Donegal 3 (64-164)
16-K-15	Down, Armagh, and Tyrone 4

An example from these parish maps can be seen online at: http://dnausers.d-n-a.net/dnetcRrI/mdrol4.jpg which is the parish map of Magheredril in the Barony of Kinealerty in Co. Down.

For the list of maps included in this chapter I partly drew on an elaborate catalogue produced by Adams auctioneers for the auction of the maps of the late Dr Barry Hewson sold in 2010, available at: http://www.adams.ie/documents/Mapsalesmall.pdf p.23 et seq.

2. Many of the Books of Survey and Distribution have been published – and there are also different manuscript sets at different locations – but for an almost complete manuscript set you could consult the Annesley Manuscripts on microfilm in the National Library in Dublin, using the following reference numbers.

NLI M/F Pos 267-8:
1 Kilkenny
2 Waterford and Kerry
3 Kildare and Carlow

4 Wexford

NLI M/F Pos 269-270:
5. Longford and Louth
6. Mayo
7. Tipperary

No. 8, 10-14, NLI M/F Pos 270-272:
Monaghan and Armagh,
Limerick
Westmeath,
Clare,
Roscommon

No. 15-20, NLI M/F Pos 272-274:
Galway,
Cork,
Down and Antrim,
Leitrim and Sligo,
Cavan and Fermanagh

NLI M/F Pos 274-275:
21. Offaly and Laois
22. Dublin and Wicklow
23. Donegal, Derry and Tyrone

3. John C Lyons, *The Book of Surveys and Distribution of the estates in the County of Westmeath* (Ladistown, 1852), p.34, under Roconnell Parish in the Barony of Moyashell and Magheredernon. The acres 'profitable' do not add up to 136-2-16 because there remained, for some reason, 8-0-5 acres undisposed.

CHAPTER 5
The Vertical Problem

The simplest way to explain this problem might be to take a hypothetical land transaction from modern times. Lets say that John Smith buys a house on a patch of land for £10,000 from Pat Murphy in Kells in 1981. He finds that he has to pay £10 annual ground rent, hypothetically, to Lord Carlingford and also he took a mortgage on the property, for £9,000, from the Bank of Ireland. Furthermore he actually went to live in England and let out the house year to year to a tenant who lived in it, Liam Lynch. For the sake of argument we will say that a similar situation existed for Pat Murphy when he owned it, he also let it out to somebody else year by year, Joe Reilly, also had a mortgage, from Ulster Bank, but in his case his, hypothetical, landlord for the ground rent was Lord Headfort. (This is because in 1979, we will say, Lord Carlingford married the heiress of Lord Headfort and in turn received the old rents of Kells from his father-in-law.) So if we were to draw that up as a simple table it might look something like this:

Type of Landholding	1977	1982
Original old landlord, receiving the ground rent	Lord Headfort	Lord Carlingford
the main substantial owner of the property	Pat Murphy	John Smith
a bank holding a mortgage over the property	Ulster Bank	Bank of Ireland
short term lease, the actual person who lives on the property	Joe Reilly	Liam Lynch

That then is what we are calling a 'vertical' type of landholding structure, we have multiple types of owners of the same property cascading down that table. So where we have in the 'horizontal problem' described a person looking over a fence at a townland stretched across the horizon, here we have a notional vertical structure stretching upwards out of that townland, the accumulated owners who own some type of ownership rights over the exact same land. This pattern, like in the above table but more complex, is what happens in the 18th century Irish deeds. When you analyse your notes from the Registry of Deeds you should arrange the owners in a table like that and think about that kind of structure as you read the deeds.

This unfortunately is a problem without much of a solution, you just have to be conscious that a lot of the time the land is being traded horizontally in a table like the above (as if in modern times, as an example, Bank of Ireland had in turn passed on its mortgage to some other bank without notifying the house owner, or indeed in the way that Lord Carlingford had got his land ownership from Lord Headfort etc.) If you think about it its almost as if the land had been subdivided and now it is being traded across ways in that table as if each type of ownership right was itself a separate parcel of land.

That might seem confusing at first but as you read down through this chapter you should become clear as to what this 'problem' really entails. It is a serious issue because Irish land in the 18th century is famously subdivided this way. There are quite frequently many 'middle men' as it were clogging up a table like the above, people who have some kind of interest in the land but are not actually the farmers of that land. Why Irish land is so prone to this kind of multiple leasing structure in the 18th century can be explained by reference to maybe six issues:

a) **Custom of long leases including the lease for lives**

In Ireland it had been from an early date, an earlier date to the 18th century,[1] the practice to transfer land either on very long leases, e.g. 99 years, or, classically, for three lives. The latter type of lease means that three people are named in the deed and when all those three people are dead then the lease is up. It was usually combined with some mention of years so that it might, usually does, state that the lease will be up if the lives are dead or if 31 years have elapsed, whichever is longer.

Surprisingly it isn't at all easy to say why exactly the three life system, or indeed these very long leases in general, became so popular in Ireland, but popular they certainly were as one commentator noted in 1827:

> "Where a settled estate has been usually let on lives, which is generally the case in Ireland, the common power of leasing is upon fines, which, as the lives or leases drop, are considered among the annual profits. (1 Burr 121.) But this practice prevails in only a few counties in England [Devon was one]... " [2]

And in 1848 we are told that:

> "The half of Ireland is said to be leased in perpetuity." [3]

Why exactly this is the case is, as I say, unknown but two theories could be put forward. One is the issue of franchises for elections mentioned in the next section but also it was thought by at least one commentator that it came about as a result of the land confiscations of the 17th century. The original Cromwellian planters faced a pretty heavy tax in the Quit Rents and to pay it they had oftentimes to face quite a slog farming in an often hostile and remote environment from what they were used to. So it seemed to have grown up as a practice among them that they would just let out the land on a very long term lease and by simply making sure that the annual sum they got exceeded the annual Quit Rent due they could live on the money in London – or Dublin – and forget about farming these inhospitable lands. This seems to be what is understood by the term 'quit rent lease' – i.e a lease that guaranteed to pay the Quit Rent – that is mentioned in the quote in the 'commercial pressures' section below. This theory is described here in an 1844 book on land and economic matters in Ireland, beginning with the mentality of the original Cromwellian planters:

> "In this state of perplexity and discontent they seized upon the crown practice of a quit rent to which they were themselves subjected, as an

example stamped with the prestige of the highest authority, and furnishing the readiest and most convenient means of relief. They granted at small rents such long leases of their lands as lives renewable for ever, and terms of 500 and 999 years. They were content in short to entitle themselves to a limited but certain income from vast possessions which were not to be occupied personally without the risk of incessant danger and incalculable losses.

The quantity of land held in Ireland on leases of lives renewable for ever, and for terms of 500 and 999 years, is enormous, and so numerous have been the intermediate leases granted at small profit rents that as many as six and seven landlords, each deriving sums of sixpence, a shilling, and half-a-crown an acre, have frequently been known to intervene between the crown and the virtual possessor of the property, that is to say, the actual holder of one of the leases referred to, and deriving under it the predominant interest in the soil.

The labyrinth of tenures with their concomitant settlements which occurs in a case of this kind, renders the transfer of property difficult and expensive, and proves a heavy bar to improvement. In the case for instance of 1000 acres of land held for 500 years and chargeable to anterior lessees with a rent of 5s an acre, while to the last lessee it is worth £1 an acre, how can improvement be expected to take place?" [4]

Here he quotes from Henry Grattan's biography of his father (vol ii p.82) and famous namesake:

"From the unsettled state of Ireland, the various confiscations and forfeitures, landed property had formerly been considered of little value; and in order to form a good tenantry and give encouragement to improve the land, this species of tenure – leases with covenants of perpetual renewal – was devised. It was said to have been introduced by the Ormonde family, and a great proportion of the property of the country was held under it. On the fall of each life in the line a fine was paid, and if the life was not substituted within a stated period (three or six months) the interest became forfeited to the landlord."

For whatever reason this is in fact the basic lease pattern of Ireland at this time and as you can see from the long quote above it led to "as many as six and seven landlords, each deriving sums of sixpence, a shilling, and half-a-crown an acre" which frequently were "known to intervene between the crown and the virtual possessor of the property". This then is our vertical problem in a nutshell. Those original proprietors who had given up these long leases nonetheless took great care to list all these lands when they were making family settlements or getting mortgages listed in the ROD. So that's why you have to become very conscious of this vertical issue when you are reading these deeds. Just because John Vicars, or whoever, lists the townland of Ballygolagh as his property in his deed of 1751 it doesn't necessarily follow that he has much right over that townland. You have to try and place him in this vertical pattern and try and track the land throughout the 18th century on each of the particular vertical planes in the leasing structure. You have to look upon it as if the lands of Ballygolagh were now divided when the long lease was given, only vertically instead of horizontally, and you now are trying to track these vertical patches of land in the same way that you solved the horizontal problem. In particular when you are reading about anybody owning land in a townland you are always asking yourself what part of that townland does the deed refer to, in this vertical sense, i.e. are they trading again in rights over the land granted in that old lease I read about in that deed from 1714 or whatever. And deeds in the ROD will frequently refer back to an earlier lease to clarify that for you and so don't forget to always note that where it occurs.

b) Swelling the voting Register

Another reason why the land in Ireland is so subdivided in this vertical sense was because it sometimes suited the landlord to rearrange his leasing pattern to give himself more voters as tenants. A potential voter in the 18th century had to satisfy certain requirements of land ownership to be allowed to vote and since a tenant who held his property under a term of lives was more likely to be able to vote it often happened that the landlord would give him that type of long lease in order to get together a good voting pool of tenants to use for political purposes. Since Catholics weren't officially allowed to take leases like that until the Catholic Relief Act of 1778 this effect on the long lives system only applies to Protestants before that date or before the franchise was extended in 1793.[5] Further details are outlined here:

"From 1727 to 1793 only Protestants with a forty-shilling freehold (a freehold worth at least 40 shillings per year above the rent) or above qualified to vote. In 1793 Catholics with at least a forty-shilling freehold were given the vote. Forty-shilling freeholders, whether Catholic or Protestant, had the vote between 1793 and 1829. In 1829, all 40 shilling freeholders lost the vote, and from that date a £10 freehold was required to qualify to vote. From 1832 through 1884 a series of reform acts extended the franchise somewhat, but it was not until 1918 that all adult males (over age 21) were given the vote. In the 1920s women over age 21 gained the same privilege in both Northern Ireland and the Irish Free State (now the Republic of Ireland)."[6]

By 'freehold' they mean land owned outright by the voter or land held under a lease of lives. Land held under a short term lease – and sometimes all leases that specified a term of years only, it varied somewhat in response to various bits of legislation – did not qualify the tenant to vote. Hence the great incentive to give tenants leases for lives, who needless to say would be expected to vote in response to their landlord's wishes. Our aforementioned 1844 commentator talks about what happened after the 40 shilling freeholders lost their vote and also points out the historical background:

> "Passing over leases for 21 and 31 years, and one or more lives in reversion, which were general when a forty shilling freehold conferred the parliamentary franchise, but which have fallen rapidly into disuse since that privilege was taken away...
>
> The Irish forty shilling freehold was first granted in the reign of Henry VIII, and was abolished in the reign of Geo. II when, as Primate Boulter stated, the Roman Catholics being five to one were found to be growing too strong for the English interest. The elective franchise from this freehold was conceded in the year 1793 as an instalment of Catholic Emancipation, and again extinguished when that measure was conceded in 1829." [7]

It seems then that there is quite a history in Ireland of this phenomenon of rearranging estates to increase the franchise, which makes this whole issue a potential partial origin of the three lives system itself. Whatever about that overall historic question the point here is obviously that this franchise issue is also giving us another reason why Irish landholding was so complicated in this vertical sense. Some tenants were in theory given land, but only under complicated artificial leasing arrangements from their landlord which makes the real land transactions difficult to disentangle. Sometimes people in rural Ireland can even point out to you given fields that were parcelled out of estates deliberately to give tenants an artificial 'forty shilling freehold', which only serves to show again what difficulties the modern historian has in understanding these deeds.

c) Commercial Pressures

As you move through the century the pace of industrial and financial development quickens quite a bit of course, its in this century that modern banking and the Industrial Revolution begins. So while there was a need for sophisticated financial tools like cheques, or the ability to put money into long term investments that would yield a standard annual interest, these instruments were not available in Ireland in the same manner as say London or Amsterdam. Clearly Ireland lacked the great trading environment of those countries but it still was advanced enough that it really needed those instruments.

So, to a degree, what happens is that these financial instruments go into land ownership whereas in London or Amsterdam it would have gone into overseas trade or South Sea shares etc. The person who still requires a cheque like payment will frequently find himself trading in IOUs based on rents due for land, and the person who wants to invest in a long term annuity will sometimes invest in land to get himself that kind of financial instrument. It seems to me that this happens more often in Ireland in the 18th century because the more regular banking arrangements of say London are apparently lacking. We can see this in an anecdote relating to a businessman in Dublin in the early 19th century who seems to be using a custom that related to Ireland of the 18th century:

> "...for such is the force of custom, that fresh leases of this kind [very long, e.g. for lives renewable for ever and over 99 years] are made even in our time, and purchasers of these quit or head rents, as they are called, are always in the market, who prefer them as modes of investment on account of the superior security they offer for the payment of the interest created.
>
> ...
>
> A recent instance of the kind may be worth mentioning. A Dublin merchant after realising a sum of £60,000 resolved, a few years ago, to retire from business. Soon afterwards an estate in one of the Midland Counties was put up to auction, and he became the purchaser of it for about the sum stated. Upon obtaining possession of the property he called the tenants together and asked them to

name rents they would be content to pay if he continued them in their farms. The answer generally was a pound an acre. But if I give you a lease of thirty one years said the landlord what will you give then? Oh, twenty-five shillings for a lease, was quickly responded. And what for a lease for ever? A lease for ever! Sure your honour's joking with us, cried the astonished tenants. Not at all, replied the landlord. Here are the leases ready drawn, and he produced a little library of parchment; and I am willing to give leases for thirty one years or for ever, as may be agreed upon, to every one of you. The upshot was that the whole estate was relet on leases for ever at thirty shillings an acre." [8]

His involvement as you can see was purely to get a nice annual figure paid to him as a return on his investment in laying out the £60,000, exactly as if in modern times he was buying a bond like financial instrument. As you can also see it leads to quite a chaotic picture in the leasing of the land, here we have another party in our vertical table who is only there for commercial and not farming purposes. Back in the 18th century outright sales of land like this were probably not common in accommodating the merchant who wanted to invest his money but other ways were found for landlords to take advantage of this commercial need. A landlord could arrange with an investor to lease to him his rental income on a given named property, for a long number of years, and in return the investor would pay the landlord a large lump sum up front. This kind of thing is not unheard of in the deeds and as you can see adds again to our vertical problem not a little.

The other way that this commercial atmosphere adds to our problem is this idea of passing around rent IOUs. As an example if you read the quote in the next chapter involving Henry Grattan you can see where his tenant paid her rent – or 'fine' actually – via notes dated some months after the date she was paying him. These are rent IOUs, she gave him a document that allowed him to collect a given rent from her tenant, that was otherwise due to her 6 months hence etc, in lieu of cash. They did this a lot, it is even possible that the tenant who owed the money originally was not her tenant at all but was some other farmer who's landlord had passed the note to her in lieu of cash! This isn't a major factor in the deeds in the ROD – its a much more important factor to be aware of in understanding correspondence of the time – but it should be understood that sometimes, for example, it might specify that X person was paid a given debt via a note that authorised them to receive the rental money from Y even though Y was not actually originally X's tenant. What you need to understand is that this can be done purely for these commercial reasons, in lieu of cheques or not wishing to handle large amounts of cash or because they just didn't have ready money and could only pay in monies that are due sometime in the future. Obviously this again adds to our vertical complexity.

An example from the deeds which probably combines both these commercial issues can be seen in 1772. In that year Matthew Lougherry owed a debt to Peter Gaynor of Dublin, an 'upholder', and as a way of paying Gaynor he gave the money to Sir James Nugent of Donore who in turn undertook to pay Gaynor out of revenue, totalling £140 a year, that Nugent normally received from a number of houses in the Strand, Charles, Mass Lane, and Aran Streets in Dublin.[9] We have here both these commercial transactions because clearly you would otherwise expect Lougherry to pay the debt to Gaynor in cash, instead that money is being transferred, with the debt IOU operating as a modern style cheque. The second point is that Gaynor is now clearly laying out his money as an investment with Nugent, an up front payment that will then give him a regular annual return, and you can see clearly here how the deeds get quite complicated in the ROD as these commercial transactions work through the system.

d) The Penal Laws

These ended up creating a kind of underground gentry throughout the 18th century and this in turn meant that we have frequently, and sometimes secretly, another layer in our vertical picture here, the original Catholic owners. This is described in detail in the next chapter but is summarised here by Kevin Whelan in a ground breaking article on the subject:

> "...the enduring elite and popular memory of a prior ownership régime, the existence of an Irish Catholic nation-in-waiting overseas...created an instability over the issue of land ownership. The descendants of the old proprietors mutated into an underground gentry, the shadow lords of eighteenth-century Ireland." [10]

e) Debt

One can always speculate as to why it seems that Irish people in general, and certainly the aristocracy in Ireland in the 18th century in particular, are so prone to getting into debt but certainly no reader of Irish 18th century land transactions will be under any illusions about the extent of indebtedness across the country. The classic Irish landlord of the period – and this extends right up to the land acts of c.1900 – of course was permanently in debt, and quite possibly taking out fresh loans to pay off earlier loans etc. Needless to say then the lenders, the nascent bankers of 18th century Ireland, were very quick to get these mortgages registered in the ROD. Since debt is so common this very frequently adds on another layer in our vertical problem, the person who holds a mortgage on the estate, and further explains why Irish land is so overloaded with these layers in the 18th century.

Incidentally one of the Acts that regulate the ROD also specified that where a mortgage was paid off – which was rare enough! – it was to be recorded as such on the margin of the original transcript of the memorial of the mortgage and examples of these can be seen in the ROD.[11]

f) Marriage Settlements

Multiple layers in this pattern can also be created by multiple marriage settlements cascading down over the generations.

To clarify this lets examine, very roughly, what happens in a marriage settlement at this time. Lets assume that John Plunkett, a son of Alexander Plunkett of Ardmaghbeg, or whoever, was seeking the hand of Catherine Eustace, the daughter of Patrick Eustace of Naas, in marriage in 1764. Before the marriage (while the deed would be registered probably after the marriage) Alexander Plunkett and Patrick Eustace would get together and some fierce bargaining and negotiating would ensue. Of course normally the father of the bride, Patrick Eustace, will be expected to make a provision for the new couple out of his estate, as what is later known as a dowry, to go along with his daughter. This can be expected to be the whole estate, or nearly so, if she was an heiress otherwise it will be much smaller and in practice it may be that Alexander Plunkett will be contributing some lands or money to the deal as well i.e. the financial arrangements to settle the new couple up in some estate or property. (On that point we should be clear that the ROD entries on marriage settlements will nearly always specify money as being talked about in this deal, not lands, but actually in practice the transaction will often involve lands and leases and not cash at all, or at least not very much of it. No doubt that seems somewhat confusing but it is this writer's experience at any rate of reading these settlements. The ROD will always use words like, e.g., Patrick Eustace will give John Plunkett £20, but in fact if you get a chance to see the original transaction play out in family papers you will frequently find that Patrick Eustace actually transferred a note – or indeed a deed – that allows Plunkett to collect monies that he, Eustace, was due as rent on x or y lands, over z number of years, amounting to £20. On the ground its hardly ever cash that is transferred, and this is also true of wills by the way. Where Alexander Plunkett, or whoever, is stated in a will as receiving £20 from Joe Bloggs actually he will have got a lease of specified lands – which may be mentioned in a longer form of the will or will become clear in reading other family papers – which will, or are projected to, amount to the value of £20.)

This settlement will always specify that Catherine Eustace in the event of her husband's death, or in some cases for other eventualities such as her husband's bankruptcy (e.g. when a Dublin woolen draper was married in 1788 the bride, Judith Sweeney of Sligo, was guaranteed to receive her dower or thirds in the event "that he the said Edmond [her husband] should chance to fail in trade or business and become a bankrupt" or died before her),[12] will be entitled to land that she can call her own or at least have a life interest in. This was often about a third of her late husband's lands.

Depending on the complexity of the settlement it might go on to say that the first born child of the marriage, if there is one, is entitled to x or y lands or money and the second born will get z, etc. Then it also might state, and certainly it will be understood as some kind of a necessity, that if the new groom represents the heir to the property, the eldest son, then he will be expected to make provision of some sort for his younger siblings if they are otherwise unprovided for (some money to pay for a brother to enter the army, or a settlement for them on a small part of the estate, or some kind of dowry for his sisters etc).

It can then get more complicated again if the parties wish to use trustees for the transaction. This I think largely depends on the status of the parties, meaning that wealthy families would tend to use trustees more than poorer ones but that is not completely clear. If trustees are used it means that the estate is actually vested in these outside parties – they would be friends of the family, maybe legal friends, or non immediate relatives – and they in turn will act as a kind of escrow system to guarantee the integrity of the marriage settlement. In otherwords they will be expected to oversee the transactions of the settlement and the new couple, and their parents, will have to abide by what they say in relation to the settlement because these trustees will now officially own the lands and property transacted in it. You will easily see in the deeds in the ROD where these trustees are used because in the context of a marriage settlement – you know it is a marriage settlement because at some point the deed will mention a 'marriage to be solemnized' or words to that effect – you will notice how outsiders seem to be getting possession of the estates for no reason. If you think this places a lot of trust in the trustees then you would be right!

But to get back to the point of our chapter here, the outcome of all this is that yet more vertical layers are added on top of the land. This is particularly true of that provision that is made to our Catherine Eustace above. Her entitlement, to an annuity probably out of specified lands, in the event of her husband's death, in practice adds a new vertical layer over those lands. Then the younger children, or any of these parties, of the settlement might be entitled to some share of a lease out of specified lands etc., adding greatly to the overall complexity. There is even the trustees who may, technically, now own the land so obviously they have to be at least consulted, and possibly paid some money, everytime the land is dealt in later. A frequent new party in land created by the family settlements might be a grandmother of the groom or bride, who might be called the 'dowager', who under her own marriage settlement, possibly of as long as half a century ago, will be entitled to x or y interest in lands. Since under these kind of settlements frequently the land is not outright sold or handed over but rather some kind of lease is made then its easy to see how over the years the complexity of the land holding pattern builds up. A new heir who comes into an estate could easily find that all the provisions made for his mother, sisters, brothers probably, grandmother maybe, etc, in either wills or marriage settlements have added enormously to his debts and complexity of the landholding of his estate.

This overall point is also true of many other countries, where marriage settlements will add complexity to land holding and add to our vertical problem, but I think there are reasons to suspect that it is a particular issue in Ireland. Looking at the large number of marriage settlements in the ROD the impression you are left with is that quite poor families are using that system, moreso I suspect than other countries. Probably what's happening is that the dispossessed Catholic families are keeping up appearances even though they are now very poor. They are going through the whole rigmarole of the complex marriage settlements because that's what they were used to, when probably their small estates cannot now bear all that debt and complexity. In a way it might have continued like that all the way to the Famine after which they certainly stopped subdividing land. For this reason I think these marriage settlements created more of a vertical problem in Ireland than in many other countries.

For these six reasons then we can easily appreciate that Irish landholdings in the 18th century are very subdivided and complex in this 'vertical' sense.

Actual Examples of Irish land transactions

It may be helpful at this point to see some practical examples of landholding in Ireland at that time to see if you have mastered the different terms and the different types of ownership over land. To start on a simple example here is an advertisement of land for sale that was printed in early 1810:

"County of Westmeath
TO BE SOLD
The fee of the Town and Lands of BALLYCALROW, in the Barony of *Clonlonan*, containing 153 Acres and 7 Perches; let to the late *John Parvin*, for three Lives or thirty-one Years, at the yearly Rent of £60 per Ann. of which Lease only one Life is in being, (*Mr Wm. Parvin*, the present Occupier) the Years having expired in 1788.

Those lands are in excellent Order, well sheltered and divided with Hedge Rows. There is also a good Farm-house and Offices, Garden and Orchard, on the Ground.

They are situate in a rich, beautiful, manufacturing Country, joining the great Western Road, within two Miles of Moat, and five of Athlone, both good Market Towns.

Proposals to be received by JAMES NUGENT, Esq, *Clonlost, Kilucan*; and Messrs. HARRIS and BRYAN, *York-street, Dublin*." [13]

Nugent obviously is on the top of this particular vertical tree in that he clearly really owns the land, hence the reference to 'fee' meaning 'fee simple'. He, or his ancestor, had leased the land for 3 lives or 31 years in c.1757 i.e. 31 years before the years expired in 1788. Remember again that a lease like that, which is very common in 18th century Ireland, expires when a certain three named people are dead or after 31 years, whichever is longer. In this case we know that William Parvin is one of those lives and probably when the 1757 lease was drawn up he was listed as a 'life' because he was the son of the 'late John Parvin'. Then the seller, the aforementioned James Nugent, who was a Colonel in the British Army, received the following letter:

"Moate 18th Feb 1810

Colonel Nugent

Sir, I have Received your Advertizement, Relative to the Sale of your Estate, in this Neighbourhood (Ballykillroe). I propose to give you Sixty years purchase for them lands, at the present Rent, without any Deductions for the present lease, I am Sir with Respect your Obedient Servant

John Gibbons" [14]

When he says 'sixty years purchase' he means that the price he will give for the land is the same as the current year's rent multiplied by 60. That is a huge markup but the reason is, no doubt, that the current rent of £60 a year that Parvin is paying Nugent is considered to be very small and it will increase dramatically after the death of the last life. Hence Gibbons can be generous and make no "deductions for the present lease", meaning no deductions for the length of time that Parvin still has the lease for. Obviously this length of time is the lifetime of William Parvin but since he was named in a lease of 1757, 53 years before the time of the letter and bear in mind that he might have been aged 10 or thereabouts at that time, it might be a safe bet that Parvin has not too long yet to live.

That is a very straightforward and simple Irish land transaction but it does get more difficult! What follows is a letter that was drawn up, it seems c.1720, which states the circumstances of land held by Ridgely Nugent with a view to sending this to a lawyer and asking for advice on the case:

"State of the Case

of Ridgely Nugent gent deceased

Henry Witherell being possessed of the lands of Clogheran in the County of Dublin by virtue of a lease for ever from   Berry of Toberbarry esquire, in the year 1711 agreed with said Ridgely Nugent to set him 120 acres of arable land in said lands of Clogheran for three lives renewable for ever at 11s. 6d per acre yearly, and pursuant to said agreement perfected a minute to Nugent, which minute was registered.

Soon after John Forster esq late Lord Justice of the Common Pleas purchased said lands, and the arrears due thereon, from said Berry and distrained said Witherell's goods and laid himself in prison for arrears due by him.

Witherell's wife, to have her husband at liberty, gives up their deed to Forster.

In 1712 – Mr Nugent filed a Bill against Witherell and Forster. They answered and confessed Witherell's title and Nugent's to be both prior to Forster's purchase.

After this one James Walker, agent to Forster, comes to Mr Nugent and after some treaty Mr Nugent agreed to let him hold the lands so took from Witherell at the same rent till he said Nugent should give him warning to leave it –

And accordingly he held the same till sometime in 1716 – he came to Mr Nugent and offered 13/6 @ per acre if Mr Nugent would give him a lease of 21 years, which was not agreed and Mr Nugent going to England desired Walker to keep it at that rent till he returned.

In 1720 – Mr Nugent gave Walker warning to clear the land the 25th March following.

Before the 25th March Nugent dies first making

his will and hereby devising to William Smith all his estate and the benefit of said bargains and appoints him executor of his will.

24th March 1720 Smith gives Walker warning to clear the land –

Walker holds the possession pleading he took a lease of the lands from Lord Chief Justice Forster's son and heir.

The minute from Witherell to Nugent was lodged with Barry, Notary Public, to draw deeds pursuant thereto.

Note also Walker held the premises and Nugent's title from 1712 to 1720 and the year 1720 [sic] and never pretended any other title and Walker paid some money to Nugent on account of the surplus rent of 2/6 per acre paid from 1716 to 1720." [15]

Maybe we could draw up that 'vertical' landholding pattern in a table, starting with the situation in 1711 we have drawn up this table with the highest type of ownership at the top:

Type of Landholding	1711	1712	1720
Original owner (the fee simple)	Berry	John Forster, (having bought up Berry's interest)	Richard Forster (son and heir of John who died this year)
'a lease forever', originally from Berry, details unspecified	Henry Witherell	(Witherell was intimidated out of his interests)	
3 lives renewable forever	Ridgely Nugent	Ridgely Nugent	William Smith (heir of Nugent)
short term lease, details not specified but		James Walker (Forster's agent)	James Walker (he is trying now to ignore

101

the lease has to be given up on the demand of the lessor			the fact that Smith is in the middle here, he claims he gets the land directly from Forster)

That then is the way to understand this 'vertical' pattern of landholding, you get different types of rights over the land that cascade down this vertical path. Hence Berry gave away some major rights to Witherell, who in turn gave a 3 lives lease to Nugent, who in turn conceded only some short term lease to Walker. So when you are looking at deeds in the ROD you are actually looking at the transfer of rights like this over the land, that's why you get multiple owners of the exact same patch of land. What you are watching then when you are in the ROD is the horizontal transfer across this type of table, the transfer of specific rights over the same patch of land.

Notice too how Witherell was basically intimidated out of his rights, a by no means uncommon occurrence in the 18th century when you are dealing with powerful people such as the Lord Chief Justice John Forster.

Another thing to note is how Walker originally ends up both sides of the vertical tree in 1712 in the sense that he is Forster's agent, and therefore above Nugent, but then he ends up underneath Nugent as his tenant. The bizarre reality is that he then pays Nugent a rent and Nugent then pays him back some of that money because Nugent owns some rent money to Forster and Walker is Forster's agent (or in practice, as the letter indicates, Walker pays Nugent only the 'surplus money', i.e., probably, the money left over after you deduct Nugent's rent to Forster from Walker's rent to Nugent). This kind of thing is by no means uncommon in the 18th century, in many cases because the landowner might be desperate for some reason to get the lands back off some tenant who has a long lease and if the tenant doesn't want to hand it up, as in this case, then the only recourse he has is to take the lands from that tenant and become, in a way, the tenant of your own tenant on the same land!

Another example of that phenomenon in a complicated land structure in early 18th century Ireland can be seen here in this legal memorandum from Westmeath:

"Memorandum

Mr Palles took a lease of twenty one years from Col Robert Nugent of the lands of Foyran, signed sealed and delivered with three or four credible witnesses. Mr Palles set a small part of the said Foyran for said term of twenty one years to Matthew Fagan which amounted to about £13 per annum by a sufficient well drawn lease, well witnessed and perfected as the former. The said Mr Palles set Edmund Scally the remainder of the whole farm to commence the May following by a lease of twenty one years, well drawn and perfected as aforesaid, for the whole rent due to Col Robert Nugent whereby said Mr Palles had Fagan's said holding clear profit by the farm. In some years after said Scally took the farm he made over his interest in it to said Col Nugent and cleared accounts with him, whereby said Col Nugent was tenant for the whole rent himself and by his agreement with Scally owed the whole rent, so that he was then landlord and tenant.

After said Fagan held his land holding for several years in his own occupation, as said Mr Palles is informed, he the said Fagan told said Mr Palles, when he demanded his rent of said Fagan, that he had set a part of his holding to Col Nugent, and that he could not pay said Mr Palles till the Col would pay him, said Mr Palles being an entire stranger to his dealing with the Col until said Fagan gave him an account of it when he wanted his rent. Said Fagan run in arrear with said Mr Palles about eighty pounds and still as he demanded the same said he could not get the rent of that part of his holding, and as soon as he could receive it that he would pay Mr Palles."

So far so good, clearly Colonel Nugent had decided to get back the lands he had leased out and the only way he could was to become a tenant of Scally, who seems to have been superceded here, and of Fagan. Fagan cooperated with him but that left Palles. In theory there is nothing wrong with Palles being in the middle here, i.e. he has Nugent above him, or would have if the Scally lease didn't clear his rent to Nugent, and Fagan and now Nugent himself below him. The problem is that in practice, as opposed to in theory, this creates a lot of problems. You can imagine that Colonel Nugent is not best thrilled to have his farm encumbered by all these middlemen and now that he is both tenant and landlord, as it were, he can play a few games. Since it is his money that starts off this vertical structure he can cut the money off by not paying his rent, as you have just read, so putting financial pressure on the middlemen, and secondly since he is also the overall large landlord of the neighbourhood he has some legal clout which can be brought to bear, in this case he ran the Manorial court of Carlanstown and could use that to squeeze his over mighty underlings. This is how it then develops and if you read the rest of this text – contained in the footnote – bear in mind that Fagan is cooperating with Colonel Nugent, and his brother Captain Michael who is the father of Viscount Clare, against Palles who is also actually the brother in law of Captain Nugent, although they are obviously not on good terms.[16]

We will now tackle a genuinely complicated 1726 ROD memorial. This memorial begins by outlining these three parties to the deed:
Bryan Cooke of Bellamadim, Co Dublin
Matthew Cooke of Kilbridge [Kilbride] Co Cavan
Tom Bayly of Killnacrott Co Cavan
Lord Baron of Dunsany under his seal demised to Connor Cooke, late of Kilbridge, the lands of Tullyboy, Barony of Clanmahon and County of Cavan, for 31 years @ £9 per annum and "after the wars then between England and Ireland were ended" it was to go to £10 per annum.
George Lowther, late of Kilrue Co Meath, esquire, had demised to Connor Cooke that part of Kilbride called Derrymadin

for 31 years at £60 sterling per annum.

George Plunkett of Dogstown Co Meath by a lease did demise to Bryan Cooke the land of Gallanbane, Barony of Clanmahon, for 21 years at £9 5s per annum.

The said Connor Cooke being indebted to Thomas Reilly, deceased, with his son the said Bryan Cooke, by deed assigned to Reilly Tullyboy and Kilbride, alias Derrymadim, but Reilly (Thomas) acknowledged a clause of redemption which would allow the Cookes to retrieve their land in the event of paying back the debts.

Connor Cooke was also indebted to Bryan Reilly of Ballinrink and also to Miles Reilly, merchant, and Bryan Reilly also paid a sum of money to Thomas Reilly and then took over his interests in these lands.

Connor Cooke made a will and assigned Bryan Cooke and Matthew Cooke and the said Bryan Reilly to be the executors.

Then

> "the said Thomas Reilly had paid to the said Bryan Reilly the said sums due to him and had taken an assignment of the said securities from the said Bryan Reilly, the said deed of which this is a memorial.
>
> Witnesseth that in consideration of the said sum of £191 and 12 shillings due from the said Bryan Cooke and Mathew Cooke, executors of the said Connor Cooke, and for the better securing the repayment thereof, and in consideration of 5 shillings to them paid by the said Thomas Bayly, they, the said Bryan Cooke and Mathew Cooke, did give grant bargain and sell, assign and confirm unto Thomas Bayly, his executors, administrators and assignees, all their estates, rights, titles, terms and interests in and to the said town and lands of Tullyboy, Kilbride alias Derrymadin, and the gallon of Kilbride, and Gallonbane, all lying in the County of Cavan, subject nevertheless to the proviso or condition of redemption in the said deed, of which this is a memorial, contained."

witnessed by:

Robert Fleming of Kilnacrott aforesaid [relatives of the Bayly's], gent

Patrick Nugent of Cunlin in the County of Cavan gent, and

Michael Reilly of Oldcastle in the county of Meath gent.

Henry Buckley, of Dublin, was the public notary who handled it and Nugent swore to the memorial when it was being registered in Dublin.[17]

So to analyse that we can break it down into maybe four parts:

i) First of all you can see how the Cookes are inching their way back into these lands by taking long leases – before the Penal Laws had kicked in – from the Plunketts and Lowther. This in all probability is an example of a Catholic family trying to get back some of their old lands. This part of the memorial shows the old, as it were, title deeds of the family in regard to these lands. So in our vertical structure here you have the Plunketts and Lowther at the top but with the effective ownership now resting with the Cookes.

ii) Then they get into debt with the Reillys who now come on the scene with some rights of ownership over the land, a common way that people come into the vertical leasing structure of land as pointed out above.

iii) The Reillys in turn seem to swap the land between themselves and back again. This is not at all surprising, its exactly what these families do, as pointed out above they are swapping around leases in the way that nowadays people might use cheques. These are IOUs that they will pass around in lieu of cash, hence it seems that Thomas owed money to Bryan Reilly and so passed him this lease and then when Thomas was more flush with cash he bought his interests in the land back from him. By the way you can take it that all of these Reillys listed are descendants of Colonel John Reilly who led the Reilly regiment in the Williamite wars and who settled in Co. Meath just across the border from these Cavan lands.

iv) But now look at the role of Thomas Bayly, he seems to get all the interests in the land assigned to him for a whole 5 shillings? That reads suspiciously like as if Bayly is now acting as a fake Protestant owner, helping out these Catholics by agreeing to be the nominal owner of the land. Certainly going by his name and the fact that he was a member of the Williamite Cavan militia during the late war, and indeed the fact that his son held an important position in the treasury in Dublin Castle, Deputy Clerk of the Pells, in the 1730s and 40s, we can safely assume that he was Protestant.[18] From the phraseology of the deed ("for the better securing the repayment thereof") we might suspect that Bayly was also a little involved in banking or at least in acting as a land agent for some landlords – which his son did on a large scale – but probably that was not the primary role he was fulfilling here. This then is our final owner in the vertical structure.

At any rate that seems to be the vertical pattern that we can establish here. I suppose some readers might think that most land transactions are surely not as complicated as all that, that the above 'vertical' issues only relate to small amounts of land? Well I am afraid it can get really complicated in the 18th century and as an example of this I will present here a letter sent on the 7th of November 1719 by Ignatius Palles (the ancestor of Chief Baron Palles incidentally, a famous Irish legal expert particularly on land law) outlining the circumstances under which he holds some land in South Cavan, with my own commentary added in in italics:

Lands of Ignatius Palles in 1719

"I just now had an account from Tullystown and Carlanstown, they are all very well thank God. I gave you the trouble of a scroll before this to entreat you to get me about £1,000 at 6 per cent interest to pay off my debts, or even £600 to pay off Major Hampson with the best terms you can procure. And I now take the freedom to put you in mind of it again and I believe you will have a good opportunity amongst so many moneyed men that expect to purchase the lott of Finea, for they cannot all have it.

And of course if he can get that money then the new creditor will be added on as another type of owner over his land, and no doubt will get it registered in the ROD.

I am further to acquaint you that my good brother Dowdall is now going to sue me (of I suppose) for a lien of my estate; or something else, that I do not at present comprehend but if I understand his meaning his notion is as follows:

First observe – that before the war of 88 my grandmother married her daughter Jane to my uncle Barnewall and gave him a rentcharge of £500 on her concerns (that I now possess) with a proviso that if the said Jane should die without issue that two hundred pounds of the said five hundred pounds should revert back again to her.

Showing how the estates get progressively encumbered with all the provisions of the family settlements.

After the said wars uncle Barnewall was indicted and outlawed lost his estate, and my grandmother and other friends were afraid he would lose his portion too; being the aforesaid £500: And my grandmother sometime after made her last will and Testament and to preserve my uncle Barnewall's said portion, bequeathed or devised the aforesaid £500 by the said will to cousin Taafe; in trust for my aunt Jane, aforesaid; without mentioning the former rentcharge lest it should be discovered and they ordered uncle Barnewall to stifle or conceal his said rentcharge and to acknowledge no other title but the will; which he did accordingly.

Two things to observe here:

a) Notice how the extent of Barnewall's lands and assets are artificially reduced by his relatives in anticipation of his outlawry, a common manoeuvre which in turns adds complexity to the land holdings.

b) Also now you can see how another type of owner comes on the scene holding the land only as a kind of secret trustee, here cousin Taafe, and if you are watching this kind of transaction in the ROD you will not know at first that it is a sort of fraudulent transaction.

And my grandmother ordered in her will pursuant to the aforesaid rentcharge that in case my aunt Barnewall should die without issue that two hundred pounds of the said five hundred pounds should revert and devised one hundred pounds of them to my sister Dowdall. It is also ordered in the said will and likewise in the said rentcharge that uncle Barnewall should have but 8 per cent for the said five hundred pounds till my grandmother would pay him off though the rentcharge was given him when money was at 10 per cent.

Notice that while they are talking about cash, £500 and the interest on it, actually it is to be paid as a rentcharge on the estate which shows you that at the time land charges were being used instead of our modern financial instruments. As you can see this itself can complicate the ownership structure if that rentcharge was to be registered in the ROD at any point.

In sometime after my uncle Barnewall died without issue whereby my sister Dowdall became entitled to one hundred pounds of the said £500 for which I punctually paid her eight pound a year till she was married. Then upon her intermarriage there were articles of intermarriage perfected and my father, Mr Dowdall, my sister and I are parties to them a copy of which I here enclosed send you.

By the said articles I obliged myself to pay down that hundred pounds at a time that no man else would give near hand the money for it; for at that very time Coyne pretended to redeem this mortgage and insisted that the land owed us nothing but that we received our money out of the main rates of the land. Notwithstanding, I had that regard for my sister's welfare, and her husband telling me that the said eight pound a year that my sister received would do him no good, that he could not set up without a sum of money upon which I articled to pay him down that hundred pounds and strained myself very much to get it for them to set them up. And paid it punctually according to articles and got the enclosed discharge for it (that is to say) the enclosed is a true copy of it.

Now I suppose Mr Dowdall got a notion that; that hundred pounds is a hundred pound of the first mortgage money and that my estate being all mortgaged first for £1,500 that he ought to have the 15th part of my estate or some such stuff as I am informed. Now in reality it is not so, it is a £100 of my uncle Barnewall's rentcharge as aforesaid. And if it were otherwise I think the enclosed Articles of Intermarriage and the enclosed discharge cuts it off; besides my purchasing the right of redemption from the Earl of Cavan.

Actually the whole land that they are referring to here came into Palles' ancestors from the ancestors of this Earl of Cavan c.1640, via a mortgage, and it seems from the Coyne family also by mortgage. These Catholics found that only this land, which was therefore nominally owned by a Protestant, was all that they had left after the Cromwellian confiscations of the 1650s. Then the Earls of Cavan in the 18th century tried to get the lands back, showing you how the land ownership of this century was further complicated by the land confiscations/Penal Laws of even the mid 17th century. The right of redemption Palles is referring to is where he bought out Lambert's right to ever claim that the mortgage had been paid off and hence he should receive the lands back.

Now he proceeds to describe his 'title deeds', i.e. an outline of how he came to own the lands plus the accompanying documents:

My title is thus: my grandmother Jane Plunkett settles all her right in that mortgage on Mr Stephen Taafe without any exception by a deed. She afterwards makes a will and orders cousin Taafe to pay five hundred pounds to my aunt Barnewall in manner aforesaid, money to my mother etc. Cousin Taafe gave me a declaration of trust importing that settlement to be made on him for my use, I paying off the several persons according to the will. In sometime after, the estate in law being in cousin Taafe ['s name] purchased the right of redemption from the Earl of Cavan in cousin Taafe's name and cousin Taafe also gave me a declaration of trust as to the right of redemption and I afterwards levied fines and suffered a common recovery above eight years ago.

Having secured proper ownership, by paying off Lambert and getting the right documents from his trustee Taafe, then he moved to secure the property completely by going for a Common Recovery as you read about in chapter 2.

My cousin Taafe if he be in town can inform you particularly; so could uncle Barnewall as to the rentcharge. I beg sir you will take advice as to this affair or if these articles or discharge be sufficient. You see there is a penalty of a thousand pounds in the articles for performance and for indemnifying me and giving me any further assurance that my counsel would...[lost in fold]...a bill in Chancery against my father and me but he...yet I am convinced that if Major Palles had not winked at this proceeding Mr Dowdall would not dare breed any such disturbance.

A 'bill in Chancery' was how a court case would probably start. It consisted of a written complaint, the 'bill' addressed to the Lord Chancellor seeking relief from this or that party for such and such a wrong, which the person accused could then reply to with an 'answer'.

You may remember my uncle Barnewall insisted before, on the same point, for the same money, and we referred it to Counsellor Hussey, uncle Barnewall's own cousin germane [first cousin] and he gave it against him and told him he could have no more by his rentcharge than his money and that he could not deny taking of it and he drew an instrument himself to that purpose obliging my uncle Barnewall at any time to receive his money from me otherwise I would not give interest or principle...your care in this will add to your many former favours to

Dear Sir

Your truly affectionate brother [in-law] and most obedient humble servant

Ignatius Palles.

Matty and all friends here join in our very humble services to you,

we all long to see you." [19]

That last point about referring it to Counsellor Hussey is where the parties to a dispute would sometimes bring it to a third party, usually two relatives one from each side, or maybe a legal expert, who would give a judgement as a kind of arbitration in order to save on the time and expense of a court case. Of course the point is that Catholics could not easily go to the main courts – in theory anyway, actually some were quite litigatious! – to prove their ownership over land because they were always scared of the Penal Law implications, hence they particularly would like to settle things out of court.

Which brings us to the question of the Penal Laws, the subject of our next chapter.

Footnotes

1. For example there is mention of a lease for 3 lives dating from 1693 in the ROD at: 358-112-239146.

2. J H Thomas, *A systematic arrangement of Lord Coke's First Institute of the Laws of England* (Philadelphia, 1827) vol II, p.512.

3. Thomas Alcock MP, *The Tenure of Land in Ireland* (London, 1848), p.15.
This writer in 1851 takes another stab at trying to understand why very long leases were so common in Ireland:
"The inconvenient tenure of leases for lives renewable for ever (under which more than one-seventh of the entire land in Ireland is or was until very recently holden) was, we believe, another consequence of the extensive engrossing of estates by absentee proprietors, unwilling or unable to depart with their seignorial dominion of the soil, and incapable, from the obligation of stronger ties to England, to discharge the duties it demanded, and therefore under the necessity of interposing between them and the occupiers of the soil, a class who would virtually represent the fee-simple, and yet be amenable to the obligations of a tenant, and to the statutable remedies incident to the reversion, which that tenure left in the proprietor of the fee. Lord Redesdale, once Lord Chancellor of Ireland, states that leases with covenant of perpetual renewal arose in Ireland, instead of fee-farms, in consequence of persons purchasing improvable estates, without having money to carry on their improvements, and then procuring it in this manner: they paid, for example, fifteen thousand pounds for an estate, and conveyed it to another, in fee-simple, for ten-thousand pounds, taking a lease of the whole, with covenant for perpetual renewal, at a rent equal to the interest of the ten thousand pounds."
(William Dwyer Ferguson and Andrew Vance, *The Tenure and Improvement of Ireland* (Dublin, 1851), p.7.)

4. George Lewis Smyth, *Ireland: historical and statistical* (London, 1844) vol 1, p.429.

5. W. H. Crawford, *The impact of the domestic linen industry in Ulster* (Belfast, 2005), p.108.

6. http://www.progenealogists.com/ireland/freeholders.htm .

7. George Lewis Smyth, *Ireland: historical and statistical* (London, 1844) vol 1, p.432.

8. George Lewis Smyth, *Ireland: historical and statistical* (London, 1844) vol 1, p.431.

9. 1772 294-83-193897.

10. Kevin Whelan, *An Underground Gentry? Catholic Middlemen in Eighteenth Century Ireland,* in, *Eighteenth Century Ireland,* vol 10 (1995) p.8.

11. 1734 76-451-55342.

12. 1788 395-183-261497.

13. PRONI D/2620/2.

14. Ibid.

15. Ridgely was a son of Walter Nugent of Portloman Co Westmeath. The original lease from Witherell to Nugent, then described as being of Tullygraham Co Monaghan, is dated 5 Jan 1711. Also see the legacy made by Ridgely who made a will on the 6th of Feb 1720 (all from PRONI D2620/2).

16. Continuing the document which I think is worth recording in full because legal documents like this for the very early 18th century, c.1710, in Ireland are not all that common now:
"Said Mr Palles appraised his cattle for rent, and after said Mr Palles had said cattle a considerable time in Clonbockoge in topgrass, at the prayers and tears of Fagan's wife etc he returned them back to Fagan without making them pay for their trespass.

On Mr Palles' [meet?]ing Fagan sometime before his lease determined, for the arrear, said Fagan distrained the cattle of Mr Plunkett which he found on the land he set the Col, and said Fagan came to Mr Palles, and told him, as did Mr Hugh Reilly of Clonkify, that said Fagan was oppressed, wronged, and shuffled out of his right and rent by the Manor Court of Carlingstown by Mr Plunkett and those that backed him, and did not scruple to say that Capt Nugent was in the bottom of it. And he and his brother in law said Hugh Reilly of Clonkieffy advised Mr Palles to get a marked writ for said Fagan, and to send him to Mullingar Jail, and assured Mr Palles that Captain Nugent and seventy pounds of said arrears due to said Mr Palles, and that when Fagan being in jail, Captain Nugent would be touched in conscience and would pay Fagan, and that then said Fagan would pay Mr Palles. Whereupon Mr Palles took a marked writ for him but intended to execute the same by consent of Capt Michael Nugent and Fagan after an amiable manner till Mr Fagan served Mr Pallas a most scandalous prank about Mr Ffolliott [of Barcony, ancestors of the well known Irish genealogist Rosemary Ffolliott].

Whereupon Mr Palles sent said Fagan straight to jail and Mr Palles wrote to Capt Nugent to Dublin to complain of the ill usage he had from Fagan, not doubting but a brother and a friend would resent his ill usage, and Capt Nugent very well knows how generously and honourably he behaved to his brother on that occasion. Fagan hath now filed a bill against Mr Palles and alleges it was done by the advice and orders of Capt Nugent to put Mr Palles to expense and trouble, on a false report or complaint to the court that Mr Palles denied to give Fagan a stated account of said Fagan's, that lay in Mr Palles' custody. Which is all false, for when said Hugh Reilly of Clonkiffy came artfully to demand such a paper of Mr Palles, Mr Palles suspected that Fagan and said Reilly intended some foul play or trick, whereupon Mr Pallas called two or three witnesses by and bid them take notice, and bear witness, that he the said Mr Palles was ready and willing at all hours to account with Matthew Fagan, and was ready to produce every paper of his, or that concerned him, and that he had sent twenty [sic] messengers to Fagan and a hundred threats that he would send him to jail if he would not come to account.

Then Hugh Reilly said he, said Fagan, would come to account but that he apprehended Mr Palles would have him taken by a writ, but Mr Palles answered in presence of witnesses that he would give him a safe conduct under his hand and word of honour he would not molest him, and assured him he had not then any writ for him.

Mr Palles is strangely surprised that Capt Nugent should come between him and his tenant, Mr Palles made no demand on Capt Nugent for he sets him no land, nor to the Col., and would make no demand on any, but on Fagan. And if Capt Nugent had any demand on his brother, the said Mr Palles, he might civilly ask him to account with him, and behave like a brother, which his brother would not refuse to do. And if Fagan had any demand on Capt Nugent he might account with said Fagan or deal with him without using Mr Palles ill, but instead of that he like a good natured brother bearing bail for Matthew Fagan, and, if Fagan or his messengers tell truth, prompted said Fagan to fill a bill and makes a tool, or instrument, of Fagan, and he is not worth one groat, to put Mr Palles to trouble and expense, and to lose his good money for bad, and to hinder Mr Palles of his just debt.

Mr Palles is persuaded that Fagan represented the state of this case very falsely to Capt Nugent but Mr Palles thinks that Capt Nugent should have examined himself, and known it from him, before he would proceed after the ill natured manner he did in favour of a person whom he knows himself, and after declared, to be a litigatious knave.

And though Fagan falsely reported he was battered and bruised by twenty strokes by one single person who apprehended him with a writ, which is as false as the rest of his allegations, the person took him civilly by the shirt and told him he was the King's Prisoner, but Fagan being better horsed galloped off and thought to make his escape, and as he was making off the person made a stroke at him, and the top of his shirt touched him in the back of the head, and his horse stumbling the person seized him, and carried him off."
(Nugent Section, Stowe Papers, Huntington Library.)

17. 29th July 1726, 51-200-33361, registered 25th November 1726.

18. *Notes and Queries,* 17th May 1924, p.354.

19. Ignatius Palles writing to Captain Michael Nugent 7th of November 1719, Stowe Papers Huntington Library.

CHAPTER 6
Penal Laws

The Penal Laws are of course very important in understanding the role of land in Ireland in the 18th century and in fact the act that setup the Registry of Deeds was originally part of those laws, as stated here by Joseph Maguire who worked in the ROD c.1900:

> "The Act of Anne was ancillary to the penal laws against Catholics, and was designed to prevent secret conveyances which were commonly made by Catholics to Protestant trustees, who held the lands as owners in the eye of the law, while they allowed the beneficial ownership to be enjoyed by their Catholic cestuis que trustent ['as the beneficiaries of the trust']." [1]

For the early years of the ROD it seems that this was their guilty secret at least that appears to be why Sir William Betham was so adamantly opposed to printing extracts from the ROD in the Irish Record Commission books published in the early 19th century:

> "Such printing may do much harm by exciting the discontents of the descendants (whether real or pretended) of the attainted proprietors"

and

> "would furnish a weapon as well as a motive with the fractious to irritate the public mind and embarrass the government." [2]

It seems therefore appropriate that we should describe here what the Penal Laws actually were and how they were practically applied in the 18th century.

The dates of the Penal Laws

The first thing to note about the 18th century Penal Laws against the Catholics in Ireland is that they were actually the culmination of many anti-Catholic laws that had been passed since Queen Elizabeth's time. A summary of the latter laws, as passed in England, are available in this quote from the Catholic Encyclopaedia:

"The Penal Laws began with the two Statutes of Supremacy and Uniformity by which Queen Elizabeth, in 1559, initiated her religious settlement; and her legislation falls into three divisions corresponding to three definitely marked periods:

– 1558-70 when the Government trusted to the policy of enforcing conformity by fines and deprivations;

– 1570-80 from the date of the excommunication to the time when the Government recognized the Catholic reaction due to the seminary priests and Jesuits;

– from 1580 to the end of the reign.

To the first period belong the Acts of Supremacy and Uniformity (I Eliz. 1 and 2) and the amending statute (5 Eliz. c. 1). By the Act of Supremacy all who maintained the spiritual or ecclesiastical authority of any foreign prelate were to forfeit all goods and chattels, both real and personal, and all benefices for the first offence, or in case the value of these was below 20 pounds, to be imprisoned for one year; they were liable to the forfeitures of Praemunire for the second offence and to the penalties of high treason for the third offence. These penalties of Praemunire were: exclusion from the sovereign's protection, forfeiture of all lands and goods, arrest to answer to the Sovereign and Council. The penalties assigned for high treason were:

– drawing, hanging and quartering;

– corruption of blood, by which heirs became incapable of inheriting honours and offices; and, lastly

– forfeiture of all property.

These first statutes were made stricter by the

amending act (5 Eliz. c.1) which declared that to maintain the authority of the pope in any way was punishable by penalties of Praemunire for the first offence and of high treason, though without corruption of blood, for the second. All who refused the Oath of Supremacy were subjected to the like penalties. The Act of Uniformity, primarily designed to secure outward conformity in the use of the Anglican Book of Common Prayer, was in effect a penal statute, as it punished all clerics who used any other service by deprivation and imprisonment, and everyone who refused to attend the Anglican service by a fine of twelve pence for each omission." [3]

It was a matter of some controversy as to whether these laws applied to Ireland, and if so to what extent, as you can see at the end of the following quote which describes the situation in Ireland in 1642. This is a contemporary document of that date, a memorandum prepared by the Catholic citizens of Galway and submitted to the Archbishop of Tuam:

"2. That ye children of Catholics falling out to be wards, are forced in their youth to such puritanism, and are married to Puritans, to the great peril of their souls, as woeful experience daily teacheth, &c.

3. That such as are to sue livery are not admitted by laws thereunto without swearing an oath contrary to their conscience if Catholics, whereby is given full cause either of loss of estate or eternal damnation, or, at ye least, an evil omen of thriving where the heir, to redeem his fortunes, begins with perjury.

4. No Catholic native is admitted to learn in any Catholic school within this Kingdom, or is hardly suffered, where the parents are able to find them, to go to foreign Catholic countries to learn, whereby barbarous manners and ignorance in all human and Divine learning is brought into the

introducing of Atheism, heresy, and incivility.

5. No Catholic native, however deserving, is capable of service near his Prince, or advanced in church, arms, arts, science, law, places of judicature, clergyship, even of a justice of peace, mayor, or headborough, by which means the minds of men are dissuaded from walking the ways of honour and virtue; and base, corrupt, and ignorant strangers supply their rooms, to the unspeakable loss of this unfortunate Commonwealth, &c.

6. All attempts to introduce in this Kingdom by Parliament all the laws of England enacted against recusants failing, printed declarations, warranted by Parliament in England, do report that Ireland is bound by the Acts of Parliament of England, though in the making thereof this Kingdom hath no concurring voice, whereby they are made subject to the laws made in England against recusants." [4]

Although the practical environment as faced by Catholics of course varied a lot in the 150 years or so from the reformation to the 18th century nonetheless that quote captures many of the problems that they faced throughout this time. This pre-18th century situation is also outlined here along with the later 18th century Penal Laws:

"There were in force against the Catholics at the time of the Treaty [of Limerick]:-

1. An Act against the authority of the See of Rome. It enacts that no person shall attribute any jurisdiction to the See of Rome; that the person offending shall be subject to a premunire; and that all who have any office from the king, every person entering into orders, and taking a degree in the university, shall take the oath of supremacy.

2. An Act restoring to the crown the ancient jurisdiction over the state, ecclesiastical and spiritual. It likewise enacts that every ecclesiastical person, and every person taking office, shall take the oath of supremacy.

3. An Act for the uniformity of common prayer. It enacts that every person, having no lawful excuse to be absent, shall, every Sunday, resort to some place of worship of the established church, or forfeit 12d.

4. An Act by which the chancellor may appoint a guardian to the child of a Catholic.

5. An Act by which no Catholic schoolmaster can teach in a private house without a license from the ordinary of the diocese, and taking the oath of supremacy.

6. The new rules by which no person can be admitted into any corporation without taking the oath of supremacy.

The acts subsequent to the Treaty [of Limerick] were:-

1. The 7 Will. III. c. 4. [1695] which deprived the Catholics of the means of educating their children either at home or abroad, or of being guardians of their own or of any other person's children. It was of this act that Burke remarked,-

"Whilst this restraint upon foreign and domestic education was part of a horrible and impious system of servitude, the members were well fitted to the body. To render men patient under a deprivation of all the rights of human nature, everything which could give them a knowledge or feeling of those rights was rationally forbidden. To render humanity fit to be insulted, it was fit that it should be degraded." – *Letter to a Peer etc.*

2. 7 Will. III c. 5. [1695] An Act to disarm the Catholics, and to limit the binding of Roman Catholics as apprentices.

3. 9 Will. III c. 1. [1697] An Act to banish Roman Catholic priests.

4. 9 Will. III c. 3. [1697] An Act to prevent

Protestants from intermarrying with Papists.

5. By 10 Will. III c. 8. [1698] an Act for the preservation of game, it was declared unlawful to employ a Papist as a gamekeeper.

6. 10 Will. III c.13. [1698] An Act to prevent Papists from being solicitors.

7. 2 Anne, c. 3. [1703] An Act to prevent Popish priests from coming into the kingdom.

8. 2 Anne c. 6. [1703] An Act to prevent the further growth of Popery. [This is probably the most important of the penal laws affecting Catholics: "It excluded them from Parliament, from the local government corporations, from the learned professions, from civil and military offices, and from being executors, or administrators, or guardians of property. It prevented Catholics from buying land and from leasing land for more than thirty-one years.

The act required the estate of a Catholic to be "gavelled" at his death, meaning divided among all his sons rather than inherited by one son (unless one son was a Protestant). The act allowed a son in a Catholic family to convert to Protestantism ... and thereby take over the whole family property."]

9. 2 Anne c. 7. [1703] An Act for regulating the Popish clergy.

10. 4 Anne, c. 2. [1705] An Act to amend the Act for registering Popish clergy. [Parish Priests had to be registered, in so far as they were allowed in the country at all, and incidentally the registration lists, with the two guarantors for each priest, were printed at the time and are now available in the *Irish Ecclesiastical Record*, vol.12 (1876), p.299-550.]

11. 6 Anne, c. 6. [1707] An Act to amend the Act for preventing Papists from being solicitors.

12. 8 Anne, c. 3. [1709] An Act to explain the Act for preventing the further growth of Popery.

This tightened the laws against property and introduced the 'Protestant Discoverer'.

13. 12 Geo. I c. 3. [1725] An Act making it felony for a Popish priest to celebrate marriages between Protestants and Papists.

14. 1 Geo II c. 22. [1727] An Act for regulating the admission of barristers at law, six clerks, and attornies, and for better strengthening the Protestant interest: forbids the admission of any person to these professions who shall not prove that he has been a Protestant for two years.

15. 7 Geo II c. 5. [1733] An Act for the amendment of the law relating to Popish solicitors.

16. 7 Geo II c. 6. [1733] An Act to prevent converts from Popery or persons married to Popish wives or educating their children in the Popish religion from being justices of the peace.

17. 13 Geo II c. 6. [1739] An Act to amend and render more effectual the Act of William III for disarming Papists.

18. 19 Geo II c. 7. [1745] An Act for more effectually preventing his Majesty's subjects from entering foreign service and for publishing the Act of William III to prevent foreign education.

19. 19 Geo II .c XI. [1745] An Act for better regulating the election of members to serve in parliament.

20. 19 Geo II c. XII. [1745] An Act for the better regulating of corporations.

21. 21. Geo II c. 10. [1747] An Act to amend and make more effectual the two preceding Acts.

22. 23 Geo II c. 10. [1749] An Act for rendering more effectual the Act to prevent marriages by Popish priests.

23. 23 Geo II c. 14. [1749] An Act in relation to the appointing high and petty constables.

24. 29 Geo II c. 5. [1755] An Act to prevent the return of such persons as now are, or hereafter may

be in the service of the French king." [5]

Then beginning in 1772 the laws were gradually relaxed:

"1772 An Act of emancipation (11 & 12 Geo. III c. 21) allowed Catholics to reclaim and hold under lease for 61 years fifty acres of bog but it should not be within a mile of any city or market town.

...

1778 An Act (17 & 18 Geo. III c. 49) was passed repealing the provision in the 1703/4 Act (2 Anne c. 6) whereby a son could convert to the Church of Ireland and take over the family property. The 1778 Act relieved those Catholics who took the oath [of allegiance to the King] prescribed under the 1774 Act from certain restrictions contained in the 1704 and 1709 Acts. Catholics who took the oath were no longer limited to 31-year leases; they could hold leases for up to 999 years or five lives. A Catholic also no longer had to divide his estate among all his sons at his death.

1782 The Relief Act of 1782 (21 & 22 Geo. III c. 24) allowed Catholics who took the 1774 oath to purchase lands in fee, that is, outright ownership.

1793 A Relief Act (33 Geo. III c. 21) was passed giving Catholics the parliamentary and municipal franchise (vote) on the same basis as Protestants and admitting them to the university and to government offices. They were still excluded from sitting in Parliament and from the higher offices, but in other respects they were placed on a level with Protestants.

1829 The Catholic Relief Bill was passed. Catholics were admitted to Parliament and local government corporations; but they were still excluded from some of the higher offices. Further, the franchise was raised to ten pounds, so the forty-shilling freeholders were disfranchised." [6]

This is then the basic story of the Penal Laws in the 18th century, various laws that were brought in during the first decades of the century, building on earlier laws that actually dated from Queen Elizabeth's time, which were gradually wound down from c.1780 on.

The Penal Laws and the Registry of Deeds

As you can see in the quote from Maguire at the head of this chapter the idea behind bringing the ROD into the application of the Penal Laws was simply to police and maybe spy on land transactions in Ireland to make it easier to enforce the laws against Catholic landowners. Clearly the powers that be saw the peculiar advantages, in this sense, of the system that had just been rolled out in Yorkshire in England. Obviously having a central registry of all land transactions has got to speed up the surveillance of the Catholic landowners which no doubt was seen to be a central plank of the Penal Law system.

At any rate as far as we are concerned now in our study of the ROD deeds the Penal Laws come into the picture in three ways:

a) You will see mention of the Penal Laws (sometimes referred to as 'Popery Acts') on occasion in the deeds. Watch out for references to a 'Protestant Discoverer', this person is mentioned in the Laws and refers to the first Protestant who discovers Catholics owning land illegally and who gets a reward of those lands for informing on the Catholics. So much for the theory, actually what tended to happen was that Catholic landowners secretly paid off some tame Protestant to agree to act as a fake Protestant Discoverer in order to anticipate a real Protestant Discoverer or indeed just to use him to get real, as opposed to life tenure only, ownership of land i.e. to save the cost of a Common Recovery (as described in Chapter 2 infra).

Examples of this in the deeds include a reference to a Bill filed on the 19 December 1765 in the Court of Exchequer, "founded on the Popery Acts", mentioning that inter alios "Ignatius Blake and Margaret his wife, at the suit of the said Dugal Swiney [a yeoman from Dublin] as the first Protestant Discoverer" and with reference to the lands of Rathaspick in Co. Westmeath.[7] A possible example of a fake Protestant Discoverer used "in trust" to defeat the Penal Laws can be seen in 1734 in a deed involving the lands of Tonemegeragh and Cunlin Co. Cavan and the parties of Richard Poole, a Dublin joiner, Miles Reilly of Tonemegerah, and Richard and Anthony Malone of Dublin. Poole states in the deed that his name was used 'in trust' for Miles when he exhibited a Bill against the Malones in the Court of Exchequer as a Protestant Discoverer. The Malones were probably working with Reilly, as his lawyers, on this considering that they later transferred their interest in the lands to Reilly.[8]

An example of a Protestant Discoverer being used "to cut and destroy the tail remainders" is provided by a 1760 deed involving Richard Hall of Gt Britain St in Co. Dublin and Wyndam Madder of Dublin and the lands of Robinstown in Co. Westmeath.[9]

b) A simple point of course is that it means that Catholics are less prominent in the ROD at least in the early years. Many Catholic families certainly did trade in land throughout this time and indeed are mentioned in the ROD but of course it stands to reason that an institution set up as part of the Penal Laws would not be the most favoured place for Catholics at least in the early part of the century. Where they are mentioned you can also see an absence of deeds in excess of 31 years and sometimes an overall anti-Catholic emphasis can be detected although in practice this is not very evident. One deed involving the lands of Turin and the family of Carpenterstown Co Westmeath specified that the tenant was "not to set the premises or any part thereof to any Papist or Papists." [10] (Its a curious thing that the lands of Carpenterstown, north of Castlepollard, remained off limits to Catholics until c.1900. The current owners, Cooneys originally from Walshestown, could only buy the lands by using a Protestant intermediary, the Mitchell family, because even at the c.1900 period the land could not be sold to a Catholic.[11])

But in general all this can be very exaggerated, one should not assume for a minute that Catholics are somehow not mentioned in the 18th century ROD, in fact that is very far from the truth.

c) Finally it adds significantly to our 'vertical problem' described in the previous chapter. In a way the Laws created a kind of underclass of dispossessed Catholics who wanted to get back or hold onto their old lands but who were prevented by these laws. So they often take up a kind of shadow existence between the real farmers of the land and the large Protestant landlord. They become, in some cases, the famous 'Catholic Middlemen' of the 18th century. (By the way this class is frequently criticised throughout the century as being uncouth, money obsessed, hard drinking, uneducated boorish types! as you can see in some comments by Arthur Young quoted in the next chapter.) Typically these are the old Catholic proprietors of the land who are hanging on by clinging onto some old long leases from the Protestant owners of the land, and then in turn they give back to the small farmers patches of land on short leases. It turned out this way partly because those old Catholic families were simply around in the area in the early and mid 18th century period when the Protestant landlords were handing out those long leases and partly because they were desperate to get back their old lands and went to great lengths to get a foothold there. For example the family of Donore Co Westmeath in 1735 rewarded Joseph Byrne of Ballneclunagh with a lease of that land because of Byrne's good offices "in prevailing upon the Right Honourable the Lord Baron of Athenry to surrender a lease which he had of Ballneclunagh" to the Donore family.[12]

It does tend to be a hidden kind of class as well because of course under the Penal Laws they weren't really entitled to simple long leases and had to rely on the discretion of their neighbours and the sense of solidarity among the Catholic community in general to hold onto the land. (One writer in 1752 said that "the acts relating to purchases made or leases taken by papists are so eluded by perjuries, trusts in Protestant names and other contrivances that they are of little significance." [13]) After all they call this whole milieu the "Hidden Ireland" and the way that this community supported the Catholic clergy and hierarchy when it was illegal to do so is similar to the way they in part held onto land even where it was also illegal to do so.

In any case from the point of view of our analysis of the deeds it should cause us to read between the lines a little bit to see can we spot an old Catholic family holding on, usually, as stated, in the middle between the now Protestant proprietor and the real farmer of the land. As an example of this kind of detective work consider this anecdote from the memoirs of the famous Henry Grattan. In 1780 he sponsored a Bill in the Irish Parliament in which confirmed the holders of leases for lives in their property because they had otherwise been threatened by a decision of the House of Lords in London. That legal decision could have made many landlords in Ireland rich, including Grattan himself as he relates here:

"I deserve," said he, "some credit for what I did then. I was poor, and I had in the county of Westmeath an estate under this tenure, that produced about £170 a-year. On the death of my father, it was said to be worth £800 a-year, and, at the period I speak of, it was worth more, probably £1200 a-year; but I would not avail myself of the English decision and take this property, although the tenancy was forfeited. The tenant came to me to get the lease renewed. She was a little old lady, in a green riding-habit, and a black beaver hat, and a large steel buckle fastening her belt. I had been out in the fields, and came in cold and wet, and I sat down by the fire to warm myself, and to avoid laughing at so comical a figure. I gave her the renewal, and I took £80 "fine" (I think it was) instead of £1,200 a-year. She did not seem to give me much credit for what I was doing, and as I was signing the deed, she looked at me very suspiciously, and said,

'I hope, Sir, you and this other gentleman (the attorney) will not cheat me, as I am a poor lone woman.'

She then proceeded to pay me, and her mode of payment was singular; she gave me three bills for this sum of £80 at six, and twelve, and eighteen months." [14]

In order to try and figure out who this potential 'middle person' is we are helpfully told by Grattan's son that:

> "The granddaughter of the individual here mentioned, is married to Mr. Trevor, Viscount Dungannon, and member of Parliament for the town of Durham."

A little research in the usual sources will tell you that the 'old woman' was Elizabeth Nugent, daughter of Richard Nugent of Robinstown which is on the eastern shore of Lough Ennell in Co Westmeath. She married Judge D'Arcy in July 1765 and had a daughter Elizabeth D'Arcy who died in 1829. This daughter married Major Georges Irvine (of Castle Irvine Co Fermanagh) in 1788 and they had a daughter Sophia Irvine (1799-1880) who in turn in 1821 married Arthur Hill Trevor, 3rd Viscount Dungannon, who was MP for Durham in 1831-2, 1835-41 and 1843. Hence this is an interesting insight into the old Catholic families, of which her family was a famous example – they were the direct descendants of an executed Catholic judge –, hanging onto the land via old long leases. Of course they never really warmed to the idea that somebody else now owned the land which accounts for the somewhat offhand attitude she had towards Grattan!

And its not just the Catholic landowner who is sometimes hidden here don't forget that Catholic clergy could be mentioned in the deeds but without their clerical titles, and even possibly members of the Wild Geese could turn up, again stripped of their foreign military titles. One family in whose ranks many officers in the Wild Geese are to be found was the Bracklyn branch of the Nugent family in Westmeath. A 1795 ROD deed of this family, living then in Balcarrow, was witnessed by a person described only as "Lavallin Nugent of Vienna" who in fact later became a famous field marshal in the Austrian army.[15]

So basically one effect of the Penal Laws is that it brings a whole 'Hidden Ireland' atmosphere to the 18th century ROD, where you have to observe carefully in order to trace out the somewhat discreet and secretive world of the Irish Catholics of the time.

Practical Application and Effect of the Laws

Well what was the practical situation like for the old Catholic families under these laws in Ireland? In truth it is different for each family but to outline an overall picture I would suggest two phases in their response to the 18th century Penal Laws:

a) Initially I think the laws made little enough difference to those Catholic families. After all the laws are clearly geared to wear down families over many decades, they don't have a particular short term impact e.g. even the laws against bearing arms didn't have a great impact initially because some families could continue to carry arms under the terms of their surrender at the end of the Williamite wars. Also during this initial stage there was great solidarity among the Catholic families who had just fought in that war and this made a great difference to the operation of the laws. If no heir to the lands was close to breaking ranks and become Protestant then a lot of the laws became mute, similarly if the younger sons didn't create waves then the gavelkind law became valueless etc etc.

Another point was that if a given Catholic was to fall foul of those laws and lose his estate a lot depended on how to assess the extent of this estate. As has been pointed out in the previous chapter, a lot of the estates were encumbered with annuities that had to be paid to family members, and with debts and old leases etc etc so it could be difficult to actually say who exactly owned what land. So if Alexander Plunkett, say, was going to lose his estate under these laws then you can imagine that all of the other Plunketts will rally around and ensure that the overall figure for the extent of his estate becomes artificially small (because they can claim that this or that farm was really held by such and such a relative under this old will etc etc). And conversely they can do the opposite with a family that for some reason was immune to confiscation. So for example back in the 17th century they exaggerated the landholding of families that had got 'Innocency' certificates under the Court of Claims c.1660 (again by simply reversing the previous process, they would claim that under x or y old will or family settlement the said family owned a vast estate!) and then they did the same thing for those families who had become Protestant and used them to protect the Catholic ones. Hence, legally speaking, the protestant Dunsany branch of the Plunkett family were said to own lands that were actually owned by the Catholic Fingall Plunketts. In the same way some lands owned by the Dease family in Cavan were officially listed as owned by their relatives the Protestant Nugent family of Mountnugent, and then when the Penal Laws ended both lands were handed back to their real owners. It wasn't just that simple mechanism either, a Catholic Nugent parent would use that Protestant family as nominal guardians of their children for example, and state as such in their wills, in order to get around the laws against Catholic guardians etc.

As you can see then a lot depended on the sense of solidarity within those old Catholic families, so long as they stuck together they could continue to bamboozle the system!

b) Then from c. the mid 1740s until the easing of the laws c.1780 you get a gradual erosion of that solidarity which in turn impacted on their ability to resist the Penal Laws. First of all its obvious that the only reason why these families resisted the laws was because they felt that taking the Protestant oaths would impact negatively on their immortal soul. There is no reason to be cynical about this, that is the only reason why any of these families stayed Catholic throughout those long centuries when it certainly wasn't in their political or economic interests so to do. But as you get into the mid to late 18th century you get two drifts that are eating away at these religious convictions:

– Firstly the economy in Britain and Ireland grew rapidly at this time as you see the first shoots of the industrial revolution and this harsh money obsessed environment in turn seemed to make obsolete and almost silly these old religious convictions.

– Secondly a lot of these old Irish Catholic families had family serving in the military abroad, the Wild Geese, and these were influenced by the lax moral standards of that time on the Continent, particularly during the dying embers of the ancient regime in France. For them again it looked old fashioned and pointless holding onto these religious convictions and they in turn were an influence on their Irish relatives.

So you can see the religious sense weakening at this time and that phenomenon, allied to the basic point that the Penal Laws were bound to be more effective over time as the original owners died off and as their heirs felt the full rigour of the laws which focused a lot on the inheritance of land, meant that those laws seemed to be more effective in this second half of the 18th century.

That might be the simplest way to understand the practical effect of the laws but there is also another controversy about these laws which is worth mentioning here: Its often been said that the Penal Laws were not actually enforced effectively and hence it was a bit of a dead letter etc etc. So for example we are told that on the one hand no Catholic could become a member of the guilds in the towns but actually what happened was that those guilds set up special types of membership, quarterage, which in practice meant that Catholics became members in all but name.

It seems to me that this approach is only partly true. Yes it is the case that the actual enforcement of the Penal Laws was spasmodic, as it was in fact all the way back to the Reformation because it was simply impractical for the British government to heavy handedly compel the Irish Catholics to abide by all these laws bearing in mind the small minority that the Protestant religion represented across most of Ireland. But that isn't the whole story. The real issue here is that the Penal Laws were focused on land ownership and since time immemorial land ownership documents and practices are conservative, meaning that landowners like to dot their 'i's and cross their 't's when it comes to the legal documents that prove their ownership of lands. So you can imagine how a Catholic heir to an estate feels when he gets land into his possession. Yes its not very likely at all that the government authorities are going to scrutinise the lengths of his leases or the degree of profit he made on them (the actual profit level of some leases was also specified under one of the penal laws, to ensure that Catholics weren't using nominal leases to get around the laws) etc, nor, as the 18th century wore on, was it at all likely that a genuine 'Protestant Discoverer' was going to take his lands from him but nonetheless it might be said that under the strict interpretation of the Penal Laws he wasn't the proper owner of the land. This tended to gnaw away at them quite a bit and you will find therefore that the Catholics did in fact fear these laws and act to protect themselves from them even when the state itself was not very active in enforcing them.

Another point is that a spasmodic enforcement of the law was all that was needed here, if a family was hoping to hold onto a farm over the 70 odd years of the 18th century Penal Laws then that's an awful long time to go unnoticed from the gaze of a government official! and they knew this and again it made them nervous about those laws. For these reasons then I think it would be unwise to accept that the laws were in practice a dead letter, even if they were only enforced periodically.

Certainly Irish writers of that time and a little later were quite adamant about the devastating effect of the Penal Laws on many of the great Irish aristocratic families. For example in the Appendices you can read a long quote on this from the *Reminiscences of an Emigrant Milesian*, the memoirs of Andrew O'Reilly, a brother of Edward O'Reilly the lexicographer and Paris correspondent of The Times in 1853.[16]

As an example of the practical response of families to the laws it might be interesting at this point to read a legal opinion prepared in 1732 for a Catholic bride and her Protestant groom by Richard Malone, a scion of a famous legal family in Westmeath who did so much work in defending Catholics during the Penal Laws:

> "State of John Nugent esq's Case
>
> That said John Nugent a late protestant convert now in possession of a considerable estate as tenant for life is upon a Treaty of Marriage with Catherine Eustace a papist of a considerable fortune.
>
> 1st Query – Do the said parties or either of them incur any and what penalties in case they do intermarry and the said Catherine continues still a

papist.

2nd Query – If they or either of them incur no pains or penalties do they or either of them incur any and what disabilities by their so intermarrying and the said Catherine's still continuing a papist.

3rd Query – Can such papist wife be entitled to accept of a jointure or dower or any other and what settlement and security from such protestant husband.

4th Query – is such protestant convert by such intermarriage made liable and subject to any further disabilities, than a person bred a protestant from his infancy would be liable to by the like intermarriage." [16]

That's the legal problem that they want Malone's opinion on and he responded thus:

"In case the above named John Nugent who is a protestant intermarrying with Catherine Eustace, or any other papist, he will for ever after, be disabled and rendered incapable of being heir, executor, administrator, or guardian, to any person and to sit in either house of parliament and from bearing any office or employment civil, or military, unless within one year after such marriage he procures her to be converted to the protestant religion and obtains and files a certificate thereof, under her hand and seal of the Bishop of the Diocese, the Archbishop of the Diocese, or the Lord Chancellor of this kingdom. And he is also, in case of such marriage, without obtaining and filing such certificate, to be deemed a papist or popish consort to all intents and purposes; which latter words, as I conceive, will by him incur [?] all such incapacities and disabilities as papist or popish ...sants [?persons?] were under at the time of making the act of parliament of the 9th of King William, to prevent Protestants, from intermarrying with papists and no others. But I am of opinion that those several disabilities must arise, upon a conviction to be had, upon the statute for making first [or 'such'?] marriage; and that by law, the same cannot in[?]curr, before such b[e h]ad.

I conceive that a convert, is as to this point, upon the same sort with any other protestant. And cannot ... , any other forfeitures or disabilities, in this respect, than what any other protestant may, and as there is no disability or incapacity, deemed upon any popish woman, who marries a protestant. I apprehend Catherine will be entitled to Dower, of any article of inheritance, which the husband shall be actually seized of during the coventus [marriage]. But she will not be capable of taking a joincture, without being subject to a discovery, upon the popery acts. She will however be capable of taking a provision, to be secured, out of, or by the interest of any, or by any personal [?] security.

27th of March 1732

Richard Malone" [18]

As you can see from that the Penal Laws were by no means some kind of dead letter but there were ways around some of the issues, such as the problem of setting aside a jointure for the Catholic wife. This is another legal opinion on the Penal Laws from the Malones, in this case in reply to a query from the Savage family of Portaferry in Co. Down and dated 2nd Dec 1749:

"If the lands demised by these leases were set at less than 2/3rds of the improved yearly value they are certainly interests discoverable on the Acts against Popery

...

And if Mr Andrew Savage causes a bill to be filed in the name of another Protestant as the first Protestant Discoverer in trust for himself he will be thereby able to avoid these interests and bargains..." [19]

The fake Protestant Discoverer being the great standby of the Catholics in trying to dodge the bullet of the Penal Laws,[20]

although they didn't avoid it in this case anyway because the Savages became Protestant. The Malones were an interesting legal family who sometimes got little thanks for their efforts in trying to protect Catholics from the Penal Laws as you can read in the account of Kedagh MacGeoghegan given in Appendix G.

So much for the Penal Laws which are an unstated but real influence on the ROD on the 18th century, we will now turn our attention to what is very much to the fore in the registry, the value of the monies listed in, and the economics lying behind, the 18th century deeds.

Footnotes
1. Joseph Maguire, *Land Transfer, Registration of Deeds and Title*, read 17th Feb 1922 and published in the *Journal of the Statistical and Social Inquiry Society of Ireland*, vol XIV, p.163-4.
The Penal Laws of the 18th century were all too effective in reducing the land ownership of Catholics:
"Thus between the 1690s and 1790s the amount of land in Catholic hands fell from c.15% to c.5%."
(Séan J Murphy, *A Most Valuable Storehouse of History*, in, *History Ireland*, vol 17 no.1 (Jan-Feb 2009), p.24.)

2. *Irish Historical Studies*, vol 7 no.25 (March 1950), p.26.

3. http://www.newadvent.org/cathen/11611c.htm .

4. Brian Nugent, *An Creideamh* (Oldcastle, 2009), p.251-252.

5. George Lewis Smyth, *Ireland: historical and statistical* (London, 1844) vol 1, p.125, and the quote relating to the 1703/4 act is from http://globalgenealogy.com/globalgazette/gazkb/gazkb68.htm .

6. http://globalgenealogy.com/globalgazette/gazkb/gazkb68.htm .

7. 1765 249-205-160130.

8. 1734 77-288-53719 and 1734 77-289-53726, and see also 1734 76-222-53727, 1738 92-85-63993 and 1738 92-160-64216.

9. 1760 206-600-137399.

10. 1718 21-463-12140 involving Walter Nugent of Carpenterstown.

11. Id like to thank the Cooney family for this information.

12. 1735 82-411-58357.

13. *Dialogue between a Protestant and a Papist* (Dublin , 1752), p.10, quoted in Kevin Whelan, *An Underground Gentry? Catholic Middlemen in Eighteenth Century Ireland,* in, *Eighteenth Century Ireland,* vol 10 (1995) p.11. That latter article contains a lot more detail on the subject of these Catholic middlemen, with many good quotes agreeing with the basic position outlined infra.

14. Henry Grattan, *Memoirs of the Life and Times of the Rt. Hon. Henry Grattan* (London, 1839-46) vol ii, p.84.
In the published *House of Commons Journals, Ireland,* under the 25th October 1703, p.74, we find that Richard Nugent of Robinstown wants to be heard because his son Nicholas Nugent of the same place had petitioned the House that his father "intends to disinherit him upon account of his being a protestant."
Probably another example of teasing out this underground gentry can be seen in an 1802 deed involving the Marquis of Buckingham, and including the lands of Kiltomb in Co Westmeath, where it was revealed that in 1767 Hugh O'Reilly was named the purchaser of land that was actually bought in trust for Lord Clare – who employed O'Reilly as his solicitor in Dublin – who in turn was using the 'proper money' of John Nugent of Kiltomb – probably a Catholic – who was the real owner (565-119-376876).

15. 1795 476-341-314786. The Bracklyn family went there on land leased to them on a long lease by the Tuites of Sonnagh, they left Bracklyn after a shooting incident at the gate leading to the house.

16. In the second half of Appendix C.

17. PRONI D552/B/2/1/74.

18. Ibid.

19. PRONI D/552/B/2/1/169.

Another legal opinion from the Penal laws, this time an opinion on draft marriage articles drawn up for the intended nuptials of Lady Emilia Plunkett and Robert Nugent of Carlanstown, as arranged between the latter's father Michael and Theobald, Earl of Carlingford, the bride to be's uncle, July 1730:
"It seems to me that the following particulars in this draught are dangerous with respect to the Popery Acts:

First, the clauses for charging the estate with portions for younger children.

2ndly, the clause for sale of particular lands to raise money for the better securing the provision intended for the Lady, and,

Thirdly, the clause whereby the young gentleman is to take particular lands in lieu of his annuity of £800 per annum, during his father's pleasure.

Wherefore I apprehend the agreement concerning the lands [?]tsaded to be given in satisfaction of the annuity should be struck out: And that instead of the Agreement to sell, and the covenants for charging your stake with portions for younger children, part of your estate should be [letters lost]ed, so as to make way for statute bonds of the staple, whereby the lady, as well as the younger children, may be provided for.

Cornelius Callaghan."
(Nugent part of Stowe Papers, Huntington Library)

20. Another example of a fake Protestant Discoverer can be seen in the case of the Murphy family of Ballinlough Big, Ballinlough Co. Meath. They were sued in 1754 by John Games who alleged that they, Papists, had purchased the lands of Ballinlough Big from Charles Wild for a lease that was too long for Catholics and for a rent that was undervalued. They then proceeded to sell the property to Robert Nugent, of Farrenconnell Co Cavan, who was a Protestant, to screen it from a Discovery under the Popery Acts in order to deprive the plaintiff of the benefit he was entitled to under said Acts of Parliament (Munimenta Nugentiorum, NLI M/F Pos.6849 no.92).

Yet another example of a Protestant discoverer is William Vicars, who acted only "in trust" for Matthew Fox with respect to lands in Ballinderry Co. Westmeath, as mentioned in a deed at 1765 239-284-15787.
(John Ainsworth, *Sidelights on 18th Century Land Tenure*, in JRSAI 1949, p.268.)

CHAPTER 7
Irish Economy and Prices in the 18th century

One issue that obviously arises in trying to understand the 18th century deeds is the overall economic background of the country. It seems to this observer that you cannot hope to put yourself in the shoes of the transactors of these deeds without knowing the cost of things and the economic background in Ireland in the 18th century. What follows in this chapter then are some long quotes from commentators on this economic background and finishing with contemporary accounts which will give the reader a grasp of 18th century Irish prices.

Firstly here is a simple quote from Louis Cullen who is a recognised expert on Irish conditions in the 18th century:

> "The fact that many 21-year leases and 31-year leases fell in between 1717 and 1730 was responsible for a significant rise in landlord's incomes at that time.
>
> ...
>
> Rent movements were uneven in the difficult 1730s and 1740s. While estimates suggest a rise from £1.6 or £2.0 million in the 1720s to £2.5 million in 1753, it is likely that the bulk of the increase took place after the mid 1740s, reflecting the new found buoyancy of the economy in the late 1740s and early 1750s. This was the beginning of a strong upward trend: the aggregate rental doubled or more than doubled between the mid-1740s and the mid-1770s, the rents on individual renewals, or more unevenly on entire estates, amply confirm the force of the upward trend. By 1815 rents had probably doubled again to £12 million. There was to be no comparable rise in the 19th century. This gives added point to the period from the late 1740s to 1815 as one in which landlord incomes enjoyed a unique buoyancy. The late 1740s to late 1760s was perhaps the period of sharpest rise; unequalled before or since, not even excluding the prosperous

138

years of the Napoleonic Wars. It stands out all the more because the appropriation of middlemen's profit rents by head landlords had made relatively limited progress at this stage." [1]

The leases for lives, in general, became popular – although these are actually an ancient type of lease in Ireland – from about the 1730s and are still to be met with towards the end of the century but you will find their popularity waning, among the landlords, by the end of it. In my opinion where a lease for lives occurs towards the end of the century it should often be looked upon as a quasi outright sale of land, but actually where 'lives' type leases occur in the earlier part of the century sometimes the landlords seem to have underestimated the degree of ownership of the land they were signing away. Hence the generally hostile way they would view those leases by 1800, except, as I say, as just an archaic way of registering a sale of land.

This latter type of lease caused not a little confusion in Irish landholdings by the middle of the 19th century because a lot of the land owners forgot to renew the leases in the way proscribed.[2] To take a simple hypothetical example: if John Smith granted a lease to Joe Murphy, for a 'consideration' of £1,000, of Clonbrackin in 1790, for three lives renewable forever at a fine, on the occasion of the necessity to add a life to the lease, of one peppercorn, then obviously what is happening here is that the land is in practice being sold off by Smith to Murphy and they just word it as a lease for three lives seemingly as a legal archaism. But since both parties probably view it in practice as an outright sale naturally Murphy might forget to pay the peppercorn, or indeed just forget to add a 'life' to the deed every time the life has to be renewed, and what happens then? The question of whether or not he then forfeits the land became the topic de jour among the legal fraternity in Dublin in the 19th century. Other than these simple points to bear in mind about leases and about what Cullen states above about the overall economic story, the rule is that there is no rule!, in the sense that the leases you will encounter can take all shapes and sizes throughout the century.

Undoubtedly though the most vivid and authoritative account of the 18th century economy in Ireland comes from the pen of

Arthur Young, an English writer very interested in agriculture who toured Ireland during the years 1776-1779. Rather than present some kind of colourless summary of his impressions it seems best to present to the reader here some long extracts of this work, which is so helpful in understanding the economic background underpinning the 18th century deeds in the Registry of Deeds:

Arthur Young's Tour of Ireland 1776-1779

"From hence took the road to Summerhill [Co. Meath], the seat of the Right Hon. H. L. Rowley. The country is cheerful and rich; and if the Irish cabins continue like what I have hitherto seen, I shall not hesitate to pronounce their inhabitants as well off as most English cottagers. They are built of mud walls eighteen inches or two feet thick, and well thatched, which are far warmer than the thin clay walls in England. Here are few cottars without a cow, and some of them two. A bellyful invariably of potatoes, and generally turf for fuel from a bog. It is true they have not always chimneys to their cabins, the door serving for that and window too. If their eyes are not affected with the smoke, it may be an advantage in warmth. Every cottage swarms with poultry, and most of them have pigs.

...

In conversation with Lord Longford I made many inquiries concerning the state of the lower classes, and found that in some respects they were in good circumstances, in others indifferent; they have, generally speaking, such plenty of potatoes as always to command a bellyful; they have flax enough for all their linen, most of them have a cow, and some two, and spin wool enough for their clothes; all a pig, and numbers of poultry, and in general the complete family of cows, calves, hogs, poultry, and children pig together in the cabin; fuel they have in the utmost plenty. Great numbers of families are also supported by the neighbouring lakes, which abound prodigiously with fish. A child with a packthread and a crooked pin will catch perch enough in an hour for the family to live on the whole day, and his lordship has seen five hundred children fishing at the same time, there being no tenaciousness in the proprietors of the lands about a right to the fish. Besides perch, there is pike upwards of five feet long, bream, tench, trout of ten pounds, and as red as salmon, and fine eels. All these are favourable circumstances, and are very conspicuous in the numerous and healthy families among them.

Reverse the medal: they are ill clothed, and make a wretched appearance, and what is worse, are much oppressed by many who make them pay too dear for keeping a cow, horse, etc. They have a practice also of keeping accounts with the labourers, contriving by that means to let the poor wretches have very little cash for their year's work. This is a great oppression, farmers and gentlemen keeping accounts with the poor is a cruel abuse: so many days' work for a cabin; so many for a potato garden; so many for keeping a horse, and so many for a cow, are clear accounts which a poor man can understand well, but farther it ought never to go; and when he has worked out what he has of this sort, the rest of his work ought punctually to be paid him every Saturday night.

...

From Mullingar to Tullespace [Tyrellspass?] I found rents in general at twenty shillings an acre, with much relet at thirty shillings, yet all the crops except bere were very bad, and full of weeds. About the latter-named place the farms are generally from one hundred to three hundred acres; and their course: 1. fallow; 2. bere; 3. oats; 4. oats; 5. oats. Great quantities of potatoes all the way, crops from forty to eighty barrels.

...

In conversation upon the subject of a union with Great Britain, I was informed that nothing was so unpopular in Ireland as such an idea; and that the great objection to it was increasing the number of absentees. When it was in agitation, twenty peers and sixty commoners were talked of to sit in the British Parliament, which would be the resident of eighty of the best estates in Ireland. Going every year to England would, by degrees, make them residents; they would educate their children there, and in time become mere absentees: becoming so they would be unpopular, others would be elected, who, treading in the same

steps, would yield the place still to others; and thus by degrees, a vast portion of the kingdom now resident would be made absentees, which would, they think, be so great a drain to Ireland, that a free trade would not repay it.
...

Having now passed through a considerable extent of country, in which the Whiteboys were common, and committed many outrages, I shall here review the intelligence I received concerning them throughout the county of Kilkenny. I made many inquiries into the origin of those disturbances, and found that no such thing as a leveller or Whiteboy was heard of till 1760, which was long after the landing of Thurot, or the intending expedition of M. Conflans. That no foreign coin was ever seen among them, though reports to the contrary were circulated; and in all the evidence that was taken during ten or twelve years, in which time there appeared a variety of informers, none was ever taken, whose testimony could be relied on, that ever proved any foreign interposition. Those very few who attempted to favour it, were of the most infamous and perjured characters. All the rest, whose interest it was to make the discovery, if they had known it, and who concealed nothing else, pretended to no such knowledge. No foreign money appeared, no arms of foreign construction, no presumptive proof whatever of such a connection. They began in Tipperary, and were owing to some inclosures of commons, which they threw down, levelling the ditches, and were first known by the name of Levellers. After that, they began with the tithe-proctors (who are men that hire tithes of the rectors), and these proctors either screwed the cottars up to the utmost shilling, or relet the tithes to such as did it. It was a common practice with them to go in parties about the country, swearing many to be true to them, and forcing them to join by menaces, which they very often carried into execution. At last they set up to be general redressers of grievances, punished all obnoxious persons who advanced the value of lands, or hired farms over their heads; and, having taken the administration of justice into their hands, were not very exact in the distribution of it. Forced masters to release their apprentices, carried off the daughters of rich farmers, and ravished them into marriages, of which four instances happened in a fortnight. They levied sums of money on the middling and lower farmers in order to support their cause, by paying attorneys, etc., in defending prosecutions against them; and many of them subsisted for some years without work, supported by these contributions. Sometimes they committed several considerable robberies, breaking into houses, and taking the money, under pretence of redressing grievances. In the course of these outrages they burnt several houses, and destroyed the whole substance of men obnoxious to them. The barbarities they committed were shocking. One of their usual punishments (and by no means the most severe) was taking people out of their beds, carrying them naked in winter on horseback for some distance, and burying them up to their chin in a hole filled with briars, not forgetting to cut off their ears. In this manner the evil existed for eight or ten years, during which time the gentlemen of the country took some measures to quell them. Many of the magistrates were active in apprehending them; but the want of evidence prevented punishments, for many of those who even suffered by them had no spirit to prosecute. The gentlemen of the country had frequent expeditions to discover them in arms; but their intelligence was so uncommonly good by their influence over the common people, that not one party that ever went out in quest of them was successful. Government offered large rewards for informations, which brought a few every year to the gallows, without any radical cure for the evil. The reason why it was not more effective was the necessity of any person that gave evidence against them quitting their houses and country, or remaining exposed to their resentment. At last their violence arose to a height which brought on their suppression. The popish inhabitants of Ballyragget, six miles from Kilkenny, were the first of the lower people who dared openly to associate against them; they threatened destruction to the town, gave notice that they would attack it, were as good as their word, came two hundred strong, drew up before a house in which were fifteen armed men, and fired in at the windows; the fifteen men handled their arms so well, that in a few rounds they killed forty or fifty. They fled immediately, and ever after left Ballyragget in peace: indeed, they have never been resisted at all without showing a great want of both spirit and discipline. It should, however, be observed, that they had but very few arms, those in bad order, and no cartridges. Soon after this they attacked the house of Mr. Power in Tipperary, the history of which is well known. His murder spirited up the gentlemen to exert themselves in suppressing the evil, especially in raising subscriptions to give private rewards to whoever would give evidence or information concerning them. The private distribution had much more effect than larger sums which required a public declaration; and Government giving rewards to those who resisted them, without having previously promised it, had likewise some effect. Laws were passed for punishing all who assembled, and (what may have a great effect) for recompensing, at the expense of the county or barony, all persons who suffered by their outrages. In consequence of this general exertion, above twenty were capitally convicted, and most of them executed; and the gaols of this and the three neighbouring counties, Carlow, Tipperary, and Queen's County, have many in them whose trials are put off till next assizes, and against whom sufficient evidence for conviction, it is supposed, will appear. Since this all has been quiet, and no outrages have been committed: but before I quit the subject, it is proper to remark that what coincided very much to abate the evil was the fall in the price of lands which has taken place lately. This is considerable, and has much lessened the evil of hiring farms over the heads of one another; perhaps, also, the tithe-proctors have not been quite so severe in their extortions: but this observation is by no means general; for in many places tithes yet continue to be levied with all those circumstances which originally raised the evil.

...

To Arthur Buntin's, Esq., near Belfast; the soil a stiff clay; lets at old rents 10s., new one 18s., the town parks of that place 30s. to 70s., ten miles round it 10s. to 20s., average 13s. A great deal of flax sown, every countryman having a little, always on potato land, and one ploughing: they usually sow each family a bushel of seed. Those who have no land pay the farmers 20s. rent for the land a bushel of seed sows, and always on potato land. They plant many more potatoes than they eat, to supply the market at Belfast; manure for them with all their dung, and some of them mix dung, earth, and lime, and this is found to do better. There is much alabaster near the town, which is used for stucco plaster; sells from £1 1s. to 25s. a ton.

...

At Clonells [Clonalis], near Castlerea, lives O'Connor, the direct descendant of Roderick O'Connor, who was king of Connaught six or seven hundred years ago; there is a monument of him in Roscommon Church, with his sceptre, etc. I was told as a certainty that this family were here long before the coming of the Milesians. Their possessions, formerly so great, are reduced to three or four hundred pounds a year, the family having fared in the revolutions of so many ages much worse than the O'Niels and O'Briens. The common people pay him the greatest respect, and send him presents of cattle, etc., upon various occasions. They consider him as the prince of a people involved in one common ruin.

Another great family in Connaught is Macdermot, who calls himself Prince of Coolavin. He lives at Coolavin, in Sligo, and though he has not above one hundred pounds a year, will not admit his children to sit down in his presence. This was certainly the case with his father, and some assured me even with the present chief. Lord Kingsborough, Mr. Ponsonby, Mr. O'Hara, Mr. Sandford, etc., came to see him, and his address was curious: "O'Hara, you are welcome! Sandford, I am glad to see your mother's son" (his mother was an O'Brien): "as to the rest of ye, come in as ye can." Mr. O'Hara, of Nymphsfield, is in possession of a considerable estate in Sligo, which is the remains of great possessions they had in that country. He is one of the few descendants of the Milesian race.

...

Price of Provisions [in Limerick]
Wheat, 1s. 1d. a stone
Barley and oats, 5¾d. to 6d.
Scotch coals, 18s.; Whitehaven, 20s.
A boat-load of turf, 20 tons, 45s.
Salmon, three-halfpence.
Trout, 2d., very fine, per lb.
Eels, 2d. a pound.

Rabbits, 8d. a couple.
Wild ducks, 20d. to 2s. a couple.
Teal, 10d. a couple.
Plover, 6d. a couple.
Widgeon, 10d. ditto.
Hares, 1s. each, commonly sold all year.
Woodcocks, 20d. to 2s. 2d. a brace.
Oysters, 4d. to 1s. a 100.
Lobsters, 1s. to 1s. 6d., if good.

Land sells at twenty years' purchase. Rents were at the highest in 1765; fell since, but in four years have fallen 8s. to 10s. an acre about Limerick. They are at a stand at present, owing to the high price of provisions from pasture. The number of people in Limerick is computed at thirty-two thousand; it is exceedingly populous for the size, the chief street quite crowded; many sedan chairs in town, and some hackney chaises. Assemblies the year round, in a new assembly-house built for the purpose, and plays and concerts common.

Upon the whole, Limerick must be a very gay place, but when the usual number of troops are in town much more so. To show the general expenses of living, I was told of a person's keeping a carriage, four horses, three men, three maids, a good table, a wife, three children, and a nurse, and all for £500 a year:

A footman 4-4-0 to 6-6-0
A professed woman-cook 6-6-0
A house-maid 3-0-0
A kitchen-maid 2-0-0
A butler 10-0-0 to 12-0-0

...

Average of nineteen years export [from the port of Cork], ending March 24, 1773

Hides, at £1 each	£64,000
Bay and woollen yarn	294,000
Butter, at 30s. per cwt. from 56s. to 72s.	180,000
Beef, at 20s. a barrel	291,970
Camlets, serges, etc.	40,000
Candles	34,220
Soap	20,000

Tallow	20,000
Herrings, 18 to 35,000l. all their own	21,000
Glue 20 to 25,000	22,000
Pork	64,000
Wool to England	14,000

Small exports, Gottenburg herrings, horns, hoofs, etc., feather-beds, palliasses, feathers, etc.

35,000

£1,100,190

Average prices of the nineteen years on the custom books. All exports on those books are rated at the value of the reign of Charles II.; but the imports have always 10 per cent. on the sworn price added to them. Seventy to eighty sail of ships belong to Cork. Average of ships that entered that port in those nineteen years, eight hundred and seventy-two per annum. The number of people at Cork mustered by the clergy by hearth-money, and by the number of houses, payments to minister, average of the three, sixty-seven thousand souls, if taken before the 1st of September, after that twenty thousand increased. There are seven hundred coopers in the town. Barrels all of oak or beech, all from America: the latter for herrings, now from Gottenburg and Norway. The excise of Cork now no more than in Charles the Second's reign. Ridiculous!

Cork old duties, in 1751, produced	£62,000
Now the same	140,000

Bullocks, 16,000 head, 32,000 barrels; 41,000 hogs, 20,000 barrels. Butter, 22,000 firkins of half a hundredweight each, both increase this year, the whole being

240,000 firkins of butter,

120,000 barrels of beef.

Export of woollen yarn from Cork, £300,000 a year in the Irish market. No wool smuggled, or at least very little. The wool comes to Cork, etc., and is delivered out to combers, who make it into balls. These balls are bought up by the French agents at a vast price, and exported; but even this does not amount to £40,000 a year.

Prices

Beef, 21s. per cwt., never so high by 2s. 6d.; pork, 30s., never higher than 18s. 6d., owing to the army demand. Slaughter dung, 8d. for a horse load. Country labourer, 6d.; about town, 10d. Milk, seven pints a penny. Coals, 3s. 8d. to 5s. a barrel, six of which make a ton. Eggs, four a penny.

Cork labourers, cellar ones, twenty thousand, have 1s. 1d. a day, and as much bread, beef, and beer as they can eat and drink, and seven pounds of offals a week for their families. Rent for their house, 40s. Masons' and carpenters' labourers, 10d. a day. Sailors now £3 a month and provisions: before the American war, 28s. Porters and coal-heavers paid by the great [grate]. State of the poor people in general incomparably better off than they were twenty years ago. There are imported eighteen thousand barrels annually of Scotch herrings, at 18s. a barrel. The salt for the beef trade comes from Lisbon, St. Ube's, etc. The salt for the fish trade from Rochelle. For butter English and Irish.

Particulars of the woollen fabrics of the county of Cork received from a manufacturer. The woollen trade, serges and camlets, ratteens, friezes, druggets, and narrow cloths, the last they make to 10s. and 12s. a yard; if they might export to 8s. they are very clear that they could get a great trade for the woollen manufactures of Cork. The wool comes from Galway and Roscommon, combed here by combers, who earn 8s. to 10s. a week, into balls of twenty-four ounces, which is spun into worsteds of twelve skeins to the ball, and exported to Yarmouth for Norwich; the export price, £30 a pack to £33, never before so high; average of them, £26 to £30. Some they work up at home into serges, stuffs, and camlets; the serges at 12d. a yard, thirty-four inches wide; the stuffs sixteen inches, at 18d., the camlets at 9½d. to 13d.; the spinners at 9d. a ball, one in a week; or a ball and half 12d. a week, and attend the family besides; this is done most in Waterford and Kerry, particularly near Killarney; the weavers earn 1s. a day on an average. Full three-fourths of the wool is exported in yarn, and only one-fourth worth worked up. Half the wool of Ireland is combed in the county of Cork.

...

Rode to the mouth of Cork Harbour; the grounds about it are all fine, bold, and varied, but so bare of trees, that there is not a single view but what pains one in the want of wood. Rents of the tract south of the river Caragoline, from 5s. to 30s.; average, 10s. Not one man in five has a cow, but generally from one to four acres, upon which they have potatoes, and five or six sheep, which they milk, and spin their wool. Labour 5d. in winter, 6d. in summer; many of them for three months in the year live on potatoes and water, the rest of it they have a good deal of fish. But it is remarked, at Kinsale, that when sprats are most plentiful, diseases are most common. Rent for a mere cabin, 10s. Much paring and burning; paring twenty-eight men a day, sow wheat on it and then potatoes; get great crops. The soil a sharp, stony land; no limestone south of the above river. Manure for potatoes, with sea-weed, for 26s., which gives good crops, but lasts only one year. Sea-sand much used; no shells in it. Farms rise to two or three hundred acres, but are hired in partnership.

...

The state of the poor [near Tarbert Co. Kerry] is something better than it was twenty years ago, particularly their clothing, cattle, and cabins. They live upon potatoes and milk; all have cows, and when they dry them, buy others. They also have butter, and most of them keep pigs, killing them for their own use. They have also herrings. They are in general in the cottar system, of paying for labour by assigning some land to each cabin. The country is greatly more populous than twenty years ago, and is now increasing; and if ever so many cabins were built by a gradual increase, tenants would be found for them. A cabin and five acres of land will let for £4 a year. The industrious cottar, with two, three, or four acres, would be exceedingly glad to have his time to himself, and have such an annual addition of land as he was able to manage, paying a fair rent for it; none would decline it but the idle and worthless.

Tithes are all annually valued by the proctors, and charged very high. There are on the Shannon about one hundred boats employed in bringing turf to Limerick from the coast of Kerry and Clare, and in fishing; the former carry from twenty to twenty-five tons, the latter from five to ten, and are navigated each by two men and a boy.

...

Palatines [German immigrants] were settled here [near Adare Co. Limerick] by the late Lord Southwell about seventy years ago.

They preserve some of their German customs: sleep between two beds. They appoint a burgomaster, to whom they appeal in case of all disputes; and they yet preserve their language, but that is declining. They are very industrious, and in consequence are much happier and better fed, clothed, and lodged than the Irish peasants. We must not, however, conclude from hence that all is owing to this; their being independent farmers, and having leases, are circumstances which will create industry. Their crops are much better than those of their neighbours. There are three villages of them, about seventy families in all. For some time after they settled they fed upon sour-crout, but by degrees left it off, and took to potatoes; but now subsist upon them and butter and milk, but with a great deal of oat bread, and some of wheat, some meat and fowls, of which they raise many. They have all offices to their houses, that is, stables and cow-houses, and a lodge for their ploughs, etc. They keep their cows in the house in winter, feeding them upon hay and oat straw. They are remarkable for the goodness and cleanliness of their houses. The women are very industrious, reap the corn, plough the ground sometimes, and do whatever work may be going on; they also spin, and make their children do the same. Their wheat is much better than any in the country, insomuch that they get a better price than anybody else. Their industry goes so far, that jocular reports of its excess are spread. In a very pinching season, one of them yoked his wife against a horse, and went in that manner to work, and finished a journey at plough. The industry of the women is a perfect contrast to the Irish ladies in the cabins, who cannot be persuaded, on any consideration, even to make hay, it not being the custom of the country, yet they bind corn, and do other works more laborious. Mrs. Quin, who is ever attentive to introduce whatever can contribute to their welfare and happiness, offered many premiums to induce them to make hay, of hats, cloaks, stockings, etc. etc., but all would not do.

...

To Sir William Osborne's, three miles the other side Clonmel.

From a character so remarkable for intelligence and precision, I could not fail of meeting information of the most valuable kind. This gentleman has made a mountain improvement which demands particular attention, being upon a principle very different from common ones.

Twelve years ago he met with a hearty-looking fellow of forty, followed by a wife and six children in rags, who begged. Sir William questioned him upon the scandal of a man in full health and vigour, supporting himself in such a manner: the man said he could get no work: "Come along with me, I will show you a spot of land upon which I will build a cabin for you, and if you like it you shall fix there." The fellow followed Sir William, who was as good as his word: he built him a cabin, gave him five acres of a heathy mountain, lent him four pounds to stock with, and gave him, when he had prepared his ground, as much lime as he would come for. The fellow flourished; he went on gradually; repaid the four pounds, and presently became a happy little cottar: he has at present twelve acres under cultivation, and a stock in trade worth at least £80; his name is John Conory.

The success which attended this man in two or three years brought others who applied for land, and Sir William gave them as they applied. The mountain was under lease to a tenant, who valued it so little, that upon being reproached with not cultivating, or doing something with it, he assured Sir William that it was utterly impracticable to do anything with it, and offered it to him without any deduction of rent. Upon this mountain he fixed them; gave them terms as they came determinable with the lease of the farm, so that every one that came in succession had shorter and shorter tenures; yet are they so desirous of settling, that they come at present, though only two years remain for a term.

In this manner Sir William has fixed twenty-two families, who are all upon the improving hand, the meanest growing richer; and find themselves so well off, that no consideration will induce them to work for others, not even in harvest: their industry has no bounds; nor is the day long enough for the revolution of their incessant labour. Some of them bring turf to Clonmel, and Sir William has seen Conory returning loaded with soap ashes.

He found it difficult to persuade them to make a road to their village, but when they had once done it, he found none in getting cross roads to it, they found such benefit in the first. Sir William has continued to give whatever lime they come for: and they have desired one thousand barrels among them for the year 1766, which their landlord has accordingly contracted for with his lime-burner, at 11d. a barrel. Their houses have all been built at his expense, and done by contract at £6 each, after which they raise what little offices they want for themselves.

...

In general, I was informed that the trade of the place [Waterford] had increased considerably in ten years, both the exports and imports—the exports of the products of pasturage, full one-third in twelve years. That the staple trade of the place is the Newfoundland trade. This is very much increased; there is more of it here than anywhere. The number of people who go as passengers in the Newfoundland ships is amazing: from sixty to eighty ships, and from three thousand to five thousand annually. They come from most parts of Ireland, from Cork, Kerry, etc. Experienced men will get eighteen to twenty-five pounds for the season, from March to November. A man who never went will have five to seven pounds and his passage, and others rise to twenty pounds; the passage out they get, but pay home two pounds. An industrious man in a year will bring home twelve to sixteen pounds with him, and some more. A great point for them is to be able to carry out all their slops, for everything there is exceedingly dear, one or two hundred per cent. dearer than they can get them at home. They are not allowed to take out any woollen goods but for their own use. The ships go loaded with pork, beef, butter, and some salt; and bring home passengers, or get freights where they can; sometimes rum. The Waterford pork comes principally from the barony of Iverk, in Kilkenny, where they fatten great numbers of large hogs; for many weeks together they kill here three to four thousand a week, the price fifty shillings to four pounds each; goes chiefly to Newfoundland. One was killed in Mr. Penrose's cellar that weighed five hundredweight and a quarter, and measured from the nose to the end of the tail nine feet four inches.

There is a foundry at Waterford for pots, kettles, weights, and all common utensils; and a manufactory by Messrs. King and Tegent of anvils to anchors, twenty hundredweight, etc., which employs forty hands. Smiths earn from 6s. to 24s. a week. Nailers from 10s. to 12s. And another less considerable. There are two sugar-houses, and many salt-houses. The salt is boiled over lime-kilns.

There is a fishery upon the coast of Waterford, for a great variety of fish, herrings particularly, in the mouth of Waterford Harbour, and two years ago in such quantities there, that the tides left the ditches full of them. There are some premium boats both here and at Dungarvan, but the quantity of herrings barrelled is not considerable.

The butter trade of Waterford has increased greatly for seven years past; it comes from Waterford principally, but much from Carlow; for it comes from twenty miles beyond Carlow, for sixpence per hundred. From the 1st of January, 1774, to the 1st of January, 1775, there were exported fifty-nine thousand eight hundred and fifty-six casks of butter, each, on an average, one hundredweight, at the mean price of 50s. Revenue of Waterford, 1751, £17,000; 1776, £52,000. The slaughter trade has increased, but not so much as the butter. Price of butter now at Waterford, 58s.; twenty years' average, 42s. Beef now to 25s.; average, twenty years, 10s. to 18s. Pork, now 30s.; average, twenty years, 16s. to 22s. Eighty sail of ships now belonging to the port, twenty years ago not thirty. They pay to the captains of ship of two hundred tons £5 a month; the mate £3 10s. Ten men at 40s., five years ago only 27s. Building ships, £10 a ton. Wear and tear of such a ship, £20 a month. Ship provisions, 20s. a month.

...

Farms about Ballycanvan, Waterford, etc., are generally small, from twenty and thirty to five hundred acres, generally about two hundred and fifty. All above two hundred acres are in general dairies; some of the dairy ones rise very high. The soil is a reddish stony or slaty gravel, dry, except low lands, which are clay or turf. Rents vary much—about the town very high, from £5 5s. to £9, but at the distance of a few miles towards Passage, etc., they are from 20s. to 40s., and some higher, but the country in general does not rise so high, usually 10s. to 20s. for dairying land.

The poor people spin their own flax, but not more, and a few of them wool for themselves. Their food is potatoes and milk; but they have a considerable assistance from fish, particularly herrings; part of the year they have also barley, oaten, and rye bread. They are incomparably better off in every respect than twenty years ago. Their increase about Ballycanvan is very great, and tillage all over this neighbourhood is increased. The rent of a cabin 10s.; an acre with it 20s. The grass of a cow a few years ago 20s., now 25s. or 30s.

An exceeding good practice here in making their fences is, they plant the quick on the side of the bank in the common manner, and then, instead of the dead hedge we use in England on the top of the bank, they plant a row of old thorns, two or three feet high, which readily grow, and form at once a most excellent fence. Their way also of taking in sand-banks from the river deserves notice. They stake down a row of furzes at low water, laying stones on them to the height of one or two feet; these retain the mud, which every tide brings in, so as to fill up all within the furze as high as their tops. I remarked, on the strand, that a few boatloads of stones laid carelessly had had this effect, for within them I measured twelve inches deep of rich blue mud left behind them, the same as they use in manuring, full of shells, and effervesced strongly with vinegar.

Among the poor people the fishermen are in much the best circumstances. The fishery is considerable; Waterford and its harbour have fifty boats each, from eight to twelve tons, six men on an average to each, but to one of six tons five men go. A boat of eight tons costs £40; one of twelve, £60. To each boat there is a train of nets of six pair, which costs from £4 4s. to £6 6s.; tan them with bark. Their only net fishery is that of herrings, which is commonly carried on by shares. The division of the fish is, first, one-fourth for the boat; and then the men and nets divide the rest, the latter reckoned as three men. They reckon ten maze of herrings an indifferent night's work; when there is a good take, forty maze have been taken, twenty a good night; the price per maze from 1s. to 7s., average 5s. Their take in 1775, the greatest they have known, when they had more than they could dispose of, and the whole town and country stunk of them, they retailed them thirty-two for a penny; 1773 and 1774 good years. They barrelled many, but in general there is an import of Swedish. Besides the common articles I have registered, the following are: pigeons, 1s. a couple; a hare, 1s.; partridges, 9d.; turbots, fine ones, 4s. to 10s.; soles a pair, large, 1s. 6d to 1s.; lobsters, 3d. each; oysters, 6s. per hundred; rabbits, 1s. to 1s. 4d. a couple; cod, 1s. each, large; salmon, 1¼d. to 2d.

A very extraordinary circumstance I was told—that within five or six years there has been much hay carried from Waterford to Norway, in the Norway ships that bring deals. As hay is dear here, it proves a most backward state of husbandry in that northerly region, since the neighbourhood of sea-ports to which this hay can alone go is generally the best improved in all countries.

...

Dancing is very general among the poor people [in the vicinity of Lough Derg on the Shannon], almost universal in every cabin. Dancing-masters of their own rank travel through the country from cabin to cabin, with a piper or blind fiddler, and the pay is sixpence a quarter. It is an absolute system of education. Weddings are always celebrated with much dancing, and a Sunday rarely passes without a dance. There are very few among them who will not, after a hard day's work, gladly walk seven miles to have a dance. John is not so lively, but then a hard day's work with him is certainly a different affair from what it is with Paddy. Other branches of education are likewise much attended to, every child of the poorest family learning to read, write, and cast accounts.

[One has to wonder at this point at the integrity of his informants!] There is a very ancient custom here, for a number of country neighbours among the poor people to fix upon some young woman that ought, as they think, to be married. They also agree upon a young fellow as a proper husband for her. This determined, they send to the fair one's cabin to inform her that on the Sunday following "she is to be horsed," that is, carried on men's backs. She must then provide whisky and cider for a treat, as all will pay her a visit after mass for a hurling match. As soon as she is horsed, the hurling begins, in which the young fellow appointed for her husband has the eyes of all the company fixed on him. If he comes off conqueror, he is certainly married to the girl; but if another is victorious, he as certainly loses her, for she is the prize of the victor. These trials are not always finished in one Sunday; they take sometimes two or three, and the common expression when they are over is, that "such a girl was goaled." Sometimes one barony hurls against another, but a marriageable girl is always the prize. Hurling is a sort of cricket, but instead of throwing the ball in order to knock down a wicket, the aim is to pass it through a bent stick, the end stuck in the ground. In these matches they perform such feats of activity as ought to evidence the food they live on to be far from deficient in nourishment.

...

To judge of Ireland by the conversation one sometimes hears in England, it would be supposed that one-half of it was covered with bogs, and the other with mountains filled with Irish ready to fly at the sight of a civilised being. There are people who will smile when they hear that, in proportion to the size of the two countries, Ireland is more cultivated than England, having much less waste land of all sorts. Of uncultivated mountains there are no such tracts as are found in our four northern counties, and the North Riding of Yorkshire, with the eastern line of Lancaster, nearly down to the Peak of Derby, which form an extent of above a hundred miles of waste. The most considerable of this sort in Ireland are in Kerry, Galway, and Mayo, and some in Sligo and Donegal. But all these together will not make the quantity we have in the four northern counties; the valleys in the Irish mountains are also more inhabited, I think, than those of England, except where there are mines, and consequently some sort of cultivation creeping up the sides. Natural fertility, acre for acre over the two kingdoms, is certainly in favour of Ireland; of this I believe there can scarcely be a doubt entertained, when it is considered that some of the more beautiful, and even best cultivated counties in England, owe almost everything to the capital, art, and industry of the inhabitants.

...

Before I conclude this article of the common labouring poor in Ireland, I must observe, that their happiness depends not merely upon the payment of their labour, their clothes, or their food; the subordination of the lower classes, degenerating into oppression, is not to be overlooked. The poor in all countries, and under all governments, are both paid and fed, yet there is an infinite difference between them in different ones. This inquiry will by no means turn out so favourable as the preceding articles. It must be very apparent to every traveller through that country, that the labouring poor are treated with harshness, and are in all respects so little considered that their want of importance seems a perfect contrast to their situation in England, of which country, comparatively speaking, they reign the sovereigns. The age has improved so much in humanity, that even the poor Irish have experienced its influence, and are every day treated better and better; but still the remnant of the old manners, the abominable distinction of religion, united with the oppressive conduct of the little country gentlemen, or rather vermin of the kingdom, who never were out of it, altogether bear still very heavy on the poor people, and subject them to situations more mortifying than we ever behold in England. The landlord of an Irish estate, inhabited by Roman Catholics, is a sort of despot who yields obedience, in whatever concerns the poor, to no law but that of his will. To discover what the liberty of the people is, we must live among them, and not look for it in the statutes of the realm: the language of written law may be that of liberty, but the situation of the poor may speak no language but that of slavery. There is too much of this contradiction in Ireland; a long series of oppressions, aided by many very ill-judged laws, have brought landlords into a habit of exerting a very lofty superiority, and their vassals into that of an almost unlimited submission: speaking a language that is despised, professing a religion that is abhorred and being disarmed, the poor find themselves in many cases slaves even in the bosom of written liberty. Landlords that have resided much abroad are usually humane in their ideas, but the habit of tyranny naturally contracts the mind, so that even in this polished age there are instances of a severe carriage towards the poor, which is quite unknown in England.

    A landlord in Ireland can scarcely invent an order which a servant, labourer, or cottar dares to refuse to execute. Nothing satisfies him but an unlimited submission. Disrespect, or anything tending towards sauciness, he may punish with his cane or his horsewhip with the most perfect security; a poor man would have his bones broke if he offered to lift his hands in his own defence. Knocking-down is spoken of in the country in a manner that makes an Englishman stare. Landlords of consequence have assured me that many of their cottars would think themselves honoured by having their wives and daughters sent for to the bed of their master; a mark of slavery that proves the oppression under which such people must live. Nay, I have heard anecdotes of the lives of people being made free with without any apprehension of the justice of a jury. But let it not be imagined that this is common; formerly it happened every day, but law gains ground. It must strike the most careless traveller to see whole strings of cars whipped into a ditch by a gentleman's footman to make way for his carriage; if they are overturned or broken in pieces, no matter, it is taken in patience; were they to complain they would perhaps be horsewhipped. The execution of the laws lies very much in the hands of justices of the peace, many of whom are drawn from the most illiberal class in the kingdom. If a poor man lodges a complaint against a gentleman, or any animal that chooses to call itself a gentleman, and the justice issues out a summons for his appearance, it is a fixed affront, and he will infallibly be called out [challenged to a duel]. Where manners are in conspiracy against law, to whom are the oppressed people to have recourse? It is a fact, that a poor man having a contest with a gentleman, must—but I am talking nonsense, they know their situation too well to think of it; they can have no defence, but by means of protection from one gentleman against another, who probably protects his vassal as he would the sheep he intends to eat.

The colours of this picture are not charged. To assert that all these cases are common would be an exaggeration, but to say that an unfeeling landlord will do all this with impunity, is to keep strictly to truth: and what is liberty but a farce and a jest, if its blessings are received as the favour of kindness and humanity, instead of being the inheritance of right?

Consequences have flowed from these oppressions which ought long ago to have put a stop to them. In England we have heard much of White-boys, Steel-boys, Oak-boys, Peep-of-day-boys, etc. But these various insurgents are not to be confounded, for they are very different. The proper distinction in the discontents of the people is into Protestant and Catholic. All but the White-boys were among the manufacturing Protestants in the north: the White-boys Catholic labourers in the south. From the best intelligence I could gain, the riots of the manufacturers had no other foundation but such variations in the manufacture as all fabrics experience, and which they had themselves known and submitted to before. The case, however, was different with the White-boys, who being labouring Catholics met with all those oppressions I have described, and would probably have continued in full submission had not very severe treatment in respect of tithes, united with a great speculative rise of rent about the same time, blown up the flame of resistance; the atrocious acts they were guilty of made them the object of general indignation; acts were passed for their punishment, which seemed calculated for the meridian of Barbary. This arose to such a height that by one they were to be hanged under circumstances without the common formalities of a trial, which, though repealed the following session, marks the spirit of punishment; while others remain yet the law of the land, that would if executed tend more to raise than quell an insurrection. From all which it is manifest that the gentlemen of Ireland never thought of a radical cure from overlooking the real cause of the disease, which in fact lay in themselves, and not in the wretches they doomed to the gallows. Let them change their own conduct entirely, and the poor will not long riot. Treat them like men who ought to be as free as yourselves. Put an end to that system of religious persecution which for seventy years has divided the kingdom against itself; in these two circumstances lies the cure of insurrection; perform them completely, and you will have an affectionate poor, instead of oppressed and discontented vassals.

A better treatment of the poor in Ireland is a very material point of the welfare of the whole British Empire. Events may happen which may convince us fatally of this truth; if not, oppression must have broken all the spirit and resentment of men. By what policy the Government of England can for so many years have permitted such an absurd system to be matured in Ireland is beyond the power of plain sense to discover.

...

For a country, so very far behind us as Ireland, to have got suddenly so much the start of us in the article of roads, is a spectacle that cannot fail to strike the English traveller exceedingly. But from this commendation the turnpikes in general must be excluded; they are as bad as the bye-roads are admirable. It is a common complaint that the tolls of the turnpikes are so many jobs, and the roads left in a state that disgrace the kingdom.

The following is the system on which the cross-roads are made. Any person wishing to make or mend a road has it measured by two persons, who swear to the measurement before a justice of the peace. It is described as leading from one market-town to another (it matters not in what direction), that it will be a public good, and that it will require such a sum per perch of twenty-one feet, to make or repair the same. A certificate to this purpose (of which printed forms are sold), with the blanks filled up, is signed by the measurers, and also by two persons called overseers, one of whom is usually the person applying for the road, the other the labourer he intends to employ as an overseer of the work, which overseer swears also before the justice the truth of the valuation. The certificate thus prepared is given by any person to some one of the grand jury, at either of the assizes, but usually in the spring. When all the common business of trials is over, the jury meets on that of roads; the chairman reads the certificates, and they are all put to the vote, whether to be granted or not. If rejected, they are torn in pieces and no further notice taken; if granted, they are put on the file.

This vote of approbation, without any further form, enables the person who applied for the presentment immediately to construct or repair the road in question, which he must do at his own expense; he must finish it by the following assizes, when he is to send a certificate of his having expended the money pursuant to the application; this certificate is signed by the foreman, who also signs an order on the treasurer of the county to pay him, which is done immediately. In like manner are bridges, houses of correction, gaols, etc. etc., built and repaired. If a bridge over a river which parts two counties, half is done by one and the other half by the other county.

The expense of these works is raised by a tax on the lands, paid by the tenant; in some counties it is acreable, but in others it is on the plough land, and as no two plough lands are of the same size, is a very unequal tax. In the county of Meath it is acreable, and amounts to one shilling per acre, being the highest in Ireland; but in general it is from threepence to sixpence per acre, and amounts of late years through the whole kingdom to one hundred and forty thousand pounds a year.

The juries will very rarely grant a presentment for a road which amounts to above fifty pounds, or for more than six or seven shillings a perch, so that if a person wants more to be made than such a sum will do, he divides it into two or three different measurements or presentments. By the Act of Parliament, all presentment-roads must be twenty-one feet wide at least from fence to fence, and fourteen feet of it formed with stone or gravel.

As the power of the grand jury extends in this manner to the cutting new roads where none ever were before, as well as to the repairing and widening old ones, exclusive, however, of parks, gardens, etc., it was necessary to put a restriction against the wanton expense of it. Any presentment may be traversed that is opposed, by denying the allegations of the certificate; this is sure of delaying it until another assizes, and in the meantime persons are appointed to view the line of road demanded, and report on the necessity or hardship of the case. The payment of the money may also be traversed after the certificate of its being laid out; for if any person views and finds it a manifest imposition and job, he has that power to delay payment until the cause is cleared up and proved. But this traverse is not common. Any persons are eligible for asking presentments; but it is usually done only by resident gentlemen, agents, clergy, or respectable tenantry. It follows necessarily, that every person is desirous of making the roads leading to his own house, and that private interest alone is considered in it, which I have heard objected to the measure; but this I must own appears to me the great merit of it. Whenever individuals act for the public alone, the public is very badly served; but when the pursuit of their own interest is the way to benefit the public, then is the public good sure to be promoted; such is the case of presentment of roads: for a few years the good roads were all found leading from houses like rays from a centre, with a surrounding space, without any communication; but every year brought the remedy, until in a short time, those rays pointing from so many centres met, and then the communication was complete. The original Act passed but seventeen years ago, and the effect of it in all parts of the kingdom is so great, that I found it perfectly practicable to travel upon wheels by a map; I will go here; I will go there; I could trace a route upon paper as wild as fancy could dictate, and everywhere I found beautiful roads without break or hindrance, to enable me to realise my design. What a figure would a person make in England, who should attempt to move in that manner, where the roads, as Dr. Burn has well observed, are almost in as bad a state as in the time of Philip and Mary. In a few years there will not be a piece of bad road except turnpikes in all Ireland. The money raised for this first and most important of all national purposes, is expended among the people who pay it, employs themselves and their teams, encourages their agriculture, and facilitates so greatly the improvement of waste lands, that it ought always to be considered as the first step to any undertaking of that sort.

At first, roads, in common with bridges, were paid out of the general treasure of the county, but by a subsequent act the road tax is now on baronies; each barony pays for its own roads. By another act juries were enabled to grant presentments of narrow mountain roads, at two shillings and sixpence a perch. By another, they were empowered to grant presentments of footpaths, by the side of roads, at one shilling a perch. By a very late act, they are also enabled to contract at three-halfpence per perch per annum from the first making of a road, for keeping it in repair, which before could not be done without a fresh presentment.

...

The only divisions which a traveller, who passed through the kingdom without making any residence could make, would be into people of considerable fortune and mob. The intermediate division of the scale, so numerous and respectable in England, would hardly attract the least notice in Ireland. A residence in the kingdom convinces one, however, that there is another class in general of small fortune—country gentlemen and renters of land. The manners, habits, and customs of people of considerable fortune are much the same everywhere, at least there is very little difference between England and Ireland, it is among the common people one must look for those traits by which we discriminate a national character. The circumstances which struck me most in the common Irish were, vivacity and a great and eloquent volubility of speech; one would think they could take snuff and talk without tiring till doomsday. They are infinitely more cheerful and lively than anything we commonly see in England, having nothing of that incivility of sullen silence with which so many Englishmen seem to wrap themselves up, as if retiring within their own importance. Lazy to an excess at work, but so spiritedly active at play, that at hurling, which is the cricket of savages, they shew the greatest feats of agility. Their love of society is as remarkable as their curiosity is insatiable; and their hospitality to all comers, be their own poverty ever so pinching, has too much merit to be forgotten. Pleased to enjoyment with a joke, or witty repartee, they will repeat it with such expression, that the laugh will be universal. Warm friends and revengeful enemies; they are inviolable in their secrecy, and inevitable in their resentment; with such a notion of honour, that neither threat nor reward would induce them to betray the secret or person of a man, though an oppressor, whose property they would plunder without ceremony. Hard drinkers and quarrelsome; great liars, but civil, submissive, and obedient. Dancing is so universal among them, that there are everywhere itinerant dancing-masters, to whom the cottars pay sixpence a quarter for teaching their families. Besides the Irish jig, which they can dance with a most luxuriant expression, minuets and country-dances are taught; and I even heard some talk of cotillions coming in.

Some degree of education is also general, hedge schools, as they are called, (they might as well be termed ditch ones, for I have seen many a ditch full of scholars,) are everywhere to be met with where reading and writing are taught; schools are also common for men; I have seen a dozen great fellows at school, and was told they were educating with an intention of being priests.

Many strokes in their character are evidently to be ascribed to the extreme oppression under which they live. If they are as great thieves and liars as they are reported, it is certainly owing to this cause.

...

In the country their [the wealthier class] life has some circumstances which are not commonly seen in England. Large tracts of land are kept in hand by everybody to supply the deficiencies of markets; this gives such a plenty, that, united with the lowness of taxes and prices, one would suppose it difficult for them to spend their incomes, if Dublin in the winter did not lend assistance. Let it be considered that the prices of meat are much lower than in England; poultry only a fourth of the price; wild fowl and fish in vastly greater plenty; rum and brandy not half the price; coffee, tea, and wines far cheaper; labour not above a third; servants' wages upon an average thirty per cent. cheaper. That taxes are inconsiderable, for there is no land-tax, no poor-rates, no window tax, no candle or soap tax, only half a wheel-tax, no servants' tax, and a variety of other articles heavily burdened in England, but not in Ireland. Considering all this, one would think they could not spend their incomes; they do contrive it, however. In this business they are assisted by two customs that have an admirable tendency to it, great numbers of horses and servants." [3]

Irish 18th century prices, from household accounts

The deeds in the Registry of Deeds are always very specific about the exact monies that changed hands but that data is not very helpful unless you can match it to a picture of what things cost in 18th century Ireland. For this purpose then what follows here are some prices that are gleaned from household accounts preserved among various manuscript collections in Ireland and the UK.

1687
Yearly accounts of the lands of Ballycor (or Ballycar) Co Meath owned by the Fitzgeralds and passed to James Nugent of

Clonlost Co Westmeath
   for tobacco 0:3:1
   for aquavitae [whiskey] 0:4:0
   for pipes 0:0:6
   for nails 0:1:6
   for boards 0:10:1
   for making two coffins 0:5:0
   to the cow boy 0:2:4
   to the servant boy 0:7:8
   to Father Nicholas [Moran, PP of Killinan] 1:10:0

1693
Accounts by Christopher Darcy relating to the land of Cussenstown Co Westmeath
one barrel of wheat and shoeing the horse that carried the wheat 0:12:8
   for one pick-axe 0:2:8

1712
An account of works done for Esq Nugent at the Red Lyon in Trim.
   paid Conor Graney for going to Westmeath 0:1:6
   paid for fish 0:6:6
   paid John Flynn for straw 0:5:8
   Ale to your servant Nicholas Coffy going to Dublin 0:5:8
   to Robert Might for drawing boards from Dublin 0:5:8
   paid for 50 still dales [deals i.e. wood] and [a] half at 1:7 per board 0:8:8
   at the same time for 4 whole dales 0:5:4
   more [than a] 100 of nails 0:0:10
   more 100 of nails [doubtless a different type] 0:0:5
   paid for barrel of wheat 1:8:0
   5 pound of iron for hooks [and] hinges 0:1:0
   paid for glue 0:0:1
   paid Christy Monaghan for working at stone [and?] of Iron 0:2:0
   Ned Makaney 3 days drawing of straw [no doubt the straw for the roof] 0:2:0

half a hundred of nails 0:0:2 half
paid Luke Dillon for thatching 7 days 0:7:0
paid Constant [sic] Smith the mason 0:10:2
paid Mr Proudforth for straw 6 loads 0:8:0
for drawing them home 0:2:6
19 days work fro Bryan Mulkearan 0:12:8
12 days work to Michael Smith 0:8:0
paid for iron 0:3:6

1753

These accounts from 1753 to 1769 – excluding the legal account of 1764 – were paid to the executors of the estate of the late John Nugent – who might be the then recently deceased Earl of Westmeath – by, it seems, one Walter Nugent, or possibly the other way around as it isn't very clear from the surviving documentation. '@' obviously indicates the price of each individual item, hence this entry: "20 1/4 pounds English Jamaican refined sugar @ 15 pence @ 1:5:5 half" means that the sugar is priced at 15 pence a pound and they purchased 20 and a quarter pounds of it which came to £1, 5 shillings and 5 and a half pence.

58 1/2 pounds Hops at £6 @ 3:2:8
20 pounds English powder sugar 1:1:8
2 pound 5 ounces fine green tea and canister 1:7:9
6 pounds Turkey coffee 0:15:0
1 pound Durham mustard 0:3:0
4 pounds nutmeg 0:2:6
2 ounces mace 0:2:0
1/2 ounce cloves 0:0:9
2 ounces cinnamon 0:2:4
7 pounds barly 0:1:9
7 pounds rice 0:2:0
1/4 pound pepper 0:1:10 half
1/2 pound anchovies and pot 0:2:8
1 pound alispice 0:1:8
21 pounds new curran[t]s 0:9:0
14 pounds new raisins 0:5:0
16 pounds 14 ounces best powder loaf sugar at 2 @ 0:10:10

1 pound best plain green tea 0:10:0
20 1/4 pounds English Jamaican refined sugar @ 15 pence @ 1:5:5 half
28 pounds powder loaf sugar @ 12 pence per pound 1:8:0
28 pounds fine Jamaican Sugar 0:14:0
2 pounds best chocolate 0:8:0
1/4 pound white pepper 0:1:4
1 1/2 pound black pepper 0:2:3
a pan of sturgeon weight 4 pounds 0:4:8
1 basket of salt 0:1:0
1 dozen of best oranges 0:1:0
a basket and crock for sturgeon 0:1:6
1 pound capours and pot 0:2:2
1 pound samphire [an edible plant] and pot 0:1:4
1/2 t[?] bottle best oil 0:2:2
6 dozen oranges 0:4:6
1 dozen lemons 0:1:2
1/2 pound green tea and canister 0:6:4
1 bottle orange flower water 0:1:4
2 1/16 gallons strong Jamaican Rum and Cask paid 1:0:1
1 1/16 gallons brandy and cask 0:6:6
42 pounds shott 0:9:0
14 pounds blasting powder 0:16:4
7 1/2 pounds best powder @ 18 per 0:11:3
1 cask for ditto 0:1:1 half
1/2 pound a hundred flint 0:1:4
1 pound best powder blue 0:1:4
1 bottle olives 0:2:0
4 flasks best oil 0:6:0
2 pound and 5 ounces French Capours and pot 0:4:10
5 1/8 gallons vinegar and cask 0:9:4 half
10 5/8 gallons best shrub [a fruit juice drink] and cask 3:11:3
7 pounds best starch 0:2:0
4 pounds Flanders starch 0:2:0
1 pound salt peter 0:1:4
1 pound Tsing [?] Glass 0:3:6
1/2 pound Allspice 0:0:9
2 pound 5 ounces best Hyson Tea 2:12:0

3 pound 1 ounce fine green tea 1:16:9
2 pounds 6 ounces plain green tea 1:3:9
1 pound 2 ounces best Bohea Tea 0:6:9
1 pound white ginger 0:1:2
4 canisters 0:4:2
1 basket 0:0:4
1 hamper 0:1:6
1-0-14 pounds best English hops 6:3:9
1 pound truffles and morels 0:12:0
2 baskets salt 0:2:0

1763
35 yards of gum [?] worsted shag @ 2/8 4:13:4
20 yards ditto [meaning 'gum'?] living serge @ 1/3 1:5:0
12 yards stripe flannel @ 1/10 1:2:0
12 yards white serge @1/3 0:15:0
4 dozen livery buttons 0:4:0
3 1/2 yards R[?]efine blue cloth @ 10/6 1:16:9
5 yards blue serge @ 1/5 0:7:1
  1 1/2 dozen Coat and [two letters here, jointly look like a capital N]Vest buttons 0:1:0
  two shammy skins 0:2:6

1764
3 1/4 yards bearskin rug @ 8/ 1:6:0
1 yard fine serge 0:1:10
1/4 yard [illegible] 0:4:6
Trimmings [word illegible] 0:8:4
  2 1/2 yards super fine drab [sic, or maybe 'arab'] English cloth @ 21/ 2:12:6
  1 yard super fine scarlet cloth 1:4:0
5 yards superfine drab serge @ 2/ 0:10:0
2 yards guy [sic] linen @ 4/4 0:8:8
a piece of black silk webb 1:16:6
1/2 yard of black serge @ 1/3 0:1:10
3 yards broad white fustian @ 1/7 0:4:9
1/4 yards fine black serge @ 2/5 ?
2 1/2 yards white linen @ 2/4 0:5:10

1 gold hat lace loop and button 0:11:1
7 yards silk and cotton Holland @ 5/6 1:11:6
4 yards gum [?] corduroy @ 13/6 2:14:0
cash paid for flax seed 3:2:0
cash paid for a plumb cake 1:7:7
3 yards Cambrick @ 6/6 0:19:6
3/8 yards Ticken @ 3/8 0:5:0
1/4 yards strong diaper @ 4/7 0:5:0
1/2 hundred [weight, presumably] nails 0:1:1
20 Ozs thread 0:3:0
1 pair nut crackers 0:2:6
2 groce corks 0:4:0
1 pewtor dish 0:5:2
brass for a coach bridle 0:0:8
1 plate basket and hair comb 0:3:9 and a half
2 yards cambrick and 2 dozen shirt buttons 0:17:0
2 day books and 6 wax candles 0:17:2
2 large thongs for whips 0:2:8
remitted to England 19:10:7

1764

Helpfully this account, which was rendered by Hugh Reilly, a Dublin solicitor, to his client Lord Clare in 1764 details exactly what it cost to register a deed in the Registry of Deeds in the 18th century.

April 9 – Redrawing a deed of release from John Nugent esq. to you, of the lands of Clontiduffy [Co. Cavan] – 2:2:0.

Fee to Councillor [i.e. a legal councellor, a solicitor or barrister] O'Brien to settle it – 2:2:0.

Engrossing two parts of it, four skins each – 2:0:0.

Paid for parchment – 0:5:0.

Lease for a year engrossing and parchment – 0:5:0.

Memorial engrossing parchment and registering – 0:10:0.

Drawing bond and warrant – 0:5:0.

Paid search of the Registry for the dates of the deeds to William and George Garnett etc – 0:3:0.

Paid for search in the Exchequer and King's Bench to know what court judgements was [sic] entered – 0:10:0.

[Total:] 8:10:0.

To [should be 'for'?] entering judgement at your suit in the King's Bench against Captain Nugent – 1:18:8.

To drawing draft of an Article [?] from you to Denis O'Brien of lands in the County Clare and two copies – 0:10:0.

[Total:] 10:18:8.

Received the contents in full this 22nd of April 1764 four [sic] Hugh Reilly.

1765

1 quire fine paper 0:4:0

2 dozen Tree Mason [deliberate mistake for 'Free Mason'? It certainly isn't an 'F' on the manuscript] glasses 0:13:4

1 stone whiting 0:0:6

shoes 0:7:4

4 pair ribbed stockings 1:4:0

drugs 0:1:7

china and basket 0:10:6

waters 0:4:11

wax candles and box 0:15:6

1 stone groats 0:2:2

hat and cane 0:18:9

blackwood for shoes 0:6:0

a brush etc 0:1:7 half

cash paid to blackwood for shoes 2:1:9

one barrel herrings 1:10:0

9 yards of fine gray linen @ 2/2 0:19:6

9 yards Wilton Druggett [a type of carpet] @ 7/6 3:7:6

2 9/16 yards black double Lutherine @ 8/6 1:1:9

cash paid for 6 cloak brush and Pomatum 0:1:7

3 yards silk damascus @ 5/6 0:16:6

thread needles and tape 0:3:2

silk for a gown 7:11:9

muslin 0:15:11

4 pairs cotton stockings 0:19:4

2 pairs silk stockings 1:2:9

tooth powder and brush 0:5:5

shoes 0:9:9

cash paid for leather 0:5:6
tape lather and Hungry water [described elsewhere as 'Tape Hungary Water etc'] 0:3:2 half
cash gave Milly 1/3£ silk and petty coat 1:3:5
15 yards coffee coloured livery cloth 8/ 6:0:0
24 yards coffee coloured livery serge @1/5 1:14:0
5 1/2 dozen hatcoat buttons 0:5:6
4 pair rib worsted stockings @ 6/ 1:4:0

1766
4 gallons Netts foot oil 0:13:4
beans and peas 0:8:11
shoes and seeds 1:4:2
muslin 0:9:1 and a half
livery lace 0:3:0
cash paid for hoop petty coat 0:9:9
2 1/4 yards blue and white flannel @ 2/6 0:5:6 and a half
2 1/4 yards padua serge @ 1/4 0:3:0
1/16th [sic] yard crimson dutch velvet @ 20/ 0:1:3
1 gross moulds 3 [d]oz[en?] thread 0:0:10 [sic]
1/4 yard scarlet english rug @ 13/ 0:16:3

1767
one bottle Turlington drops
ditto...........Cappelier   } 0:5:5
cash paid stage [coach] 0:1:1
3/4 yard silk damascus @ 5/6 0:4:1 and a half
1 yard yellow stripe silk damascus 0:4:0
Nine Ash trees have been blown down by a storm which Mr Dardis has sold for £3:4:10, a very good price and above the valuation. I received a proposal this day for the Ash Grove, 610 trees £220.

1768
20 pairs stockings 1:13:11

1769
repairing 2 hats 0:2:8: half

box and carriage 0:3:3
box and stage 0:3:11 half
1/2 realm of cut paper and 1 quire of gilt [paper] 0:10:0
2 quire paper and a hat 0:11:7 half
1 yard cambrick and 2 pencils 0:9:7
white lead oil etc 1:4:3
dress shoes and a velvet cap 0:18:4
James's Powders and stage 0:9:2.

1808
Household accounts from a house associated with the Clonlost family, near Trim.
15 side dessert knives 14:4:4
15 side dessert forks 11:10:6
wax taper 0:18:6
silver sugar tongs 0:19:5
1 p[ound? piece?] plat[ed?] chamber candles 3:19:7
1 dozen F H [a hallmark?] dessert spoons 8:5:6
a plat[ed?] ink stand 2:10:6
6 best plat[ed?] egg cups @ 5/11 each 1:15:9
1 dozen green han[dled?] knives and forks 3:8:3
a pair of steel snufflers 0:6:6
a plated tray for d[eserts?] 0:14:6
a silver soup ladle 6.2 [?, quality of the silver?] 3:13:8
an office seal 0:16:3

Discount for prompt payment [is listed here as] 4:12:9 half [on a bill of] 53:3:3 half.

1 shamey skew (3/3) and plate powder (2/2) [used to clean silver plate and sometimes containing mercury].[4]

Footnotes
1. Louis M Cullen, *Economic Development, 1750-1800*, which is chapter VII in, *A New History of Ireland* (Oxford, 1986) Vol IV, p.177-178.

2. There was also a special law passed on the 19th and 20th George III c.30 seeking to alleviate this problem.

3. Arthur Young, *A Tour in Ireland* (London, 1897), p.23, 25-26, 28, 29, 33-37, 54, 57-58, 63, 72-73, 80-82, 85-86, 116-117, 118-119, 124-125, 130-132, 136-

139, 146-147, 156, 164-169, 172-176, 180-182, 183, available at http://www.gutenberg.org/files/22387/22387-h/22387-h.htm .)

4. These various accounts, or photocopies of them, are from PRONI D/2620/2, Clonlost Papers, with the exception of the legal accounts listed under 1764 which are from the Essex County Record Office D/DU/502/5.
The reference to trees at the end of the 1767 entries is from the Nugent section of the Stowe Papers, Huntington Library, James Fagan at Lickblea writing to Viscount Clare with respect to the estate at Carlanstown Co. Westmeath 27th Nov 1767.

CHAPTER 8
Case Study of a Family History using the ROD and other sources

He stumbled home from Clifden fair
With drunken song, and cheeks aglow.
Yet there was something in his air
That told of kingship long ago.
I sighed -- and inly cried
With grief that one so high should fall so low.

He snatched a flower and sniffed its scent,
And waved it toward the sunset sky.
Some old sweet rapture through him went
And kindled in his bloodshot eye.
I turned -- and inly burned
With joy that one so low should rise so high.
-- *High and Low,* by James H Cousins

In this chapter I hope to give a real world example of a family history so that readers can judge for themselves how feasible it is to trace an Irish family through the 16th to the 19th centuries using the ROD among the other usual sources. The 'other sources' are obviously not strictly necessary to describe for a book on the ROD but I felt that most readers anxious to acquaint themselves with the operations of the ROD in the 18th century would probably welcome a real world example of the use of these 'other sources' – particularly folklore, newspapers and court cases – as well. Also I have sought to quote from sources that will hopefully add some colour to illustrate more authentically the political, social and religious history of those times in Ireland through the at times tumultuous lives of this family.

To begin with we have this monument that G V Du Noyer tripped across at St Mary's Church in Fore Co. Westmeath which he described as a

"Monumental slab of the family of Nugent, Barons of Delvin, from the east wall of the ruined church of St Mary's, at Fore, in the county of

Westmeath. The inscription, which is intended to be a clear and succinct account of the pedigree of some families of this branch of the Nugents, is so completely the reverse, that I transcribe it as a genealogical curiosity:–" [1]

THES . MONUMENT . WAS . FIRST .
BEGUN . FOR . OLIVER . NUGENT .
OF . BELENA . IN . THE . COUNTY
OF . MEATH . ESQ . BROTHER . TO
THE . HONORABLE . RICHARD .
LORD . BARON . OF . DELVIN . BY .
CHRISTOPHER . NUGENT . HIS
SON . AND . HEIR . WHICH . OLIVER
DIED . THE 17 OF . MARCH 1589 . AND
WAS . HERE . ERECTED . AT . THE . COST
AND . CARE . OF . ROBERT . NUGENT . OF
CLONEGIRACH . AND . XPHER . N$^{T.}$
GRANDCHILDREN . TO . THE . S$^{D.}$
XPHER . OF . NICHOLAS . & ROBERT
SON . OF . OLIVER . N$^{T.}$. OF . WILLIAM
XPHER . EDMOND . & RICHARD
SONS . OF JAMES . N$^{T.}$. BOTH . NEPH
EUS . TO . THE . S$^{D.}$. AND . OF . EDMOND
N$^{T.}$. GRANDCHILD . TO . THE . S$^{D.}$ XPHER
& THOMAS . HIS . SON . FOR . THE
INTERRING . OF . THEM . & THER
POSTERITY . ANNO . DOM. 1689
GOOD . XPIANS . PRAY . FOR
THESE . HERE . INTERRD.

So this is our mission, should we choose to accept it!, to unravel out from the milieu of the surviving Irish records the authentic history of the family marked out on this monument. In order to keep the reader in suspense (!) we will begin by tracing out the cadet branches of this family and then the main line and finally we will look at the surviving ROD entries to see to what extent they illuminate this history.

Farrenconnell Family

We will start with the Farrenconnell family which is the only well known family in the usual sources, like Burke and Lodge etc. On the monument where it says "Of Nicholas and Robert, son of Oliver Nugent" it is referring to Nicholas, who founded the Enagh family, and his younger brother Robert, who founded that of Farrenconnell, and it goes on to say that their father Oliver and James [of Dungimmon] were nephews of Christopher, the son of Oliver Nugent the founder of the Ballina family. Oliver and James were in fact the sons of William who was a younger half brother of Christopher, William was a son of Oliver and his second wife Anne Browne. Because the basic pedigree of this family is so well documented I will just confine myself to describing the various soldiers in this overwhelmingly military family, beginning with:

Christopher (1747-1821), the son of Robert who died in 1770, purchased an ensigny in the 46th regiment, paid £1,500 to become a captain and retired in 1774 but before that:

> "Christopher fought two duels for his lady love, in one of which he was wounded in the breast. He eventually gained the hand of his fair friend, but left her on the night after his marriage and never saw her for 20 years afterwards."

He lived in "The Big House" in Gneeve, which was also occupied at some time by Thomas Reilly esq but in the late 19th century was in ruins. He died in September 1821 and was probably buried in the family plot at Fore.

His brother Richard (1745-1794) started as a lieutenant in the 31st foot in the British Army but

> "continued for nearly 20 years in the Russian service which he had joined without the knowledge of his family. He was in the retreat from Constantinople in which the Russians endured fearful hardships, so great that even in his description of it to his family the tears would roll down his cheeks."

He fought with the Russian and Austrian armies against the Turks during the years 1754-1772.[2]

Major General St George Mervyn Nugent, (the son of Oliver, who was the son of Christopher Edward John Nugent, an officer in the 33rd light dragoons, who was the son of Oliver (1741-1813), a first lieutenant in the Manchester volunteers in 1759 and later high sheriff for Cavan, who was the son of Robert (1703-1770) also high sheriff for Cavan and for whom Farrenconnell became known as Bobsgrove, the son of Oliver (1676-1749) a land surveyor, the son of Robert (1640-1692) whose brother was Nicholas who founded the Enagh family etc) entered the army c.1842, was injured in the Battle of Sobraon against the Sikhs in 1845, was invalided home and returned to India at the close of 1848. In 1861 he was appointed Assistant Quarter Master General of the Army in North America and in 1867 had the same job in Dublin. In 1875 he was made Adjutant and Quarter Master General and Chief of Staff in Malta and after various other posts he retired with the rank of Major General in 1881. He had four sons and a daughter: Christopher (1857-58), St George (1859-65), Oliver (1860-1929), the general who was born in the camp at Aldershot 9th Nov 1860, Cyril (1862-1889) who was born in Halifax Nova Scotia, and his daughter was Henrietta who married George Irvine.[3]

As an interesting piece of real, if personal, history his son Oliver wrote to his uncle the historian in May 1884 to tell him that his father was dying and it seems that, somewhat characteristically, the historian wrote back asking about his spiritual state. The reply he got, on the 5th of May 1884, was:

"I cannot tell you dear brother of my spiritual state, why? Dear brother, I have the very simplest faith. "Hath liest on Him the iniquity of us all." I am of the 'all'. "Cleanseth from all sin," that includes mine. Some on broken pieces of [undeciphered word] but so it was, they all escaped safe to shore and I will be in that all, this is no doubt poor theology but it is my stay." [4]

Also in the spirit of trying to get underneath the skin of this family, rather than just relaying a dry list of names and dates, I will give here some extracts from his diary:

"Tues 22nd May 1855

Walked about St Georges's Hill and Demesne of Lord Ellesmere's with R. and A. [probably his brother Richard, the historian, and his wife], and was indeed enchanted with it, being kept evidently as a shooting lodge and covered with heath, fern and Scotch Pine, so like Dear Dear Farren Connell; although greatly pleased to wander through its pretty hills and dells, and to enjoy its delightful stillness and solitude, yet I could not help feeling at times infinitely sad reminding me as it did so forcibly of days gone by, never alas to return, when in silence and solitude I wandered through the woods of my own happy home, unclouded by care, a stranger to anxiety, and all else save the affectionate love of my beloved family. Now strangers possess that which was <u>my</u> home, and that sweet word is for[ever] erased from my vocabulary, such is my return to my own land. I find no resting place for the sole of my foot.

...

Wed 30th May 1855

...talking over happy days gone by forever, met Robert O'Reilly, and had Joe Lynch today who each gave me a most sad account of dear F[arren] C[onnell].

Thurs 31st

Not at all well...called on Mr Joy Q.C. to leave a card and note only, on Count Nugent 40 Belvedere Place who had gone to Clontarf, on Lord Westmeath 39 Upper Mount St who was at dinner.

Tues 11th September 1855

Drove to my brother's house Gloucester Terrace, and after dressing went to call on the

Littons in the hope of finding my dear companion able to go out walking with me but unhappily she had engaged herself to go out with some friends to see the London docks, and I only saw her for a very few moments indeed to my infinite disappointment, feeling very lonely as a consequence and sorry that I had anticipated time in coming to London.

Wed 12th
Breakfasted with the Littons and accompanied them to the Crystal Palace, where I spent a most happy day indeed with my own darling girl as my companion, and unrestrained converse with her my occupation and delight, the more as at times I flattered myself my words did not fall on unwilling ears. Remained there the entire day which nevertheless seemed then all too short for sight and speech to exhaust themselves, dined with them on my return and so close a most delightful day.

Thursday 13th
Breakfasted and spent the forenoon with the Littons. Then went to the club to write letters and to see the list of killed and wounded officers in the storming of Sebastopol, 140 in number but only 23 killed, one regiment, the 23rd, having no less than 14 killed and wounded. Afterwards went to see an Exchange Agent to try and get out of my infernal Regt., the 96th, into some decent respectable Regt., likely to go into active service, the more as I this day heard the 96th had left Dublin and gone to the Curragh to play at soldiering, the only thing they are fit for or even likely to do. In the afternoon walked with my beloved girl in Hyde Park and as usual when with her enjoyed it extremely although at times I could not help feeling sad that a long time must elapse ere I could hope again to see her

> or enjoy familiar converse with her. After an early dinner accompanied them to Drury Lane Theatre...but my eyes and thoughts were far otherwise employed in watching over and thinking over my precious companion from whom I was, at their close, called upon to part and for a very uncertain period for who can tell or dive into the future of this world. Left her at the theatre door sad and wretched and drove home to my solitary abode gloomy and dejected." [5]

You will be reassured to hear that he afterwards married Emily Litton.

To his brother Richard we particularly owe a great debt of gratitude because he was the family historian and without his diligence is preserving and cataloguing old letters we would never have had access to this colourful history. He collected information on all the various branches of the Nugents and received a few interesting letters from Nugent's at home and abroad, including this one from a Count [Christopher James] Nugent [of Killasonna, who served in Austria as aide de camp to Field Marshal Count Nugent of the Bracklyn family] then of 40 Belvedere place Mountjoy Square, of c.1877, which discussed the politics of Bismarck in Germany and concluded:

> "Now my dear Nugent I have endeavoured to reply to your letter, to best ability – I derive most of my knowledge from the "Augsburg Gazette" – It is marvellous the deep knowledge it displays on English affairs. The circulation, exceeds any European paper – A traveller on the borders of Russian and Austrian Poland – Ready entered a coffee house and asked for two things and was immediately served – The Augsburg Gazette and a bottle of Guinness stout, and both were served – Now adieu with kindest remembrances to my two young friends.
>
> C Nugent" [6]

For the life history of this historian we have here some extracts from a printed memorial card that was distributed after his death:

"From very young he gave his life to the Lord, and never flinched or swerved from his allegiance, glorifying it always.

...

His choicest friends were Rev William Pennefather, and his sister, the Honourable Mrs S Maxwell. A lake separated the two homes, which were closely linked by choicest ties. Even as early as 1842 when only 20 years of age he went about the country speaking at meetings for the Church Missionary Society and the Jews Society.

...

And in the campaign of 1868 he never ceased urging upon Disraeli to make it [the Protestant Cause] the banner. Where it was so made in Lancashire the Conservatives had great victories, and he had the acknowledgement of Mr Disraeli to this effect, thanking him for his share.

He was trained for the law but delicate health broke up the prospect of any profession, so that, although cut off from pecuniary advance, his life was free to serve in voluntary effort.

...

Everything that had to do with Ireland had of course his warmest interest and when the awful Famine of 1846 and 1847 broke out, the National Club, under his working, collected a large sum for the relief of the starving people. He was deputed to go over with it and arrived at the house of the Bishop of Meath, Edward Stopford. It was an eventful visit, for there he met her who became his wife, a daughter of the Bishop, a helpmeet [sic] for life; in every point in full and entire and intelligent sympathy with him in his views and aims and in the fervent desire to make their Master's interests the Law of their lives, regardless of worldly prospects. She was called home just twelve years ago.

The deepest interest of the last 20 years of his life was the Church of Ireland Sustenation Fund (London Committee). He keenly felt the dishonour to God of the Irish Church Act [which disestablished the Church of Ireland], and felt that England owed it to her scattered Protestant brethren to help in enabling them to maintain their religion. He therefore formed the London Fund, under the first presidency of the late beloved Earl of Harrowby. The Representative Body of the Church of Ireland have already passed a minute recording their sense of deep loss at his death." [7]

The reference to his friendship with Lady Farnham and his speaking as a kind of lay preacher shows that he must have been caught up in what became known as the 'Second Reformation" in Cavan. Apparently it started in September 1826 in a strange incident outlined here by James McQuige writing in February the following year:

"It originated thus. My son in law, Thomas McDowell, observed 3 men standing on the bridge of Cavan one day, in close conversation. He at length went to them, and brought them to an explanation, shewing. That they were 3 school masters, who were employed also in reading the Irish testament of the B[ritish] and F[oreign] B[ible] S[ociety] for the poor. That the priests attacked them: saying they must cast those books away! They replied, they would not, until they had proved that it is not as good a book as the Doway [meaning the Douai-Rheims Bible, the authoritative version for Catholics] – The priests were cruel – The Countrymen firm – The priests excommunicated them, and the 3 men thus cast out, *because they had been born blind, but had now received their sight!* – came away to Cavan Town, to take counsel together, to know what steps they should take to preserve life and save their souls. McDowell gave them their dinner, and then took them to Lady Farnham who heard their story at which she wept. They were told, they should be protected. The Sunday following the 3 men read their recantation, and that day eight days [later], they brought 6 masters more, in the same predicament, who read their recantation; and they were followed by the People in numbers as the papers shew. This is not a thing done in a corner, confined to one neighbourhood such as Cavan. His light is breaking forth, where ever the oracles of God have been opened. A few days ago 46 in Roscommon, 12 in Leitrim, etc." [8]

Needless to say this whole thing ignited a huge religious controversy at the time with some Catholics also weighing in to argue the opposite case, including just outside Cavan, James Martin, a poet labourer from Millbrook Co. Meath who fulminated against these evangelists in some of his poems. These Bible study groups etc survived and prospered until the aftermath of the Famine when their zealousness in combining food with the right religious opinions gave them the name of 'soupers' and they were mostly discredited thereafter. The Cormeen family preserved some folklore about this in particular in relation to the White family in Castlerahan who were relatives of theirs. (Sally White, a Protestant, had married into the Keogan family of Cornacrave, one of whom, Sarah, married Thomas Joseph Nugent.) The story goes that relatives of these Whites who lived near Donabate in Co. Dublin came to visit their Cavan relatives at this time and got on well until Sunday. On that day they realised for the first time that their hosts were preparing to go to a Protestant service at which point they left precipitously for Dublin never to return.

In any case you can see that Richard Nugent was very interested in theology and politics, two lively subjects that tend to recur in describing the different branches of the Ballina family. One person left out of this account incidentally is General Oliver Nugent, the son of the General whose diary you have read and a nephew of the historian. In truth he needs no introduction since he is very well known as the commander of the Ulster Division at the Battle of the Somme etc etc. His son was also an army officer but died of TB around the same time as his father and as such the very distinguished male line of the Farrenconnell family unfortunately passed away in the early 20th century. It is this family incidentally who gave their name to the town of Mountnugent.

Dungimmon Family

The other nephew of Christopher of Ballina listed on the monument is James, from whom the monument lists four sons: William, Christopher, Edmond, and Richard. This James was known as Seamus Dubh de Nuinseann, a Gaelic poet who used to pit his poetic wits against Dr Thomas Dease, the then Bishop of Meath (for whom see Patrick Fagan's book *Éigse na hÍarmhí*) and who was originally of Kiltomb Co. Westmeath but who went on to found the Dungimmon family in Cavan.

This family is described in a printed appeal case to the London House of Lords, i.e. Walter Pollard Appellant versus Thomas Nugent and Alice Nugent his wife. Alice was from the Dungimmon family and only from the ROD, 1716 19-1-9081, do we find out that Thomas was originally of Portlick Co. Westmeath (if this is the Portlick on the banks of the Shannon then he came a long way to get to Dungimmon?). Nearly all these Ballina Nugents had to take court cases at some stage against the Pollards for the reasons outlined here in a Chancery Bill of Oliver Nugent, of Farrenconnell, versus Walter Pollard 16th October 1713:

> "Your Supplicant further sheweth that there being a Commission of Grace for remedy of defective titles issued in this Kingdom in 1684 and Walter Pollard of Castle Pollard Co. Westmeath being reckoned a man very knowing in business and being an active stirring man and being also a person who possessed a great deal of friendship and kindness for and to said Nicholas and Robert Nugent and being their neighbour and seeming to be very much inclined to serve and befriend them and having an intention at that time to pass patent

of such estate as then belonged to himself on said Commission of Grace in order to amend his title thereto he the said Walter Pollard did in 1684 apply himself to said Nicholas and Robert Nugent and they being both easy country gents no ways acquainted with or conversant in law business easily made them believe that their Title to said lands was very defective and there was then an said Commission of Grace a good opportunity for them to amend and make good their title to said lands and as easily prevailed on them to make to him the said Pollard a Deed or Conveyance of the said lands of Enagh and Farrenconnell. Whereby same were conveyed to him and his heirs to the intent that he the said Pollard should be enabled to pass same in said Letters Patent which he was then preparing to apply to the Commissioners appointed to execute said Commission of Grace. Your supplicant further sheweth that although the title which said Nicholas and Robert had to said lands was good and sufficient enough without obtaining any Letters Patent for same yet said Pollard having told them the contrary and seeming to make said proposal to them out of friendship and with an intent in appearance to serve them and proposing then to have no more from said Nicholas and Robert but their proportion of the expenses he should be at in passing the said Patent they did agree thereto but at the time of the making of said Conveyance to said Pollard to enable him to pass said Patent as aforesaid they took an obligation or Instrument in writing from said Pollard which he perfected under his hand and seal bearing date 17th October 1684. Whereby he the said Pollard reciting said Conveyance so made to him by the said Nicholas and Robert Nugent and the intent of making same did oblige himself to pass Patent thereof for said Nicholas and Robert Nugent and upon their paying him their proportion of the expenses which he should be at in doing thereof to convey said lands back again to them and their heirs according to the said several rights thereto which obligation or instrument your supplicant hath left in the hands of Richard Geering esq his clerk in this cause for said Defendant to view before he answers this Bill in case he answers in Dublin or in case he answers by Commission." [9]

The political background by the way is that one of the well known tricks of the Stuart monarchs was to question the land titles of the aristocracy and then receive large fees from the same aristocracy as they "remedy" any "defects" in their titles and that is the real origin of the Commission of Grace.

In any case this seems to have happened to all the Nugent families in South Cavan at that time, i.e. that they had agreed that Pollard was to be the nominal owner of the land under the Commission of Grace, simply to save the expense of their applying to that Commission individually, but had got Pollard to sign a deed acknowledging their real ownership, as you have just read. Unfortunately for them Pollard welched on the deal and so they all had to sue him in court to get proper title to their lands and while it seems these court cases went smoothly enough, bearing in mind the aforementioned deed they had to show the court, nonetheless it must have been very difficult as Catholics, as they all were in the very early 18th century, and expensive as small farmers, to go to court like this.

So to clarify, there are then at least two legal minefields that all these Nugent and allied families – particularly Pallases and Deases – had to go through to get ownership of their own land at this time – late 17th early 18th century –, the Pollard and the Lambert court cases. The Lambert court cases derive thus: in the run up to the 1641 rebellion Robert Nugent of Carlanstown and Jane Countess of Westmeath (née Plunkett and known as 'scraping Jenny', her family were the master craftsmen at holding onto land in Co. Meath) gathered together monies from various Nugent families around Westmeath/Meath, but particularly the various branches of the Ballina family, and used this money to offer to fund a mortgage for Charles Lambert, Earl of Cavan, and using Lambert's lands in Cavan as collateral. Lambert never paid it back so these Nugents each got a parcel of the Cavan lands. Then throughout the late 17th and early 18th centuries Lambert continually brought all these families to court claiming that the mortgage must be paid off by now, but in fact he doesn't seem to have got the lands back because the Nugents were able to say that during the Confederate period they only earned a little money from the land and so not enough to claim that the mortgage was paid off etc etc. This land was pretty much all that the Nugents had then in Cavan because almost all the rest was lost under the Cromwellian confiscations, a fate which these lands avoided because they were nominally under the ownership of Lambert, a loyal Protestant. In fact you'd wonder if this was the deliberate idea behind this mortgage, because in the year or two before the 1641 rebellion the Nugents might very well have predicted what was to happen, based on their experience with previous confiscations including that of the Ulster Plantation, and they felt that having a Protestant nominally owning their land might be beneficial.

But to bring us back to the Pollard case, it seems that when the Dungimmon family won in the courts in Ireland against Pollard he appealed it all the way up to the House of Lords in London, obviously hoping that the family could not sustain the expense of going that far with the case. The resulting printed case file is the primary source for the Dungimmon family and from which we know that:

James, the Gaelic poet, got the lands from Robert Nugent of Carlanstown according to the documents of the Lambert mortgage. He in turn had as children: William, Christopher, Edmond, Richard and Mary who married Edward Plunkett.

6th of May 1659

James signed marriage articles for the marriage of his son William with Mary Sherlock and assigned William a third of the lands of Dungimmon, known as Ballyeaghter. The Registry helps us out here because according to ROD 592-49-400471 in 1807 we find that Ballyeighter is called Mountpalles or Little Mountpalles and was then held by Andrew Palles. (It must be stressed again that the ROD is very good at tracing obscure non-townland placenames. Obviously the townland names you can get from other sources, particularly the Ordnance Survey.)

1673
William died, and soon after James his father, with William leaving as children James, Oliver and Richard and four daughters, Alice, the respondent in the court case, Catherine, Margaret and Anne. On William's death his widow Mary now held Ballyeaghter in her and her children's right.

20th April 1676
The said younger brothers of that William, i.e. Christopher, Edmond, Richard the elder, James the elder, Edward Plunkett and the widow Mary, leased Dungimmon to Pollard for 21 years for £41 for the first year and £49 each year hereafter, and out of this rent the widow Mary got £16 10 shillings.

1681
Pollard bought out Richard Nugent the elder's share.

1684
The family fell under Pollard's Commission of Grace swindle. James Nugent the younger, Catherine and Margaret died without issue.

1686
Alice bought out Oliver Nugent and Richard Nugent the Younger's share, and soon after married Thomas Nugent of Portlick Co. Westmeath.

1699
Pollard acted as the owner of the land and only paid the widow Mary £8 a year
> "deducting the rest for improvements, and when the lease was expired he refused to reconvey or deliver up the possession according to the said

bond and agreement [the Nugent's got him to sign a bond of £900 that he would have to pay if he didn't give the lands back after registering them with the Commission of Grace and after the term of the lease] and sometimes paid the said Mary Nugent the widow and her children £10 sometimes £12 and at other times £14 a year, and hath paid no rent since the year 1710."

1708
Mary Nugent the widow died and her interest in the lands, and that of James Nugent the elder and William Nugent, was granted to Thomas and Alice.

3rd March 1711
Daniel Kelly married Anne Nugent and "for a valuable consideration" transferred his interest in the lands to Tom and Alice.

May 1711
"The Appellant [Pollard] sent for the Respondent Thomas Nugent [married to Alice] and tendered to him a Deed ready engrossed whereby the Respondents in consideration of an annuity of £5 a year, were to convey their interest in the said Lands to the Appellant who declared that if the Respondents would not execute the same, he would find out other means to deprive them of all the said Mortgage Money."

7th Dec 1713
The Nugents win a judgement against Pollard in the Court of Exchequer in Ireland and they are to get back Ballyeaghter and from this Pollard is appealing to the House of Lords in London.

We then find out from the Registry of Deeds, 1716 19-1-9081, that Pollard transferred Ballyeighter into Nugent's name in March 1716 so it seems that the latter won the case. There are many other letters and documents and actually numerous ROD memorials on this family but these extracts from the House of Lords case will have to suffice.

Enagh Family

As pointed out under the Farrenconnell family, where the monument says: "Of Nicholas and Robert, sons of Oliver Nugent", they are referring there to Nicholas Nugent of Enagh (who died in 1708) and his younger brother Robert (1640-1692) of Farrenconnell. Nicholas married Anne Sankey of Offaly and had two sons and a daughter:

– William (who died 19th of August 1745) married in March 1704 Mabel the daughter of John Nugent of Killasonna Co. Longford. He went to the continent to fight with the Wild Geese as you can read here in a reference that he got from the Franciscans of Louvain in 1719, translated from the Latin:

> "Captain, is a man illustrious both by family, nobility, and his constant and unshaken profession of the Catholic religion for which cause his property in Ireland is in modern times falling into such ruin, that he holds it necessary for the preservation of the same to fly to some excellent men his relations, who are fighting in the Emperor's army [Charles VI] and are of high repute, for the purpose of committing himself and his affairs to their counsels and intervention." [10]

He had one son John (1715-1761), who died without issue, and a daughter Anne who married a Captain Therry. When that John died he left Enagh to the Farrenconnell Nugents but the will was disputed and his nephew John got the land but only for his lifetime after which it reverted to Farrennconnell.[11]

– Robert (who died 25th March 1754) married Grace the daughter of Colonel John O'Connor of Offaly and had two sons Maurice and John Nugent. In later life Robert is described as of Kiltomb or sometimes of Streamstown Co. Westmeath (which he got by lease from the Nugents of Clonlost), and also sometimes of

Johnstown Co. Westmeath. John his son, of Kiltomb who farmed Enagh until his death, died in 1792 leaving a son Christopher, and Maurice the other son of Robert had died sometime earlier.

– Alison who married James Nugent of Ballinea.

Its a curious twist of history that the main historical records we have of this family are of some fierce internal disputes, heightened of course by the difficulties engendered by the Penal Laws. Firstly William seems to have been a brash soldier type who didn't much care how he treated his younger brother Robert while he was off soldiering or breaking up the family estate. Robert got nothing out of the family property and he was quite conscious that under the Penal Laws as a Catholic technically he should have received an equal half of the property alongwith his elder brother .i.e. under the gavelkind provision of the laws. Nonetheless he didn't pursue the matter in the courts until his nephew, his brother's heir, turned Protestant in which case the gloves were off and he proceeded to sue him. Also while his brother was alive he sent him this passionate – and as such historically very interesting – letter on the 20th of June 1728:

> "Where was your dear friend [being ironic], or any other, when I lent you £90 to extricate yourself out of Pollard's claws. Where was he when I gave you £30 to go to Germany, where was he when I paid Mr Lambert etc about £30 to make you easy, where was he when I gave you everything you wanted, 'till April 25th you abused me at Fore, I leave you to guess who was the occasion; far be it from me, to do you, or any other, an injustice according to my understanding, but one thing I assure you, if all the dribs and drabs I received out of Enagh, these nine years past, were never accounted for nor applied to any debt, it should not be thought either unjust or unreasonable considering I am a son of the same father and mother with you and never got anything from him in his lifetime nor from you after.
>
> I am that son that managed for him in his

infirmity, took care of his little affairs like a bailiff both early and late, when I ought to be at my books. I managed so well for him that no man on earth could say he owed him a crown when you returned from Savoy. This is the way I was diverted, when happy you were, in England, Flanders, France, Germany, and the Alps pissing against the wall the product of my dear father's industry before the wars.

Excuse me for not mentioning Savoy, with other places of pleasure. If I forgot not you told me that sweet meat must have sour sauce. You went naked through the town of Turin, and in jail was forced to make buttons and live on raw turnip, and cabbage, which must consequently be a judgement for leaving my dear father in distress with Colonel Nugent [of Carlanstown] and Mr Lany. If they could speak and tell, your ugly condition abroad being represented to my dear father [he] remitted money to bring you home, after you landed borrowed money to clothe you, and £50 from Mr Tuite to make you and me graziers [?].

...

Even when my dear father died I was denied the old blankets, and the old feather bed he lay on the earth [meaning presumably that the 'bed' means just the mattress]. I had not one penny worth of furniture, therefore you can't say that your low condition is due to your good nature. Except in staying with good company.

I cannot avoid saying something here of your usage to your dear father, my sister, and me, for in some time after the money was borrowed from Tuite he had an occasion to call it in. There was nothing left to pay it, but the marrow of your back. He then, my dear father, was carried a match making [meaning he might get some money if he married off his son, as dowry with the future daughter in law], hoodwinked, and was forced (by your damning yourself that you would leave the kingdom) to settle immediately his little affairs on you, making little or no provision for himself and three children, but your oath that he should have all in his own power, during his life. Which was soon forgot and often threatened, when a little brandy prevailed, to be turned out of the house, and your only brother ill used.

...

My dear father was for some time bed rid in which spring water was his common comfort, he died about May and you broke up house soon after to live with your mother in law, and left poor Pilgarliek [a servant?], and his poor unhappy sister Joan, to shift." [12]

William's son John went to Italy to serve in the Wild Geese under his uncle on his mother's side, Major General Christopher Nugent of Killasonna Co. Longford who had been at various times the Governor of Corfu, Dalmatia and Verona under the service of the Venetian Republic. It seems that on the death of General Christopher in early 1742 John had come home and tried to help sort out the General's estate in Ireland which seems to have run into controversy. Apparently then as part of these enquiries, and following his father's advice, he went to London to petition his Nugent relatives to help in this matter. You can read here in his letter home from London of the 19th of April 1742, writing to Robert Nugent of Farrenconnell, how he fared:

"I expected to be able to write to you somewhat sooner, but an illness coming on me hindered my knowing enough [sic] for that purpose, nor am I well enough, or knowing enough even now to write, but that I would not miss the opportunity of Mr Matthew Reilly and Mr Tuite's going that way. I have waited of Mr Robert Nugent [of Carlanstown, later President of the Board of Trade] in this manner (for to the Parliament he does not go, being a country man which party doesn't now attend):

I went to an alehouse of [unclear word] house and sent a porter to watch when he came from walking, who delivered him my letter, and he sent for me to a convenient coffee house where I was. I no soon[er] came to the house, but was told he went out. I fretted a little, and abused my messenger at the very door and was going, but he sent after me, received me in his study, Bashane like, and entertained me with a parade of his interest, and that he would not leave a stone unturned to do his cousin of Killasonna justice with regard to my uncle's effects. I showed him we did not dread his proud mightiness, though as civilly as I would; then he grew more tractable and made me offers of service – a la mode de cour ['in the style of being from his heart', but obviously John was unimpressed]. I thanked him in the same style and so got rid of a mighty little good without his enquiring after either friend or acquaintance. I wrote all the particulars as I thought 'twod be amusing to you.

'Twas not so with the worthy Lord of Delvin. As soon as two desperate fevers, which had like to carry him off, were over with him, he was patient to see one. Inquired after your family very kindly and spoke and advised with friendship: 'tho I did not let him know my bottom.

My cousin Hugh Maguire is gone to Scotland with his regiment before I came to London, so that now you may guess I must shift, which I believe would be over now but for my illness. I offered to enlist here but the first question was about my religion but I would not deny mine, so there I fell down: but hope to be up again by going to sea aboard a merchant man to the Straits, by making a push at Venice, or at worse being a sailor: I only want the answering a draft drawn on my uncle for

£10 payable to Mr Thomas Luttrell the 10th of May which I hope will be answered and by the means of Mr Matt Reilly I shall get it. I have wrote to my sister but have had no answer from her, and what my father is doing. I hope you have got my pacquett by Philiys Fanans son Bryan. I pray to know how Christopher Nugent goes on and how Mr Oliver does, all whom I pray God preserve and be assured none can have a more grateful memory of your kindness than...etc..

John Nugent" [13]

The money troubles that he was obviously having in London in fact got much worse as he relates in this later letter to his father William dated 15th July 1745. In fact I don't know of a better letter that really shows the desperation that drove some people to abandon their religion during the Penal Laws, he had to join the British army, which was about to go to war against the Stuarts in Scotland, simply to survive and that meant abandoning his religion:

"I never to the last took any step but with your consent, 'twas by your directions I went to Italy, 'twas at your desire I left the best of uncles, and a certain fortune, to come home for the sake of a cunning ambitious sister, 'twas to assist her you sent me this last happy journey [being ironic]; but how kindly she has requited our good nature may appear by reflecting on the care she has taken to hinder our partaking any share of a fortune, which we might at least hope some pleasure of seeing it come to her, if there had been no other right – our fond mistake, her chief industry was to conceal her intentions 'till she ever put it out of her own power to dispose of anything...her keeping me in suspense in so dear a place as London is, I count a downright cruelty; where expense, sickness and straights had wrought me to almost to desperation; when providence directed me this way of life; which I hope you'll approve – seeing 'twas a last remedy, and that all my best things were pawned for subsistence, when I made interest to get into the Troop I now am in, and was three days after I took on, that I had the remittance from you.

...

To give you a proper idea of my present circumstance 'tis necessary you should know three things that were needful to come at my present bread:

– first to deny my country, for that countrymen are (without vast interest on their side) for the most (without distinction of principle) denied,

– next I changed my name to be more out of knowledge, and of course what bred up to. [i.e. so he could be more anonymous. Note these are two reasons, he doesn't have to mention the last one because its obviously his religion that he denied, and this would have been a big blow to his father so he doesn't labour the point.]

But notwithstanding these and other precautions I am shrewdly suspected in all. My country I now don't deny as my language betrayed me, my name is [found out], by the name Nugent I am judged not of the Established Church, through my education, particularly my speaking foreign languages and understanding something of the military, they think me some French officer." [14]

This later letter of his to Robert Nugent of Farrenconnell of the 27th of October 1745 clarifies the circumstances under which he wrote to his father:

"...I wrote soon after to my father at large, which I believe you approve, seeing I would not write to him (and at the same time keep him in the dark) [presumably he was asked to write to his father but not mention his change of religion, he seems to have done this literally but by writing it cleverly he got the point across] without my manifestly abusing him, and which I am too well convinced his nature would not bear. However I hope if my reasons are not sufficient, yours will help to convince him of the necessity of my proceedings and may depend on my never being concerned in any low, or mean action; and which principle I hope (God willing) to continue in, so that I hope to be no more ashamed of my behaviour when J.P. [his new disguised name] than when I was or may be J. N.

I have not heard from my sister a great while, nor do I much desire it as I expect no help to my Cont:[?] from that quarter. I had two letters from her after her marriage, full of her usual designs, but never answered any, both that I might get rid of her ill nature, and at the same time avoid shocking her husband, which the kindest truth I would write must do, and a letter to her must unavoidably come first to his hands." [15]

He died unmarried a few years later and seems to have suffered ill health as a result of his time in those wars, including the 1745 uprising in Scotland during which he fought with Cumberland's troops. The Enagh family vanish off the scene sometime later with those lands incorporated into that of Farrenconnell.

Gneeve

Although seemingly not listed on the Fore monument nonetheless for the sake of completeness I think I should mention also the family of Gneeve (pronounced 'Greeve'). Gneeve is a small townland in Cavan just beside the Meath border, near the road that goes from Oldcastle Co. Meath to Mountnugent Co. Cavan, as is the location of nearly all these places. In or around 1680 we are told that an Oliver Nugent of Gneeve (who died sometime between 1673 and 1680), the grandson and heir of Christopher of Ballina – his father is never mentioned –, who married Honora O'Reilly, the daughter of Philip from Shesriagh in Co. Leitrim, was attempting to assert his rights over some of the old Ballina land.[16] This Oliver was in the thick of it during the tumultuous events of the 1641 rebellion in Cavan, as outlined here by the governor of Cloughoughter Castle in Cavan in his complaint of these proceedings among the 'depositions' of the rebellion:

> "Sayth that on Saturday the 23 of October last between the hours of 7 and 8 a clock in the evening, one Thomas Pallatt, an Englishman, repaired to this deponent from Cavan town and told him that there were several rebels with some Scotch forces which had taken Clownis in the County Fermanagh and killed Mr Arthur Champion at (his) house at Shanocke. And that Mr Edward Alderiche with others had fled for their lives and were at Cavan; where Captain Baylie was, as he [was] preparing to resist the rebels.
>
> And that Milmore mac Edmond Rely [Myles the Slasher], the then high sheriff of that county, with divers others in his company, had repaired to Farnham Castle to seize on such arms as were there to arm men for the prosecution of the said rebels, as also for the defence of the country. For in that castle there was, as this deponent has been credibly informed, complete arms and armour for forty men at least, it being a castle belonging to the heir of Sir Thomas Waldram who is an undertaker [planter] in that County of Cavan. The said Pallatt had scarcely done his relation when the high sheriff of that county, Milmore mac Edmond Rely, with divers in his company, knocked at this deponent's door and required entrance. And conferring with the said deponent for the speedy advancement he had for some service for his Majesty this deponent nothing suspecting him opened his doors. And immediately there rushed in divers men with skeanes, swords, pistols, and pikes, and told this deponent that he must yield

himself, his arms, and ammunition, into their hands: for he had a commission (from his Majesty) to disarm all the British.

Being by me, the deponent, demanded the reason of it, they said, the intention of his majesty was by their means to bring into subjection the puritan faction of the parliament of England, and that they would right the Queen's majesty for aspersions laid on the Royal progeny, too bold for them to speak, or without any modesty to be related. Having thus, with naked weapons at the breast of this deponent, seized him, they told him if there were resistance made by any that their commission was to kill their wives and children before their faces, to burn their houses, and afterwards to kill the parties resisting. And on this they demanded the key of the Castle of Clowater [Cloughoughter] which was a strong tower situate in the midst of a lough some musket shot from this deponent's house, which this deponent refusing to do because it had the name of a fort. Without maintenance or allowance they were ready to have murdered this deponent until one Anthony Culme, a kinsman of this deponent who then had the key of the castle in his custody, desired them to hold their hands and he would deliver them the key which accordingly he did. Immediately upon this Milmore mac Edmond Rely, the then high sheriff, and Edmond mac Milmore Rely, the said sheriff's father, called for a bible and charged this deponent on peril of his life to depose whatsoever arms, or other ammunition, he had in his house. Unto which I replied I would hide nothing from them, and bade them to search which accordingly they did.

Immediately they told me that I must forthwith be carried to that uninhabited and comfortless castle of Clowater, there to remain with a strong guard till they had subdued the whole kingdom.

And their pleasures were further known, the deponent's poor afflicted wife, who was but lately before delivered of a child, with tears did solicit their favour that I the deponent might stay in my (his) house till the next morning with a safe guard. But in that rebellious route neither words nor tears would avail but away both she and I were carried that night to the castle where I was (they were) left with a strong guard about us. And one Owen Mac Turlagh Rely was left Captain, or Chief Commander of that guard, whom for ought that ever I could perceive was a most civil man much troubled at them distempers and under God during his imprisonment, which was of six months, a continual preserver of his life. The chief men which I the deponent marked and knew at (his) apprehension the 23rd of October was Milmore mac Edmond Rely, the high sheriff, and Edmund mac Milmore Rely, the said sheriff's father; who were the only men that spoke the words afore rehearsed. There was likewise present that was armed and assistants to them: John mac Phillip mac Milmore Rely of Lismore, Mr Oliver Nugent, grandson to Mr Nugent of Ballaimagh in the County of Meath, Owen mac Turlagh Rely, who was left Captain of Clowater Castle, Shane mac Oweny Sheridan of Carbratan, William mac Owen Bane Sheridan and Shane mac Owen Bane Sheridan of Killekerie, and one Brian Modder Rely." [17]

Oliver in turn had a son James of Gneeve who in 1700 is listed as being of Tullygullen in Co. Cavan.[18] Other than that its unclear what happened to this family although in the mid to late 18th century we find another family of Nugents living in this small townland. In particular, going by the Farrenconnell papers catalogued by Joe Ainsworth in the 1950s, we seem to have these four brothers and two sisters:

– Thomas who died in 1765 and is buried in Killeagh (as will be noted below, the Gneeve family plot in Killeagh is close to that of the Mountprospect family);

– James, who is dead by 1765 and had a son Thomas and daughter Mary;

– John who inherits the first mentioned Thomas' interest in the lands of Gneeve and Farrenconnell;

– Matthias who had lands in Beelaghy and an interest in lands in Barcony (Co. Cavan) and Ballinrink (Co. Meath). He married Lucy Cook of Francis Street in Dublin and he died c.9/09/1769, and she on the 10/3/1770, as noted in the Freeman's Journal for those dates, and we are told that he specified in his will that: "his four sons may be bound apprentice when at a suitable age to some decent genteel business." Oliver Reilly of Garryross was his executor and Oliver Nugent of Bobsgrove was the guardian of his children;

– Some unnamed daughter who seems to have married an Allen and had four children: James, Mary, Jane and Catherine Allen;

– Catherine who seems to have married E Carty of Ballynenagh, and her husband had a sister Barbara Carty who in time inherited her brother in law Thomas Nugent's interest in the lands of Ballinrink.

The confusing thing is that this family would surely be descendants of that James, the son of Oliver who was in turn a grandson of Christopher. However complicating this question is the following note added to a pedigree of the Nugents owned by Myles Stoney of Farrenconnell and written by Patrick J O'Reilly (a Dublin solicitor who did extensive research into the identity of Myles the Slasher O'Reilly and whose notes are currently housed in the Royal Society of Antiquaries of Ireland in Dublin):

> "This gentleman [Oliver Nugent of Farrenconnell] is mentioned in the wills of two out of four brothers James, John and Thomas of Gneeve and Matthias Nugent of Ballynenagh Co. Cavan and Hilltown near Fore Co. Westmeath. John (without giving him anything in trust) appointing Oliver Nugent "a trustee for my children" and Matthias more reasonably saying "I

hereby direct that Oliver Nugent of Bobsgrove may leave power and direction over my children and do recommend them to his protection." John and Matthias Nugent, who were cousins of Oliver Nugent's father, died in the same year as the latter (1770), with whom they were contemporary, being sons of the younger brother of Oliver who married Catherine Reilly."

Another note O'Reilly adds was in regard to Mary Nugent:
"my father's grandmother was the last Nugent buried in St Mary's Fore. She was a daughter of Matthias Nugent of Ballynenagh, son of the younger son (James) of Robert of Farrenconnell who died in 1690."

This then is presumably the ancestry of the later family in Gneeve, although earlier, as we have seen, this was certainly the mainline of the Ballina family (and they have the first names to match and also seem to deal in the old Ballina lands of Lismacanigan and Cunlin).

Which by a circuitous route brings us back to the beginning of this family. Here we shall attempt to trace the mainline beginning with Oliver who founded the Ballina Nugent clan in Tudor times:

Oliver Nugent of Ballina and Down Enouse Co. Meath/ Carpenterstown Co. Westmeath

Oliver Nugent, a brother of Richard Nugent Baron of Delvin and uncle of Christopher Nugent, the Baron of Delvin who died in 1602, went to live in Ballina (but pronounced 'Bellaney', hence the monument has 'Belena') which is in Co. Meath directly south of Oldcastle, the last townland before entering Westmeath on the Castlepollard road. A few known facts about him include:

– According to Lodge he was also of Clonigerah, which is just across the border in Co. Westmeath and includes the later houses of Sallymount and Hounslow.

– His daughter Marion married Alexander Plunkett of Tathrath Co. Meath.[19]

– He was the cessor of the Barony of Corkaree in Westmeath in 1577,[20] making the mistake of subsuming his own morality into the state's necessity:

> "Sheweth unto your lordship your supplicant Thomas Nugent now prisoner in her Majesty's Castle of Dublin, that one Oliver Nugent, cessor of the Barony of Corkery, younger brother to your supplicant (by whose furtherance he is grown to wealth, and yet nevertheless forgetting the fear of God, the danger of the law, and the duty he oweth unto his said brother) hath and doth daily by uncivil means, practice the utter destruction of your supplicant, his followers and tenants within the said Barony. And to that end hath bought the said office, by colour whereof he doth daily overload them with soldiers, kerne and other charge without any commission, so that all your supplicant's inheritance in that Barony is like to be waste, which partly appeareth by the copy of a letter which your supplicant of late delivered unto your honour, and by a supplication which your supplicant exhibited before the Lord Deputy for the spoil of a town of his, in which he procured Captain Collier to be assistant unto him by subtle means and in divers other things here too tedious to report, the determination whereof was remitted to your Lordship.
>
> And now of late the said Oliver having taken up all such cess as was due in said Barony of Corkery (whereof one James Nugent was receiver) upon your supplicant's inheritance, and the rest of the Barony (your supplicant is manurane in the town of Moynstown only excepted [meaning he is the manor lord of the barony, except for

Moynestown]) for to have again to himself, he distrained a plough of garrons [horses] of your supplicant's tenants and the same hath detained, till a big pot of your supplicant's goods was pledged therefor. Wherefore your said supplicant prayeth that the said cessor be driven to account with him and what he shall prove to be due upon your supplicant he will the same pay, beseeching also your Lord that for the respects aforesaid he be discharged of his office." [21]

– His lands were set to be confiscated as a result of the 1581 rebellion of the Nugents which he was implicated in.[22]

– He died on the 15th of March 1589 and is, as we have seen, buried behind a monument to him and the Ballina family in general at Fore in the graveyard behind St Mary's, the modern Catholic Church.

– On the 6th of May 1592 he was mentioned, posthumously, in the William Nugent versus Sir Robert Dillon court case.[23] It was stated there that in 1585 he was, alongwith John Barnewall of Moylagh, in charge of the disbursement of government money to parties who had been successful in apprehending rebels, known as the 'head money'. This was important because William Nugent, Oliver's nephew, was using this to prove that a rebel for whom head money was paid out was a close friend of Sir Robert Dillon which, alongwith many other proofs, served to prove Dillon guilty of treason. In these documents Oliver is described as being of Carpenterstown and also of Doune Enouse.[24]

– He married firstly Anne Plunkett of the Dunsany family and secondly Anne Browne daughter of Richard Browne of Kilpatrick Co. Westmeath. From the first marriage he had Christopher, of whom we follow below, and Fr Robert Nugent SJ (c.1575-1652), a leading figure in the Jesuits in Ireland in the early 17th century, and from the second marriage he had Fr Nicholas Nugent SJ (1586-1656) and William Nugent. This William Nugent, of Enagh and Ratheever Co. Cavan, was in turn the father of Oliver and James Nugent, the former was the ancestor of the Nugents of Enagh and Farrenconnell and the latter – an Irish poet known as Seamus Dubh – was the founder of the Dungimmon family.

– As mentioned, two of his sons, Nicholas and Robert, became leading Jesuits in Ireland. This is especially true of Robert who was a poet and correspondent in Latin (with many of his original Latin letters to Rome now preserved in Dublin), in Irish (he was a good friend and correspondent of the Irish poet Bonaventure O'Hussey), and English (one of Fr Robert's poems "extolled the pure generosity of Ormond.") as well as being an authority in mathematics and music (he even changed the arrangement of the Irish harp). He was the head of the Jesuits in Ireland at the time of the 1641 rebellion and he was an early supporter of the Confederation of Kilkenny, sending two Jesuits as ambassadors from the Confederation to Belgium and France, Fr Henry Plunkett and Fr Matthew Hartegan respectively.[25] He was also placed in charge of the printing press of the Confederation, with which he wanted to print Fr Stephen White's historical works but as a Jesuit he couldn't print anything without the permission of his superiors in Rome and that took time to get during the rebellion.[26] As the Cromwellian advance slowly crept across the country he had to relocate first to Galway and then, after an aborted attempt to flee to the Continent, he got shelter in the still Irish held island of Inishboffin where he died on the 6th of May 1652. A few extracts from his letters might be of interest, summarised from the Latin by Fr Leo Hicks SJ, starting with this appraisal of Fr Thomas Macarius that he sent to Rome on the 20th July 1640 and then going on to describe the onset of the 1641 rebellion and subsequent wars:

> "All who know him well assert that what was written to you was true: only superlatives are to be avoided; they say he is learned in lit. ltam[?] and fit to profess each in any university as he did in Flanders, Belgian province – whence fuller information can be obtained. Well versed in Greek and Hebrew, in sacred and profane history; an

excellent preacher – though more feeling is wanting. A good businessman but he is choleric, and too imperious: but admonished by me he humbly promised to amend. Rather eager to acquire things without becoming discretion; addicted to prayer; observer of rule and constant in his vocation."

12th of November 1640:
"We are between hope and fear here at present, though religious issues were not treated of in Parliament expressly at present: they seem to be going to do so and so dangerous times are apprehended."

24 March 1642
"Words cannot express the misery of this kingdom. Nothing seen or heard of here, especially in Eastern parts of the Kingdom, than depredations, slaying of children, women and men; fires destroying the furniture and property of whole families. Such is the fury of the English and our own people that the realm cannot only be pacified it seems by the destruction of one or the other. The English breath out slaughter against Catholic religion and our Catholics unless they abjure the faith. Ours have taken up arms in defence. Though the Irish are greater in number they are almost without arms and I do not see how they can defend themselves in a just cause and holy war, against an enemy very well armed, unless Catholic princes, and above all his Holiness, supply arms and powder. Our little flock is dispersed and each lives privately among friends. Have no certain news as to what has happened to ours in Dublin and the Pale. I fear the English may slay many, bul[?]fors will be done. It will be very difficult I see to send letters or recover them in

future but I shall not neglect any opportunity of writing about the state of this Kingdom." [27]

As the Cromwellian armies closed in on the Irish Catholics the church authorities were particularly anxious to rescue Fr Robert, as you can read in this document drawn up on the 22nd February 1652 which is entitled "Rationes ob quas P. Robertus Nugentius periculoso hoc tempore in transmarinas partes mittetur" ["Some of the reasons for which Fr Robert Nugent is in danger at this time and should be sent overseas"]:

"1. He was for 22 years Superior of the Mission and therefore knows intimately the foundations, property, state and persons of the residences. This fact is well known to the enemy and hence he is in the greatest danger. Were he captured he might be compelled by torture to reveal all – which would be very harmful to the society and dangerous to us. If he leaves Ireland the danger to his person ceases.

2. He was zealous in promoting this Catholic war. He alone of the Society [Jesuits] signed the public condemnation of the peace – with bishops and heads of other religious orders. He was intimate with the Nuncio to which prelate we all, following directions from Rome, showed all service etc. He gave the Nuncio a large sum of money for the prosecution of the war – money that is for the most part belonging to the foundation of our residence of Cashel. [But the money originated with the will of Elizabeth Fitzgerald née Nugent, the Countess of Kildare, Fr Robert's first cousin once removed and a close friend of his. He had assisted her by getting a retrospective dispensation for her marriage from Rome, because her mother was a Fitzgerald and she realised after her marriage that she was just inside the forbidden bands of consanguinity. (See his letter of the 12th of Feb 1611.) He frequently stayed at her castle at Kilkea Co. Kildare and as such it became for a while the de facto HQ of the Jesuits in Ireland.] He

for several weeks entertained the Nuncio as a guest in a castle [Kilkea] in the country – together with all his suite, the generals of the army and very many prelates during the whole time of the unsuccessful siege of Dublin (by the Catholic forces) was being conducted. Later other public business was committed to him which gave occasion for the hostility of Catholics and heretics to him and for their evil speech of him. These matters without doubt would make it very dangerous, were he to fall into the hands of the enemy.

Hence it is that he is among the first in the Catalogue drawn up by heretics, to whom no favour or hope of pardon is to be extended." [28]

Christopher Nugent of Carpenterstown Co. Westmeath/ Downe Enouse and Ballina Co. Meath

Oliver's son and heir was Christopher Nugent, of whom we know the following:

– He married Anne, daughter of Thomas Nugent of Ross Co. Meath (a descendant of William Nugent, a brother of Christopher, the Baron of Delvin who died in 1602) and Mary Plunkett of Loughcrew.

– His daughter Catherine married Edmond O'Reilly, the second son of Hugh Connallach O'Reilly, who was reported to have died in 1635 at Kevitt Castle near Crossdoney in Co.Cavan. This is via a funeral entry in the Ulster King-of-Arms Office – the Irish Heraldry Office – in Dublin but in fact Edmond was alive in the 1640s. His son Myles who became the sheriff of Co. Cavan in 1641 is undoubtedly the famous 'Myles the Slasher' and this accounts for Oliver of Gneeve being so close to these O'Reillys at the time of the 1641 rebellion.[29]

Above is an Ancient Order of Hibernians banner in honour of Myles the Slasher and on the next page you see the monument in Finea and below that a plaque in the wall of Ross Castle Co. Meath. This serves to show how important he is to Cavan history and bear in mind that when that monument in Finea was erected c.1910 it attracted a number of monster meetings, and some disputes, involving the United Irish League (who were allied to the Irish Parliamentary Party and semi secretly backed by the Ancient Order of Hibernians) and the emerging Sinn Féin Party (which was secretly supported by the Irish Republican Brotherhood). Even the O'Rahilly, who died in 1916, weighed in with some historical research seeking to establish his identity.

In memory of
MYLES O'REILLY
(THE SLASHER)

THIS ANCIENT CASTLE IN WHICH
THE CELEBRATED MYLES O'REILLY
KNOWN AS THE SLASHER
IN 1644 PASSED THE NIGHT
PREVIOUS TO THE BATTLE OF FINEA
AT WHICH HE WAS KILLED
HAVING FALLEN INTO RUIN
WAS PARTLY RESTORED BY
HIS LINEAL DESCENDANT
ANNA MARIA DEASE O'REILLY
1864

– Owen son of Shane Og O'Rourke of Cloncorrick Co. Leitrim married Elizabeth Nugent, a daughter of this Christopher. Shane died on the 7th of May 1635 and is buried in Dromlohan Co. Cavan.[38]

– His brother Gerrott Nugent (and another unnamed brother) were killed on Her Majesties service during the 9 years war.[39]

– A letter from his first cousin Christopher Nugent Baron of Delvin to the Irish Council in Dublin of the 7th of August 1596 says he was carried off a prisoner by the sons of Sir Thomas Nugent of Carlanstown, who were fighting on O'Neill's side during the 9 years war:

"My very good lords I am sorry that I can not at this time advertise to your lordships of a good success in service as heretofore I have done. The next Thursday after I apprehended the two brethren of the Nugents, a brother of theirs, called Christopher, who gave a show of dutifulness while they rested in rebellion, most treacherously joining with the younger brother, and some kerns, entrapped my cousin Edmund Nugent, of Carlanstown, Sir Thomas Nugent's heir, and Christopher Nugent FitzOliver, my cousin germane [first cousin], who they carried with them prisoners.

And upon intelligence sent me from Bryan McMona[?] O'Ferall that they returned from O'Rourke's country into Inchmore, an island in the Co. of Longford, accompanied with 20 kerne only (for at the apprehension of their two brethren their company dispersed), I sent certain of my kinsmen and household, which made in number 50, to see if they might on the sudden assault the said island. But understanding of Granard that the former intelligence was not true, and there staying for further intelligence, were this day morning very early suddenly assaulted by certain of the Farrells accompanied with a great number of shot belonging to O'Rourke and the Reillies, as is reported, by means of which shot 16 of the company were presently slain, whereof two were my cousin germanes, and mine uncle James' eldest son hath his arm broken with a bullet, and is shot into the body, whereof if he shall recover or not, God only knoweth.

My loss herein is great, and to me grievous, but greater is like to ensue to me and the country if your lords do not with speed prevent the same; for one of my spies who accompanied Phillip (O'Reilly) when he met the Earl (of Tyrone) at Enniskillen, heard the Earl say that he expected O'Donnells being with great force here in Delvin."[40]

In case the Tudor terminology is a little unclear, what happened was that Christopher and Edmund Nugent of Carlanstown were kidnapped by other Nugents of Carlanstown and brought to an island in Longford. The Baron felt he could rescue them but the rescuing party were ambushed by the forces allied to Hugh O'Neill and many were killed. It seems that sometime later Christopher escaped because he certainly lived a long life after this.

– We are told about him in a letter of the 24th of November 1599 that:

"Upon Tuesday last Christopher Fitz Oliver (Nugent) a gentleman of Westmeath, nearly allied to O'Reilly's wife, and having certain intelligence of the enemy's purpose to overrun the country, met them by the way, and of himself demanded the cause of this great envy towards the Lord of Delvin. Tyrone [Hugh O'Neill] answered him that the Lord of Delvin was the only block that hindered him overrunning the whole kingdom, and vowed that he would never leave Westmeath until he had overrun him".[41]

By 'O'Reilly's wife' the letter means the wife of *the* O'Reilly, i.e. the chief of the O'Reillys. He must therefore have been a prominent figure in the diplomacy between the O'Reillys, who were fighting with Hugh O'Neill, and the Baron of Delvin, who was fighting for the Queen, during the 9 years war. The Baron was really very isolated in Westmeath as he tried to resist O'Neill at this time and the latter obviously felt that the Baron was a serious nuisance to him.

– In a list of (false) charges prepared against the Baron of Delvin on the 19th of November 1601 it was claimed that when Hugh O'Neill was marching south to Kinsale our Christopher "came to Tyrone [i.e. Hugh O'Neill] at Gortloney and brought with him four garron loads of bread and ale and aquavita".[42]

What happened was that although the Baron was an enthusiastic supporter of the Queen during the war nonetheless it seems the Dublin government was still very anxious to destroy the Baron by fixing false charges on him. Probably because he was a staunch Catholic and quite a leader of the Pale in preserving that religion in Ireland – which greatly aggravated the Dublin government – they tried to claim (completely falsely) that he was a secret supporter of O'Neill. This idea that his cousin was happy to supply O'Neill was then part of that picture they were trying to create.[43]

– In a similar list of the 9th of June 1602 it is said that he was the "chief instrument from the Baron to the Archtraitor". It also states that his father was of 'Carpinstown'.[44] At this stage the government was busy prosecuting the Baron for treason, during which the Baron died while under house arrest in Dublin.

– It seems it is he that is described as a merchant in Fore Co. Westmeath in an undated Chancery Bill (O 108) in the National Archives in Dublin:

"To the Right Honourable the Lord Chancellorie [sic]

Humbly complaineth unto your honour, Patrick Maning of the Navan, in the County of Meath, merchant.

That where your supplicant was a 15 years past did bail unto Sir[?] Christopher Nugent of Fore in the County of Westmeath, merchant, 9 quarters and 12 pounds of fine [word lost] value £14 sterling lawful money of England, one hundereth sheepskins [?, this word, and the two other 'skins', are hard to make out and unfortunately little more than a guess] value 40 shillings of like money, one hundereth lambskins 20 shillings of like money and one hundereth calf skins value 30 shillings of like money, to be rebailed to the complainant when he should require the same.

And sundry times after the said bailment, the complainant requested the defendant to redeliver the said varine [?] sheepskin, lambskin and calfskins, which to do he always refused and yet doth wrongfully and to the damages of your complainant of £24 sterling.

The premise considered, if it please your Lordship for as much as the defendant is greatly allied and befriended in the County of Westmeath, from whence the tocalling [?] in this [word lost] should come by turn of common law, and your supplicant a mere stranger and unknown in that country, to grant her Majesty's writ of sub[poena] against the said Nugent, joining him upon a pain to redeliver unto your supplicant the said parcels, otherwise to appear before your Lordship to tell why he should not, and your supplicant shall pray etc."

The end of that document where he describes how Christopher was "greatly allied and befriended in the County of Westmeath" while true enough no doubt is not to be taken too seriously. This plea was before the Court of Chancery in Dublin which in simple terms would operate like the modern Irish Supreme Court. In other words you couldn't plead before this court the normal operations of the law, rather the court was to provide 'equity' –

i.e. justice – in cases where the normal course of Common Law could not be expected to give you that justice. So in this case Patrick Manning acknowledges that in the normal course of law he should take the case to the courts in Westmeath but he is claiming here that because Christopher is so powerful in Westmeath, and he a "mere stranger and unknown in that county", that he couldn't reasonably expect justice there hence he has to go to the Court of Chancery. But in truth this is probably just a legal excuse to allow him to take the case conveniently in Dublin and is very commonly used in Chancery pleadings, more common than it would be if it were a genuine reason, in this writer's opinion in any case.

– Described as of Carpenterstown in an Irish Chancery Pleading (U 121) where he sued Oliver Tuite with respect to land in Gneeve (Co. Cavan), lands that he rents from Tuite for £6 a year sterling which is "far more than the land is worth".

– In 1610 Christopher Nugent of Downensosse Co. Meath, clearly our man, was granted by Letters Patent two polls of land in Lisvecanegan [Lismacanigan] and one poll of land in Finewoeh [Finaway] in Co. Cavan.[45]

– He leased Bellananagh and Gortachurk in Co. Cavan to the Flemings c.1641.[46]

He died in 1671 or thereabouts as an old man probably in his nineties if not over a hundred. He is mentioned in some of the documents relating to the Cromwellian confiscations where it is claimed, probably quite accurately, that he was bed ridden and very aged at the time of the 1641 rebellion and therefore took no part in it, however his land was confiscated regardless. He was succeeded in his turn by his son James of whom we know:

James Nugent of Ballina/Annagh Co. Meath and Lismacanigan/Cornamucklagh/Clontiduffy Co. Cavan

– He is reported to have married Anne a daughter of James Nugent of Ross.

– Described as of Annagh in a bond, alongwith his father Christopher of Ballina and with respect to Robert Brady, a debt listed in the Dublin Staple books of the 17th of May 1631.[47]

– Also described as of Annagh, which is beside Ballina in Co. Meath, in a 1638 deed preserved in the Nugent section of the Stowe papers in the Huntington Library in San Marino California. This deed also mentions that he owned land in Lismacanigan and Cornamucklagh in Co. Cavan.

– Then in 1640 we find a James Nugent of Lismacanigan Co. Cavan turning up in the records and its clearly this James. We know this because, for example, he is named, and given that address, in the marriage articles of his sister Margaret and Richard Tuite of Rathmore Co. Meath dated 29th of May 1640.[48]

Luckily enough we have then some exact dates from which we can say that this family moved into Cavan between 1638 and 1640. And helpfully enough we have even some folklore on this. It seems that this old Nugent estate of Lismacanigan became known in the 18th century as the estate of Mountprospect which is a typically 18th century 'fancy name'. The Mountprospect family in turn preserved some traditions of how they came to Cavan. In the early 1960s a Gaelic scholar called Canon Coslett Quinn came to the house in search of an old pedigree of the Dempseys and recorded this simple tradition of the origin of the house:

> "At some undetermined date, a long time ago, Lord Westmeath, whose family name was Nugent, said to one of his nephews, who was at a loose end, that he had better go down to that rough place in County Cavan, and reclaim it. The estate of Mount Prospect thus came into being. The last of the line was Thomas Nugent." [49]

– In any case continuing our account of this newly made Cavan man, James Nugent, we find that he owned all of Lismacanigan and Cornamucklagh in 1640 as recorded in the Books of Survey and Distribution for Cavan, which were then all confiscated in the Cromwellian confiscations and given to Cuppage and Burton.[50]

– He was accused in a 1641 deposition of being involved in the robbery of horses from a Thomas Hodges, where he is described as being a JP from near Daly's Bridge (Mountnugent):

> "Castabell Hedges, wife to the fore deposed Thomas Hedges, duly sworn deposeth: That fourteen of the horses and mares of which this deponent's husband was robbed about the 24 day of October last were taken away by James Nugent, a Justice of peace, near Dalyes bridge, in the County of Cavan. And that threescore of his sheep, and 12 of his cows, and linen worth 40 s., and wool worth £3 and pewter worth 30 s., and other household stuff worth 40 s. were taken away by Cahir O Rely of Drumcro in the parish of Don in the County of Cavan. And other of his goods were taken away by Patrick O Sheredin of Aghwhie in the parish of Killidrumfartan in the County of Cavan, and Phillip o Lincy of the same. And further she cannot depose
> [her mark]
> Castabell [mark] Hedges" [51]

– We have some further details of James' activities during the war from this piece of folklore recorded in the Anglo-Celt in the 1920s, bearing in mind that Cornamucklagh is right beside Lismacanigan and both were owned by James:

> "When Ballaghanea "Court" or "Castle" was burned in 1642 a sad event is supposed to have occurred in the vicinity. The Nugents then lived in a stronghold at Cornamucklagh, and one of them – "Big Shaemus" – was then a lieutenant in the confederate army of Owen Roe [O'Neill]. Previously Shaemus Nugent wooed and won the

hand of a winsome maiden named Sheila Lynch, who resided near the "Court" of Ballaghanea.

Local history tells that a flank of English forces on their way to the "Battle of Scrabby" halted at Cornamucklagh to carry off prey and booty, where a "speaking magpie," whose tongue was split with magic silver, told them the whereabouts of Nugent's future bride. The story is still credited that the maiden referred to – Sheila Lynch – then met her death at Ballaghanea in trying to escape to the cave of Slieve Rinan, that she stumbled and fell dead, while meeting the soldiers face to face.

How true this tradition is no one can say, but at all events, the uncanny tale survives. Some say that often in the midnight hours the banshee croons around Ballaghanea while a "magpie" perches and hovers at the spot where this maiden fell dead. The extensive possessions in Cornamucklagh of "the Nugents, Irish Papists," were forfeited to the Crown in the 17th century." [52]

– Described as being of Clontiduffy Co. Cavan he was charged £3 12 shillings subsidy tax, on goods of £27, in the subsidy rolls of 1662 and other years.[53] He had moved onto Clontiduffy after the Cromwellian Wars because that was part of the lands allocated to him under the Lambert mortgage and therefore these were probably all the lands he had left in Cavan.

– On the 7th of October 1670 Oliver Nugent of Enagh granted lands to his second son Robert Nugent the division of which was to be decided, in the event of disagreement, by this James Nugent of Clontiduffy or his son Robert [of Clonigeragh].[54] Also in regard to Oliver Nugent of Gneeve, the grandson of Christopher of Ballina, there is a reference to his uncle James Nugent of Clontiduffy in a document dated the 17th of April 1673.[55]

Between the death of James and the beginning of the contemporary documents that list the Nugents settling in Cormeen and Mountprospect circa 1720 we have unfortunately only a few scattered references to go by. One is a pedigree of the family that was written by William Skey who was St Patrick Pursuivant, a kind of deputy to the Ulster King of Arms who was the chief herald of Ireland, circa 1840.[56] That Skey pedigree follows on the line of Robert Nugent of Clonigerah, a son of our James of Annagh/Lismacanigan etc, who is said to have married Elinor a daughter of Edward Nugent of Bracklyn Co. Westmeath esq, and he had a daughter Catherine who married Matthias Nugent of Clontiduffy, and a son, Thomas Nugent of Clonigerah, who died without issue and who was succeeded in Clonigerah by his 3rd cousin Oliver Nugent of Bracklyn.

This Thomas Nugent of Clonigerah was mentioned alongside his brother in law Matthias Nugent of Carlanstown in a list of debts from what seems to be Jacobite bankers, Richard and Andrew Dalton, in a bond of the 9th of August 1688. He is also listed alongside his brother in law in a list of outlawries, a record of those who were outlawed because of their participation on the Jacobite side in the Williamite Wars, and it seems that both Thomas and Matthias were officers in James's army with Matthias being variously described as a Captain and later a Major.[57]

But it gets a lot more interesting when we throw in a little more folklore. The later traditions of the Cormeen family state that they had extensive lands prior to the Penal Laws which they entrusted to a Nugent Protestant relative, as fake Protestant owners to protect them from the Penal Laws. This was a close relative, a brother or cousin etc, but unfortunately the deal wasn't honoured and this family escaped with the lands that should have been owned by the Cormeen Nugents. These lands included property which was later owned by the Pallas family, possibly Mountpalles, of whom the judge Christopher Pallas was a descendant.[58] It seems likely that this is a reference to the two brothers in law above, possibly Major Matthias took over these lands from Thomas Nugent of Clonigerah although he had only married in here, and it seems that Thomas did have descendants or at least close relatives who were also of the Ballina family. I believe then that the later Mountprospect/Cormeen family are descendants from this Thomas or at least from a close relative of his.

Major Matthias was originally from Carlanstown Co. Westmeath and later lived in numerous places including, it seems, Arnegrosse Co. Westmeath,[59] Ballynascarry, Co. Westmeath,[60] which is beside Tullystown – where a branch of the Baltrasna Reillys lived – on the southern shore of Lough Sheelin, also of Foyran Co. Westmeath,[61] of Clontiduffy (as stated in Lodge's peerage) and then probably of Legavoge, which is a part of Barcony in Co. Cavan which he leased from Lord Massereene and later Lord Farnham [62] and where he seems to have lived when he made his will in 1721 and in which he is described as a merchant.

In answer to one of the many court cases of the early 1700s he describes how he got the lands of Clontiduffy and Rathclaghy via an assignment from Thomas Nugent, a son of Robert Nugent of Clonigeragh, who was a son of James Nugent of Co. Cavan [obviously he of Annagh/Lismacanigan/Clontiduffy] who in turn got it by assignment from Richard and James Tuite, who in turn had got it by dowry from the marriage of [the last named James' sister] Margaret Nugent to Richard Tuite, the lands in question being owned by Margaret's father Christopher Nugent of Ballina who had got these lands via monies he had lent to Robert Nugent of Carlanstown Co. Westmeath c.1640 which in turn were spent in funding a mortgage of these lands from Lambert, the Earl of Cavan, who was continually trying to get the lands back by claiming that the mortgage had been paid off.[63] (If that sounds convoluted unfortunately it is! As this book has hopefully outlined, land dealings in Ireland are often like this.) This is what leads me to believe that it was this Matthias who took over these old Ballina lands in Cavan and the presence of the first name Thomas, which is so common in the Cormeen/Mountprospect families, makes me think that they were the descendants of this Thomas, the son of Robert of Clonigeragh.

This Major Matthias Nugent was a granduncle of the well known Robert Nugent who you have met before when John Nugent of Enagh sought his assistance in London in 1742.[64] Robert in turn took an interest in these lands, giving various loans to two British army officers of this Clontiduffy family i.e. Major John Nugent (who served in the West Indies) and Lieutenant Michael Nugent (of the 34th Regiment of Foot who wrote a letter to Robert Nugent's son in law the then Lord Lieutenant of Ireland dated 23rd Oct 1789),[65] the sons of Robert Nugent of the same place who was in turn a son of that Major Matthias.[66] Hence in answer to our piece of folklore my guess is that it was this Robert Nugent, who later in practice took over these lands via the loan he gave to his relatives, who effectively shut out the mainline Ballina family from these lands.[67]

All this will hopefully serve to show that the Mountprospect/Cormeen family continue the main Ballina line, so hence we will now describe the line of Mountprospect:

Dominic Nugent of Mountprospect Co. Cavan

– In the letter book kept by John Bayly, working in the treasury in Dublin Castle and moonlighting as a land agent for many landlords including the Grattans, he includes this short notice of a letter he sent on the 22nd Jan 1739 to his brother in law Patrick Nugent of Cormeen:

> "Mr Pat Nugent
> In answer to his nephew Dominick Nugent's letter." [68]

Which, bearing in mind the absence of the first name Dominic among the Nugents of this locality and the proximity of Cormeen to Mountprospect, leads us to assume that this is the relationship between the Cormeen and Mountprospect families.

– In the Quit Rent Office Ledgers preserved in the National Archives in Dublin Dominic is listed as paying the Quit Rent on the Mackin's patentee lands in Barcony.[69] As you will have read in earlier chapters the Quit Rent was a state tax imposed on land transferred during the Cromwellian plantation and for the 18th century it is quite interesting to read these old tax returns to see who was the overall landlord, as it were, of a parcel of land, because they were usually those that paid the Quit Rent.

– Giving their address as Legevogi [an old name for part of Barcony, or near there], the following children of Dominic and Jane Carlton were baptised by the Catholic priest in Castlerahan:

13/4/1756
Joan Nugent, sponsors: Andrew Pallas and Mary Nugent.

18/3/1759
Thomas Nugent, sponsors: Christopher Spinks and Elizabeth Reilly.

25/1/1761
Mary Nugent, sponsors: Mary Nugent and John Flood.

– Dominic died and was buried in 1779 as recorded here in the Freeman's Journal:

> "A few days since a Clergyman of the established church, attended pursuant to notice sent him, by one of the family of the church of Killeagh in the county of Meath, in order to inter the remains of Mr Dominick Nugent, of Prospect in the county of Cavan, a very respectable gentleman, who was a convert to the church of England, had married a protestant of good family, and bred up his children in that faith, the funeral was attended by several respectable persons of the neighbourhood, and a number of popish priests, the procession proceeded to the church yard with great decency, but when the clergyman attempted to officiate, he was in a most outrageous manner assaulted and prevented from doing his duty by a riotous mob, and under an immediate necessity of saving himself by flight – then they forcibly buried the body with all the usual ceremonies of the church of Rome, contrary to the last desire of the deceased, and in opposition to the repeated remonstrances of his children; it is unnecessary to

make any comment upon such violent proceedings." [70]

As you can see the Ballina family was always enmeshed in religious controversy! A few things about this account do not entirely ring true though. Firstly note the entries in the Catholic parish register given above, obviously most of the children seem to have been raised Catholic. Secondly it is worth considering that part where it says "the funeral was attended by ...a number of popish priests". While certainly possible it is nonetheless unlikely that a 'number' of Catholic priests would, during the Penal Laws, attend the funeral of a non Catholic. The chances are he was Catholic and only some member of his family, maybe his son Thomas, wanted to bury him as a Protestant, quite possibly to save any trouble that might arise in land ownership if he was acknowledged as a Catholic at his funeral. He was in turn succeeded by his son Thomas.

Thomas Nugent of Mountprospect Co. Cavan

– June 1767

When John Makeinson and William Spinks were getting a lease of lives from Lord Farnham on this date they specified the lives of William Spinks, the lessee, Thomas Makeinson, the son of John Makeinson, and Thomas Nugent, the eldest son to Dominic Nugent and aged 13 years. This is from the farm accounts held by the Earl of Farnham rather than ROD entries.[71]

– 1st September 1784 his sister Jane married Richard Dempsey of Scalestown Co. Meath.[72]

– 10th Sept 1784, he received a long lease of the lands of Cormeen from Lord Farnham, consisting of 49 acres 1 rood and 12 perches and for a rent of £39 9s 2d. This was for the lives of Thomas himself and William Henry Spinks, aged 5 years, and Thomas Spinks, 4 years old, the first and second sons to Charlton Spinks of Derry in the parish of Denn and County of Cavan. Within three years he had to build a structure 40" long, 16" wide and 10" high, and was not to alien more than 10 acres [i.e. let to under tenants] under penalty of £10 additional rent.⁷³

– In c.1790 he subscribed for a copy of George Parker, *Life's painter of variegated characters* (Dublin, c1790), as listed in that book.

– There was a story told about the Nugent landlords of Mountprospect in the National Schools folklore project of the 1930s including a reference to this Thomas [but unnamed here] who wasn't popular with some but liked enough by those in the environs of his house. He was shot by highwaymen near the entrance to his lane, the Ჟeata bán (i.e. the White Gate), and he buried his horse, the Capall bán, near the spot:

> "Over one hundred years ago the townland of Mountprospect was owned by a man named Nugent. He was very peculiar in his ways but was very popular with his tenants and labourers even though he was a great tyrant. He owned other lands besides those of Mountprospect, but he had not such a good reputation in those districts. The entrance to his residence was called the Ჟeata bán and along the gate were two high walls.
>
> One night as landlord Nugent was returning to his home, after probably inspecting the lands and stock, he was followed by two highwaymen on horseback. Nugent was mounted on his Capall bán, his favourite horse and noted for its speed. As Nugent was nearing the entrance to his residence from the road, a shot from the highwaymen aimed at Nugent struck the horse. Just at that moment Nugent faced his horse for the wall which he cleared. This gained a second or two for his master and took the pursuers by surprise. The horse though maimed galloped madly down the avenue leading to the house, bearing its master to safety. As the hall-door was reached the poor horse fell dead.

Next day Nugent ordered his men to make a grave for the dead horse. This grave was to [be] lined carefully with moss. The horse was buried and over the grave Nugent planted four sycamore trees, one at each corner. The four trees grew and are to be seen to this day close together in the lawn of Mr Nixon, the owner of that part of Mr Nugent's lands. These four trees mark to this day the grave of the Capall bán and the spot is always referred to by that name." [74]

In reading this newspaper account from the *Freeman's Journal* of the 14th March 1820 you can judge just how truthful and accurate Irish 'folklore' actually is (in my opinion its *never* consciously fiction as such):

"Robert Gannon, Michael Gannon, and Patrick Gannon, indicted, for that they, at Baltrasna, in the Co. of Meath, on the 10th of January last, did assault Ann Read, and take from her person, silver tea spoons, 48 ten penny tokens, 3 bankers notes, each for one pound, several broaches, rings and other articles, the property of William Read.

...

[Anne, the wife of William Read] left her own home on that evening and was preparing to go to Athlone; left her house about six or seven o'clock on a jaunting car in company with her two daughters; the car was driven by a neighbour of hers, some men met her on the road near Baltrasna, it was a dark night, saw three men, they called on the driver to stop, that he was the King's Prisoner [probably a ruse to disguise themselves as bailiffs], each of them had a pistol; they made her and her daughters get out of the car [and robbed her.]

...

Thomas Nugent esq examined – This gentleman says he recollects the 10th of January last; on the evening of that day an attempt was made to stop him by four men; they were in front, and opened as if to let him pass; was coming from Oldcastle fair; rode smartly; this was about 5 o'clock, and about 3 miles from where Mrs Read was robbed, the said 4 men met him; one of them, Robert Gannon, the prisoner, seized the reins, and said he was the King's Prisoner; he put spurs to his horse and escaped being robbed; two shots were fired after him when he had got about a perch, one of which entered the horse's ribs; lodged information before Mr Battersby, and identified prisoner in Mullingar gaol.

Cross examined by one of the Gannons – Did you not in Trim gaol refuse to identify me? No, but I said I would do so when necessary; I could not be mistaken in you; you were in my employment.

Questioned by prisoners – Now, sir, was it not in consequence of my threatening to bring an action against you, that you are now prosecuting? No. The witness here explained the conduct of the prisoner and his family while in his employment – they conducted themselves very improperly, lazy and roguish; this the prisoner extracted from him.

...

[The Judge summing up:] but Mrs Read's evidence was strongly supported by the testimony of Mr Nugent. This gentleman has brought the prisoners altogether in number, as described by McCann, within a short distance of where Mrs Read was robbed; he has sworn positively to one of them; the Jury, his Lordship was sure, would consider their verdict, if guilty, they would say so; and if they had a reasonable doubt, they would acquit the prisoner."

After twenty minutes consideration they were found guilty by the jury. Geata bán, the Whitegate, is well known as a placename in the area and used to be a traditional meeting place for Irish travellers who were welcome to stay there, with their horses, for the night.[75] (This seems to be a tradition with this family the idea being, as in often said with some old families, that we were all travellers once, meaning a reference to the era after the Cromwellian confiscations no doubt.⁷⁶) The trees, now three rather than four, are still there immediately behind the modern house at the Whitegate. The prevalence of these 'bán's is a little perplexing, its even the case that a relative of this family (or at least the Cormeen family), Patrick Nugent living in Castlerahan townland c.1910 was known as "Popabán", seemingly the "seed of the white"?

– In one of the most curious of the references from folklore we find that either he, or the Cormeen family, must have harboured the escapee from the famous Betta Manna hangings in Delvin in the 1820s. The story is told here by Hannah Fitzsimons in her authoritative work *The Great Delvin*:

> "Three men, Mumford, Gilligan and Forde were hanged in Glaxtown, in a field called Sorachan, in 1822. The gate leading into the field has ever since been called "Gallows Gate". The story as follows was told by the late John Masterson, of Bracklyn. Mumford was an illegitimate son of a Yeoman captain who had settled in Johnstown, and who had illicit relations with Betty Manny a local woman of notorious character. Mumford, tired of Betty's many demands, refused to give her sufficient corn to sow her garden, when she approached him for this. In revenge she threatened to report Mumford as being a member of a secret society, which he was not. In retaliation Mumford and three other men who were members of the society decided to frighten her out of this course by violently assaulting her. They went to her house and "carded" her. Her anger knew no bounds and she went straight to the police and laid information against the men. Four men, Mumford, Gilligan, Forde and Kelly were arrested but Kelly escaped and avoided further arrest by jumping the river Deel. The other three were brought to Mullingar

jail to await trial. Before this came off, the police sergeant went to the parish priest of the time, in Delvin, telling him if he would write out a good reference for Betty, such as would satisfy an employer, he would get the woman out of the district altogether. Happy at the thought of ridding his parish of this notorious woman, he gladly complied with the sergeant's request and no more was seen or heard of Betty, the police giving the word around that she had left the country. But, when the trial came off, in Mullingar, to everyone's amazement, the police produced Betty as a witness. The Defence protested against the word of so notorious a woman being accepted, but the prosecution produced for the Court the reference of good character which the priest had been tricked into giving. The men were convicted on the strength of Betty Manny's word and were sentenced to be hanged close by their own homes. When the day appointed for the hanging arrived, the unfortunate men were taken to the field. There were both soldiers and police in attendance, but the soldiers refused to do the hanging, whereupon, the police took off their belts and, with these, swung the bodies. Mumford's sister asked for her brother's body, but her request was refused, the three bodies being taken away by the soldiers and buried in Mullingar jail. In the nineteen twenties, while men were turf-cutting on Glaxtown bog, they came across the fairly well-preserved body of a red-haired woman and the bulk of local opinion had it that it was the body of Betty Manny. (Betty had red hair). There was the mark of a fracture on the head and of a stab in the back. John Masterson did not think it was Betty's body. He was of opinion that she had been sent to Barbadoes by the British Government for he knew a man named Reilly, from Glaxtown, who had joined the British

Army, and whose regiment had been drafted there. He (Reilly) said that there was a place at some distance from their camp, where they had to go for rifle practice, and that several times, on his way to the range, he had seen Betty Manny." [77]

A fascinating story I think you will agree but the interesting twist we are focusing on comes from this reference from Mary Anne Callan of Caddagh, Mullingar, in the National Schools folklore project of the 1930s:

"When the police were following him [John Kelly] he jumped across the Deal and it was twenty two feet wide at the place. He escaped and got work with a man named Nugent who lived in Co. Cavan. He used to go to mass to a church named Castlerahan where there was no police to follow him." [78]

The story goes on to say that he was later pardoned on the recommendation of Fetherston. With that description it would have to be either the Cormeen or Mountprospect families that harboured him, which is not a little curious. Castlerahan is really quite some distance from Delvin and there is no connection between this family and the Kellys, as far as I know, so one could speculate that, somewhat romantically!, this family still felt a kind of paternalistic affection for the Nugent home place of Delvin and sought, after a manner, to protect its inhabitants?

– He died in 1840 as reported here in *The Gentleman's Magazine* under 'lately', September 1840:

"At his seat, Mount Prospect, Mount Nugent, Ireland, Thomas Nugent, esq. During a life of nearly 100 years he sustained the character of a high-minded, benevolent, and truly honourable man."

His estate passed to a Dempsey family and from them to Nixons. The Nixons were pushed out by the Land Commission in the 1960s and the old house was then destroyed,[79] meanwhile the Cormeen lands were sold off by that Nugent family in c.1990.

Relevant Registry of Deeds entries

We will now get around to what we promised in the introduction to this chapter, to see what Registry entries we can hope to find which will illuminate this history bearing in mind that this is by no means an exhaustative analysis of these families or a complete record of what is available in the memorials, restrictions obviously necessitated by considerations of time and space. The date that precedes the ROD numbers below is, unless otherwise stated, the date on the deed, not the date of registration, and the text that is written as italics is done to show that it is my interpretation or commentary on the memorial and not information that is in the memorial itself.

Farrenconnell
I am afraid there are just too many entries in the ROD to even give a short account of them here. You can expect any Protestant landlord family – landed that is in the one location for a long period – to be very well represented in these deeds, so well in fact that you could probably trace father to son etc all through the 18th century using ROD entries alone.

Dungimmon
Again there are in fact too many entries related to this family to list here, but a flavour of them include:

1716 19-1-9081
Walter Pollard of Castlepollard Co Westmeath sold, in virtue of a decree from the Court of Exchequer in Ireland, the third part of Dungimmon called Ballyeighter to Thomas Nugent of Portlick Co. Westmeath. Witnesses include Lewis, William, and Tempis Pollard.

registered 1728 60-36-39786
After referring to the above deed from Pollard to Thomas Nugent, Edmund Nugent of Dungimmon demises to the Honourable Robert Napper esquire Major General of His

Majesties forces in Ireland for £800 the lands of Dungimmon as held by him and his father before him. This sale has the proviso that if Edmund or his heirs pays back Napper before 1729 the £800 plus interest at £7 per annum then the land will revert back to the Nugents.

That last reference is what you would call a clause of redemption and is quite common, the old landed families were very reluctant to part completely from their old lands and dreamed of being able to pay back these debts at some point in the future. Otherwise it could be some legal trickery to disguise Edmond's continuing ownership of the lands.

1735 78-353-56437

Edmond Nugent of Dungimmon, and Frances his wife, "with the consent of Naper" leases to Benjamin Barrington of Dublin esquire 172 acres in Dungimmon and Ballyeighter. The witnesses include George Reynolds of Loughscur Co. Limerick [sic] esquire.

Actually this is in Co. Leitrim and George was a son of Anne Nugent, a sister of Edmond's wife Frances of the Carlanstown family. It is reported that this George was the main inspiration for O'Carolan to begin putting words to his music, starting with a song on the local dispute of the fairies of the two hills Sheemore and Sheebeg, that George described to him.

In 1786 George's son, George Nugent Reynolds, was murdered by a lawyer called Robert Keon and his son in turn, again George Nugent Reynolds, became a well known poet and songwriter. The circumstances of the murder are described here:

> "These two gentlemen went out to fight a duel; and when Mr. Reynolds, previously to coming to action, was in the act of saluting Mr. Keon, with his hat in his hand, wishing him a good morning, the latter fired his pistol, and shot him through the head. Upon this Mr. Plunkett, Mr. Reynolds's second, called out, "A horrid murder!" On which Mr. Keon's brother replied, "If you don't like it, take that," and snapped his pistol at Mr. Plunket, which luckily did not go off. The jury found Mr.

Keon "guilty" in November last; but his counsel moved an arrest of judgment, and pleaded several errors in the different proceedings, to stop the sentence. The Court, after the most solemn arguments, over-ruled all the objections, and passed sentence of death upon him, according to the verdict, and he was executed on the sixteenth of the following month." [80]

1737 147-499-101145
William Naper of the City of Dublin esquire demised to Edmond Nugent of Dungimmon that part of Dungimmon, containing 72 acres 2 roods, situated on the South West side of the road leading through the said lands of Dungimmon from Oldcastle to Daly's Bridge, for 31 years and the lives of Christopher, William and Robert Dardis, sons of Michael Dardis of Higginstown Co. Westmeath. The rent is £30 sterling per annum.

registered 1793 457-386-300842
Parties:
Andrew Palles of Ballykinave Co, Mayo esquire;
James Campbell of Castletown Co. Westmeath esquire;
Alicia Nugent of the City of Dublin spinster.
The memorial recites that Naper made Nugent a party to a deed and she with those rights demised to Palles and Campbell the lands of Dungimmon containing 170 and a half acres 'for a life long sum'.

Meaning presumably an annual sum for the rest of her life. Again, adding to the earlier deed, it seems likely that at some stage Naper was acting as a type of trustee for this family. However another possibility is that the Napers come into it via the marriage of Anna Maria Naper and Dillon Pollard Hampson of Castlepollard.[81]

Enagh
Although not completely certain nonetheless it seems that it is this family that are consistently recorded as being of Johnstown

Co. Westmeath in the ROD entries, as they are in some of the documents from Farrenconnell House calendared by Joe Ainsworth in the 1950s.[82]

1773 294-638-196026

The grantor is John Nugent of Johnstown Co. Westmeath, the grantee is Aungier Brock of Batstown Co. Westmeath and the witnesses include Garret Nugent also of Johnstown.

1781 343-89-229697

Thomas Nugent of Johnstown Co. Westmeath is leasing to John Nugent of the island of St. Croix in the West Indies lands including:
Johnstown, which it seems Thomas holds partly from an old lease involving Lewis Montford,
Culvin Co. Westmeath, via a lease from Anthony Nugent and Alice McAuley [?],
Mullagheray Co. Westmeath, via a lease from the Earl of Westmeath,
witnessed by John Wilson of Dublin and Andrew Nugent esq of Glenidan Co. Westmeath.

1783 355-66-237716

The grantor is Catherine Nugent of Johnstown Co. Westmeath, widow of John Nugent who in the 14th year of King George II received land in Roscommon via a court judgment against Hugh O'Donnell, late of Newport Co. Mayo, and Henry McDermott late of Greyfield Co. Roscommon, both deceased. His lands in Roscommon fell to Garret Nugent deceased and are now held by his widow who is leasing it to George Jennings of Dublin. Francis Nugent of Johnstown is a witness.

1786 384-159-254392

John Nugent of Johnstown leasing Johnstown, Mullaghere and the demesne and lands of Culvin Co. Westmeath to John Shiel of the same place.
This date could be an error because John seems to have been dead by 1786?

1786 466-532-298958

Thomas Nugent of Johnstown Co. Westmeath leasing to Cornelius O'Brien of Prospect Co. Tipperary five acres in the "Bog of Carney Brack next to the Castle division at Carney" in the Barony of Lower Ormond in Co. Tipperary. There is a 'consideration therein mentioned' in the deed but not in this memorial and the rent is for one peppercorn every year for 99 years.

Obviously then it is really an outright sale of the land and for a price that we don't know without seeing the deed.

1787 505-125-324198

Thomas and his wife Anne of Johnstown leasing the farm that had been held by John Waters, 25 acres, to David Cambie of Castletown Co. Tipperary.

1791 441-149-284037

Thomas Nugent of Johnstown Co. Westmeath, and Anne Nugent née Gamble his wife, are leasing land called Camey in the Barony of Lower Ormond Co. Tipperary to General Manus O'Donnell of N[unclear word] Castle Co. Mayo.

Gneeve

1727 77-433-54264 (and registered 1734)

Walter Burton of Dublin is leasing land in Lismacanigan and Barcony to James Nugent of Gneeve, land previously held by James and his father John. Witnesses include Christopher Reilly of Ballynea Co. Meath.

1734: 80-175-55401, 2, and 3

These three deeds have a grantor John Hart of Cunlin Co. Cavan and a grantee James Nugent of Gneeve Co. Cavan. Also the witnesses to the three deeds are John Sterling of Dublin and William Legard of Dublin. The lands leased are Rathclaughy Hart, Clontiduffy Hart, and Gneeve and Farrenconnell, respectively. The 57 acres leased in Rathclaughy Hart are bounded on the west by the high road leading from Oldcastle Co.

Meath to Garrirobuck Co. Cavan, on the east by Dungimmon, on the south by Rathclaughy Nugent, and on the north by Garrirobuck.

1746 130-33-87601

Elinor Nugent, the daughter of James Nugent of Gneeve Co. Cavan, is set to marry Patrick the son of Bryan Daly of Millcastle Co. Westmeath. Bryan will settle £600 on his son consisting of an old bond of £302, plus the interest, due on Mr Pollard, and Bryan's lease of Corballies, leased from Walter Nugent, which joins Ballycomoyle and Luke Daly's holding. James undertook to give £100 to his daughter. The witnesses include John Nugent of Gneeve.

On the face of it it looks like John Nugent had to put up less money into this marriage than Bryan Daly which is surprising obviously because the father of the bride would be expected to pay somewhat more. However it may be that John's money was ready cash and that the bonds from Pollard could be considered difficult to call in. (This however is just guesswork because where it states an exact cash figure in these deeds it doesn't necessarily follow that it was actually cash, maybe John Nugent will also be giving leases and bonds instead of real cash to his daughter.)

1750 141-528-98209

Thomas Hart of London leased to James Nugent of Gneeve the lands of Clontiduffy Hart formerly in the possession of Robert Nugent gent. Also lands in Gneeve, Farrenconnell and Rathclaughy in as ample a manner as the said James Nugent or his undertenants then held it. Witnesses include John Nugent of Gneeve.

The aforementioned Robert Nugent must be the son of Major Matthias Nugent of Clontiduffy, but originally from Carlanstown Co. Westmeath, a granduncle of Earl Nugent.

1751 140-275-94675

William Naper of Dublin and Thomas Nugent of Gneeve let that part of Dungimmon on the North side of the road leading from Oldcastle to Daly's Bridge [Mountnugent] which had been late in the possession of John Nugent, brother of the said Thomas, containing 97 acres 1 rood and 26 perch, for 31 years commencing the 29th of September last and at a rent of £40 sterling per annum.

Note that terminology: 31 years commencing 29th of September last. It seems that this very common phrase in the ROD might have its origin in the way Catholics dealt with the Penal Laws. Under those laws no Catholic could get a lease for that length or longer but under this wording the actual length of the lease is just short of the 31 years, because it is backdated as you can see.[85]

1756 193-131-137249

A revision to the marriage settlement of a marriage which has already taken place. Matthias Nugent of Crossdrum Co. Meath married on the 22nd of December 1755 Lucy Cooke the daughter of Easter Cooke and her late husband James Cooke a woollen draper of Dublin. Easter, who is "otherwise Walsh otherwise Reilly", is an executrix of her husband alongwith Garret Reilly of Rathaltan Co. Wicklow. As was mentioned earlier in this book her son Ambrose was sickly and as a result the amount she agreed to pay as dowry has changed.

Its a curious fact that only a few years after this date an old chalice was found beside the skeleton of a priest inside a cave in that same townland of Crossdrum. It is remarkable because the description on the chalice, which is dated 1635, mentions a Stephen Cooke.[86]

1783 343-518-237892

James Nugent leasing to his brother John of Dublin the lands of Hilltown Co. Westmeath. These lands were demised by George Paul Monck to Thomas Church of Dublin but

> "the said lease was taken in trust of Matthias Nugent formerly of Mount Eagl [sic] in Co. Meath, gentleman deceased, by which said deed James Nugent, one of the sons of said Matthias, did for £50 transfer to John Nugent of Dublin City, one other son of said Matthias,"

all his interest in the land.

Presumably Church was holding these lands for Matthias Nugent to get around the Penal Laws which had been relaxed somewhat by 1783.

1784 376-255-250686
John Nugent of Dublin leasing to James Allen of Gneeve 22 acres 1 rood and 25 perch in Hilltown Co. Westmeath, as formerly held by Owen Sheridan farmer, for 11 years from the 1st of November next "provided the interest of the said John Nugent therein shall so long continue," for 9 shillings per annum per acre. In an endorsement on the back of that lease dated 23rd Feb 1785 John agreed to abate the rent by 3 shillings 9 pence per acre. Witnesses include James Bartly of Ballencree Co. Meath, school master, and Thomas Allen the son of the said James Allen.

This deed was registered in 1786 which accounts for the memorial being able to register the endorsement as well as the deed itself. Writing on the back of deeds like this was quite common, it was convenient just to write on the back and get both parties to sign it because it saved the expense of more parchment. These two parties are no doubt close relatives which probably accounts for John's generosity!

Mountprospect
1736 87-92-60717
John Maxwell of Dublin [from the Farnham family] is leasing away, "for ever" for £180, to Boleyn Whitney of Dublin his interest in the third or retrenched part of Legawoge (part of Barcony), lands which he purchased from Lord Massereene, the said lands currently held by Dominic Nugent at £8 a year rent.

It looks like Whitney is operating here as a trustee, and possibly a fake Protestant owner, on behalf of Dominic Nugent. Boleyn Whitney (1686-1758), 'a councellor at Law' (see 1719 24-451-14325 and 1724 41-378-26395) from Newpass Co. Westmeath was related to the Bayly family from Kilnacrott and friendly with John Bayly in Dublin (Boleyn's son, George Boleyn Whitney, married John Bayly's daughter Elizabeth) who in turn was a brother-in-law of Patrick Nugent of Cormeen. Boleyn

Whitney and Andrew Wilson of Piercefield Co. Westmeath had earlier traded in the Lismacanigan and Legavoge lands in 1719, see 24-451-14335.

1788 387-312-261508

Thomas Nugent of Mountprospect (who sealed the document) gave over to Jane Nugent [his mother, née Charlton] of the same, widow, his "household stuff, implements of husbandry, furniture and stock". Witnessed by:

James Farquhar, Dublin

George Bell, Dublin, clerk to Farquhar,

Catherine Nugent of Mountprospect, spinster, witnessed the memorial only.

Notice how Catherine went to Dublin to swear to this memorial, unfortunately my guess is that her brother Thomas was stuck for money and needed to get this signed over quickly. But what's interesting about this are those two witnesses Bell and Catherine Nugent. It turns out that Catherine Nugent (who died 11th December 1824 and was certainly of the Mountprospect family) married George Bell of Bellevue, near Enniskillen Co. Fermanagh around this time so you'd wonder if romance blossomed as she related her sad tale to Farquhar's clerk! Their son Henry Nugent Bell became a famous genealogist.

1794 475-574-307955

Jane Nugent of Prospect, widow, and her son Thomas of Prospect Co. Cavan, are leasing their interests in the lands of Legawouge and its subdenominations to Thomas Kinsley, a druggist of Dublin, for 31 years or until they can redeem a certain debt.

These lands were leased on the 2nd Dec 1765 by George Boleyn Whitney to Dominic Nugent for 31 years or three lives at £5 sterling per annum. But as part of this lease the Nugents were under the obligation of an equity of redemption relating to it. There was a judgement against Thomas Nugent in the Court of Exchequer for £600 owed to Kinsley in 1785 and at that time Thomas received money from his mother to pay off the debt. It seems then that this lease can be ended if they pay off that lump sum to Kinsley now, otherwise it will run for the 31 years. The witnesses include James Farquhar of Dublin.

If that seems a little confusing its because the memorial wasn't completely clear but nonetheless it certainly clarifies the earlier memorial. The right of redemption is where, for example, a person who contracts a mortgage has the right to get the lands back if they pay back in full the original debt.

1805 (and registered 1810) 579-94-388726

Thomas Nugent of Mountprospect gave a rent charge of £34 to Mrs Mary Squire of Clontarf Co. Dublin, charged on the lands of Cormeen as held by the under tenants of Nugent namely Bernard MacManus, Thomas Dolan, James Heery and Nicholas Cunningham, in return for £325, payable in the City of Dublin in four quarterly payments starting on the first day of December next.

Probably this MacManus lived in Cormeen cottage which was bought – back? – by the Nugents of Cormeen from the MacManuses. By tradition we are told one of whom was a doctor, or at least a dentist, after the Famine. One of these MacManuses living in that house gave a submission to the Devon Commission which made extensive enquiries into pre Famine Ireland.

The Squire family, the first of whom was a lawyer, had acquired a very long lease of the lands of Garryross, which adjoins Cormeen, from the Grattan family and held it as such throughout most of the 18th century.[87]

This deed is probably an example of an investor giving money up front in return for a steady annual income, just like a modern person would invest in bonds.

1805 576-56-384866
Parties:
1) Thomas Laracy of Killnacrott Co. Cavan farmer
2) Thomas Nugent of Mountprospect in said County esquire.

Mentions a lease of the 1st of August 1802 made between Charles Morton, then of Drumrora Lodge Co. Cavan, and Laracy whereby Morton had leased to him lands including Kilnacrott for 21 years or the life of Laracy, whichever was longer, for £32 per annum. The unexpired part of this lease is now given by Laracy to Nugent and is witnessed by:

James O'Neill, City of Dublin attorney at law

James Nugent of Mountprospect yeoman.

The Laracy family, in this case from Athboy but it is a very rare surname, were related to the Nugents of Cormeen in the 20th century, probably building on this earlier link.

1817 715-933-489468

Parties:

1) Thomas Nugent of Mountprospect

2) James Nugent and Robert Nugent late of Mountprospect.

Thomas lets to the above two persons his lands in Mountprospect, Lismacanigan, and Barcony, 120 acres or thereabouts, with the crop of grain and potatoes sewn thereon, with the old dwelling house of Mountprospect and the use of a stable, for three years at a rent of £300 sterling a year. Thomas specifies that the land cannot be broken up – i.e. tilled – save what is now in tillage and if they do they have to pay him £10 per annum per acre so tilled. He reserved to himself the new dwelling house of Mountprospect and the use of a stable and also annexed a list of farm goods and implements and furniture in the old house that was to be given to James and Robert (which is not in the memorial). Witnessed by Edward Lynch and Michael Reilly.

This obviously gives us an approximate date for the house of Mountprospect and confirms that at least one of the outlying buildings is older than it.

1820 750-439-51374

Parties:

1) Thomas Nugent of Mountprospect of the first part and

2) George Bell of Belview in the Co. of Fermanagh of the second part,

3) Thomas Smyth, a merchant in Kells Co. Meath.

With the consent of George Bell, Nugent leased to Smyth his lands in Legawouge, Cormeen, Barcony, and that part of the lands of Lismacanigan late in the possession of Robert and James Nugent.

When it says "with the consent of" it obviously means that Bell has some interest in the lands which requires his consent for this transaction, possibly he was a trustee in some marriage settlement or long lease holder or whatever. Clearly the Bells are now involved because of the aforementioned marriage but its interesting also to see again references to James and Robert Nugent because actually when Thomas died he left the lands to the family his sister had married into, it seems he had no male heirs? Its also a little curious that he doesn't state the exact relationship they are to him here, or in the previous memorial. While no doubt scandalous thoughts on this might have occurred to some! my guess is that they might have later emigrated to America, and on that I notice this in the Anglo-Celt of the 17th July 1909:

> "Edward J Nugent and his nephew Edward J Callan of Fulton Ave, Mount Vernon in the US stayed in Mountprospect Co Cavan for a few months to see the old country where their ancestors were from."

In the list of lands you can see how Cormeen seems to be a traditional part of this estate. Another document that confirms that is this notice of a sale of lease of lands from the Freeman's Journal 18th July 1807:

> "To be Let, from the 1st day of August, or 29th day of September next, for the Term of Seven Years, the House and Demesne of Mountprospect, containing about 80 acres, part of Barcony, containing about 20 acres, part of Lismacanigan, containing about 12 acres; all ad-joining the Demesne. – And also part of Coorneen, containing about 40 acre; the Tenant can be accommodated with Meadow, Oats, Turf, and Potatoes, at a Valuation.
>
> Mountprospect is situated in a Sporting Country, near Loughsheelin, within five miles of Oldcastle, a good Market and Post Town – Proposals will be received by John Tatlow, esq, Crover; Hugh Brady, esq, Oldcastle; and Mr

Christopher Spinks, Mount-Nugent."

Note in that the very strange spelling of 'Coorneen' for Cormeen which phonetically matches somewhat the name in the 1609 map: Coruine. My guess is that this list was compiled from the old documents in the possession of the family among which there was presumably an old deed using a very old name for the townland, which would show again that Cormeen was a very old part of the estate.

1819 750-439-510375

The first two parties are the same as above and there is also Hugh Brady of Oldcastle listed, and Michael Reilly of Mountprospect witnessed it. This refers to an insurance policy of 1819 taken out with the Atlas Assurance Company of London.

Cormeen

Its a curious fact that although we know from other sources that this family were in Cormeen almost for the duration of the existence of the ROD they are not it seems mentioned there before c.1900, except for the Mountprospect reference mentioned above. Nonetheless it transpires that the ROD entries are critical for understanding this family. We will consider here three ROD entries and one will abstract, from the Betham abstracts of Prerogative Wills of Ireland preserved in the National Archives in Dublin:

1722 44-126-27946

James Lowan of Cavan town, carpenter, of the one part and Thomas Bayly of Killnacrott Co. Cavan of the other. A marriage settlement on the soon to be solemnised marriage of Lowan with Elizabeth Connelly, a niece of Bayly's, and refers to a lease of Killnevara [on the outskirts of Cavan town] and to a house in the town.

Witnesses:
Thomas Bayly jnr, son of said Thomas Bayly
Patrick Lynchy of Derilahan, County Cavan
Witness to the memorial only:
Patrick Newgent, Lissmecanican, gentleman.[88]

1725 68-502-49272

Thomas Bayly junior of Cornhill Co. Cavan, and referring to lands in the parish of Drung and Barony of Tullygarvey Co. Cavan in a memorial which mentions Thomas Bayly senior [his father but neither relationship nor address stated here].

Witnessed by:

James Nugent and Patrick Nugent of Co. Cavan gents,

Memorial witnessed by Patrick Nugent and John Hankinson

1726 51-200-33361

registered 1726

This memorial has already being described at length in chapter 5 but suffice to say that it involves a lease of lands that the Cooke family passed to Thomas Bayly of Kilnecrott and is witnessed by:

Robert Fleming of Kilnecrott,

Patrick Nugent of Cunlin Co. Cavan gent (who also witnessed the memorial),

Michael Reilly of Oldcastle Co. Meath,

And witnessing only the memorial was Henry Buckley of Dublin, Public Notary.

Betham's will abstract of:

Thomas Bayly of Kilnecrott in Co. Cavan esq dated third of November 1731 and proved 12th of September 1733.

wife Cecily

eldest son (by first wife) John Bayly

youngest son Fleming Bayly

Thomas Fleming of Bellville in Co. Cavan esq [mentioned in the will]

2nd son Thomas Bayly

daughter Sarah wife of Patrick Nugent of Cormeen in Co. Cavan, gent.

granddaughter Mary Nugent.

From that last reference it is obvious that the Patrick Nugent who witnesses the earlier ROD memorials is the son-in-law of the Thomas Bayly senior who is mentioned in each of these memorials. We can naturally assume it would be the Patrick Nugent of Cormeen who is his son-in-law rather than any other Patrick Nugent. This then gives us a fascinating glimpse of a person who seems to move across these different townlands in the South East corner of Cavan: in 1722 he is Lismacanigan, in 1725 alongwith a James Nugent – maybe his brother, the father of his nephew Dominic? – he is just described as of Co. Cavan, in 1726 he is on the shores of Lough Sheelin at Cunlin, and by 1731 he has settled in Cormeen. What is really fascinating here is that those two townlands of Lismacanigan and Cunlin are the ancient property of James Nugent of Lismacanigan, the son of Christopher of Ballina, that is mentioned above and listed as such by him in his deed of 1638.[89] So you can actually see him hanging on to the edges of the old family property, maybe carving out a living as a trader or shopkeeper while he no doubt curses the Cromwellian planters on his old estates? (Notice how he seems to go to Dublin to register the memorials, going by the fact that he is selected to witness them as opposed to just the deeds, which may indicate a person who shops in Dublin for wholesale goods that are then sold when he is back in Cavan? The main branch of the Cormeen family later had a shop for which they imported goods from Drogheda.) In any case the ROD entries have proven critical in establishing here a relationship between the old Ballina/Lismacanigan family and that of Cormeen.

So you can hopefully see from the above how the Registry of Deeds entries, if combined with a little bit of detective work and using other sources to compliment it, can be a very exciting addition to the Irish historian of the 18th century. It is true though that some references are very cryptic, for example it would be nice to read the actual documents relating to the insurance policy listed above under Mountprospect because the memorial does not really tell us what it is about, but nonetheless you can learn a lot especially if you are acquainted with the pattern of the entries in the ROD and in 18th century Irish deeds in general. The trick is also to wait until your other research is done because its only when you are well acquainted with the various lands and family relationships that you can really understand the deeds properly and harness their full value.

Footnotes
1. Transcribed by G V du Noyer, *On Early Irish and Pre-Norman Antiquities*, no.98, in JRSAI vol 9 (1864-66), p.423-444. Incidentally a not very helpful, somewhat corrupt, account of this Ballina family was given in the first edition of Lodge's Peerage from which we get this pedigree in Francis Nichols, *The Irish Compendium or Rudiments of Honour* (London, 1756):

Matthias Nugent, brother of Edmund MP for Mullingar in 1689 (his son and heir was Robert, and Robert's nephew, a son of his brother Michael, was Robert Nugent Viscount Clare etc), was a son of Robert Nugent of Carlanstown, who was active in 1641, and his mother was a daughter of Kedagh Geoghegan of Syonan in Co Westmeath. He was a captain in King James' army and married Catherine, daughter of Robert Nugent of Clonigerah, the second brother of James Nugent of Ballynea, and had Robert his heir who married Elizabeth Barnewall of Creve in Co. Longford. (p.42)

This is the text of the pedigree given on p.47 which is at least in some respects inaccurate:
"James, son of Oliver of Ballinea, by the daughter of Lord Dunsany, married Anne, daughter of James Nugent of Ross, esq; and had issue by her Oliver, Robert of Clonigerah, and Thomas; Thomas, married ___ daughter of ___ and had issue, Garret, who married Maud, daughter of Gerald Faye of Trumere, esq; and had issue by her Christopher, who married Anne, daughter of Mr Geshill, who had issue by her John, Thomas and Michael; John married Catherine, daughter of Colonel Magnus O'Donnell of the County of Mayo; Robert, who settled at Clonigerah, married Helen, daughter of William Nugent of Bracklyn, esq; and had issue by her Thomas, who died without issue, and Catherine, married to Matthias Nugent of Clontiduffy esq; second son of Robert Nugent of Carlanstown, esq; Oliver, the eldest son of James of Ballinea, married Mary, daughter of John Reilly, esq; of Shesiagh in the County of Leitrim, and had issue by her James, who married Alison, daughter of Nicholas Nugent of Enagh esq; by whom he had John, who died in France without issue."

It's hard to know at what date this family severed all connections with Bellaney but maybe this reference is the last to refer to a Nugent "of" Bellaney:
"Mr Nugent of Bellanae will supply this branch."
(NLI Ms.122, previously Phillips Ms 15216, "Lindsay Papers", p.14, possible date for the original behind this document provided by the statement in it on the Dysert pedigree referring to Andrew Nugent: "who now enjoys the estate". That Andrew was the father of Lavallin who was born in 1722. Incidentally this document, on p.12, says that Robert, the son of Major Matthias Nugent of

Carlanstown, was married to Elizabeth Barnewall.)

This family are obviously then a branch off the Barons of Delvin who have a long history starting with the Counts of Perche in France. They also were on occasion Lord Deputies of Ireland, famously so in 1528.

In that year the then Baron of Delvin was Lord Deputy and suffered the indignity of being kidnapped by O'Connor of Offaly, one of the largest Irish lords at that time, because he refused to pay to him the almost blackmail money that he normally got called the cíor ḋuḃ. This was quite a moment in Irish history because it was the apogee of Gaelic power as they fought back against the Normans in the long centuries during which the Black Death, the Hundred Years War, and the Wars of the Roses had weakened the colony. After that it was again downhill all the way until Cromwell some 100 years later finally destroys all power in the native Irish.

But in 1528 all that was in the future and instead we find this Gaelic Lord almost holding the whole state to ransom as you can read here in the account that Walter Wellesley, the Prior of Connell, writes back to the Council in Dublin after parlaying with O'Connor. His account was in Latin which was later translated here by Richard Nugent the historian:

"In receipt of your most reverend lordships letters I immediately went to the Lord O'Connor, whom I found in the confines of his patrimonial estate. And I have presented these letters (of the Council) and explained the tenor to him word by word.

To which he replied that very often he offered peace, and his homage to the Lord Baron, and he sought him by every means in his power, not to compel him, through the retaining or withdrawing the Royal grant, which was wont to be given to him and his predecessors, or to give him occasion to make a league or confederacy with the Irish powers, from whom he kept himself aloof, through love for the English of this land.

But the Baron not only refusing peace and homage of this kind, but also retaining the grant for himself, brought forward many reproaches and much abuse against the same O'Connor. And amongst other things what he hardly endures, that a squire whom he had sent to Dublin in his embassy the same Baron arrested, and only sent him to his master after some persuasion of the Lords (of the Council).

And on the day of this parley he offered (to place) all his hostages in the hands of Thomas, son of the Earl of Kildare, for all complaints and demands of the Lord Baron, and the Baron declined any such offers (inducias aliquas) as O'Connor himself asserts. And refused to make any truce, which further throws all the blame of any calamity which may happen, and of those things which may follow from it, upon the Baron, saying that he was compelling him to make and strengthen a league and a party with O'Carroll and several other Irish, without whose advice he neither could nor would make peace or truce.

And so asking him (O'Connor) to make peace he finally answered, and this is what he desires, viz.: that the Royal grant should be paid to him in ready money, at the times fixed for the payment, and that the payment should not be delayed owing to the fault of any of his (O'Connor's) servants, except he himself had committed the same, and if any of his servants shall be convicted, or shall have confessed any wrong, by taking anything belonging to the Lord the King, he should compel him to restore it, or make amends for it.

He desires it also to be settled that whenever anyone in Offaly had discontinued the tribute (called Black rent) and had ceased from its payment either for a short or long time, he be released from the rest (for the future?) without any condition whatever, even by change of time.

And when I asked him to fix a time with a truce, within which your most Reverend Lordships might summon a Council, and deliberate upon this matter, he refused a truce (saying) that it was of no advantage to supplicate one who is powerful, unless the supplicant be more powerful, or equally powerful. He considers that the English territory (the Pale) was so destitute of defenders, that whenever he should approach with his army, he will have no resistance. So as quickly as it can be done the King's Majesty is to be consulted, without the protection of whose defence he says that our ruin cannot be repaired. And in the mean time measures should be taken ability [?] and with all strength.

I conversed with him about the Churches and their (cemeteries) in case that war should be waged. He said he wished that the Churches and their cemeteries should enjoy full immunity, if he had security that the deputy coming (into his country) should not invade his Churches.

The man was so elated at the success of what he had done that it is to be feared he will hand over the border towns of Athboy and Mullingar, and also Trim, to the flames. He intends, if he can, unless God shall hinder it, to reduce us to so great ruin, that for a long time we shall not be able to recover ourselves.

I took with me the Lord Abbot of Clonard, who willingly accepted the labour for the common good, and he is witness of this thing.

From Ballibogan, 15th May, anno, 1528,
Your humble Orator Brother
Lord Prior of Connell

Addressed to the Most Reverend Father in Christ and Lord, the Lord Hugh, Archbishop of Dublin, Primate of Ireland, and Lord Chancellor, give these."

(PRONI D3835/A/6/481-4.)

2. PRONI D3835/A/6/123-121, as regards the Russian officer the historian says his source was a: "verbal note communicated to me by C.E.J. Nugent and taken down at the time."

3. PRONI D3835/D/3/1/85, referring to the Daily Express 8th of June 1884 and The Times 4th June 1884.

4. PRONI D3835/D/3/1/76.

5. PRONI D3835/D/2/4/3 p.465, 466 and 486.

6. PRONI D3835/D/3/1/5.

7. PRONI D3835/D/3/1/439, the card was based on an account of Richard Nugent in "The Record" and "The English Churchman".

8. Pádraig de Brún, *Scriptural Instruction in the Vernacular: The Irish Society and Its Teachers* (Dublin, 2009), p.95.

9. PRONI D3835/B/4/2/7. Going by the end of it it seems that Oliver Nugent of Farrenconnell wrote this himself, he was well acquainted with the procedure because he had great difficulty holding on to his lands in the teeth of the opposition of Lord Lambert, the Earl of Cavan, and also he worked as a land surveyor. Oliver was a grandson of Oliver Nugent of Rahiver Co. Cavan, who in turn was a grandson of Oliver Nugent of Ballina through his son William, and the Nicholas and Robert mentioned are his uncle, of Enagh, and his father Robert.

The idea of mixing in lands with another person to save the cost of a seperate patent was not that uncommon it seems, going by this letter sent c.1675-85 by Thomas Nugent esq of Clonlost Co. Westmeath to Sir Thomas Nugent of Moyrath Co. Meath and Taghmon Co. Westmeath:
"I have received yours wherein you give me an account that you find by your grandfather's settlement, and your father's, that he has settled Bolecalroe with other lands in the Barony of Clonlonan upon your father. Your desire is to know how come I by it, the state of it is thus:

My father had eleven hundred acres of land which he had purchased before the Court of Claims, which he lost at the said Court. Then your grandfather having several other deficiencies, my father entrusted him to put his in along with his own, and pass patent, for what he could recover. Your grandfather put in for a great many acres, but according to what he recovered, of what my father's proportion, came to Bolecalroe, which was a great deal short of what my father expected. Immediately after your grandfather had passed patent, he made the same lands Bolecalroe over by deed which I am sure is prior to your deed of settlement and I know 'tis a mistake in having Bolecalroe in your settlement.

Soon after the death of your father, your mother sent to me to know what title I had to that land, I then produced my deed to her counsel, who gave his opinion that she had no right thereto. Any further satisfaction in the assurance of this that you are pleased to desire of me I am ready to produce unto you upon demand, which is all from Sir
Your humble servant etc."
(PRONI D2620/2 photocopy.)

10. PRONI D3835/A/1/7.

11. PRONI D3835/A/6/153.

12. PRONI D3835/D/1/3/2.
You can see the way that this family operated almost more like a clan than a normal family by seeing how this Robert Nugent of Streamstown enlists the help of the Baron of Delvin to recover monies owed to him for cattle, this is from a letter by the Baron of the 25th July 1746 from Clonin to his niece living in Portaferry Co. Down:
"One Thomas Ray an Innkeeper at Dungannon, bought last November seventy cows from Mr Robert Nugent of Streamstown, for which he trusted him for a great part of the price; of which he is still in debt to him £77-18s-8d. Mr Nugent sent very often for the money; and Ray constantly promised to pay in a very little time; but never does. Mr Nugent though the money is so long due is unwilling to go to law and would endeavour to get it by fair means; and thinks that if Mr Charles Ecklin, who I take to be his landlord, or Mr Knox, would write to Ray to do Mr Nugent justice that he would pay him. I must therefore desire the favour of you to speak to Mr Ecklin and Mr Knox to endeavour to get such letters; and enclose them to me, and Mr Nugent will immediately send a man with them to Dungannon. If you see Charles Ecklin you may tell him 'tis a favour I beg of him. My humble service to Mr Savage and believe me with the greatest love and esteem
Dear Niece
Your most affectionate uncle,
and obedient servant,
Delvin.
The man's name is spelt Rea. My Lord Westmeath, and Mr Nugent, who is here give you and Mr Savage their humble service, and Mrs and Mr Reilly are both very well."
(PRONI D552/A/2/6/10)

This is the paper deed, dated 21st Sept 1710, in which he received Johnston:

parties:

James Nugent of Newbridge [Clonlost] Co. Westmeath,
Robert Nugent of Enagh Co. Cavan

James let to Robert, Johnston in the parish of Killulagh and Barony of Delvin for 21 years...the rent changes with respect to if or not the war continues i.e. that between Queen Anne and her allies against France and Spain.

rent:
£45 @ and after the war £50

witnessed by:
Tom Reyly
John Lorkan
Walter Nugent

sealed by:
Robert Nugent, a cockatrice without bars or ermine.
(PRONI D2620/1 pt B.)

Much later in 1832 a James Nugent of Streamstown, but writing from 138 Dorset Street Upper, was sued for debt by Andrew Nugent, I assume of Dysert, and James became an insolvent debtor (PRONI D552/A/7/1/17-18.)

Here are two Betham abstracts of wills on what I take to be this family:
"John Nugent of Johnstown Co. Westmeath gent,
dated 9th Oct 1773 and proved 23rd Dec 1774,
wife Catherine Nugent otherwise O'Donnell,
daus Anne and Elizabeth,
sons Garret, Thomas and John,
nephew John McEvoy,
nephew in law Edmund Armstrong of Clara, Kings Co. esq."
and
"Catherine Nugent of Johnstown Co. Meath [sic but obviously a mistake] widow,
dated 16th April 1790 and proved 18th Dec 1790,
husband John Nugent of said place gent,
dau Elizabeth,
dau Anne McKiernan, John eldest son of same,
son Garrett,
Margaret Nugent, natural daughter of said son Garrett,
son Thomas."
(Betham Abstracts of Prerogative Wills, vol.53, no.3 and 266.)

13. I regret I do not have to hand the PRONI reference number for this letter.

14. PRONI D3835/D/1/4/1, also see *Analecta Hibernica* no.20, p.189.

15. PRONI D3835/D/1/3/4. Another letter touching on some military details is D3835 ADD.

16. *Munimenta Nugentiourum* No.18 and 22, NLI M/F Pos 6849.

17. 9/5/1642, TCD Cavan depositions, MS 833, fols 127r et seq.

18. Incidentally following on from a pedigree of the Nugents by William Skey of the mid 19th century (NLI M/F Pos 6849) it seems that this James, the son of Oliver and Honora Reilly, was married to Alison, a daughter of Nicholas Nugent of Enagh, and had a son John who is said to have died in France without issue in 1738, at which we are told that "the direct line of the Ballina family was extinguished and the residue of his property, after paying his debts, was left to his kinsman Robert Nugent of Farrenconnell". Possibly also, going by some ROD entries, he had a brother John who in turn had a son James?

Here is a relevant Betham will abstract:
"Matthias Nugent,
dated 7th Aug 1769 and proved 13th Jan 1770,
wife Lucy,
youngest daughter Rose,
youngest sons Matthias and Thomas,
eldest sons James and John,
niece Mary Allen."
(p.98, no.240.)

These are the Gravestones at Killeagh, Co. Meath, near the Mountprospect table tomb:
"This small token of esteem was erected by M.... Also of Mount Nugent to perpetuate the memory of his grandfather Mr James Nugent of Greeve who departed this life April the 22nd 1759 aged 82.
Also his grandmother Mary Nugent who departed this life Feb 7th 1753 Aged 59 years, his uncle John Thomas Nugent who..."

Another gravestone near there:
"Here lies the body of John Nugent * W...
Died * August the 12th Day *
In the * 22 Year of his Age
Anno...."

The Mountprospect table tomb:
"Sacred to the memory of
Thomas Nugent of Mount Pr...
who departed this life the 17th April 184..
Aged 82 years

Also here interred....
Ellen Dempsey who died September 11...
Richard Dempsey esq Mountprospect
who died Dec 29 1877
Redeemed
Blessed are the dead who die in the Lord."

19. Genealogical Office Manuscript number 70, p.492.

20. PRONI D3835/A/4/60.

21. PRONI D3835/A/4/60, Thomas Nugent to the Lord Chancellor and endorsed 18th July 1577. It was countersigned by the three Nugents held in Dublin Castle at this time: Thomas, James and Lavallin Nugent, all brothers of the previous Baron of Delvin and uncles of the then Baron.

22. PRONI D3835/A/4/230, also see Brian Nugent, *Shakespeare was Irish!* (Co Meath, 2008), p.168 and 176-177.

23. For which see Brian Nugent, *Shakespeare was Irish!*, Appendix E.

24. PRONI D3835/A/6/10/408 and 413.

25. See Robert's letter of the 24th of April 1642, preserved in the Irish Jesuit archives. The reference to the Ormond poem is from PRONI D/3835/A/6/188.

26. Letter of 20th January 1646.

27. See also Brian Nugent, *An Creideamh*, chapter 1642, for some more letters of Fr Robert's.

28. Also from the Jesuit Archives in Dublin.

29. G.O. Ms 69, p.290.

Myles the Slasher

Since this means that Myles the Slasher's mother was of this family it possibly accounts for the great traditions that the Nugents preserved in relation to the famous Myles. His story is however one of the most complex and intricate controversies of Irish local history so only a few brief notes will have to suffice here. Myles the Slasher is the great Rob Roy type figure of Cavan, he was said to be a great swordsman who, among many other feats, held up the entire Scottish army with a single handed defence of the Bridge of Finea which connects Westmeath and Cavan. During the course of this heroic defence he is said to have beheaded a Scottish soldier while he had his own sword in his mouth. What we know of him in recorded history is:

Myles O'Reilly's father, Edmond, was at least for a time recognised as the chief of the O'Reillys who were obviously the old rulers of Cavan. He was brought up in his father's castle known as Kevitt which is near Crossdoney in modern day Co. Cavan. According to the elaborate traditions that survive about him it was said that his great physical prowess manifested itself even while very young growing up in Kevitt, with stories told about his great feats of leaping etc while there. (Many of these traditions are preserved by the Smith family who live in the modern house at the site of the castle. This family is itself quite distinguished with in particular three well known brothers from that house: Louis, an economist in Dublin; Myles, and then his widow, solicitors in Cavan and Ballyjamesduff; and Daragh who was a highly regarded optician in Cavan town.[30])

To keep this digression brief we will just quote a contemporary description of this Myles which comes to us from the pen of Dr Thomas Fitzsimons at one time the Vicar General of the Diocese of Kilmore. Dr Thomas looked after the affairs of the diocese in the absence of a bishop but he fell foul of some church politics and resigned in disagreement with St Oliver Plunkett the then Archbishop of Ireland and Primate of All Ireland. He retired to Louvain and decided to spend his time in c.1673 writing in Latin a genealogy of the O'Reillys which is preserved in an Irish translation from which we have this quote:

> "Maolmórḋa m Emoinn m Maolmórḋa m Aoḋ Conallaiġ caipitín 7 coloneal marcfluaġ ar maiṫiḃ na hÉireann: fínire rin ar ḃrireḋ Croire Riaḃaiġ ionnar ġaḃ nó ionnar marḃ nó ar cuir a raon maóma rect xx marcac do Gallaiḃ 7 ġan aiġe act deicneaṁar ar 20 ḋá ṁuintir féin; fínire ar ḃrireḋ na ḃinne ḃuirbe 7 Lior na Srian 7 ar ḃrireḋ Sléiḃe Ruiréal mar a raiḃ Caiptín Ġallḃraic 7 ḋá oificeac déaġ maille leir 7 do cuir oifacaiḃ orrṫa ġan buille nó urcor do ṫaiḃairt ar aon neac act ar Maolmórḋa Macemoinn aṁáin.
>
> Ġiḋeaḋ do cuaiḋ ġan fuileḋ ġan foirḃerġaḋ aníor 7 ríor trí huaire tríora act an cloiḋeaṁ do cuireḋ tríd a pluic do conġḃáil eroir a fiacla é ġur ceilġ do aon ḃéim an cloiḋeaṁ 7 láṁ an ṁarcaiġ ġo talaṁ.
>
> Ar nimṫect ar Éirinn dó féin 7 do cáċ ir iomḋa cáḋur 7 onóir do fuair ó ríġ na Spáine 7 ó na ṁac 7 fór ó ríġ na Frainċe ar fá ḋeóiḋ aġ dul ar an ḃFrainċe dó ġo Flandenr cum a ḃeit na Máiġirtir Campa ann do glac tinner é ġo ḃfuair bár a mainirtir na ġCapurin Éirennach ran mbaile ḋá nġointer Carlonr A. D. 1670."

Translated into English:

> "Maolmórdha, son of Edmond, son of Maolmórdha, son of Aodh Conallach, was a captain and a colonel of Horse, one of the best in Ireland. The witness of that statement is in the defeat of Crossreagh, where he captured, or killed, or

253

routed, seven score of enemy Horse, having with him but ten over a score of his own Company. Likewise be its witness on the defeats of Benburb, of Lisnasrian, and of Sliabh Russell, where were engaged Captain Galbraith and twelve other officers. In this last Maolmórdha, son of Emonn, so manoeuvred that not a stroke nor shot was directed against any person but himself. For he dashed up and down through them three times without a scratch or a wound. But holding between his teeth a sword which had slashed his cheek, he struck off the sword and the officers arm, with one blow to the ground.

When he and many another with him had left Ireland, he received the highest honours and distinctions from the King of Spain, and from his son; likewise from the King of France. But at length, leaving France for Flanders, in order to serve as a Maestro di Campo there, he took sick, and died in the monastery of the Irish Capuchins in the place which is named Charleville, A. D. 1670." [31]

That then is a detailed contemporary account confirming the great traditions about Myles the Slasher with only two changes from the normal account i.e. Fitzsimons states that he didn't die at the battle where he used the sword in his mouth, as indeed authentic tradition always stated,[32] and he gives a different location, Sliabh Russell, for the battle that tradition states occurred at Finea where Myles is said to have single handedly saved Ireland by holding off the Scots at that bridge in the town for a whole day. The tradition is so adamant in respect to Finea that one feels that the good doctor might have been somewhat in error on that last point.

Luckily we have another important contemporary account, from the Scottish General Monroe himself who describes how his cavalry went to take the bridge on Sunday the 7th of July 1644. This date is very significant because it is the day before the well known Battle of Finea, i.e. some of the historical confusion is caused by historians focusing on the next day when the Irish were defeated, and hence seemingly making a mockery of the tradition, when in fact Myles had held the bridge for that crucial one day on the Sunday.

It was crucial because Monroe had staked everything on a lightning raid south through Cavan to loop around Owen Roe O'Neill's army which was making its way from Louth through into North Meath and on this day was due to arrive in the Kells area. Monroe thought that he could get around O'Neill by charging along the Finea bridge and using the open good road into Westmeath he would hope to get beneath the Irish troops – and the creaghts, the peasant class that accompanied and slowed down O'Neill's army – and so prevent them from escaping into the bogs of Offaly, which was Owen Roe's usual tactic when he was hard pressed by the Scots. When Monroe did get through on the Monday he set off to Carlanstown Co. Westmeath and there surveyed the scene and decided to turn around and go back with his mission not accomplished.

The fact was that Owen Roe was now concentrated at roughly the Portlester, Trim, Kinnegad area, just beside the great Midland bogs, that one day's grace had allowed him to escape to safety!

This is Monroe's very words describing the battle on the Sunday which began with a race to the bridge between the Scottish cavalry and the Irish who were loitering on the Cavan side:

> "Then one of them [the Irish cavalry] terming himself a Captain amongst them, called to our men to know if there were ever a captain amongst them who durst change a pair of bullets with him.
>
> ...
>
> Captain Bruff charged home near to the pass, the chief man of them he run him quite threw the body with his rapier, and killed him, and so retired himself and his men without hurt, and he had no more alarms that night.
>
> ...
>
> The same day as the battle some of the Irish dead were buried the same day at a church some 6 miles from thence, as we got intelligence by other prisoners which we took afterwards." [33]

You have to of course read between the lines a little bit here to find out what actually happened because obviously Monroe is veering a little into propaganda. The crucial point is that there was a battle on this Sunday where Monroe tried to get across the bridge and didn't succeed, the rest is his window dressing for this set back. But the other telling point is that Irish captain challenging all to a duel on the bridge and that sounds an awful lot like our traditions of the great Myles the Slasher!

The Myles the Slasher controversy has been a great quagmire bamboozling Cavan historians for over a century because alongwith this confusion as to the date (remember historians had approximately five contemporary accounts of the Monday battle showing it to be a heavy Irish defeat and hence seemed to contradict tradition) they were also misled by a Clare genealogist of the late 18th century:

In 1786 a famous Spanish general from Baltrasna in Co. Meath – at one time he was in supreme command of the Spanish army –, Alexander O'Reilly, set off to establish his ancestry in Ireland in preparation for the marriage of his eldest son into the very proud Spanish nobility.[34] For this he engaged the services of one Chevalier O'Gorman who was considered the leading expert on the subject of Irish genealogy, and paid him the enormous sum of 1,000 guineas to compile his family history "without deviating in the least from the Rules of Truth and Equity." [35] In fairness to O'Gorman he really did set about the task with some skill and in particular got translated a lot of old Irish manuscripts on the O'Reillys including the account quoted above by Dr Thomas Fitzsimons. But unfortunately for us he then realised he had a golden opportunity to spice up his history because on the one hand he knew that the ancestor of Alexander who flourished during the Confederate Wars was one Myles mac Brian Reilly and on the other hand he had Fitzsimons' fulsome account of his contemporary Colonel Myles mac Eamonn Reilly. So he simply did a swap, he imported Fitzsimons' account of Myles mac Eamonn and attached it to Myles mac Brian, Alexander's ancestor. We know he did this deliberately because we have some notes by O'Gorman on this genealogy where he has a description of Myles mac Brian which only states that he was a captain involved in those wars,[36] without any details, and he knew that Fitzsimons – which he proceeded to copy almost word for word – was very specific in attaching this account to Myles mac Eamonn. The level of confusion this caused in the centuries since is quite incredible with for example numerous newspaper controversies flaring up over the years etc.

While this must seem quite a digression from the subject of this book nonetheless it is important to see the sort of frauds and difficulties that arise in researching 18th century and earlier Irish history. But also Myles the Slasher comes into the story of this Nugent family to quite a degree, as pointed out here in a modern website:

> "It would appear, therefore that until research can unearth a reliable obituary date for Myles the safest course to adopt is to go along with another local tradition which has it that Myles, having slept in the de Nogent castle at Ross overlooking Lough Sheelin on the night before the battle, returned there afterwards had his wounds attended to and subsequently made his way back to the stronghold of the O'Reillys in mid Cavan where he married and raised his family." [37]

In the Nugent castle of Ross there is even a plaque on the wall commemorating his visit to the castle at the time of the Battle of Finea. Furthermore it seems that the various branches of the Ballina family also preserved traditions relating to their cousin Myles the Slasher. The current head of the Farrenconnell house for example is Myles Stoney who was christened Myles because of these old traditions. He also states that an old heirloom of the Farrenconnell Nugents included a golden chatelaine – a kind of ornamental key chain – which was passed onto the Nugents after they married into the O'Reillys and was owned by Myles the Slasher.

Even the Cormeen family preserve these traditions in Co. Cavan. This branch of the Nugents, which is related to that of Mountprospect which we will discuss later, preserve an old story from c.1910. At that time Patrick Nugent observed his father Thomas Joseph talking one morning to a man who had spent the night in Cormeen. He was a journeyman blacksmith, or farm labourer, and Thomas referred to him as the last of the Slasher O'Reillys and revealed that he was in some sense a cousin of theirs and was always to get employment on the farm if possible. The phrase 'Slasher O'Reillys' comes with its own difficulties because it seems impossible to state whether that would relate to the Baltrasna O'Reillys, as we have seen the 'fake' Slasher O'Reillys, or if the phrase was applied to the real heirs of the authentic Slasher.

Incidentally the Nugents and the O'Reillys because of these links in South Cavan and North West Meath have a kind of tradition that they are allied clans, a tradition preserved to this day.

30. Many thanks to the Smith family, and other Cavan residents, for assisting me in gathering these traditions.

31. Fr Paul Walsh, *Irish Chiefs and Leaders* (Dublin, 1960), p.171-173, quoting TCD Ms H i 15, 850.

32. See for example the *Anglo-Celt* 12th of November 1927 for a letter by Thomas O'Reilly of Loughduff and this approach, that the Slasher did not die at Finea, seems to have been supported by Bridie Smith who was very much the expert on Cavan folklore, in the same newspaper of the 19th of November 1927. This is a letter on the subject by that Tomás Ó Raghallaigh of Loughduff Co. Cavan:
"I believe Myles McEdmond is the "Slasher" of tradition. If so, Dr Comey is right. Myles McEdmond it was who, from the death of Owen Roe O'Neill, by his military skill and the prowess of his strong right arm, preserved from destruction the faithful remnant of the people of Breffney during the last years of the Cromwellian war. Issuing from his woody fastnesses, he inflicted defeat after defeat upon his foes as opportunity presented itself, and finally, when driven to bay in the mountains beyond Ballyconnell, in the month of June, 1652, he and his gallant followers did not surrender without a battle, but charged resolutely into the van of an overwhelming army of Cromwellians. His fortified retreat in Garadice Lough is called by the peasantry to this day Myles the Slasher's Island.

His status in the Catholic army was higher than that of his kinsman, a proof of superior merit. Moreover, the tradition of old men of my people, who were noted historians, states that the Slasher's father's name was Emen, a famous swordsman.
...
From Captain Myles McBrian, above mentioned, descended Count Alexander O'Reilly of Spain, the hero who captured Algiers, and who employed Chevalier Thomas O'Gorman to compile a history of the O'Reillys, for which he paid him £1,137 10s. This is the Book of Cavan, compiled in 1786. Thus it would not be a matter of surprise if to the ancestor of Alexander much of the fame as well as the soubriquet of Colonel Myles McEdmond were transferred.

The Bridge of Finea was an important military position. At least two battles were fought at it during the Confederate Wars.

Mr Rahilly deserves great credit for his labours in the field of Irish history. He will find it a most entertaining work.

Tomás Ó Raghallaigh
Loughduff, Cavan
22nd June 1909."
(*Irish Independent*, 24th of June 1909.)

33. Robert Monroe, *A full relation of the late expedition of the Right Honourable, the Lord Monroe, Major-General of all the Protestant forces in the Province of Ulster* (London, 1644), p.5-6.

34. See AFM vol vi p.2245.

35. TCD Ms 3411, p.301.

36. NLI Ms 8750 (29).

37. http://www.irishidentity.com/stories/myles.htm .

38. G.O. Ms 69.

39. PRONI D3835/A/4/425.

40. PRONI D3835/A/4/370.

41. PRONI D3835/A/4/403.

42. PRONI D3835/A/4/41.

43. For which see Brian Nugent, *Shakespeare was Irish!*, appendix D.

44. PRONI D3835/A/4/474.

45. Phillip O'Connell, *The Parishes of Munterconnaught and Castlerahan*, Briefne vol II no. III, p.267.

46. Oliver Davies, *Castles of Co. Cavan,* pt II, published in the, *Ulster Journal of Archaeology* (1947-8), p.94.

47. Jane Ohlmeyer and Eamonn O Ciardha, *The Irish statute staple books, 1596-1687* (Dublin, 1998). As regards the reference to Christopher and the 1641 rebellion I cannot unfortunately remember the reference to this document which is referred to in a recent publication.

48. *Munimenta Nugentiorum* no.18 and 22, NLI Ms 16,520 and NLI M/F Pos 6849.

49. Canon Coslett Quinn, *A pedigree of the O Dempsey family,* published in, *Éigse,* no.10 (1961-3) pt 4, p.309-12, and I would like to thank his son John for this reference.

Was it this James who assisted the first Earl of Westmeath in his land dealings in Cavan in the 1630s/40s, as recorded in the papers submitted by the 2nd Earl of Westmeath to the Court of Claims in the 1660s?
"The claimant further seteth forth that Phillip McHugh O'Rely, late of Belancarge, county Cavan, esquire, being seized in fee of and in the premises in the fifth part of the schedule mentioned, did in consideration of £100 paid by John Dowdall of Kells, merchant, grant and convey the same unto the said Dowdall and his heirs upon condition of redemption, pro ut per deed patet, by virtue whereof the said Dowdall entered and was seized of the premises, whose estate by mean conveyances is come unto the claimant [the second Earl of Westmeath].

The claimant further sets forth that the said Phillip O'Rely, being seized of the premises in the sixth part of the schedule mentioned, did in consideration of £200 paid unto him by James Nugent of Clonin, gentleman, grant the said premises unto the said James and his heirs upon condition of redemption. That the said James accordingly entered and was seized of the premises in fee, whose estate is now come unto the claimant, who was also seized and possessed thereof until outed by the usurpers [Cromwellians]."
(Geraldine Tallon, *Court of Claims, Submissions and Evidence 1663* (Dublin, 2006), p.230.)

Also in an indenture and marriage settlement dated the 13th of July 1635 involving Andrew Nugent of Clonlost and Thomas McArt McGeoghegan of C[?]omerstown in Co. Westmeath it refers to "James Nugent steward to the Earl of Westmeath" (PRONI D/2620/1 pt B).

Clonin of course is beside Delvin where the Earl of Westmeath had his castle and, I think, there was no James Nugent of that family as such. Hence, dealing in lands in Cavan like this, and the lands of Cormeen itself were owned in 1640 by a Dowdall and presumably before that by an O'Reilly, it seems likely that it is our James of Ballina/Annagh who presumably was helping out the Earl, his second cousin, at this time. This might neatly tie into the story of the Earl being the inspiration behind him going to live on the lands in Cavan, that Quinn mentions.

This incidentally is the full 1638 deed involving James Nugent of Annagh:

"The second day of April in the year of our Lord God 1638...James Nugent of Annagh in the County of [Meath, Westmeath?]...one part, and Robert Nugent of Carolanstown in the said county esquire of the other part, witnesseth that whereas Christopher [Nugent of Ba]lana in the county of Meath Esq, father to said James hath by his deed indented, bearing date the eighth and twentieth day of September last past 1637. Leased unto the said Robert Nugent the townes and lands of Achanasheash, Moinnrey [?], Cunlin and Cavanacholter [?] with their etc [sic] containing by estimation two poles and a half be it more or less for the space of ninety nine years for the assurance of a mortgage of two hundred pounds sterling unto the said Robert his heirs and assigns, as by the said deed of demise is that behalf more at large appeareth.

Now know yee that the said James Nugent hath given granted and confirmed, like as by these p[?, oints? particulars?] he doth give grant and [word crossed out] unto the said Robert Nugent the yearly rentcharge of 20 pounds sterling, now money of and in England, to issue and grow due out of the town and lands of Lismacanagan and Cornamucklagh with their appurtenances in the county of Cavan containing by estimation two poles to be paid yearly at May and at Hallowtide by even and equal portions to have and to hold the said rentcharge to him the said Robert his heirs and assigns forever.

And if it fortune the said yearly rentcharge or any part thereof to be behind hand or unpaid for the face of one month next after any the said feasts or days of payment that then it shall and may be lawful to and for the said Robert his heirs and assigns unto all and singular the towns and lands aforesaid of Lismacanagan and Cornamucklagh XXXXXXX [sic] enter and distrain, and the distress or distresses then and here found to lead, drive away and detain, until the said rentcharge and arrearages thereof (if any happen to be due) he and they be fully satisfied, content and paid.

And the said James Nugent doth covenant, promise and grant for him his heirs executors administrators and assigns, to and with the said Robert his heirs and assigns, that he the said Robert Nugent his heirs and assigns may from time to time, and at all times quietly and peaceably leaun[?] and receive the said yearly rentcharge according [?to?] the purport of this deed, well and truly acquitted and saved harmless from all grants, feoffments, fines, recoveries, dowries, jointures, wife's thirds, of and from all manner of incumbrances and entanglements in law or equity whatsoever.

And that he the said James his heirs and assigns shall and will from time to time and at all times may suffer, and do, or cause to be made suffered and done, all and every such further and other assurance and assurances, act and acts whatsoever be the same, by matter in fact or of records or both, for the better assuring of the said rentcharge as aforesaid to [?] the said Robert his heirs and assigns at his ask[?] or request and cost in law, such as his and their learned counsel shall adjust and devise; provided always, and the true intent and meaning of all parties to this present [?] deed, is and always hath been, that if the said Robert Nugent his heirs and assigns shall from time to time and at all times quietly and peaceably, and without any manner of disturbance, have and receive the issue, and profits of all and singular the lands contained in the above recited deed of demise, so far as the said lands are purposed for the assurance of the said mortgage, that then this deed and all covenants, clauses, and conditions therein contained to be void.

But if it happen the said Robert Nugent his heirs and assigns be any way disturbed from the enjoying of the benefit of the said recited assurance, that then and thenceforth, the said Robert his heirs and assigns from that time forward may distrain for the said rent from thence forward to grow due according the purport of this deed [sic].

Provided always likewise that whensoever the said James Nugent his heirs and assigns do satisfy content [?] and pay, or cause to be satisfied, contented or paid unto the said Robert his heirs or assigns at one whole and entire payment the just and full sum of two hundred pounds sterling in pure [or pounds?] silver current money of and in England with the arrearages now due from and after the said disturbance (if any happen then to be due) that then and from thence forward this rentcharge and the said demise and endrie the [?] matters in each of the said assurances contained be void,

In witness whereof the said parties have to these points [?] interchangeably put their hands and seals this day and year first above written

signed and delivered in presence of us
La... Archbold
Ro..........se

James (Loco Signilli) Nugent

This is a true copy of the original thereunto compared this day the 13th of April 1649 by me
Madam Notaripublicus[?] ...Waterford"
(Nugent Section of Stowe Papers, Huntington Library, San Marino, California.)

50. Phillip O'Connell, *The Parishes of Munterconnaught and Castlerahan*, Briefne vol II no. III, p.280.

51. Cavan no.13 vol 1 p.50 dorso, and Ms 833 4v.

52. Bridie M Smith, *Castlerahan and some of its clans*, published in the, *Anglo Celt*, 5th October 1927.

53. O'Reilly notebooks in the RSAI vol 14, p.37.

54. *Munimenta Nugentiorum* no.13, NLI Ms 16,520 and NLI M/F Pos 6849, and see also John Ainsworth, *Nugent Papers*, published in *Analecta Hibernica* no.20 (1958), p.154.

55. Nugent Papers ibid, p.155.

56. The Skey pedigree is available at: NLI M/F Pos 6849.

57. The Dalton debt is from Margaret Griffiths, *Calendar of Inquisitions, Co. Dublin* (Dublin, 1991), p.433. The list of outlawries in Westmeath of those who were part of the Jacobite army, noted by J G Simms in *Analecta Hibernica* no.22 1960, p.28, lists inter alia:
Matthias Nugent of Carlanstown
Thomas Nugent, Clognegarrah, gent.

Also there is this from the researches of the well known historian John D'Alton with respect to the Williamite land confiscations in Co. Cavan:
"Those who were subsequently and effectively attainted, and their estates confiscated, were...[mostly O'Reillys, the main Jacobite lords]...Richard Nugent of Annagh and Thomas Nugent of the City of Dublin...all whose estates were hereat granted to patentees..."
(*Anglo-Celt,* 26th Oct 1849, p.1.)

58. This tradition is preserved by Geraldine Smith of Lavey, Co. Cavan, B.L., whom I'd like to thank.

59. From the 1688 bond op.cit.

60. As noted in a newspaper clipping of c.1711 listing those Catholics allowed to bear arms under the Treaty of Limerick, pasted into TCD Beresford Munday/O'Reilly Ms 3396 p.5.

61. ROD 5th of August 1709 8-17-1666.

62. NLI Ms 11,491.

63. "Matthias and Oliver Nugent their confession[?] same date.
Says as to the Pole of Clontiduffy and Rathclaghy, Richard Earl of Westmeath and Countess his wife made them over to Christopher Nugent and Margaret Nugent [his daughter] for £100 subject to redemption and payment of said sum. And said lands came to Richard Clute [i.e. Tuite] of Co. Meath and to James Tute his son, and by assignment from them came to James Nugent of Co. Cavan, who after his death came descended to Robert Nugent of Clonegeragh Co. Westmeath son of said James Nugent, and he being seized thereof said lands of Clontiduffy in 1688, by assignment from said Robert Nugent and Thomas Nugent, son of said Robert, came to this defendant. And since hath enjoyed the same excepting the time of late trouble 1688."
("*Substance of the Bill of Charles Earl of Cavan preferred May 12th 1699*", PRONI D3835/B/4/2/2.)

Major Matthias Nugent, the brother of Edmond, had an eldest son Peter as well as a second son Robert, presumably Peter died young. This is from the Remainder list at the end of the 1699 marriage settlement for the wedding of Mary Fleming of Staholmock and Robert Nugent of Carlanstown. After these immediate relatives the Remainder lists:
Walter Nugent of Portlomon,
Thomas Nugent merchant,
Richard Nugent of Aughnegaron [Co. Longford],
Earl of Westmeath.
(Nugent section, Stowe deeds, Huntington Library, San Marino California.)

64. For further details on Robert Nugent see Appendix G infra.

65. British Library Additional Ms 40,180 ff168.

66. From the Nugent section of the Stowe papers in the Huntington library, San Marino, passim, and in particular the letters from Robert Nugent of Bobsgrove dated 10th of October 1764 and 19th of December 1767, and PRONI D3835/A/6/127. Summing up then, this Robert of Clontiduffy had two sons and four daughters:
Major John Nugent of the British Army based in the Caribbean mostly, Lieutenant Michael Nugent of the 34th Regiment who lived in Bath for a while but is buried in Bray Co. Wicklow and who petitioned his relative the Duke of Buckingham when he was Viceroy of Ireland,[83] Jean, described as about 30 and not settled in a letter of 1764, Catherine, who at that time lived with the Browne family of Bushtown, and Mary and Anne who were collectively given £100 by their brother John and with that opened a milliner shop in Mullingar.[84]

67. To clarify then why we can say that the Cormeen/Mountprospect family was of the original house of Ballina:

a) Because Patrick Nugent is variously described as of Lismacanigan and Cunlin before Cormeen, and those previous two places are recognised as properly the lands of the Nugents of Ballina as described in the aforementioned 1638 deed of James Nugent of Annagh. (As described under the ROD entries for Cormeen in the main text of this chapter infra.) Also that James Nugent clearly lived later in Lismacanigan so when Patrick Nugent is living there he is residing in the old home place of his family. Its possible also that the part of Mountprospect townland that includes the old house might have been originally part of Lismacanigan – obviously Mountprospect is a modern townland name and it adjoins Lismacanigan at that spot but it is difficult now to be absolutely sure of the old townland boundaries – which would mean that Mountprospect house was continually occupied by the one family.

From the tradition recorded by Canon Quinn we know that Mountprospect must be an old established house of the Nugent family, and the only such branch that this could realistically be would be that of Lismacanigan and Cornamucklagh, which border Mountprospect. This then in turn would mean that the Mountprospect – and hence Cormeen – and old Lismacanigan families were of the same stock, i.e. the main line of the Ballina family.

b) Because this family buried in Killeagh, in the townland of Moat near Oldcastle Co. Meath. This can be seen from the 1779 newspaper account of the burial of Dominic Nugent of Mountprospect, and this is quite a central and obvious place for the Nugents of Ballina to bury in. Also the grave of the Nugents of Mountprospect in that graveyard (a table tomb) is right beside that of one of the Nugents of Gneeve from the early 18th century. As can be seen above with respect to Oliver Nugent and Honora Reilly, we know that at least one family that settled in Gneeve was of the mainline of the Ballina Nugents.

c) From the prevalence of the Thomas first name in the mainline of the Ballina Nugents and in the later Cormeen/Mountprospect families. It is true that there are some other Nugent branches that use this first name, including the Earls of Westmeath and the Nugents of Moyrath and Clonlost, but these families are located a long distance from the area south east of Lough Sheelin where all these above mentioned places are located, like Clonnageeragh, Ballina, Annagh, Gneeve, Clontiduffy, Lismacanigan etc. Of the numerous different Nugent families that are located in that district the first name Thomas is only used, as far as I know, in relation to the Cormeen/Mountprospect family and that of Ballina/Clonnageeragh. (And, interestingly, in the case of a member of the Gneeve family.) Those readers acquainted with Irish genealogical practice will realise that this is quite significant, many Irish families took care to use different first names in order to mark out the different branches.

That Thomas was a very popular first name among the Mountprospect/Cormeen family we can see from the following facts: the Dominic Nugent listed below, of Mountprospect, was succeeded by his son Thomas who died a very old man c.1840 (and was succeeded by the Dempseys who were in turn c.1910 succeeded by the Nixons in Mountprospect). In respect to the Cormeen families you have Richard and his three sons Thomas, Patrick, and Richard listed in the 1821 census for Cormeen, Castlerahan Co. Cavan. Patrick was a blacksmith who worked in his smith above the parochial house on the lane leading to the old graveyard of Castlerahan and he had one son who he called Thomas, who became a priest in Folsom California, Richard went to live in Mullaghmore in the same parish, and Thomas worked as a carter hauling goods from the port of Drogheda to a shop they owned below the parochial house, on the same side of the road as that house opposite the modern church. This Thomas in turn had a son Thomas Joseph, who was an only child, and he lived in Cormeen Cottage which was purchased by his mother after his father's death from the MacManus family and he had five sons starting with Thomas, then James, then Patrick (and you can see how those latter two names were important for the family history, Patrick being the name of the first Nugent in Cormeen and James the first who went into Cavan), then Bartholomew (of Coventry) and then Michael (of Dublin). The eldest son Thomas had no children but James (of Summerbank Co. Meath) had only one son and he called him Thomas (of Trim). The Patrick (of Corstown Co. Meath) listed had three sons: Thomas (of Edmonton in Canada), Patrick (this writer's father as it happens), and Norbert (called after the Norbertine Order who moved into Kilnacrott) who died young. Hence you can easily see how they were determined to preserve the name Thomas. Its also not surprising that they do not have Roberts or Christophers or Olivers in the family because if they did it would cause confusion with the Farrenconnell and indeed Dungimmon Nugents who used those first names a lot. (They were quite conscious of this, for example when Richard Nugent went to live in Mullaghmore they no longer used the first name Richard because they said he had taken the name Richard with him, in other words only his descendants could use that first name from then on.)

Incidentally on this there are also some interesting accounts preserved among the Farnham Papers, in particular:

Rent rolls of the Massereene estates owned by Lord Farnham
1720, one year ending May, rents and fees
Barcony	Matthew Nugent £8 5s 4d
Barcony	Michael Mackin £4 2s 8d
Claure	Richard Nugent £15 10s 00d
Cormine	Matthew Nugent £39 5s 4d

1728
| Cormine | Patrick Nugent 19.00 |

1734, half year ending May
| Cormine | Mr Nugent 18.00.0 |

(Farnham Papers, Rent Rolls, 1718-1790, NLI Ms 11,491)

The Matthew Nugent listed above is probably the Major Matthias Nugent of the Carlanstown family and you can see how his lease of Cormeen seems to pass to Patrick Nugent of that place. (I dare not guess the origin of the Claure and Richard Nugent reference though, although he is doubtless related.) This neatly ties in with the reference in the fragment of the Kilmore will index, preserved in the National Archives Dublin, to a Matthias Nugent of Legawoge making a will circa 1721 (as you can see from the later references of Mountprospect, Legawoge was certainly tied in with the Mountprospect/Lismacanigan estate) which would explain why he disappears from these records between 1720 and 1728.

This in turn serves to indicate the close relationship between the Major Nugent, again of the Carlanstown family who married the sister of Thomas of the mainline of the Ballina clan, and the later family of Cormeen. But this Patrick is certainly not a son of Matthias – Matthias' son Robert and later descendants are well known and are described above in footnote 66 – and probably not a relative on the Carlanstown side of his family – because the Carlanstown Nugents are a very important and powerful branch with well established genealogies that do not show a Nugent relative of theirs in Cormeen – so probably he is related to Matthias' wife of the Ballina/Clonigeragh family.

We don't know definitively, incidentally, that the Matthias Nugent of Legavoge of 1721 was Major Matthias of the Carlanstown family but it is a reasonable assumption bearing in mind that he did take over some at least of the Ballina lands in Cavan, as pointed out earlier, and married into that family, and Matthias is not at all a common name among the Nugents of this locality.

68. NLI Ms 16,139.

69. 2A-4-127 vol no.79.

70. *Freeman's Journal* of the 2nd January 1779.

71. NLI Ms 11,491.

72. National Archives, Betham Abstracts, Marriage Licenses, volume IV/5 D. 1703-1799, E. 1630-1742.

73. NLI Ms 11,491.

74. Account by Bridie Bray of Mountprospect, Folklore Library, UCD, Ramonan National School, Cavan reel no.6, 1937-1939, Vol 996, p.176-177.

75. As explained to me by Roby Nixon of Drogheda.

76. For example that seems to have been the approach of Patrick Nugent of Corstown Co. Meath who was of this family.

77. http://longfordancestry.net/longford-articles.php?ver=16&op=3 .

78. Killough School, parish of Delvin (Killulagh) vol 726, p.128.

79. Also told to me by Roby Nixon.

80. John Gideon Millingen, *The History of Duelling* (London, 1841) vol 2, p.130. The O'Carolan reference is from the Very Rev M J Canon Masterson, *Turlough O'Carolan*, in the, *Ardagh and Clonmacnoise Antiquarian Society Journal,* 1929, vol 1 no.2, p.75.

81. See ROD 93-508-66580.

82. Published in *Analecta Hibernica* no.20.

83. Dated 23rd Oct 1789 British Library Additional Ms 40,180 ff168.

84. See the 1764 letter from Robert Nugent of Bobsgrove to Robert Nugent of Carlanstown preserved in the Nugent/Stowe collection in the Huntington Library, San Marino.

85. This is the conundrum which faced Catholics and the ROD:
"by forbidding the registration of transactions in the only type of property which the law allowed Catholics to hold [that is less than 21 year leases], the [ROD] act attempted, with demonstrable success, either to expel them or to induce their conformity in matters of religion."
(Peter Roebuck, *The Irish Registry of Deeds: A Comparative Study*, published in, *Irish Historical Studies*, vol.18 no.69 (March 1972), p.64.)
But remember its over 21 year leases that could be registered but it is less than 31 year leases that Catholics could take out.

86. See *The Irish Ecclesiastical Record*, Ser. 5, Vol. LXIX, p.125-134, February, 1947.

87. PRONI M/F 71/3 passim.

88. *Briefne*, vol v, no.20, (1980-1981), p.470.

89. As preserved in the Stowe papers in the Huntington Library.

Maps
The following pages show the:
1) 1609 map of the Lismacanigan area prepared for the Ulster Plantation (National Archives, Kew, MPF/1/55);

2) and below it the Down Survey Baronial map for the same district, of the 1650s, (and note the building marked here);

3) then the old 6" Ordnance Survey Map (of c.1829-42);

4) a map among the Grattan papers, by James Graham in 1749, which was "an original map annexed ...lease 28th April 1821" (East Riding Record Office, via PRONI MIC 71/3), and includes the following additional information:
\# - Lands Supposed Take[n] off here
[Meaning in this sense the map is inaccurate? The letters that accompany this map do talk about it being defective, where is Cormeen anyway?]
* - Part supplied taken off Garryross

10a 0r 0p
[This seems to refer to land that the Earl of Farnham added to his lands in Cormeen when he got a mortgage or long lease of adjoining lands in Garryross from Grattan.]
Further details about this map can be gleaned from the text of a lease dated 30 July 1751 (registered at ROD 153-107-101830) for 90 years from James Grattan to Revd Edward Sterling which mentions:
"Henry Grattan's part of the lands of Barcony formerly held and enjoyed by the widow Nugent" – 25 acres, lease had map annexed.

Then from a summary, probably made by Henry Grattan, son of the famous Henry, of various letters from his agent in Cavan trying to get to the bottom of what land and timber had been alienated from the Grattans during the long time when it was held by lease by the Sterling family, dated 1st January 1821, we are told that:
"Garryross contains by survey made 12 years ago and by a McLoughlin survey 203 acres including bog and bottoms – says 8 or 9 acres were taken off Barcony Grattan and added to Barcony Burton in the time of Ann Nugent widow – Alexander Stuart aged 94 now resident in Co. Monaghan lived [?] with Edward Sterling till his death – Thomas Nugent of Mount Prospect was the person who acted in selling the trees – McManus was party [?] at their taking off the roof and slates of the House – the timber was oak –
1. Barcony Grattan
2. Barcony Burton and now Capt Nugent's of Bobsgrove where the lost ground lies
3. Barcony Cuppaidge now Mr O'Reilly's
4. Barcony Massareene now Lord Farnham's
5. Barcony Robinson now called Rutagh
6. Barcony Mackin now Mr Whitney by new name Mount Prospect
7. Barcony Molloy [?] now Lismacankin

Another letter 4th April 1821 says from a court receipt [?] Garryross only contains 203 acres bog and all.

H Fitzsimon's letter 24th Oct 1820 – states John Reilly of Barcony says Mr Sterling made a lease of that to Anne Nugent for 31 years – and at expiration another and Pat Reilly (John's father) be at its expiration a 3d [or pounds maybe, fine at the renewal of the lease?] and John Reilly himself for 31 years which will expire [?] May 1822 and Sterling held it after he got it from our family 6 or 8 years before he set it to Anne Nugent – is 100 years in Sterling family –"
(Grattan Papers, East Riding Record Office, PRONI M/F 71/3.)

5) One of the maps prepared for the sale of the estate of Nicholas Coyne in Cavan and Westmeath, particularly Lismacanagan, c.1760 (PRONI D2784/2).

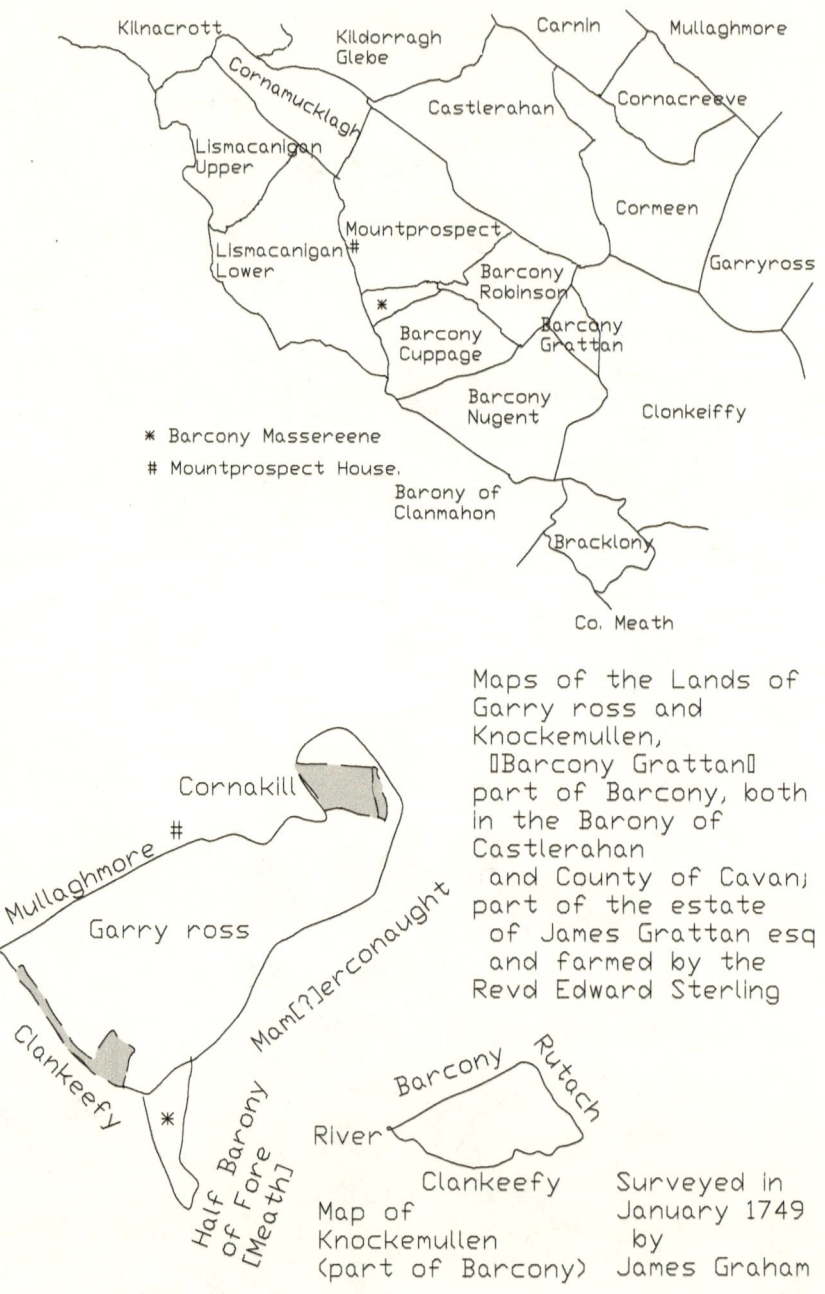

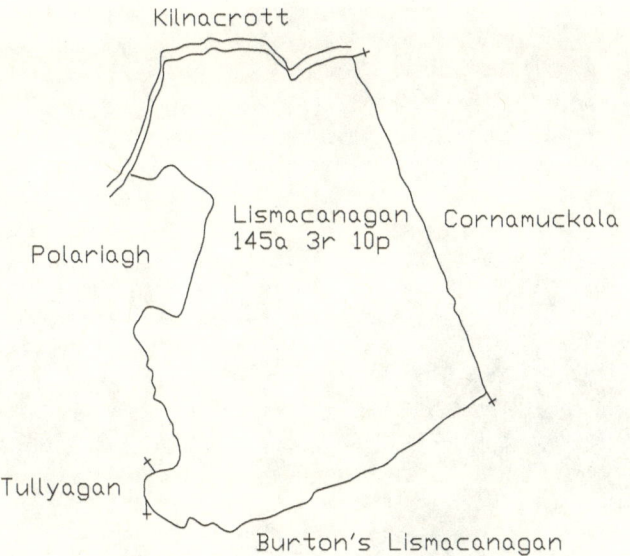

Surveyed Sept 1757 by William Coghlan, etc

Pricked off here in April 1760 by me James Campbell

This should give you some idea of what to expect from mapping in Ireland in the 17th to 19th centuries. As you can see its not always a very exact science and also the British government was pretty notorious (until the Ordnance Survey) for butchering the Irish placenames which means you have to pronounce these words phonetically to try to identify the different places.

Mountprospect House is, as you can see from the OS map, right up against the border with Lismacanigan, so the demesne and the gardens of the house, and the modern road, juts into Lismacanigan at this point. The old lane into the house follows the line of the border between Lismacanigan and Mountprospect, as you go North it continues up from the short side of the triangle of Barcony Massereene through the Whitegate which occurs at this border, while the main road turns left and then right as it circles the demesne.

Mountprospect house was destroyed by the Land Commission but luckily this old photograph and painting survives.

An old grandfather clock and wooden chest from Mountprospect House. (Incidentally I would particularly like to thank Roby Nixon, who lived in the old house, for all her assistance here.)

Above is Killeagh graveyard Co. Meath showing the proximity of the Gneeve headstone, on the ground to the left, and the Mountprospect table tomb, to the right. Below is a closeup of the Cockatrice insignia on the Gneeve headstone.

APPENDIX A
The Registry of Deeds Act

What follows is the full text of the original Act governing the Registry of Deeds for 1707 and also subsequent amendments to it which the Irish parliament passed during the 18th century.

1707 AD
(6 Anne c. 2)

AN ACT for the Publick Registring of all Deeds, Conveyances, and Wills that shall be made of any Honors, Manors, Lands, Tenements, or Hereditainents.

FOR securing purchasers, preventing forgeries and fraudulent gifts and conveyances of lands, tenements, and hereditaments, which have been frequently practised in this kingdom, especially by papists, to the great prejudice of the protestant interest thereof, and for settling and establishing a certain method, with proper rules and directions for registering a memorial of all deeds and conveyances, which from and after the twenty fifth day of March in the year of our Lord one thousand seven hundred and eight shall be made and executed, and of all wills and devises in writing made, or to be made, and published, where the devisor or testatrix shall die after the said twenty fifth day of March one thousand seven hundred and eight, for or concerning any honors, manors, lands, tenements, or hereditaments in this kingdom. We pray that it may be enacted, and be it enacted by the Queen's most excellent Majesty, by and with the advice and consent of the lords spiritual and temporal and commons in this present Parliament assembled, and by the authority of the same, That one publick office for registring memorials of deeds and conveyances, wills and devises, shall be established and kept in the city of Dublin, to be managed and executed by a fit and able person, or his sufficient deputy, such person to be from time to time nominated and appointed by the Queen's Majesty, her heirs and successors, and to continue in the said office for so long time as he shall faithfully and honestly demean [sic] himself therein.

II. AND be it further enacted by the authority aforesaid, That upon the death of any such register, and until another person be nominated and appointed in manner aforesaid, the executors or administrators of the register deceased, together with the sureties for the said register, or their executors or administrators, Shall appoint a proper person to execute the office of register; for whose demeanor in the execution of the said office, the security given for such register deceased shall be answerable.

III. AND be it further enacted by the authority aforesaid, That a memorial of all deeds and conveyances, which from and after the twenty fifth day of March, in the year of our Lord one thousand seven hundred and eight, shall be made and executed, and, of all wills and devises in writing, made or to be made and Published, where the devisor or testatrix shall dye after the said twenty fifth day Of March one thousand seven hundred and eight, for, or concerning, and whereby any honours, manors, lands, tenements or hereditaments within this kingdom may be any ways affected, may, at the election of the Party or parties concerned, be registered in such manner as is herein after directed.

IV. AND be it further enacted by the authority aforesaid, That [sic] every such deed or conveyance, a memorial whereof shall be duly registered according to the rules and directions in this act prescribed, shall, from and after the said twenty fifth day of March in the year of our Lord one thousand seven hundred and eight, be deemed and taken as good and effectual both in law, and equity, according to the priority of time of registring such memorial for or and concerning the honors, manors, lands, tenements, and hereditaments in such a deed or conveyance mentioned or contained, according to the right, title, and interest of the person or persons so conveying such honors, manors, lands, tenements, and hereditainents, against all and every other deed, conveyance, or disposition of the honors, manors, lands, tenements or hereditaments, or any part thereof comprized or contained in any such memorial as aforesaid.

V. AND be it further enacted by the authority aforesaid, That every deed or conveyance not registred, which shall be made and executed from and after the twenty fifth day of March in the year of our Lord one thousand seven hundred and eight, of all or any of the honors, manors, lands, tenements, or hereditaments comprized or contained in such a deed or conveyance, a memorial whereof shall be registered in pursuance of this act, shall be deemed and adjudged as fraudulent and void, not only against such a deed or conveyance registred as aforesaid, but likewise against all and every creditor and creditors by judgment, recognizance, statute-merchant, or of the staple, confessed, acknowledged, or entered into from and after the twenty fifth day of March aforesaid, as for and concerning all or any of the honors, manors, lands, tenements, or hereditaments, contained or expressed in such memorial registred as aforesaid.

VI. AND be it further enacted by the authority aforesaid, That all and every memorial, so to be entered or registered, shall be put into writing in vellum or parchment, and directed to the register of the said office; and in case of deeds and conveyances, shall be under the hand and seal of some or one of the grantors, or some or one of the grantees, his, her, or their guardians or trustees attested by two witnesses, one whereof to be one of the witnesses to the execution of such deed or conveyance; which witness shall by affidavit to be made before the said register or his deputy, who is hereby impowered and required to administer such oath, prove the signing and sealing of such memorial, and the execution of the deed or conveyance mentioned in such memorial, and the day and time of the delivery of such memorial, to the register or his deputy: and in case of wills, the memorials shall be under the hand and seal of some or one of the devisees, his, her, or their guardians or trustees, attested by two witnesses, one whereof shall by affidavit, to be made before the said register or his deputy, prove the signing and sealing of such memorial; which respective affidavit, the said register or his deputy is hereby impowered to take, and is hereby directed to file and enter in a book to be kept for that purpose.

VII. AND be it further enacted by the authority aforesaid, That every memorial of any deed, conveyance, or will, shall contain the day of the month and the year when such deed, conveyance, or will bears date, and was perfected, and the names and additions of all the parties to such deed or conveyance, and of the devisor or testatrix of such will, and of all the witnesses to such deed, conveyance, or will, and shall express or mention the honors, manors, lands, tenements, or hereditaments contained in such deed, conveyance, or will, and the names of all the counties, baronies, cities, towns corporate, parishes, townships, hamlets, villages, precincts, within this kingdom, where any such honors, manors, lands, tenements, or hereditaments are lying and being, that are given, granted, conveyed, devised, or any way affected or charged by any deed, conveyance, or will, in such manner as the same are expressed or mentioned in such deed, conveyance, or will, or to the same effect; and that every such deed, conveyance, or will, or probate of the same, of which such memorial is to be registered as aforesaid, shall be produced to the said register, or his deputy, at the time of entering such memorial, who shall endorse a certificate on every such deed, conveyance, and will, or probate thereof, and therein mention the certain day and time, on which such memorial is so entered and registered, expressing also in what book, page and number the same is entered, and that the said register or his deputy shall sign the said certificate when so endorsed: which certificate shall be taken and allowed as evidence of such respective registries in all courts of record whatsoever; and that every page of such register books, and every memorial, that shall be entered therein, shall be numbered, and the day of the month and the year when every such memorial is registered shall be entered in the margins of the said register-books, and of the said memorial; and that every such register shall keep an alphabetical kalendar of all counties, baronies, cities, towns corporate, parishes, and townships within this realm, with reference to the number of every memorial, that concerns the honors, manors, lands, tenements, or hereditaments in every such county, barony, city, town corporate, parish or township respectively, and of the names of the parties mentioned in such memorial and that such register, or his deputy, shall duly file every such memorial in order of time, as the same shall be brought to the said office, and enter or register the said memorials in the same order that they shall respectively come to his bands.

VIII. AND be it further enacted by the authority aforesaid, That every such register, before he enter upon the execution of the said office, shall be sworn before the lord chief baron, or some other of the barons of her Majesty's court of Exchequer, who are hereby required to administer such oath in these words:

> You shall truly and faithfully perform and execute the office and duty, that is directed and required by act of Parliament, in registering memorials of deeds, conveyances, and wills within this kingdom, so long as you shall continue in the said office.
>
> So help you God.

And that when and as often as the said register shall appoint any deputy to execute the said office, such deputy shall before he enter on the execution thereof take the said oath before the lord chief baron, or some other of the barons of her Majesty's court of Exchequer, who are hereby required to administer the same; and that every such register, at the time of his being sworn into the said office, shall also enter into a recognizance with two or more sufficient sureties, to be approved of by the lord chief baron, or some other of the barons of her Majesty's court of Exchequer, of the penalty of twenty thousand pounds unto her Majesty, her heirs and successors, to be taken by the said lord chief baron, or some other of the said barons, conditioned for his true and faithful performance of his duty in the execution of his said office; the same to be kept and to remain in the office of her Majesty's remembrances of the Exchequer amongst the records of the said court.

IX. PROVIDED nevertheless, and be it further enacted by the authority aforesaid, That when any register shall dye, or surrender his office, and that within the space of three years from and after such death or surrender [,] no misbehaviour appear to have been committed by such register in the execution of his said office; then, and in such case, at the end of the said three years after his death or surrender, the said recognizance so entered into by him, shall become void and of no effect to all intents and purposes whatsoever.

X. [Section 10 is repealed so far as relates to office hours by 25 Geo. 3. c. 47. s.1 (Ir.), and is amended as to holidays by 46 & 47 Vict. c. 20. s. 1.] AND be it further enacted by the authority aforesaid, That every such register, or his sufficient deputy, shall give due attendance at his office every day in the week, except Sundays and holy-days, between the hours of nine and twelve in the forenoon, and between the hours of three and six in the afternoon, for the dispatch of all businesses belonging to the said office: and that every register or his deputy, as often as required, shall make searches concerning all memorials that are required as aforesaid, and give certificates concerning the same under his hand, if required by any person.

XI. [See 2 & 3 Will. 4. c. 87. s. 5.] AND be it further enacted by the authority aforesaid, That every such register shall be allowed for the entry of every such memorial, as is by this act directed, the sum of six pence and no more, in case the same do not exceed one hundred words; but if such memorial exceed one hundred words, then after the rate or proportion of three pence a hundred for all the words contained in such memorial over and above the first one hundred words, and the like fees for the like number of words contained in every certificate or copy given out of the said office, and no more; and for every search in the said office six pence and no more.

XII. AND be it further enacted by the authority aforesaid, That if any such register, or his deputy, shall neglect to perform his or their duty in the execution of the said office, according to the rules and directions in this act mentioned, or commit or suffer to be committed any undue or fraudulent practice in the execution of the said office, and be thereof lawfully convicted, that then such register shall forfeit his said office, and pay treble damages, with the full costs of suit, to every such person or persons as shall be injured thereby; to be recovered by action of debt, bill, plaint, or information in any of her Majesty's courts of record at Dublin, wherein no essoign [excuse], protection, privilege of Parliament, or wager of law shall be allowed, nor any more than one imparlance.

XIII. AND be it further enacted by the authority aforesaid, That the person to be nominated as aforesaid upon the death of any register to execute the said office, during the time the same shall be vacant as aforesaid, shall before he enter on the execution thereof take the oath, herein before appointed to be taken by such register or his deputy, before the lord chief baron, or some other of the barons of her Majesty's court of Exchequer, who are hereby required to administer such oath: and that if such person so nominated be lawfully convicted of any neglect, misdemeanor, fraudulent practice in the execution of the said office during such vacancy, he shall be liable to pay treble damages, with full costs of suit to every person that shall be injured thereby, to be recovered as aforesaid.

XIV. PROVIDED also, and be it further enacted by the authority aforesaid, That this act shall not extend to any lease or leases for years not exceeding twenty one years, where the actual possession goeth along with the said lease; any thing in this act contained to the contrary thereof in any wise notwithstanding.

XV. PROVIDED always, and be it further enacted by the authority aforesaid, That where there are more writings than one for making and perfecting any conveyance or security, which do name, mention, or any ways affect or concern the same honors, manors, lands, tenements, or hereditaments, it shall be a sufficient memorial and register thereof, if all the said honors, manors, lands, tenements, or hereditaments, and the counties, baronies, cities, towns corporate, parishes, town-ships, hamlets, villages, where the same lye, be only once named or mentioned in the memorial, register, and certificate, of any of the deeds or writings made for the perfecting of such conveyance or security; and that the dates of the rest of the said deeds or writings relating to the said conveyance or security, with the names and additions of the parties, and witnesses, and the places of their abode, be only set down in the memorials, registers and certificates of the same, with a reference to the deed or writing, whereof the memorial is so registered, that contains or expresses the parcels mentioned in all the said deeds, and directions how to find the registering the same.

XVI. [So much of this act as relates to the registering of memorials of deeds and conveyances made and executed in any place not within sixty miles of the city of Dublin is repealed by 26 Geo. S. c. 47. s. 3 (Ir.).1] AND be it further enacted by the authority aforesaid, That a memorial of such deeds, conveyances, and wills, as shall be made, and executed, and published in any place not within sixty miles of the city of Dublin, shall be entered or registered by the aforesaid register or his deputy, in case an affidavit sworn before any one of the judges at the assizes, or before the justices of the peace in open court at the general quarter-sessions, or before a person commissioned, pursuant to a late act of Parliament for taking affidavits in the country in the presence of two or more justices of the peace of the same county, who are hereby required to subscribe their names as witnesses to the taking of such affidavit, be brought with the said memorial to the said register, or his deputy; wherein one of the witnesses to the execution of such deeds and conveyances shall swear he or she saw the same executed, and the memorial signed and sealed as abovesaid, or wherein one of the witnesses to the memorial of any will shall swear he or she saw such memorial signed and sealed as abovesaid; and the same shall be a sufficient authority to the said register or his deputy to give the party, who brings such memorial and affidavit to be filed and entered as aforesaid, a certificate of the registring such memorial; which certificate, signed by the said register or his deputy, shall be taken and allowed as evidence of the registries of the same memorials in all courts of record whatsoever; any thing in this act contained to the contrary thereof in any wise notwithstanding.

XVII. [So much of section 17 as relates to any forging or counterfeiting therein mentioned is repealed by 24 & 25 Vict. c. 95. s. 1.] AND be it further enacted by the authority aforesaid, That if any person or persons shall at any time forge or counterfeit any such memorial or certificate, as are herein before mentioned and directed, and be thereof lawfully convicted, such person or persons shall incur and be liable to such pains and penalties, as in and by an act of Parliament made in the twenty eight year of the reign of Queen Elizabeth of blessed memory, intituled, An act against forging evidences, are imposed upon offenders therein mentioned; and that if any person or persons shall at any time forswear himself before the said register, or his deputy, in any of the cases aforesaid, and be thereof lawfully convicted, such person or persons shall incur and be liable to the same penalties, as if the same oath had been made in any of the courts of record at Dublin.

XVIII. PROVIDED always, that in case the devisee, or person or persons interested in the honors, manors, lands, tenements, or hereditaments devised by any such will as aforesaid, by reason of the contesting such will, or other inevitable difficulty, without his, her, or their wilful neglect or default, shall be disabled to exhibit a memorial for the registering thereof within the respective times herein before limited; then, and in such case the registry of the memorial within the space of six month next after his, her, or their attainment of such will or probate thereof, or removal of the impediment, whereby, he, she, or they, are disabled or hindered to exhibit such memorial, shall be a sufficient registry within the meaning of this act; any thing herein contained to the contrary thereof notwithstanding.

XIX. AND be it further enacted by the authority aforesaid, That all persons, that shall be registers, and also all persons, in trust for whom such office shall be granted, shall be resident in this kingdom at least nine months in every year: and if such registers or persons, in trust for whom such office shall be granted, shall absent him or themselves out of this kingdom for more than three months in any one year, except in case of sickness requiring his going or staying beyond the sea for the recovery of his health, the said office to be void; any precedent grant thereof to the contrary notwithstanding.

1709 AD
(8 Anne, c.10)

AN ACT for amending an Act, intituled, An Act for the publick Registring of all Deeds, Conveyances and Wills, that shall be made of any Honors, Manors, Lands, Tenements, or Hereditaments.

WHEREAS an act made in this kingdom in the sixth year of the reign of her present Majesty, intituled, An Act for the publick registring of all deeds, conveyances, and wills that shall be made of any honors, manors, lands, tenements, or hereditaments, is of good design and publick benefit, but has been found by experience to be defective in several particulars; for remedy whereof, be it enacted by the Queen's most excellent Majesty, by and with the advice and consent of the lords spiritual and temporal, and commons in this present Parliament assembled, and by the authority of the same, That a memorial of all such deeds and conveyances, as have been made and executed since the twenty fifth day of March one thousand seven hundred and eight, being the time of the commencement of the said former act, and that shall hereafter be made and executed in the kingdom of Great-Britain, and of all wills and devises in writing where the devisor or testatrix hath died since the said twenty-fifth day of March one thousand seven hundred and eight, or shall hereafter dye, and the devisees in such will residing in Great Britain, of or concerning, or whereby any honors, manors, lands, tenements, or hereditaments, within this kingdom of Ireland, are or may be any way affected, shall be entred or registred by the register appointed by virtue of the said former act of Parliament, or his deputy, in case an affidavit swore before one of the judges of any of the courts at Westminster, or a master in Chancery, or before the justices of the peace in open court, at any general quarter-sessions in the said kingdom of Great-Britain, be brought with the said memorial to the said register or his deputy; in which affidavit one of the witnesses to the execution of such deeds and conveyances shall swear he or she saw the same executed, and the memorial signed and sealed; or in which affidavit one of the witnesses to the memorial of any will shall swear he or she saw such memorial signed and sealed; and such affidavit shall be a sufficient authority to the said register or his deputy, to give the party, that brings such memorial and affidavit, a certificate on the deed, or on a separate and distinct parchment, the deed not being produced of the registring such memorial; which certificate signed by the said register or his deputy shall be taken and allowed as evidence of the registries [sic] of the same memorials in all courts of record whatsoever; any thing in the said former act, or in this act, contained to the contrary thereof in any wise notwithstanding.

II. AND be it further enacted by the authority aforesaid, That every page of such register-books, and every memorial, that shall be entred therein, shall be numbered, and the day of the month, and the year, and hour, or time of the day, when every memorial is registred, shall be entered in the margins of the said register-books, and in the margins of the said memorial.

III. AND be it further enacted by the authority aforesaid, That in case of mortgages, whereof memorials have been already entered, or shall be entered in the said register office, pursuant to the aforesaid act, if at any time afterwards a certificate shall be brought to the said register or his deputy, signed and sealed by the respective mortgagee or mortgagees in such mortgage, his, her, or their respective executors, administrators, or assigns, and attested by two or more witnesses, one of which witnesses shall by affidavit to be made before the said register or his deputy, or persons impowered by the said former act, or by this act, for taking affidavits, (who are hereby impowered and required to administer such oath) prove such monies to be satisfied and paid accordingly, and that he or she saw such certificate signed and sealed by the said mortgagee or mortgagees, his, her, or their respective executors, administrators, or assigns, that then and in every such case the said register, or his deputy, shall make an entry in the margin of the said registry-books against the registry of the memorial of such mortgage, that such mortgage was satisfied and discharged according to such certificate, to which the same entry shall refer, and shall after file such certificate and affidavit, to remain upon record in the said register-office; for which entry the said register shall be allowed six pence, and no more.

IV. [So much of section 4 of this Act as relates to any forging or counterfeiting therein mentioned is repealed by 24 & 25 Vict. c. 95. s. 1.] AND be it further enacted by the authority aforesaid, That if any person or persons shall at any time forge or counterfeit any such certificate, as is herein before mentioned and directed, and be thereof lawfully convicted, such, person or persons shall incur and be liable to such pains and penalties, as in and by an act of Parliament made in the twenty eighth year of the reign of Queen Elizabeth of blessed memory, intituled, An act against forging evidences, are imposed upon offenders therein mentioned: and that if any person or persons shall at any time forswear him, or herself, before the said register or his deputy, or other persons impowered by the said former act, or this act for taking affidavits, in any of the cases aforesaid, and be thereof lawfully convicted, such person or persons shall incur and be liable to the same penalties, as if the same oath had been made in any of the courts of record in Dublin.

V. AND be it further enacted by the authority aforesaid, That the said former act and this present act shall be taken and allowed in all courts within this kingdom as publick acts, and all judges, justices, and other persons therein concerned, are hereby required as such to take notice thereof without special pleading the same.

VI. AND be it further enacted by the authority aforesaid, That every judge and judges of assize, at every assizes in his and their circuits, and the justices of the peace at every quarter-sessions in every county in this kingdom, within the space of three years from and after the royal assent shall be given to this act, shall cause the said former act and this present act to be read in open Court, and the same shall be then and there given in charge.

1721 AD
(8 George I. c.15)

AN ACT for explaining and amending two several acts in relation to the publick registring of all deeds, conveyances, and wills.

WHEREAS by an act of Parliament made in this kingdom in the sixth year of the reign of her late Majesty Queen Anne, intituled, An Act for publick registring of all deeds, conveyances, and wills, that shall be made of any honours, mannors, lands, tenements, or hereditaments, it is among other things enacted,

"That all and every memorial to be entered or registred, as by the said act is prescribed, shall be put into writing in vellum or parchment, and directed to the register of the office therein appointed; and, in case of deeds and conveyances, shall be under the hand and seal of some or one of the grantors, or some or one of the grantees, his, her, or their guardians or trustees:"

and whereas a doubt hath arisen, whether in case of the death of the immediate grantee or grantees in any such deed or conveyance, before his, her, or their having duly executed a memorial, the execution of a memorial by the heirs, executors, administrators, or assigns, of such grantee or grantees, be sufficient in order to the entring and registring such memorial within the intent and meaning of the said recited act: and whereas many such immediate grantees have happened to die, before they had executed memorials of their deeds and conveyances, by means whereof, and by reason of the aforesaid doubt, memorials of many deeds and conveyances have not been hitherto registred, and many hereafter may happen not to be registred, which may be to the great prejudice of many of his Majesty's faithful subjects in their estates and properties: for remedy whereof, be it declared and enacted by the King's most excellent Majesty, by and with the advice and consent of the lords spiritual and temporal and commons in this present Parliament assembled, and by the authority of the same, That where any grantee or grantees in any deed or deeds, conveyance or conveyances, made and executed since the twenty fifth day of March one thousand seven hundred and eight, or that shall hereafter be made and executed, or any devisee or devisees by any will or wills, as well in cases where the testator hath died since the said twenty fifth day of March, as where the testator shall happen to die hereafter, of or concerning, or whereby any honours, manors, lands, tenements, and hereditaments within this kingdom of Ireland are or may be any ways affected, hath or have happened, or shall happen, to die, before his, her, or their having executed a memorial of such deed or deeds, conveyance or conveyances, will or wills; it shall and may be lawful to and for the heirs, executors, administrators, or assigns, of such grantee or grantees, devisee or devisees, or for some or one of them, to sign and seal a memorial of such deed or deeds, conveyance or conveyances, will or wills; and the same shall be and is hereby declared to be as valid and effectual for the entring and registring of such deeds, wills, and memorials, from the time of entring and registring the same, as if such memorial had been signed and sealed by some or one of the immediate grantees or devisees named in such deed or deeds, conveyance or conveyances, will or wills; and that in all memorials, hereafter to be signed and sealed, the place of abode of the subscribing witness or witnesses to such memorial, who is not a subscribing witness to such deed or deeds, conveyance or conveyances, will or wills, shall be inserted in the said memorial.

II. AND whereas by the said recited act it is further enacted,

> "That every register, or his deputy, as often as required, shall make searches concerning all memorials, that are registred as aforesaid, and give certificates concerning the same under his hand, if required by any person:"

and whereas a doubt hath also arisen, whether the register, or his deputy, are obliged by the said recited act to give negative certificates: and whereas the said act would prove in a great measure ineffectual, and the intent thereof be frustrated, and purchasers rendred precarious and insecure, in case negative certificates be not given by the register, or his deputy, to the person or persons requiring the same: be it therefore further enacted by the authority aforesaid, That when any person or persons shall come to the said register-office, and require any such negative certificate to be given, he, she, or they, so requiring the same, shall deliver unto and lodge with the said register, or his deputy, a note in writing, under his, her, or their hand or hands, and mentioning his, her, or their respective places of abode, to the following effect : (viz.) [This Form is repealed by 25 Geo. 3. c. 47., a. 2. (Ir.)]

> I (or we) desire to know what memorial or memorials are entered in your office of any deeds or conveyances made to any, and what person or persons; or of any and what wills made by of or concerning any and what mannors, lands, tenements, or hereditaments, since the day of in the year of our Lord

And upon delivery of such note in writing, as aforesaid, the said register, or his deputy, shall file the said note, and shall be and is hereby required, as soon as conveniently may be, to give to such person or persons requiring the same, a negative certificate or certificates to the effect following: (viz.) [This Form is repealed by 25 Geo. 3. c. 47., s. 2. (Ir.)]

    Upon diligent search made in the register-office from the   day in the year of our Lord   I do not find any memorial of any deed or conveyance made by   to any person or persons, of any mannors, lands, tenements, or hereditaments whatsoever, entred in the said office before the date hereof, except the memorials hereinafter mentioned, (viz.) Witness my hand this   day of   in the year of our Lord

Which certificate shall be attested by two or more credible witnesses; of which the person, or one of the persons, who bring such note, shall be one; and if such register, or his deputy, shall be guilty of any fraud, collusion, or wilful neglect, in making out such certificate or certificates, whereby any person shall be agrieved or damnified, such person so damnified, his heirs, executors, or administrators, shall recover his damages against such officer, or his deputy, with full costs of suit.

III. AND whereas by an act of Parliament made in the eighth year of the reign of her said late Majesty Queen Anne, intituled, An act for amending an act, intituled, An act for the publick registring of all deeds, conveyances, and wills, that shall be made of any honours, mannors, lands, tenements, or hereditaments; it is enacted,

    "That in case of mortgages, whereof memorials then had been entred, or should be entred, in the said register-office pursuant to the said first mentioned act, if at any time afterwards a certificate should be brought to the register of the said office, or his deputy, signed and sealed by the respective mortgagee or mortgagees in such mortgage, his, her, or their respective executors, administrators, or assigns, and attested by two or more witnesses, one of which witnesses should by affidavit, to be made in manner by the said last recited act directed, prove such money to be satisfied and paid accordingly, and that he or she saw such certificate signed and sealed as aforesaid; that then the said register, or his deputy, should make an entry in the margin of the registry books against the registry of the memorial of such mortgage, that such mortgage was satisfied and discharged according to such certificate:"

and whereas satisfaction on all judgments can be acknowledged in the courts of Kings bench, Common pleas, and Exchequer, and also satisfaction on all statutes staple and statutes merchant entred in the high court of Chancery, by virtue of a warrant of attorney perfected by the parties recovering such judgments, and conusees of such statutes, for entring such satisfaction, upon oath made by one of the subscribing witnesses to the said warrant of attorney, that such warrant was so perfected by such party or conuzee: and whereas many mortgages, whereof memorials are registred in the said register-office, have been justly satisfied and discharged by accounts between mortgagors and mortgagees, their heirs, executors, administrators, or assigns, or by bills of exchange, new securities, or otherwise: yet nevertheless it hath been often found impracticable for the person or persons satisfying and discharging the same to make such proof thereof, as the letter of the said last recited act requires, and therefore satisfaction cannot be acknowledged in the said register-office, but the entries or memorials of such mortgages remain upon record, as though such money due by such mortgages had not been satisfied and paid; which is found by experience to be greatly prejudicial to the persons making such mortgages: for remedy thereof, be it further enacted by the authority aforesaid, That in case of mortgages, where memorials have already been entred and registred, or that hereafter shall be entred or registred, in the said register-office; and when the payment of the money cannot be proved, as in the said last recited act is directed, if at any time afterwards a certificate or certificates shall be brought to the said register, or his deputy, signed and sealed by the respective mortgagee or mortgagees in such mortgages, his, her, or their executors, administrators, or assigns respectively, and attested by three credible witnesses, at the least, to be named in such certificate, with the places of their abodes and occupations, importing, that the money due by such mortgages, and the interest thereof, has been duly paid and satisfied to the said mortgagee, his, her, or their executors, administrators, or assigns respectively, or to some person or persons by his, her, or their order, and such mortgagee or mortgagees, his, her, or their executors, administrators, or assigns, making affidavit in writing at the foot or on the back of such certificate before the said register, or his deputy, or before some of the persons impowered by the said two recited acts, or either of them, who are hereby required and impowered to administer such oath, that he, she, or they, do not know of any other person or persons concerned in interest in such mortgage or mortgages, and one of the witnesses to such certificate by affidavit to be made by him before the said register, or his deputy, or before some of the persons impowered by the said two recited acts, or either of them, who are hereby required and impowered to administer such oath, proving, that he or she saw such certificate duly signed and sealed by the said mortgagee or mortgagees, his, her, or their respective heirs, executors, administrators or assigns, and saw such affidavit sworn by such mortgagee or mortgagees, his, her, or their executors, administrators, or assigns, and upon the mortgager, or his heirs, executors, administrators, or assigns, his, her, or their attorney or agent, producing to the said register, or his deputy, the original mortgage so registred, cancelled, if the same be extant and in being; and if the same be lost, or accidentally destroyed, then upon such mortgagor, his heirs, executors, administrators, or assigns, leaving with the said register or his deputy, another certificate signed and sealed by the mortgagee, his heirs, executors, administrators, or assigns, that the said mortgage is lost or accidentally destroyed; which certificate to be attested by three credible witnesses at least, to be named in such certificate, with the places of their abodes and occupations, and one of the witnesses to such certificate by affidavit to be made as aforesaid, proving that he saw such mortgagee, his, her, or their heirs, executors, administrators, or assigns, duly sign and seal such certificate, for each of which affidavits so made before the said register, or his deputy, the sum of six pence, and no more, shall be taken; [Rep., Stat. Law Rev. (I.) Act, 1878.] then and in every such case the said register, or his deputy, is hereby required to make an entry on the said registry books against the registry of the memorial of such mortgage, as also at the foot or on the back of the memorial of such mortgage, that such mortgage was satisfied and discharged according to such certificate; any thing in the said two recited acts, or either of them, to the contrary thereof in any wise notwithstanding.

IV. [So much of section 4 of this Act as relates to any forging or counterfeiting therein mentioned is repealed by 24 and 25 Vic. c. 95. s. 1.] AND be it further enacted by the authority aforesaid, That if any person or persons shall at any time forge or counterfeit any such certificate, as is herein before mentioned and directed, and shall be thereof lawfully convicted, such person or persons shall incur and be liable to such pains and penalties as in and by an act of Parliament made in the twenty eighth year of the reign of Queen Elizabeth of blessed memory, intituled, An act against forging evidences, &c. are imposed upon offenders therein mentioned for forging of any false deed or writing sealed, whereby any estate of free-hold or inheritance may be molested, troubled, or defeated; and if any person or persons shall at any time forswear him or herself before the said register or his deputy, or other person impowered by the said two former acts, or either of them, or this act, for taking affidavits in any of the cases aforesaid, and be thereof lawfully convicted, such person or persons shall incur and be liable to the same penalties, as if the same oath bad been voluntarily and corruptly made in a cause depending in any of the courts of record in Dublin in a matter material in such cause.

V. AND be it further enacted by the authority aforesaid, That this present act shall be taken and allowed in all courts within this kingdom as a publick act; and all judges, justices, and other persons therein concerned, are hereby required to take notice thereof as such without special pleading the same.

1785 AD
(25 George III. c.47)

AN ACT for amending the several Laws relating to the registering of Wills and Deeds in the Registry Office of this Kingdom, and for the better regulating and conducting the Business of the said Office.

WHEREAS the registry of deeds, pursuant to an act of Parliament passed in this kingdom in the sixth year of the reign of her late Majesty queen Anne, entitled, An act for the publick registering of all deeds, conveyances, and wills that shall be made of any honors, manors, lands, tenements, or hereditaments; and also to another act for amending the same, made in the eighth year of her said late Majesty queen Anne, has been found of general and great utility; and whereas the hours heretofore appointed by the said first recited act, for the attendance of the register or his deputy, are since found to be very inconvenient to the publick; be it therefore enacted by the King's most excellent Majesty, by and with the advice and consent of the lords spiritual and temporal, and commons in this present Parliament assembled, and by the authority of the same, That from and after the twenty fourth day of June next, so much of a clause in the said first recited act, which requires the attendance of the said register or his deputy, between the hours of nine and twelve in the forenoon, and between the hours of three and six in the afternoon, be, and the same is hereby repealed; and that from and after the time aforesaid, the said register, or his sufficient deputy, shall give due attendance at his office every day in the week, except Sundays and holidays, between the hours of ten of the clock in the forenoon and four of the clock in the afternoon, for dispatch of all business belonging to the said office. [Rep., Stat. Law Rev. (I.) Act, 1879.]

II. AND whereas by an act of Parliament, passed in the eighth year of the reign of his late Majesty, King George the first, entitled, An act for explaining and amending two several acts in relation to the publick registry of all deeds, conveyances, and wills, it is enacted, That when any person or persons shall come to the register, and require any negative certificate to be given, the person so requiring the same shall deliver unto, and lodge with the register or his deputy, a note in writing, under his hand, in the words in the said recited acts particularly mentioned, or to that effect, and that on delivery of such note, the said register or his deputy shall file the same, and give to such person a negative certificate in the words, or to the effect in the said recited acts also mentioned: and whereas such form as is thereby prescribed for giving and requiring certificates, commonly called negative certificates, hath been found by experience to be attended with so much trouble, delay, and expense, by reason of the very great encrease of memorials deposited in said office, that the intent of taking out such negative certificates hath been in a great measure frustrated, and the practice thereof very much disused; and it would tend to the advantage and security of purchasers and mortgagees if the register should be at liberty to limit and confine his search, and such negative certificate as is or shall be intended to be founded thereon to particular periods of time, lands and persons: be it, enacted by the authority aforesaid, That so much of the said clause in the said last recited act as prescribes the form or tenor of such note in writing, to be delivered to, and lodged with the said register or his deputy, as a foundation for a search in the said register office, and which also prescribes the form or tenor of a negative certificate to be given thereon, be, and the same is hereby repealed; and that from and after the time of passing this act, it shall and may be lawful for every person requiring any certificate, commonly called a negative certificate, to deliver unto, or lodge with the said register or his deputy at the said office, a note or memorandum, fairly written on parchment, and signed with his name in the following words, viz.

> I desire to know what memorial or memorials are entered in your office, of any deeds, conveyances, or wills made by (*naming the person or persons*) of or concerning,   (*naming the manor, lands, tenements, or hereditaments*) in the county of   since the   day of

And upon delivery of such note, the register or his deputy shall file the same, and shall as soon as conveniently may be, give to the person requiring the same, a negative certificate to the following effect, viz.

> Upon diligent search made in the register's

office, from the   day of   I do not find any memorial of any deed, conveyance, or will made by (*naming the person*) of or concerning, (*mentioning the lands, tenements, or hereditaments*) in the county of   from the day aforesaid, until the date hereof, except the memorial herein after mentioned. Witness my hand and seal this day of   [Rep., Stat. Law Rev. (I.) Act, 1879.]

III. AND whereas the mode prescribed by the first mentioned act for registering memorials of deeds and conveyances, made and executed in any place, not within sixty miles of the city of Dublin, is uncertain and inconvenient; be it enacted, That so much of the said act as relates to the registering of such memorials shall be and is hereby repealed, and [Rep., Stat. Law Rev. (I.) Act, 1879.] that in all cases where the lands, tenements, or hereditaments contained in any deed or conveyance are not situate in the county of Dublin, or in the county of the city of Dublin, a memorial of such deed or conveyance shall be entered by the register or his deputy, in case an affidavit sworn before one of the judges at the assizes, or before the justices of the peace at the general quarter sessions of the county where such lands, tenements, or hereditaments lie, or before a person commissioned for taking affidavits in the country, pursuant to the act of Parliament in that case made and provided, and for which a sum of one shilling and six pence shall be paid, to the person or persons taking such affidavit, shall be brought with the memorial to the said register or his deputy, wherein one of the witnesses to the execution of such deed or conveyance, shall swear he or she saw the same executed, and the memorial signed and sealed as by the said act is directed.

APPENDIX B
Example of an original deed and its corresponding Registry of Deeds memorial

The spaces, bold handwriting, and, unfortunately, lack of punctuation are all true to the original.

Original Deed

This Indenture made the Eighth   day of August, in the year of our Lord one thousand seven hundred and sixty four Between Newton Radford of the City of Dublin Hosier of the one part and Edmond Nugent of the City of Westminster Esq. Lieutenant Colonel of his Majesty's   Regiment of Foot Guards son and heir apparent of the right Honourable Robert Nugent of the said City Esquire one of his Majesty's most honourable privy Council of Great Britain of the other part. **Witnesseth** that the said Newton Radford for and in consideration of the sum of five shillings sterling to him in hand paid at or before the Insealing and delivery of these presents the Receipt whereof the said Newton Radford doth hereby Acknowledge and thereof and of every part thereof doth hereby Acquit and discharge the said Edmond Nugent his heirs Executors Administrators and Assigns of **hath** granted bargained sold and Assigned and set over and by these presents **doth** part bargain sell Assign and set over unto the said Edmond Nugent, his Executors Administrators and Assigns, **All that and those** the Lands of Rashane containing fifty two acres three roods and eleven perches with their appurtenances situate lying and being in the Barony of Fore and County of Westmeath and the reversion and reversions and the remainder and remainders Rents Issues and profits of all and singular the said Premises and every part and parcel thereof **To have and to hold** all and singular the said lands and Premises above granted bargained and sold and every part and parcel thereof with the appurtenances unto the said Edmond Nugent his Executors Administrators and Assigns from the day next before the day of the date hereof for and during and until the full End and Term of one whole year from thenceforth next Ensuing and fully to be compleat and [unclear word]

Yielding and paying therefore one Pepper Corn at or upon the feast of saint Michael the Archangel next Insuing if lawfully demanded to the Intent [unclear word, two letters ending in 'o'?] by force of the statute for transferring of Uses into possession he the said Edmond Nugent, may be in the Actual possession of all and Singular the said Premises with the appurtenances and be thereby unable to take and Accept of a Grant and Release of the Reversion and Inheritance thereof to him and his heirs to the only proper use and behoof of the said Edmond Nugent his Heirs and Assigns for ever **In Witness** whereof the Parties aforesaid have hereunto put their hands and seals the Day and year first above written –

Newton [his seal] Radford

All the following writing is on the back of the deed.

Signed sealed and delivered by the said Newton Radford in presence of us
    John Smyth
    John Martin

  Received from the within named
Edmond Nugent Esq the sum of five shillings
sterling being the consideration money within } 0:5:0
mentioned the day and year within written
witnesses present
John Smyth   Newton Radford
John Martin

Newton Radford   Lease for a year of the
      to   } Lands of Fore in
Edmond Nugent Esq   the County of Westmeath

A Memorial of the within Written
Deed was Entered in the Register Office
in the City of Dublin the Tenth day of August one
thousand seven hundred and sixty four at twelve
O'Clock in the forenoon in Book 236 Page 87 and

(Number 152055 and the Execution of the said Deed
and Memorial was duly proved pursuant to an
Act of Parliament in that Case made and provided
    William Hall; Deputy Registrar.

Corresponding Memorial in the Registry of Deeds

This is the copy of the memorial of the above deed, as entered into the aforementioned book and page in the Registry of Deeds in Dublin, with the first two lines below coming from the margin of the book.

Notice how different it is from the original, it seems to be an example of the use of the penal laws to break the entail and its fascinating in that both documents, the deed and the memorial, on their own look innocent enough but put together they amount almost to a fraud. Its amazing too how cheap it was to get some person to act as a fake 'Protestant Discoverer', his pay off seems to be the main thrust of the original deed, as opposed to the memorial.

Radford to Nugent

Registered the 10th day of Aug 1764 at 12 oClock at noon

A Memorial of Indented Deeds of Lease and Release bearing date respectively the Eight and ninth days of august one thousand seven hundred and sixty four and made Between Newton Radford of the City of Dublin Hosier of the one part and Edmond Nugent of the City of Westminster Esq Lieutenant Colonel of his Majesty's Regiment of Foot Guards son and heir apparent of the Right honourable Robert Nugent of the said City Esq one of his majesty's most honourable privy Council of Great Britain of the Other part the said [deed] Reciting that Newton Radford on the ninth day of June one thousand seven hundred and sixty two Exhibited his Bill of Complaint in his Majesty's Court of Exchequer in Ireland and on the thirtieth day of June one thousand and seven hundred and sixty three his amended Bill into said Court against the Right honourable Robert Nugent the Right honourable Anthony Malone Esq William Fitzgerald gent surviving Executor of Bryan Stapleton the Elder since deceased and against Bryan Stapleton the younger Gent praying among other things to be Decreed to the fee simple and Inheritance of the Lands of Rashane Containing fifty two acres three Roods and Eleven perches situate in the Barony of Fore and County of Westmeath and to the full benefit of several Deeds and statutes staple and all other Deeds agreements and securities entered into or Executed by said Confederates in said Bill named or any of them, touching the premises and to all the Estate and Interest Granted or Conveyed or agreed to be Granted or Conveyed of in or to the premises to Michael Nugent or Robert Nugent and Reciting that by a Decree of said Court dated twenty First day of July one thousand seven hundred and sixty four Obtained in said Court it was Ordered adjudged and Decreed that said Newton Radford the first protestant Discoverer should be and was thereby Decreed to be intitled to the fee simple and Inheritance of said Lands of Rashane with the appurtenances purchased from Mr Robert Adair or his trustees or one of them by or in the name of Richard Malone Esq since deceased in trust for Michael Nugent Esq in said Decree named and that the said Newton should have the full benefit of the several Deeds and statutes staple and all other Deeds agreements and securities entered into and Executed by the said Robert Adair Richard Malone Michael Nugent Robert Nugent or Bryan Stapleton or any of them or to or in trust for them or any of them or by or in trust for them or any of them and all the Estate right title and Interest Granted or Conveyed of in or to the premises to the said Richard Malone Michael Nugent Bryan Stapleton and Robert Nugent or any of them and to the possession thereof as by said Decree Inrolled in said Court to which said release referred might at large appear and [the deed] Recites said Newton Exhibited said Bill and Obtained said Decree in said Court to which said release referred might at large appear and Recited said Newton Exhibited said Bill and Obtained said Decree in said Court at the instance of and in trust for and for the sole use and benefit of said Edmond Nugent party to said Release

 By which said Deed of Release whereof this is a memorial the said Newton Radford for and in Consideration therein mentioned did Grant Bargain sell alien release and Confirm unto said Edmond Nugent his heirs and assigns all that the said Lands of Rashane with the appurtenances and the benefit of said Deeds statutes Staple and all other Deeds agreements and securities entered into and Executed by the said several persons in said Bill and decree named or to or in trust for them or any of them or by or in trust for any of the said Defendants or any of them touching the premises and all the Estate Right title and Interest granted or Conveyed or intended to be granted or Conveyed of in or to the premises to said Richard Malone Michael Nugent Bryan Stapleton and Robert Nugent or any of them and the full and entire benefit and advantage of the said Decree and the proceedings in the said Cause or of any other future Decree or proceedings had or be had in said Cause or any other Cause Grounded on said Deed to hold said Lands and premises with said several Deeds statutes staple and securities Comprised and ordered and directed to be assigned and Conveyed by said Decree and the full and Entire benefit and advantage of said Decree and all proceedings had or to be had thereon and all money then due and which should accrue and become due thereon unto said Edmond Nugent his heirs and assigns respectively to and for this and their own proper use and benefit for Ever Which said deed whereof this is a Memorial are Witnessed by John Smith of the City of Dublin Esq and John Martin Gent Clerk to the said John Smith – Newton Radford (seal) – signed and sealed in presence of – John Smith – John Martin

The above named John Martin came this day before me and made oath that he is a subscribing witness to the Original Deeds of Lease and Release whereof the above is a memorial and also to the above Memorial and Executed by the said Newton Radford and also saw the said Newton Radford duly sign and seal the above memorial and Deposeth that the name John Martin subscribed as a witness to the said Deeds and above memorial respectively is this Deponent's proper handwriting and this Deponent delivered the said Deeds to Mr William Hall Deputy Registrar at the Registrar's Office in Dublin on Friday the tenth day of August 1764 at or near twelve oClock at noon – John

Martin swore before me the 10th day of August 1764 –
William Hall Deputy Registrar.

Footnotes

PRONI T.3046 contains a photocopy of this Irish 18th century deed in the Huntington Library in San Marino, California and the ROD Memorial is 236-87-152055.

We can tell a little bit more about the circumstances of this deed from a letter sent on the 8th of September 1764 from John Smyth, at Hot Well's Bristol, writing to Robert Nugent:

"I received the honour of your letter of the 29th of last month by Mr Dorbin, and on the 3rd instant I delivered to him as you desired the deeds and papers relative to the decree vizt. – the original Declaration of Trust on filing the Bill – The original decree enrolled and attested by the proper officer, whereby the lands are decreed to Newton Radford the Discoverer – The draught of the conveyance by lease and release from Radford to Col Edmond Nugent settled and approved of by Councillor Tench (Mr Edmond Malone who was one of the council in the Cause being gone circuit[?anuit?]) – and the deed of lease and release assigning the said decree and conveying the said lands to Col Edmund Nugent by the said Newton Radford engrossed from the said draught.

I have taken the liberty to send you in another packet the Bill of Costs of the proceedings in that Cause taxed and allowed by the proper officer for your satisfaction, – and also two other Bills of Costs for Bills of Discovery, one filed in the name of Samuel Gurwyn[?] and the other name of Joseph Thompson who are both since dead. The difficulty of getting Mr Anthony Malone to answer either of them was the reason why no decree could be obtained in either of them Causes during the lives of G[?]urwyn and Thompson. – I have also troubled you with a small Bill of Costs amounting to 3:11:2 in a suit commenced by you against Alexander Plunkett on a note of his which I long since delivered to Mr Robert Nugent [of Farrenconnell] your agent.

I have also troubled you with an abstract of the whole cost amounting to 72:1:8 Irish money which according to the Exchange at par amounts to 66:9:2 English for which I will be much obliged to you that you will please to send me a Bill as you have been so hard to mention [sic] on Bristol or London, as will be most agreeable to you, directed for me to be left at Mr Simpson's apothecary at the Hotwells Bristol, which I shall esteem as a favour. I have the honour to be with great respect sir

your most obedient and
most humble servant

John Smyth"

A further description of legal costs of this case is available here in a receipt dated the 18th of September 1764 and described as "J[ohn] Smyth the Attorney in Ireland his Receipt for Bill of Costs for Rathshane":

"The Right Honourable Robert Nugent esq to John Smyth
No.1 To Costs in the Cause of C[?]urwin against Michael Nugent esq and others 7:6:1 1/2
No.2 To Costs in the Cause of Robert Nugent esq against Alexander Plunkett 3:11:2
No.3 To Costs in the Cause of Joseph Thompson against Robert Nugent esq and others 5:16:7
No.4 To the Taxed Bill of Costs on obtaining and Enrolling the Decree in the Cause of Newton Radford against the Right Honourable Robert Nugent esq 47:18:10 1/2
No.5 To costs subsequent to the decree for money paid the Discoverer and for the Deeds Relative to the Assignment of the Decree [quite possibly the transaction outlined in this Appendix] 7:8:11
Total 72:1:8
72:1:8 Irish is 66:9:2 English"
(Both references from the Stowe Papers, Huntington Library, California.)

APPENDIX C
1703 speech against the Penal Laws and later account of the effect of those laws

It was only possible in the earlier chapter to outline the mechanics and bare effects of the Penal Laws but it might interest the reader to explore the subject in more depth. Here you get a view from both sides of the century, a speech that was made at the enactment of the harshest of the Penal Laws, speculating on what might happen, and following that is a long account by a member of one of those Catholic families who is outlining what he knew of the effects of those laws on late 1790s Ireland.

Firstly we have a speech made by Sir Theobald Butler at the bar of the Irish House of Commons on Tuesday 22nd of Feb 1703 (Old Style), petitioning on behalf of the Irish Catholics against 'An Act to Prevent the Further Growth of Popery' which went on to receive the royal assent on the 4th of March. Since this was the most sweeping of the anti-Catholic Penal Law legislation, affecting land at any rate, of the 18th century, the arguments that are rehearsed here represent quite a good summary of the various restrictions that Catholics had to face at that time.

What is not printed here is the part where he gives the history of the Articles of Limerick, under which the Catholics were supposed to have gained toleration for their religion before the surrender of that city during the Williamite Wars. Suffice to say that the criminal, and chronic, naivety of Irish politicians about this and so many other treaties is a sore affliction that the Irish populace have had to bear over the centuries!

"By the first of these clauses (which is the third of the bill), I that am the popish father, without committing any against the state, or the laws of the land, (by which only I ought to be governed) or any other fault; but merely for of the religion of my forefathers, and that which, till of late years, was the ancient religion of these kingdoms, contrary to the express words of the second article of Limerick, and public faith plighted as aforesaid for their performance; am deprived of my inheritance, freehold, &c and of all other advantages, which, by those articles, and the laws of the land, I am entitled to enjoy, equally with every other of my fellow subjects, whether protestant or popish. And though such my estate be even the purchase of my own hard labour and industry, yet I shall not (though my occasions be never so pressing) have liberty (after my eldest son or other heir becomes a protestant) to sell, mortgage, or otherwise dispose of, or charge it for payment my debts; or have leave, out of my own estate, to order portions for my other children; or leave a legacy, though never so small, to my poor father or mother, or other poor relations; but during my own life, my estate shall be given to my son other heir, being a protestant, though never so undutiful, profligate, extravagant, or otherwise undeserving; and I that am the purchasing father shall become tenant, for life only, to my own purchase, inheritance, and freehold, which I purchased with my own money; and such my son or other heir, by this act, shall be at liberty to sell, or otherwise at pleasure to dispose of my estate, the sweat of my brows, before my face; and I that am the purchaser, shall not have liberty to raise one farthing upon the estate of my own purchase, either to pay my debts or portion my daughters (if any I have) or make provisions for my other male children, though never so deserving and dutiful: but my estate, and the issues and profits of it, shall, before my face, be at the disposal of another, who cannot possibly know how to distinguish between the dutiful and undutiful, deserving or undeserving. Is not this, gentlemen, (said he) a hard case? I beseech you, gentlemen, to consider, whether you would not think so, if the scale was changed, and the case your own, as it is like to be ours, if this bill pass into a law.

It is natural for the father to love the child, but we all know (says he) that children are but too apt and subject, without any such liberty as this bill gives, to slight and neglect their duty to their parents; and surely such an act as this will not be an instrument of restraint, but rather encourage them more to it.

It is but too common with the son, who has a prospect of an estate, when once he arrives at the age of one and twenty, to think the old father too long in the way between him and it; and how much more will he be subject to it, when, by this act, he shall have liberty, before he comes to that age, to compel and force my estate from me, without asking my leave, or being liable to account with me for it, or out of his share thereof, to a moiety of the debts, portions, or other incumbrances, with which the estate might have been charged before the passing this act.

Is not this against the laws of God and man? against the rules of reason and justice; by which all men ought to be governed? Is not this the only way in the world to make children become undutiful? and to bring the grey head of the parent to the grave with grief and tears? It would be hard from any man; but from a son, a child, the fruit of my body, whom I have nurst in my bosom, and tendered more dearly than my own life, to become my plunderer, to rob me of my estate, to cut my throat, and to take away my bread, is much more grievous than from any other; and enough to make the most flinty of hearts to bleed to think on it. And yet this will be the case if this bill pass into a law; which I hope this honourable assembly will not think of, when they shall more seriously consider, and have weighed these matters.

For God's sake, gentlemen, will you consider whether this is according to the golden rule, to do as you would be done unto? And if not, surely you will not, nay you cannot, without being liable to be charged with the most manifest injustice imaginable, take from us our birth-rights, and invest them in others before our faces.

By the 4th clause of the bill the popish father is under the penalty of £500 debarred from being guardian to, or having the tuition or custody of his own child or children; but if the child pretends to be a protestant, though never so young, or incapable of judging of the principles of any religion, it shall be taken from its own father, and put into the hands or care of a protestant relation, if any there be qualified as this act directs, for tuition, though never so great an enemy to the popish parent; and for want of relations so qualified, into the hands and tuition of such protestant stranger as the court of chancery shall think fit to appoint; who perhaps may likewise be my enemy and out of prejudice to me, who am the popish father, shall infuse into my child, not only such principles of religion as are wholly inconsistent with my liking, but also against the duty which, by the laws both of God and nature, is due from every child to its parents: And it shall not be in my power to remedy, or question him for it; and yet I shall be obliged to pay for such education, how pernicious soever. Nay, if a legacy or estate fall to any of my children, being minors, I that am the popish father shall not have the liberty to take care of it, but it shall be put into the hands of a stranger; and though I see it confounded before my face, it shall not be in my power to help it. Is not this a hard case, gentlemen? I am sure you cannot but allow it to be a very hard case.

The 5th clause provides, that no protestant or protestants, having any estate real or personal, within this kingdom, shall, at any time after the 24th of March, 1703, intermarry with any papist, either in or out of this kingdom, under the penalties in an act made in the 9th of King William, entitled, *An act to prevent protestants intermarrying with papists;* which penalties see in the 5th clause of the act itself.

Surely, gentlemen, this is such a law as was never heard of before, and against the law of right, and the law of nations; and therefore a law which is not in the power of mankind to make, without breaking through the laws which our wise ancestors prudently provided for the security of posterity, and which you cannot infringe without hazarding the undermining the whole legislature, and encroaching upon the privileges of your neighbouring nations, which it is not reasonable to believe they will allow.

It has indeed been known, that there hath been laws made in England that have been binding in Ireland; but surely it never was known, that any law made in Ireland could affect England or any other country. But, by this act, a person committing matrimony (an ordinance of the Almighty) in England, or any other part beyond the seas (where it is lawful both by the laws of God and man so to do) if ever they come to live in Ireland, and have an inheritance or title to any interest the value of £500 they shall be punished for a fact consonant with the laws of the land where it was committed. But, gentlemen, by your favour, this is what, with submission, is not in your power to do; for no law that either now is, or that hereafter shall be in force in this kingdom, shall be able to take cognizance of any fact committed in another nation: nor can any one nation make laws for any other nation, but what is subordinate to it, as Ireland is to England; but no other nation is subordinate to Ireland, and therefore any laws made in Ireland cannot punish me for any fact committed in any other nation, but more especially England, to whom Ireland is subordinate. And the reason is, every free nation, such as all our neighbouring nations are, by the great law of nature, and the universal privileges of all nations, have an undoubted right to make, and be ruled and governed by laws of their own making; for that, to submit to any other, would be to give away their own birth-right and native freedom, and become subordinate to their neighbours, as we of this kingdom, since the making of Poyning's act, have been, and are to England. A right which England would never so much as endure to hear of, much less to submit to.

We see how careful our forefathers have been to provide that no man shall be punished in one county (even of the same nation) for crimes committed in another county; and surely it would be highly unreasonable, and contrary to the laws of all nations in the whole world, to punish me in this kingdom for a fact committed in England, or any other nation, which was not against, but consistent with the laws of the nation where it was committed. I am sure there is not any law in any other nation of the world that would do it.

The 6th clause of this bill is likewise a manifest breach of the second of Limerick articles; for, by that article, all persons comprised under those articles were to enjoy, and have the full benefit of, all the rights, titles, privileges, and immunities whatsoever, which they enjoyed, or by the laws of the land then in force were entitled to enjoy, in the reign of King Charles II. And by the laws then in force, all the papists of Ireland had the same liberty that any of their fellow-subjects had, to purchase any manors, lands, tenements, hereditaments, leases of lives, or for years, rents, or any other thing of profit whatsoever; but by this clause of this bill, every papist or person professing the popish religion, after the 24th of March, 1703, is made incapable of purchasing any manors, lands, tenements, hereditaments, or any rents or profits out of the same; or holding any lease of lives, or any other lease whatsoever, for any term exceeding thirty one years; wherein a rent, not less than two thirds of the improved yearly value, shall be reserved, and made payable during the whole term; and, therefore, this clause of this bill, if made into a law, will be a manifest breach of those articles. The 7th clause is yet of much more general consequence, and not only a like breach of those articles, but also a manifest robbing of all the Roman catholics of the kingdom of their birth-right; for, by those articles, all those therein comprised were (said he) pardoned all misdemeanours whatsoever, of which they had in any manner of way been guilty; and restored to all the rights, liberties, privileges, and immunities whatever, which, by the laws of the land, and customs, constitutions, and native birth-right, they, any, and every of them, were, equally with every other of their fellow subjects, entitled unto. And by the laws of nature and nations, as well as by the laws of the land, every native of any country has an undoubted right and just title to all the privileges and advantages which such their native country affords: And surely no man but will allow, that, by such a native right, every one born in any country hath an undoubted right to the inheritance of his father, or any other, to whom he or they may be heir at law; but if this bill pass into a law, every native of this kingdom, that is, and shall remain a papist, is *ipso facto,* during life, or his or their continuing a papist, deprived of such inheritance, devise, gift, remainder, or trust, of any lands, tenements, or hereditaments, of which any protestant now is, or hereafter shall be seized in fee simple absolute, or fee tail, which, by the death of such protestant, or his wife, ought to descend immediately to his son or sons, or other issue in tail, being such papists and 18 years of age; or, if under that age, within six months after coming to that age shall not conform to the church of Ireland, as by law established; and every such devise, gift, remainder, or trust, which, according to the laws of the land, and such native right, ought to descend to such papist, shall, during the life of such papist (unless he forsake his religion) descend to the nearest relation that is a protestant, and his heirs, being and continuing protestants, as though the said popish heir and all other popish relations were dead; without being accountable for the same: which is nothing less than robbing such popish heir of such his birth-right: for no other reason, but his being and continuing of that religion, which by the first of Limerick articles, the Roman catholics of this kingdom were to enjoy, as they did in the reign of King Charles II and then there was no law in force, that deprived any Roman catholic of this kingdom of any such their native birth-right, or any other thing, which, by the laws of the land then in force, any other fellow subjects were entitled unto.

The 8th clause of this bill is to erect in this kingdom a law of *gavel kind,* a law in itself so monstrous and strange, that I dare say, this is the first time it was ever heard of in the world; a law so pernicious and destructive to the well being of families and societies, that, in an age or two, there will hardly be any remembrance of any of the ancient Roman catholic families known in the kingdom: a law which, therefore, I may again venture to say, was never before known or heard of in the universe!

There is, indeed, in Kent, a custom, called the Custom of Gavelkind; but I never heard of any law for it till now; and that custom is far different from what by this bill is intended to be made a law; for there, and by that custom, the father, or other person, dying possessed of any estate of his own acquisition, or not entailed, (let him be of what persuasion he will), may by will bequeath it at pleasure: Or if he dies without will, the estate shall not be divided, if there be any male heir to inherit it; but for want of male heir, then it shall descend in Gavelkind among the daughters, and not otherwise. But by this act, for want of a protestant heir, enrolled as such within three months after the death of such papist, to be divided, share and share alike, among all his sons; for want of sons, among his daughters; for want of such, among the collateral kindred of his father; and in want of such, among those of his mother; and this is to take place of any grant, settlement, &c other than sale, for valuable consideration of money, really, *bona fide,* paid. And shall I not call this a strange law? Surely it is a strange law, which contrary to the laws of all nations, thus confounds all settlements, how ancient soever, or otherwise warrantable by all the laws heretofore in force, in this, or any other kingdom!

The 9th clause of this act, is another manifest breach of the articles of Limerick; for, by the 9th of those articles, no oath is to be administered to, nor imposed upon such Roman Catholics, as should submit to the government, but the oath of allegiance, appointed by an act of Parliament made in England, in the first year of the reign of their late Majesties King William and Queen Mary, (which is the same with the first of those appointed by the 10th clause of this act:) But by this clause, none shall have the benefit of this act, that shall not conform to the church of Ireland, subscribe the declaration, and take and subscribe the oath of abjuration, appointed by the 9th clause of this act; and therefore this act is a manifest breach of those articles, &c and a force upon all the Roman catholics therein comprised, either to abjure their religion, or part with their birth-rights; which, by those articles, they were, and are, as fully, and as rightfully entitled unto, as any other subjects whatever.

The 10th, 11th, 12th, 13th, and 14th clauses of this bill, (said he) relate to offices and employments, which the papists of Ireland cannot hope for the enjoyment of, otherwise than by grace and favour extraordinary; and therefore, do not so much affect them, at it doe the protestant dissenters, who (if this bill pass into a law) are equally with the papists deprived of bearing any office, civil or military, under the government, to which by right of birth, and the laws of the land, they are as indisputably entitled as any other their protestant brethren: And if what the Irish did in the late disorders of this kingdom made them rebels, (which the presence of a King, they had before been obliged to own, and swear obedience to, gave them a reasonable colour of concluding it did not), yet surely the dissenters did not do any thing to make them so; or to deserve worse at the hands of the government, than other protestants; but, on the contrary, it is more than probable, that if they (I mean the dissenters), had not put a stop to the career of the Irish army at Enniskillen and Londonderry, the settlement of the government, both in England and Scotland, might not have proved so easy, as it thereby did; for if that army had got to Scotland, (as there was nothing at that time to have hindered them, but the bravery of those people, who were mostly dissenters, and chargeable with no other crime since; unless their close adhering to, and early appearing for the then government, and the many faithful services they did their country, were crimes) I say (said he) if they had got to Scotland, when they had boats, barks, and all things else ready for their transportation, and a great many friends there in arms, waiting only their coming to join them; it is easy to think, what the consequence would have been to both these kingdoms; and these dissenters then were thought fit for command, both civil and military, and were no less instrumental in contributing to the reducing the kingdom, than any other protestants: And to pass a bill now, to deprive them of their birth-rights, (for those their good services), would surely be a most unkind return, and the worst reward ever granted to a people so deserving. Whatever the papists may be supposed to have deserved, the dissenters certainly stand as clean in the face of the present government, as any other people whatsoever: And if this is all the return they are like to get, it will be but a slender encouragement, if ever occasion should require, for others to pursue their examples.

By the 15th, 16th and 17th clauses of this bill, all papists, after the 24th of March 1703, are prohibited from purchasing any house or tenements, or coming to dwell in any in Limerick or Galway, or the suburbs of either, and even such as were under the articles, and by virtue thereof have ever since lived there, from staying there; without giving such security as neither those articles, nor any law heretofore in force, do require; except seamen, fishermen, and day labourers, who pay not above forty shillings a year rent; and from voting for the election of members of Parliament, unless they take the oath of abjuration; which, to oblige them to, is contrary to the 9th of Limerick articles; which, as aforesaid, says the oath of allegiance, and no other, shall be imposed upon them; and, unless they abjure their religion, takes away their advowsons and right of presentation, contrary to the privilege of right, the law of nations, and the great charter of Magna Charta; which provides, that no man shall be disseized of his birth-right, without committing some crime against the known laws of the land in which he is born, or inhabits. And if there was no law in force, in the reign of King Charles the Second, against these things (as there certainly was not), and if the Roman catholics of this kingdom have not since forfeited their right to the laws that then were in force, (as for certain they have not), then with humble submission, all the aforesaid clauses and matters contained in this bill, entitled, *An act to prevent the further growth of popery*, are directly against the plain words and true intent and meaning of the said articles [of Limerick], and a violation of the public faith, and the laws made for their performance; and what I therefore hope (said he) this honourable house will consider accordingly."

So much for the danger that was forewarned at the bar of the House of Commons when the harshest of these laws was first enacted now we can see here the result of them as related by one of the great clan of the O'Reillys who had emigrated into the North Meath/Westmeath border area after losing out all their great estates in Cavan.

The writer is Andrew O'Reilly, a brother of Edward the lexicographer, who later became Paris correspondent of the Times newspaper. His family connections meant that he was steeped in the whole atmosphere of the dispossessed Irish Catholic families of the 18th century which I think makes his testimony probably our best single source for getting beneath the skin of their history under these Laws.

He starts off with a fascinating glimpse of the kind of folklore that ran through those families in the mid to late 18th century, the curious mixture of great pride in their race, religion and country, their fixation with the always forlorn hope of help from abroad, intermingled with bitterness and collective trauma as a result of the land confiscations and then the Penal Laws.

From the first moment I began to understand the conversations held in my presence, until that which supplied me with personal acquaintance with and appreciation of the afflictions of Ireland, I had heard little else than

"Treasons, stratagems and spoils," (Henry IV, Shakespeare)

and of the conflicts of the Irish with the invaders of their soil. I heard of Fioun Mac Cuhal, and Ossian, and Oscar. I reverenced the craft, the demeanour, and the patriotism of Fioun; and admired the genius of Ossian.

I pitied Oscar for the incessant labour to which he is doomed in the other world (in a place not to be named), which consists in threshing, with a red-hot iron flail, the recusant sons of Erin as they enter. I heard of the Danes, and of Brian Boroimhe, and of his son Donogh, and of his grandson Mosogh; the three generations who fell at Clontarf, on Good Friday, 1014, in the final defeat and expulsion of the Ostmen. I heard of "the red-haired man," Mac Morogh, who, it was prophesied, would be

"Cause of grief and woe to Erin"

and of "the woman" who, the same seer foretold, would

"Lay waste the plains of Leinster;"

and I heard of her lieutenant Essex, and his doings; and of Strafford, and of his taking unto himself by forfeiture (that was the courtly phrase) in a single day the possessions of seventy-five chiefs and gentlemen of the clan of the O'Byrnes (one of them, I was told, my maternal progenitor), and which paternal adoptions constitute at present the Wicklow estates of a great English nobleman, the lineal or collateral descendant, I forget which, of the propounder of that great appropriation clause.

I heard of Maolmordha (pronounced Mecolmora) that is, Myles O'Reilly, or, as he was called, "Myles the Slasher". I heard also of Owen Roe and of (Shane) O'Neill, and of Sir Teague O'Regan, and of the wholesale colonization of Ulster, which those who were excluded persisted in terming confiscation, by that godly prince, the foe a Voutrance of Papists, witches and warlocks, James I., so expert in

"Reckoning up the several devils' names."

and who, by his autos-da-fe of hags and sorcerers, did so much towards the illumination of the world; thus setting to his granddaughter the example which she so closely imitated, in

"Roasting, just like crabs, the martyrs;"

and I heard of Glencoe, and of Mullaghmasteen; and of Oliver Cromwell, and of his Gothic revenge in battering down the north side of every tower and castle because of the heroic resistance he had encountered in the north of Ireland, and of his pious adjuration to his soldiers, to "fear God and keep their powder dry;" and of King Shumus, with (in Irish) a most contemptuous epithet thereto attached; and of "the brave, brave Duke Schomberg," who

"Lost his life. In crossing the Boyne water;"

and of Luttrell, who "sold the pass;" and of the immortal Sarsfield; and of the chivalrous Frenchman, of whom the epic poet sings:

"Saint Ruth is dead.
And all the guards have from the battle fled;
As he rode up the hill he met his fall.
And died a victim to a cannon-ball."

After them, I heard of the Rapparees, and of "the bold Freney," and of "Freney's Mountain," where he exercised reprisals on the invader; and of Father Sheeny, and of the untimely end respectively of all the jury by whom he had been found guilty; and of the Boghalawn-Bawns and White Boys.

Side by side with these, was the incessant mention of forfeitures, spoliations and confiscations, and of hangings, drawings, and quarterings, and of bills of discovery, and of Protestants and Romans, and of relapsed Papists.

These mournful recollections were occasionally relieved by the patriotic sallies and waggeries of Swift. To these quickly succeeded "the Volunteers of Ireland," and the declaration of independence, and the Duke of Leinster, and Lord Clanricarde, and Lord Charlemont, and Henry Grattan, and Henry Flood, and Edmund Burke, and Father O'Leary.

Thus prepared and predisposed, I began, although then only a child, to obtain some faint notion of the bitterness with which those references were uttered, and gathered that some party with whom I ought to sympathize had received injury. Almost suddenly, however, the interest with which domestic politics were viewed, gave place to foreign topics, or were in some sort identified with them. The French Revolution and the Bastille, and Lafayette and the National Guards were jumbled in a manner, inconceivable by me, with the volunteers, and Hamilton Rowan and Napper Tandy and the Catholic claims, and the Catholic Committee and Tom Broughall, and John Keogh and Dick McCormick, and Toby Mackinna, the latter of whom, in consequence of a pamphlet he wrote unfavourable to the claims of his co-religionnaires, was called a deserter, and of Colonel Talbot and Sir Edward Newenham.

The result of all this was the formation of what will probably appear a depraved and unwholesome taste, which grew with my growth, and strengthened with my strength; and which acquired further strength from dose and more matured observation of events, and subsequent personal intercourse with or knowledge of some of the remarkable men thrown up by the volcano.

...

Just as I was entering then on my eighth year, that is shortly before Christmas of 1790, a stranger arrived on a visit to my family, and was received as "Cousin Robin," with evidences of affection and regard. Young as I was, I regarded him with curiosity. His air, manner, language and pronunciation differed from those of the world about him.

Few facts in history are more surprising, than the rapidity and the completeness of the fall of Irish families, stricken down as that of Cousin Robin had been, by the penal laws. Reduced to beggary at once, and with habits acquired in affluence; surrounded only by contemporaries similarly crushed, or by the despoilers revelling in possession of their forfeited lands; friendless and unpitied; persecuted and insulted, rather than protected and solaced, because of the injustice and the rigour with which they had been visited, for injustice never pardons its victims; regarded as suspected persons, from the reasons for discontent so abundantly furnished them, they seemed struck with stupor or paralysis, and were rendered incapable of any effort to rise out of the abyss into which they had been precipitated. Dispirited, heartbroken, unmanned, they suffered any little personal property which escaped the fang of the soi-disant law to melt away; and were compelled to resort to the most humiliating means to prolong existence, and to accept for their helpless offspring the humblest and most common-place condition which promised a maintenance for them. "A trade" was the general resource sought for the son of the heretofore chief of a clan, or landholder, or gentleman. And this too in many cases without education; for instruction, gratuitous at least, could only be obtained through that unacceptable condition, conformity to the religion of the State. This gave rise to Swift's observation to Pope (I quote from memory): "If you would seek the gentry of Ireland, you must look for them on the coal quay, or in the liberty." Thus in my youth, "the Devoy," the head of one of the most powerful and distinguished of our septs, was a Blackinelle. I have often seen a mechanic, named James Dungan, who was said to be a descendant of Dungan, Earl of Limerick; and "the Cheevers" (Lord Mount Leinster), was the clerk of a Mrs. Byrne, who carried on the business of a ropemaker, in New Row, Thomas Street, in the early part of the present century.

With their property vanished also the moral courage, and the pride and self-respect, of the impoverished. Maddened and embittered by humiliation and suffering; renouncing all hope of recovering their alienated lands; those victims of bills of discovery or of confiscation, burned or otherwise destroyed, or threw aside as worse than useless, the records of their former possessions, the proofs of their former respectability, and seemed in fact desirous to efface all evidence of it. I know one case in which the title-deeds and other documents connected with the possession of an estate were searched for on an important occasion, and in which it appeared that they had been given to tailors to cut into strips or measures for the purposes of their trade!

So general was this indifference at the period of persecution (added to the accidental or wanton destruction of records by other means, and by other parties), that when, about the year 1815, a claim was set up to a dormant peerage [probably the Savages of Portaferry applying for the Barony of Delvin and asking the help of the O'Reillys of Ballinlough, Co. Westmeath], and a relative of mine on the point was applied to for information in support of it (an excellent authority), he said to the claimant: "You are in the condition of the descendants of very many Irish families, whose great difficulty is to prove who was their grandfather."

Two circumstances were striking in the conversation of Cousin Robin. One was, that while vaunting the loyalty and devotion of his predecessors to their King, James II., he suffered to appear a feeling of supreme contempt for that monarch. The other was, that while treating as infamous and low, Voltaire, Rousseau, D'Alembert, Grimm, and the other modern philosophers of France, he permitted himself to use language which showed that he had not escaped the contagion of infidelity, and which I well remember shocked the primitive, quiet, little circle who were his auditors.

In the first case, contempt for a sovereign who, when in Ireland, in the hour of danger, evinced none of the personal courage which he was said to have displayed early in life, was mixed up no doubt with regrets for the sacrifices made by those who followed him into exile; further increased by the unjust and unwise imputations said to have been uttered by him of them who had risked, and ultimately lost everything, by adhering to his cause.

In the second case, fashion struggled with principle. The young people of the day in France read Voltaire, and yet boasted their loyalty. They laughed with him at religion and its ministers, and they professed themselves ready to die in defence of the monarchy, of which his writings sapped the foundations.

Disappointed in his expectations in Ireland, Cousin Robin took his leave early in 1791, and returned to France. He was among the Irish who emigrated with "the princes," and fell, I believe, in the campaigns in which they were engaged, for we never heard more of him. Owing to the freedom with which he spoke on religious matters, a coldness had begun to grow up between him and his relatives, who in consequence witnessed his departure without regret, and made no effort to continue their intercourse by correspondence. Some years afterwards, however, his failings were forgotten, while his anecdotes of the Brigade were recalled with delight. Like the frozen words spoken of by that renowned and veracious voyager, Baron Munchausen, and which, when the thaw released them became audible, the narratives and gossip of Cousin Robin presented themselves with marvellous exactness to my memory many years afterwards.

Poor Cousin Robin! I have referred to certain inconsistencies in his character, but I have met with too many of his contemporaries who partook of them, and too many eccentricities in others to dwell upon those he discovered with much severity.

...

The disorganisation of society in Ireland produced by conquests, forfeitures, confiscations, and, as it was termed, religious persecution (but which, like faction, of which it was a species, was only the madness of many for the gain of a few) assumed now what the French call a fearful development. The self-proclaimed Protestant, which was frequently a misnomer, for he was a mere robber, seized and entered upon the lands and houses of the Papists, and turned them to his own use; sometimes without any form of law, and more frequently by its perversion; always, however, to the utter disregard of justice.

To encourage proselytism in the vain belief that real conversion would grow out of professed conformity, rewards were offered to children to declare against their parents, brothers against brothers, servants against masters. False friends pertaining to the State religion, to whom property was transferred in trust by Roman Catholic owners, who hoped by that subterfuge to preserve at once their worldly possessions and their faith, repaired to the Court of Chancery, and declared that fact, and as a matter of course became the proprietors.

Of this species of perfidy and baseness, a remarkable instance occurred in the vicinity of Dublin. Mr. Malpas, who erected the obelisk on Killiney Hill, which still remained in my day, and a most striking ornament of Dublin Bay it was, handed over by deed to a neighbour, and soi-disant friend, Mr. E, a very considerable landed property; of which, in the manner above described, E , possessed himself.

Not content with this spoliation, he denounced his confiding friend as a Jacobite as well as a Papist.

The effect of this system was naturally to perpetuate the hatred of the Roman Catholics for the government which prescribed and legalised these confiscations. Families hitherto respectable, affluent, hospitable, and generous, but now plundered and impoverished — nay, reduced to misery — fell into disrepute and were compelled to solicit alms of those who had been their pensioners. Honourable pride, virtue, self-respect gave way. In a few cases the Roman Catholics conformed nominally to the State religion, to save a remnant of their property. The contempt of their late co-religionists, relatives, or friends, who adhered under all the consequences to the faith of their fathers, and the maledictions of the Church, and the populace were poured upon them. Remorse and irritation did the rest. The new convert became, as usual, still more the Protestant and persecutor than he who had never professed any other creed or principles. In the majority of instances, he was crushed, worn down, broken-hearted; all pride, spirit, and self-esteem gave way, and the previous land-holders sank into the condition of the pauper or the serf. Thus, in my youth, the Devoy was a blacksmith; the Byrne of Bally manus, a woollen-draper; the Cheevers, Lord Mount Leinster, clerk to Mrs. Byrne, rope-maker, of New Row, Thomas Street.

Two examples of the working of the system, which prevailed even so lately as eighty years ago, will suffice to convey an idea of the situation of the Catholic gentry of that period.

R[obert Balfe] was a gentleman possessing a tolerably large fortune, residing in C[ortown] Castle, near Kells, in the county of Meath. He was the eldest of six or eight brothers, giants in stature, all of whom lived in the castle or its dependencies; and having no profession or pursuit, became almost of necessity, and like their contemporaries upon the adverse faction, dissolute and riotous. Towards the year 1745, his friends perceived that R B, then a man of thirty or forty years of age, displayed symptoms approaching to imbecility or folly, which declared itself in inordinate susceptibility of the tender passion. Fearing that he would contract a marriage with an inferior, his brothers pressed him to seek a wife in the circles of the gentry of the county. He said he would think of it. When pressed more closely, he desired that they would suggest to him a suitable match. They named several, all of which he declared non-receivable, on grounds the most absurd. Miss Bligh, for example, he scorned; "her family being scarcely a hundred years settled in Meath!" Alarmed at this opposition to their project, his friends became importunate, and said: "Since you disapprove all that we propose, choose for yourself"

"Now you talk common sense," said he. "I will marry the daughter of a gentleman — a pretty girl I have long loved."

"What gentleman?"

"Ned B[alfe], of N."

Whether agreeable or otherwise to his family, they acquiesced in this choice; and R B married his fair namesake, and brought her home to his castle.

At that period there lived Counsellor John O'Reilly [of Baltrasna Co. Meath]. He was a gentleman by birth, and a barrister by profession, as the title given to him indicates, and was in some respects the O'Connell of that day. He was a man of talent and energy, and had been deputed by the Roman Catholics of Ireland to represent them, I will not say at the Court of George II., but in London; holding a retainer, and interfering on the spot in matters connected with his mission, communicating the results to his constituents, and informing them whenever any new danger or attack menaced them or their property.

In the course of time, the funds to maintain Mr. O'Reilly in this position failed; his own patrimony was expended, and he returned penniless to Ireland, without having achieved much for those who had deputed him to London. "Power is too powerful," said he, "we must submit to fate."

Although unsuccessful, he was well received by the Roman Catholic gentry, whose interests he had certainly sought to maintain. Money was out of the question. They offered him hospitality, and he continued for some time the guest in succession of half the Catholic families of Meath. Among others, R B was more than kind to him; he invited him to, and domesticated him in C Castle.

An improper intimacy between O'Reilly and the lady of his host ensued, it is to be feared. Not content with their disregard of all the ties which bound them to the unhappy R B, now falling into idiocy, they sought to render him the laughing-stock of his servants, tenants, and neighbours; parading him in grotesque apparel, with his face daubed with yellow ochre.

Indignant at and fatigued by this infamous abuse of the poor man's weakness, and irritated possibly by the alienation of their brother's income for O'Reilly's benefit, R's giant relatives resolved on taking the law into their own hands — no unusual practice in those days. They imprisoned him in a chamber of his own house, therefore, and turned his faithless wife and her paramour out of doors.

The guilty pair did not quit the castle empty-handed, however. They carried with them an iron coffer, in which were preserved the title-deeds of the estate, and other documents; and these they pawned with Sir [Thomas Taylor, 3rd Baronet of Kells], grandfather of the present Lord [Headfort], for a thousand pounds.

The lender waited not repayment: "he filed a bill of discovery in the Court of Chancery,' as that process was denominated in those days.

He showed that B[alfe] was a Papist, and he himself a Protestant, and a decree was passed investing him with the estate.

The brothers of B resisted. They defended with their persons, and by the aid of their retainers, the Castle of C, and with some loss of life, I think. Overpowered, they retired at length, and perceiving that all their efforts to obtain justice were vain, one or two of them, infuriated by their wrongs, conformed to the Protestant religion, and claimed the alienated estates. After a long course of impoverishing litigation, they were beaten by the baronet, for he was not yet ennobled [he became an Earl in 1766]. One of them fell in a duel; another, I think, in retaining forcibly possession of the castle. Reduced to poverty, the survivors ended their days in obscurity and unhappiness.

The descendant of R[obert] B[alfe], the chief of the family, was in its reduced condition, apprenticed about the year 1760, to a trade, the refuge of the offspring of half the ancient Roman Catholic families of Leinster. At the beginning of the present century, he was a turner, living in Catherine Street, near Meath Street, Dublin, and emigrated to America shortly afterwards.

A gleam of hope, which over reached him in his exile, occurred some thirty years since to a relative of his, a member of the legal profession [maybe Matthew Reilly, the solicitor in Dublin, Andrew's cousin]. In reflecting upon the unhappy foil of the B[alfe]s, this cousin remembered that previously to the elopement of Mrs.R B with Counsellor John, a portion of his (B 's) estate, now of the value of four thousand pounds per annum, had been mortgaged to a Mr. N for a thousand pounds; and that Mr. N being a Protestant, and in possession, that portion of R B 's estate was not mentioned in the decree on the bill of discovery, filed by Sir ?[Taylor]. He further ascertained that Mr. N, being an honest, honourable man, or satisfied with undisturbed possession of the lands and mansion-house of —— ——, had taken no steps to legalise his holding the portion of the Papist's property over which he had a lien.

Alas! limitation had run against the claim which the lawyer was about to make for restitution of his relation's property, and that hope vanished.

One word more respecting this unfortunate family, to illustrate further the operation of the penal laws at that period. One of the Balfes, brothers of Robin, who had, as the phrase went, "turned Protestant," in order to claim and recover the family fortune, became from change of position, chagrin, privation, and resentment, an irritable, violent, desperate man, and being of huge proportions, was the terror of half the country, especially when in his cups. In a public-house brawl one night, he was beset by a roomful of half-intoxicated men, whom he had insulted. During half an hour he, with his back to the wall, defended himself resolutely and effectively, inflicting fearful wounds on the assailants. At length a window over his head was opened, and a virago armed with a churndash appeared at it. With a terrible blow, which fractured his skull, she felled the giant.

He was carried to his sister's house, where it was found that his case was desperate. Informed that his death was inevitable, Balfe, who never contemplated a real change of creed, consented to receive the visit of a Roman Catholic priest. Becoming from that fact, however, what was termed "a relapsed Papist," and the laws against Popish priests administering the sacraments of their Church, particularly to persons in his circumstances, being severe (in fact it was a capital offence), much secrecy was required in procuring for the dying man the consolations of religion, A clergyman was found, however, to brave the consequences. He arrived at the house where B lay, disguised as a woman, and seated on a pillion behind a peasant of the neighbourhood, an ex-tenant of the family, and having administered the sacraments to the dying man, he then withdrew.

The surviving relatives of B expressed their determination to take vengeance of the faction by whom he had been murdered, as they deemed it. "No," said the dying gladiator, with a last effort; "let there be no vengeance, no prosecution. I brought it on myself." Then raising himself on his elbow, and his eye momentarily flashing, as he looked upwards, he added, with the air of Altamont:

"With that black-thorn stick I struck the first blow, and it felled Jack." Having uttered this he fell back on his pillow and expired.

The second instance of the working of the penal code, in its legalisation of confiscation, and encouragement of soi-disant conversions to the established religion, which I promised, is the following:

Seventy or eighty years ago, there resided in Soho Square, London, an Irish Roman Catholic gentleman, known among his friends as "Geoghan of London." [Probably Jack 'Buck' MacGeoghegan and in reference to his elder brother Kedagh.] Pretending to be, or being really alarmed, lest a relative (Mr. Geoghegan of Jamestown) should conform to the Protestant religion, and possess himself of a considerable property, situate in Westmeath, Ireland, of which he (Geoghegan of London) was tenant for life, and of which, if I remember rightly, Geoghegan of Jamestown was the presumptive heir, Geoghegan of London resolved upon a proceeding to which the reader will attach any epithet it may seem to warrant.

He repaired to Dublin, reported himself to the necessary authorities, and professed, in all its required legal forms, the Protestant religion on a Sunday, sold his estates on Monday, and relapsed into Popery on Tuesday.

He did not effect these changes unostentatiously; for he saw no reason for mauvaise honte, as he called it. He expressed admiration of the same principle of convenient apostasy, which governed Henri IV.'s acceptance of the French crown. "Paris vaut bien une messe," said that gay, chivalrous, but some-what unscrupulous monarch. Thus, when asked the motive for his abjuration of Catholicism, Geoghegan replied: "I would rather trust my soul to God for a day, than my property to the fiend for ever."

This somewhat impious speech was in keeping with his conduct at Christchurch when he made his religious profession: the sacramental wine being presented to him he drank off the entire contents of the cup. The officiating clergyman rebuked his indecorum. "You need not grudge it me," said the neophyte; "it's the dearest glass of wine I ever drank."

In the afternoon of the same day he entered the Globe Coffee Room, Essex Street, then frequented by the most respectable of the citizens of Dublin. The room was crowded. Putting his hand to his sword, and throwing a glance of defiance around, Geoghegan said:

"I have read my recantation to-day, and any moll who says I did right is a rascal!"

There exists still, a further expression of Mr. Geoghegan, which, had the features I have traced not been preserved, would convey a perfect picture of the man; but it was a jest upon a matter too sacred to justify its repetition in print in the terms employed. The gist of it is this:

A Protestant with whom he was conversing the moment before he left home to read his recantation, said to him: 'For all your assumed Protestantism, Geoghegan, you will die a Papist."

"Fi done, mon ami!" replied he. "That is the last thing of which I am capable."

One more specimen of the operation of the penal laws, and I have done with that part of my subject. It is so ungracious that nothing but the necessity for plainly exhibiting the system, could induce me further to dwell upon it.

Mr. Geoghegan had a relative, Mr. Kedagh Geoghegan, of Donower, in the county of Westmeath, who, though remaining faithful to the creed of his forefathers, enjoyed the esteem and respect of the Protestant resident gentry of his county beyond most men of his time. Notwithstanding his profession of the Roman Catholic religion precluded his performing the functions of a grand juror, he attended the assizes at Mullingar regularly, in common with other gentlemen of Westmeath, and dined with the grand jurors.

On one of those occasions, a Mr. [George] Stepney [of Durrow], a man of considerable fortune in the county, approached him, and remarked:

"Geoghegan, that is a capital team to your carriage. I have rarely seen four finer horses — nor better matched. Here,

Geoghegan, are twenty pounds," tendering him a sum of money in gold. "You understand me. They are mine." And he moved towards the door, apparently with the intention of taking possession of his purchase. The horses, not yet detached from Mr. Geoghegan's carriage, were still in the yard of the inn close by.

"Hold, Stepney!" said Geoghegan. "Wait one moment. I shall not be absent for more than that time." He then quitted the room abruptly, and was seen running in great haste towards the inn at which he always put up.

There was something in the scene that had just occurred which shocked the feelings of the witnesses of it, and something in the manner of Geoghegan, that produced among them a dead silence and a conviction that it was not to end there. Not a word was yet spoken, when the reports of four pistol-shots struck their ears, and in a few seconds afterwards Geoghegan was perceived coming from the direction of the inn, laden literally with fire-arms. He mounted to the room in which the party were assembled, holding by their barrels a brace of pistols in each hand. Walking directly up to Stepney, he said:

"Stepney, you cannot have the horses for which you bid just now."

"I can, and will have them."

"You can't. I have shot them; and Stepney, unless you be as great a coward as you are a scoundrel, I will do my best to shoot you. Here, choose your weapon, and take your ground. Gentlemen, open if you please, and see fair play."

He then advanced upon Stepney, offering him the choice of either pair of pistols. Stepney, however, declined the combat and quitted the room, leaving Geoghegan the object of the unanimous condolements of the rest of the party and overwhelmed with their expressions of sympathy and of regret for the perversion of the law of which Mr. Stepney had just sought to render him the object.

It is hardly necessary to observe that Mr Stepney, in his offer of twenty pounds for horses that were worth twenty times that sum, was only availing himself of one of the enactments of the penal code, which forbade a Papist the possession of a horse of greater value than five pounds.

Notwithstanding this incident, old Kedagh Geoghegan continued to visit Mullingar during the assizes for many years afterwards; but to avoid a similar outrage, and to keep in recollection the cruel nature of the Popery laws, his cattle thence forward consisted of four oxen.

...

There is a story told of a lady, a member of the Clare or Westmeath family. I have heard, that she was the daughter of the fourth Earl of Westmeath, and the honourable Bellew, daughter of Lord Bellew, who for some reason which has escaped me, was strangely distinguished by the title of "Captain Moll Nugent." Perhaps it was the following circumstance that obtained for her that unfeminine title.

Generally speaking, in mixed companies, allusion to politics, to Jacobites, or Williamites, was omitted, even in those days. Sometimes, either through design or inadvertence, however, etiquette was infringed, and the Roman Catholics present were affronted, or felt themselves to be, by toasts or expressions recalling to them their defeat. Thus, at supper after the ball given at the Castle on a 4th of November, the Lord-lieutenant for the time being, gave as a toast, "the glorious and immortal memory of the great and good King William, who delivered us from brass money, Pope, Popery, wooden shoes, and slavery!"

"I'll drink your toast my Lord," said Miss, or Lady, Moll Nugent, "but with a trifling addition, if you will give me leave."

"Certainly," replied the Viceroy.

"Then," said she, "I shall add the memory of the sorrel horse that broke his neck!"

This is not a pleasant story. Much less does it furnish a type of the Irishwoman of rank of that period.

"I do not like your manly belles,
Your Chevaliers d'Eon, and Hannah Snells."

But allowance must be made for a high-spirited young woman, a rigid Roman Catholic possibly, but certainly a fanatical partisan of the expelled Stuarts, to whom, the legal possessors of the throne of those realms, her family had been faithful even to desperation, and had suffered for it in its members and in its property. All this and her daily observation of the persecution of her friends and creed, and of insults wantonly offered to her party, which none of the male sex dared resist, rankled in her bosom, and it only required the slightest spark to produce an explosion. This display of the ascendancy of the Orangemen she considered the more cowardly because chastisement of it could not be anticipated, there being no male Roman Catholic present. She rose, therefore, to protest against what she deemed a violation of the rights of hospitality and of the principles of good-breeding; for, she continued to argue, that he who gave the original toast knew there was present at least one Roman Catholic lady whose susceptibilities it was sure to wound.

She was wrong, however, in supposing that the toast in question was a volunteer. It had been ever since the overthrow of the Stuarts a charter toast at the Castle, and with all the great corporations. It was, therefore, as a matter of routine that it was given by the noble host, who moreover believed that every person present was cognisant of that fact. He inferred, therefore, that nobody would feel surprise or indignation upon his proposing the toast. Upon the present occasion, however, he reckoned without his hote, as we have seen. Viewed as the circumstance may be, now when we are all sober, the toast drunk by Captain Moll Nugent, raised her to the pinnacle of popularity with her party.

When incidents like these were possible in high places, the latitude will easily be conceived in which as regarded insult and provocation, and resistance, the inferior grades of society indulged, and the consequent state of irritation in which the country was held for a hundred years. A hundred years? Ay, and upwards; for long after the commencement of the present century there continued to exist in the front of a house in Nassau Street, Dublin, between Grafton Street and Dawson Street, a marble tablet, inserted in the wall, in which a bust of King William, of the natural size, and in bas-relief, was to be seen, and beneath it this inelegant and unworthy distich:

"May we never want a Williamite,
To kick the breech of a Jacobite."

This monument of intolerance and execrable taste was, moreover (at the expense of the city, it would seem) as regularly painted, and its epigraph as carefully picked out preparatory to each 4th of November, as the statue of King William on College Green. That it caused heartburning, I recollect well; but its removal was due only to the demolition of the entire house for the purpose of local improvement."

Footnotes
Sir Theobald Butler's speech is from Sir Henry Parnell, *A history of the penal laws against the Irish Catholics* (Dublin, 1808) Appendix no.1, p.vi-xiii, and O'Reilly's account is from Andrew O'Reilly, *Reminiscences of an Emigrant Milesian* (London, 1853), vol I: p.51-56, 75-82, and vol III: p.47-65, 76-80.

O'Reillys of Oristown/Cortown in Meath and Harold's Cross in Dublin

Andrew was but one member of a distinguished Meath family who are not very well documented which is why the current writer will try here to fill in the gaps.

The oldest reference we have to where this family seems to have come from derives from a passage in one of Edward O'Reilly's manuscripts which has made its way into the British Library in London:

"The following inscription was copied from the Base of an old stone cross in the Church yard of Kells in the County of Meath, in the year 1739, by Eoghan O'Reilly of Corstown, grandfather to the writer of this, viz Edward O'Reilly." (NLI M/F Pos 407, Egerton 146, p.27/16.)

Which Corstown he is referring to is the interesting question but I think on balance they are probably referring to Cortown, which is not far from Kells going in a south easterly direction. I say that because the account by Andrew O'Reilly that you see here mentioned talks a lot about the Balfe family from Cortown Castle, and he states that an Owen O'Reilly had married into this family so I take that to be the 'Eoghan' that Edward mentions above. Also one of the high crosses at Kells has an inscription at the base saying:
"This cross was erected at the charge of Robert Balfe of Callierstown, being sovereign of the corporation of Kells, anno domini 1688."
which possibly explains Eoghan O'Reilly's interest in these High Crosses in 1739.

It is obvious too that the well known Rev Eugene O'Reilly, who built St Mary's Church in Navan, was the first president of St Finian's College originally in Navan, and who was a nephew of Rev Laurence Reilly PP of Kildalkey – who died in 1794 and who was born in the parish of Oristown –, was a cousin and quite possibly a first cousin of our Andrew. Eugene also had a brother Matthew who later became an eminent solicitor in Dublin, and this seems to be referred to in one of Edward O'Reilly's letters (Edward refers to cousin Matthew O'Reilly, who has a profession, of Queens Street, and his son Myles died c.28th May 1828 and was buried in Mulhuddart (TCD Ms 3407, p.20)). Also Rev Bernard Flood, who was 'Dean' of Clara Frankford, or Ballybeg, born at Robertstown, Union of Kilbeg, a nephew of Fr Michael Flood PP of Kilskyre, was very closely related to Fr Eugene.

From all that we can tell that they are of a Meath branch of the O'Reillys originating from the area immediately south and east of the town of Kells. How they link from there to the great Cavan families of the O'Reillys is unclear but one commentator links them to Heath House in Co. Laois as you can read here in an obituary of Fr Eugene:

"The Very Rev. Father Eugene O'Reilly, parish priest of Navan, vicar-general and archdeacon of Meath, was born about the year 1768, and descended, in a paternal line, from the 'O'Reilly' of Heath House, in the Queen's County, and, on the maternal side, from the Maguires of Rathmore, who were closely connected by marriage with the Dunsany branch of the Plunkett family, in the county of Meath, and with the Balfes of Courtown, who were the progenitors of the Roscommon branch of the same name, against whom, being 'Papists', bills of discovery were filed by the Taylor family, now ennobled by the title of marquis, and which penal proceedings were the last instituted in this country against the rights and profession of Catholics. At the desire of his uncle, Rev. Laurence O'Reilly, parish priest of Kildalkey, he and his brother, Mr. Matthew O'Reilly, afterwards an eminent solicitor in Dublin, were sent to France in the year 1786. There, in the College of Lille, he prosecuted his classical studies with distinguished success till 1792, when he was forced, by the fury of the Revolution, to return to Ireland. Subsequently, having studied a short time in Carlow, he was amongst the first to enter Maynooth, in 1795, the year of its foundation."
(Fr Anthony Cogan, *The Diocese of Meath: Ancient and Modern* (Dublin, 1862), vol I, p.245 quoting the *Catholic Directory* of 1853.)

In any case presumably a brother of Fr Eugene's father and Fr Lawrence Reilly of Oristown settled in Dublin and it is from him that we have descent to his son Andrew – who was born at Christmas 1782 – and his brother Edward, the lexicographer. We don't have much more to say about the interesting Andrew, because of the paucity of materials, excepting that he was also a relative of a Colonel Terence O'Reilly, who was born in Dublin 4th Nov 1783, served in the Irish Brigades in France and whose sword is in the RIA (*Proceedings of the Royal Irish Academy*, vol VI (1853-57), p.445.). Also there is a reference to a great fraud that he uncovered while working as Paris correspondent of the *The Times*:

"On Oct 1st *The Times* recalled the fact that it was the 80th anniversary of its

exposure of "the most remarkable and extensive fraudulent conspiracy ever brought to light in the mercantile world." That exposure was the work of its Paris correspondent, Andrew O'Reilly, who performed the meritorious task at the risk of his life. The event is commemorated by an inscription cut over the principal entrance of *The Times* office in Printing House Square and a mural tablet in Lloyds. Andrew O'Reilly was the author of a rare and interesting work entitled *Reminiscences of an Emigrant Milesian*."
(*Irish Book Lover*, vol.XIII, No.4 (1921), p.62. For the details of this fraud see *The Literary World*, vol.4 (6th Oct 1871), p.212.)

His brother Edward — who in 1816 was of 101 New Street in Dublin —, on the other hand, is quite an important figure in Irish history of the period but in fact elaborate details of his life are also quite hard to come by. For this reason it might be helpful to reprint here what, to this writer's knowledge, is the only serious attempt to articulate his life history, from the *Irish Book Lover* of 1917-18:

"A descendant of the O'Reillys of Briefne, the time of his birth is unknown and the place disputed. Mr O'Donoghue, following the obituary notice in the *Gentleman's Magazine*, says it was in Cavan, but Dr Walsh, who knew him personally says (*History of Dublin*, 1818) that he was born at Harold's Cross, and educated in Dublin, where he had never heard Irish spoken.
...
From an interesting sketch which appeared in *The National Magazine*, Dublin, October, 1830, more than a year after his death, which occurred at Harold's Cross in Aug. 1829, we learn that he had not the advantage of a classical education, and the greater portion of his life was spent in the drudgery of a merchant's office, and subsequently in a retail business for the support of a numerous family.

From his scanty income he contrived means to possess himself of one of the largest and most valuable collections of Irish Mss ever possessed by any private individual. These Mss had been collected by speculators and brought to Dublin from all parts of Ireland in the expectation that they would have been purchased by the University under the terms of the Flood bequest. That bequest being lost, no better purchasers could be found for the cartloads of ancient Mss than the vendors of old books, from whose stalls the poor but patriotic O'Reilly had the good fortune to rescue them."

Dr Walsh is more explicit, and tells us that:—
"In the year 1794, a young man of the name of Wright, who was about to emigrate, had a number of books to dispose of, which chiefly consisted of Irish Mss. They had been collected by the industry of a man of the name of O'Gorman, who was clerk to Mary's Lane Chapel, and the person from whom Dr Young, Bishop of Clonfert, and General Vallency had learned Irish.

This man's library, which filled five large sacks, Mr O'Reilly purchased from Wright, and on examination found himself possessed of a collection of the rarest Mss, for one of which he has since refused 50 guineas. Master of this valuable repository, he commenced the study of the language, and by persevering application, has acquired a deep knowledge."

Gilbert adds that the collection William Halliday had made for lexicographic purposes came into the hands of O'Reilly, "who combined them with materials of his own" for inclusion in his magnum opus.

When in 1818 the Iberno-Celtic Society was formed for the preservation of the remains of Irish literature, by transcription and publication, O'Reilly was appointed assistant secretary. The only work issued by the Society was his "Chronological Account of Four Hundred Irish Writers," 1820, which, a contemporary declared to be "not much more than a catalogue raisonne of the Mss tracts and poems in his own very valuable library."

In 1824 O'Reilly obtained a prize from the RIA for his "Essay on the Brehon Laws," and again in 1829, for an "Essay on the Authenticity of the Poems of Ossian," published posthumously.

When the Ordnance [Survey] was instituted in 1826, O'Reilly "was employed by the Government at a miserably low rate of remuneration at the Survey Office, Phoenix Park," (Gilbert) to settle the orthography of the names for the ordnance maps, a post in which he was succeeded by John O'Donovan. Dr H. J. Monck Mason employed him to catalogue the Irish Mss in Trinity and his work was utilised in the fine catalogue edited by Dr Abbott and issued in 1900. He also prepared Catalogues of Manuscripts in other Dublin libraries...In addition he left unpublished his English-Irish dictionary; translations of the Annals of Innisfallen, a considerable portion of the Annals of the Four Masters, and a greater part of the life of Hugh Roe O'Donnell...long projected a life of O'Carolan...

"The private character of Mr O'Reilly," we are told "was honest and amiable; his temperment ardent and impassioned, and an Irish one in the strictest sense of the word. His appearance was equally characteristic of his country; and his well formed physiognomy at once bespoke the man of fine intellect and patrician Irish blood.""
(*Irish Book Lover*, vol.IX (Dec 1917-Jan 1918). For an account of the clerical O'Reillys I have also drawn on the immortal Cogan, *Diocese of Meath*.)

APPENDIX D
An Example of colourful Folklore, a poem from the 17th century

What was mentioned briefly in chapter 3 was the idea that historians should really go into the locality they are researching and take great heed of the local knowledge of history remembered there, somewhat condescendingly referred to as 'folklore'. This is such an important and oft neglected task that I thought I would print here a whole poem to show you how inspiring and colourful it can be to unravel folklore and reveal the large historical component contained therein.

But understanding folklore requires some skill just like understanding the old legal documents. Firstly it should be born in mind that Irish folklore always, invariably, has some element, maybe all of it, of truth. It is not at all the case that these old Irish seanachies swapped around consciously fictional stories and this is a mistake that many people seem to make. For this reason any comparison between a given Irish story and some fairy tale as related in the forests of Sweden or wherever is irrelevant, in the Irish case at any rate they certainly are not telling 'stories' in the sense of fictional accounts, they are always telling very real episodes but sometimes with errors and exaggerations etc. You can see this very clearly in the work of people like Douglas Hyde who published a lot of the old Irish stories as told to him c.1900 in places like Roscommon. He found out that Irish folkloric memory recorded stories very exactly similar to the accounts as preserved in written Irish texts from c.1100. The fact is that the stories would not be so exact as that unless it was the case that Irish seanachies prided themselves on accurately passing on what they saw as oral history, if it was just a story teller relating a 'fairy tale' they wouldn't take so much care with it and hence it would never have emerged so close to the written text recorded almost a millennium previously.

So that is what you must bear in mind when you are reading or listening to Irish folklore. You should assume it is true, as true, at least, as any written record but that many times it can take a twist or an error along the way which can hide that truth. For example in the Loughcrew area of Co Meath the locals were always told that the stone cairns on the local hills were created by a giant hag that hopped from one hill to the next but fell down before she got to the last one. A person unacquainted with Irish folklore and presuming that this is just story telling might think it was a tale made up quite recently but this is not the case at all. When Eóghan Ó Raghallaigh was writing his genealogical account of the O'Reillys in 1703, in which he incorporating some very old material, he referred to an O'Reilly chief called Cathaoir who owned the land around Loughcrew:

"Cathaoir who had Baile Phatrisg, Baile Hist, etc., on the far side of the mountain called the Three steps of the Hag of Beare (Trí Coircéim na Caillige béarra)." [1]

So in fact this is quite an ancient story and yet you still feel it of course couldn't be true? But then consider that modern archaeological evidence has shown that the cairns are aligned to the morning sun, and the different cairns light up in the morning during particular days – like the equinoxes – in sequence across the hills, so in a way the sun is hopping across the three hills during the dawns of the year and the cairns are there to catch it. So if you were to speculate that this 'hag' is actually a reference to the sun in old Irish pagan worship then you could postulate that Irish folklore had actually preserved a version of the truth maybe across a whole two millennia or so?

It might be helpful here to give another example of Irish folklore of more modern date to see how best to analyse it. About the middle of the 19th century a poor Irish poet called Phillip Connell wrote about an incident that he thought was dated to about 1541. He relates a story of a romance that involved the daughter of the 'Black Baron' who he knew was a Nugent who lived in Ross Castle in Co. Meath, on the shores of Lough Sheelin. He also knew that the 'Black Baron' was responsible for attacking the monastery at Fore in Co Westmeath so he naturally assumed that the date of this story was c.1541, approximately at the time of the dissolution of the monasteries under Henry VIII.

But it turns out that other folklore talks about the Black Baron *and his wife being buried standing up in Fore Abbey and this couldn't have been the Baron of the 1540 period.*[2] *Folklore also points out the very spot where the cannons were placed that attacked Fore Abbey and this spot is too far out for cannon of the early 16th century (as opposed to the mid 17th century) because the cannons just couldn't shoot that far.*[3] *We can also read in his poem about Owen Roe O'Neill and the defence of Clogh Oughter Castle from the forces of Cromwell. So to cut a long story short we can accurately date the incident in this poem to the aftermath of the surrender of Clogh Oughter on the 27th of April 1653, or at any rate sometime after the surrender of the Leinster army led by the 2nd Earl of Westmeath (the 'Black Baron', he was known as the Baron of Delvin before he became Earl in 1642 and was living in Ross – an outlying castle where cousins of his previously lived, the descendants of the poet William Nugent, a brother of the Baron of c.1580 – because he had burnt down his own castle at Clonyn on the approach of Cromwell and he must have attacked Fore Abbey at approximately the same time) on the 12th of April 1652.*[4] *During the year between these dates he was on Cromwell's side while the O'Reillys, and MacMahons, were still holding out in Cavan on the other side of Lough Sheelin. 'Sabina' in the poem below was his daughter Elizabeth – whom we know died young – and 'Orwin' was a harpist and a chief of the MacMahons,*[5] *not the O'Reillys which the poet is substituting for poetic reasons I suspect, of whom however we know very little.*

But we do know the name of the seanachie that had passed along the tale to Connell in the pre-Famine era:

> "The place [minstrel's grave] was pointed out and their tragical story told to me by James Briody of Tonagh. He was the best Irish seanachie I ever knew. He is now dead and with him is lost a wonderful fund of Irish tales, songs, facts and tracings of families. But all these stories of legendary lore are fast passing away. The old men are vanishing, the young are too anglicised to retain either the traditions of their fathers nay they nowadays [1853] feel ashamed if speaking the Irish tongue. And yet I will maintain that I know

the English language as well as most of them yet I never could pour out my feelings so forcibly in English as in Irish words." [6]

Connell was unfortunately very poor and he tells us in the same letter that he could not find employment in Manchester where he had emigrated to and consequently:

"I am advancing rapidly to the meridian of true poetical dignity, namely having my haunchbones through my pocket holes."

In any case we know now that the account in the following letter and poem by this old Irish poet is in fact basically true and is then a further example of how you should persist in verifying whatever folklore your research turns up. Again whatever folklore you have you assume to be true but you can often expect twists and turns in identifying the truth behind the folklore, just like in this case. I will quote here the whole letter and poem as an illustration of another great quality to Irish folklore i.e. it can be exciting and offer quite a bit of colour to liven up any local history! By the way the 'minstrel's grave', and headstone, is still there, and was painted by Du Noyer in the 19th century, and Ross Castle is now a guest house and the poem also refers to the remains of an old castle on an island in the lake, which is also still there. As regards corroborating some of the other facts I think I should point out that the main problem the owners of the aforementioned guest house have is the number of guests who see ghosts flitting across the lake! All of the following was written by Phillip Connell to the Earl of Farnham and he obviously formatted his letter elaborately in the hope that Farnham would like to publish the poem:

"My Lord

I have ventured to hope the accompanying poem, though in every other way unworthy your Lordship's notice, may obtain favour in your sight from the hero of the piece, the same and the writer, being all belonging to the beautiful Lake Sheelin, which I cannot help fancying can still recall in your Lordship's mind the sweet refreshing scenes of childhood.

"That bower and it rises I ne'er can forget

For oft when alone in the bloom of the year
I think is the nightingale singing there yet
Are the roses still bright by the calm Bendemeer"
(Moore's Lalla Rookh)

I must further confess my Lord that at the same time that I was apprehensive my little childish tale was beneath your Lordship's notice I was still ambitious as an humble Irishman to treat your English friends to an Irish Legend said to have occurred close by the place of your Lordship's birth and written by one of your Lordship's workmen [meaning Connell].

Perhaps after all the poem is not fit to be shown – as this your Lordship is an excellent judge – and if I have herein trespassed too far on the deep respect, honour, and, I will add, veneration, which we so justly give to your Lordship then I have no other apology to make but this: that my sole motive for writing was to try to show my gratitude for the many favours conferred on

My Lord
Your Lordship's most
Obedient Humble Servant
Phill Connell.

Orwin
and
SEBANA

A Tale

"For well I know that such had been
Thy gentle care for him who now
Unmourn'd shall quit this earthly scene
When none regards him but thou."..Byron

PREFACE

In my young days I was passionately fond of the old traditionary legends of my country of which the old men could then tell vast numbers.

One summer Sunday evening I met an old man tending his

cows by an old fort. I accepted his invitation to a grassy seat where he told me the whole story of Orwin and Sebana wherein I have made very little change, the principal being the substituting the more poetical names of Orwen and Sebana for the harsh ones he gave.

While reciting the tale he pointed out to me all the localities of the scenes together with the grave of the lovers in Mr Sommerville's grounds near the old castle.

He further said that many had seen the phantoms of the lover's walking on the waves arm in arm when the world was wrapt in sleep and the moon was low in the west.

Phil Connell

<u>Orwin and Sebana</u>
Mild shone the moon o'er Sheelin's waves,
And silent night involved the world,
When Orwin left his secret cave,
Where round his home the water's curled,

2
From splendid domes and festive halls,
By adverse war's mischances driven,
Alone he mourned his early fall,
Nor felt a hope save that of heaven,

3
The last on Brefney's mountains high,
Who dared to brave proud Cromwell's power,
Now conquered and compelled to fly,
For safety to this lonely tower.

4
Within a solitary isle
By Sheelin's murmuring waves surrounded,
The ruins of a mouldering pile,
Received him joyless and confounded,

5

An ancient fare where festals [sic] say
His father's held when wars were aver
Now seem in hoary ruins gray
Close by the shore of streamy Crover

6
Lonely he wandered on the shore,
And wept his friends in battle fallen,
Again in fancy mark'd their grave,
While fondly thus their names recalling:

7
"Mighty O'Neill thine eyes are closed,
That keenly blazed in battle danger,
Weak is that arm so long oppos'd,
To Erin's foes, her greatest avenger.

8
Green is the grave without a stone,
Within Cloughoughter's rolling waters,
Yet long will thy dear name be known,
In the sad songs of Erin's daughters.

9
Near what lone rivers are ye laid,
You great O'Donnells of the mountains,
Or do ye roam like me dismayed,
Lamenting by the moonlit fountains?

10
McMahon of the daring hand,
Sound is your sleep by winding Mourne,
The strangers now divide your land,
And Farney clansmen weep forlorn.

11
Shades of my sires who to these halls
See your sad son an outlaw driven,

While foemen in your ancient halls
Now triumph over prostrate Cavan.

12
Descend and show your pensive son
Whose heart admits but dark despairing,
Will Brefney's cause be ever won
Will freedom ever shine on Erin."

13
Thus wailed he while the moaning owl
Replied through dreary vaults rebounding,
And from afar the watchdog's howl
Came to his fears like trumpets sounding.

14
And yet one feeling cheered his heart
By every other bliss deserted,
With love's endearing visions blessed,
He clung to life though broken hearted.

15
Far o'er the waves high on the shore,
Proud Ross displayed its lofty towers;
Where she he fondly did adore
Oft wandered in its peaceful bowers.

16
Sebana was the fair one named,
The proud Black Baron's youngest daughter.
For every gentle feeling framed
And lover's alone in vain besaught her.

17
Once as along the foamy shore,
As raise the moon resplendent glowing,
She stood to hear the waters roar,
And tuneful boatmen gently rowing.

18
The winds were low the boatmen's lay [sic]
Came softly o'er the heaving bellows,
The blackbird whistled from each spray
The redbreasts sang among the willows.

19
When hark came floating from afar
Celestial sounds more to inspire
The feeling soul, than human care
Had e'er drawn from the thrilling lyre.

20
It seemed as from some fairy band
Around the island castle moving,
Now sweetly slow now rising bland
Through all the wilds of music roving.

21
Transfixed by the enchanting song,
She lean'd upon a bending willow,
Till the last diapason [sic, ?] rung
Yet pausing o'er the listening billow.

22
All night within her chamber lone
Sweet dreams renew'd them in her slumbers,
The lark who hailed the morning dawn
Seem'd to have caught the same sweet numbers.

23
Twas noon and now resolved to know
Whence the enchanting strains proceeded:
She called her page who oft would row
Her little boat, when pleasure needed.

24

Within the lonely tower they found
In respite brief from care and sorrow,
Exhausted Orwin sleeping sound
Without a hope to cheer the morrow.

25
His harp lay silent by his side,
His blue edged sword suspended o'er him
And gleaming round the dreary void
The crackling brambles burned before him.

26
Aroused he startling seized his sword
Yet paused to beauty's sovereign power
While on her knees the maid implored
A life to him dear from that hour.

27
"O pardon," cried the affrighted fair,
"A thoughtless maid whose steps unwary,
Curiosity hath urged thus far,
Whence oft before I loved to tarry.

28
My father lords the woods of Ross,
Before you kneels his youngest daughter,
There come and join the feast, the chase
And grieve no more by Sheelin water."

29
"Arise," he cried, "you 'ave naught to fear
Though now my life is in your power,
A banished outlawed rebel here
I seek concealment in this tower.

30
All cool reserve were useless now
Then to thy gentle breast appealing,

I crave no oath I ask no vow
Where eyes so mild bespeak such feeling.

31
Before you stands the man who last
opposed the regicide invader,
My armies slain, my glories lost,
Behold the home of Brefney's leader.

32
Thy father fought on Cromwell's side,
In mortal fight we once contested,
And did he know that here I hide
Soon were the days of Orwin ended."

33
"Orwin!" exclaimed the wondering fair,
Her eyes with sudden raptures beaming,
"And art thou he so famed in war,
So terrible in red fields flaming?

34
When warriors throng my father's hall,
Oft do I hear that name repeated,
Where even the Saxon chiefs extol,
Thy gallant deeds so oft related.

35
And there dwells one to shield thee too,
Whose grateful heart will love thee ever,
Since saved in bloody field by you,
When hostile spears around do quiver.

36
Before O'Neill when Saxons fled,
While formost you pursued the slaughter,
A dying foeman almost dead
You bore to safety o'er the water.

37
That foe who did such kindness share
Is my beloved and fondest brother,
Then come to Ross and meet him there
Nor shall thy name be known to other."

38
She urged in vain, then bade farewell,
Resolved with evening to return,
Each felt what either would not tell
And sighed and looked their deep concern.

39
Mild evening o'er the waters smiled
Again the boat approached the island
Again the proud Black Baron's child
I[?] on the rebel chieftain smiling

40
The feast was spread the cheering wine
Restored once more the chieftain's spirit,
And once again did brightly shine,
Each social trait he did inherit.

41
That ample heart by fortune's frown,
Contracted long – again expanded;
That gallant soul long bending down
Burst forth with native graces blended.

42
Again he touched the tuneful strings,
In soothing strains of fairy sweetness,
Then sung the wars of Erin's Kings,
And deep deplored her fallen greatness.

43

Then sung of sorrows all his own,
His luckless wars, his toils and danger,
His friends o'ercome, and he alone
Left a forlorn friendless ranger.

44
He ceased and found the maid in tears,
Well had she felt each plaintive story,
And tender pity for his cares,
Burst forth in nature's oratory.

45
The happy hours sped softly by,
Reluctantly at length they parted,
Sweet was the language of that eye,
Which modesty but half averted.

46
And from that night when chance was kind,
They oft enjoyed the stolen hours,
Till Orwin once his cave resigned,
To rove within her father's bowers.

47
There arm in arm, along the shore,
And all on earth besides unheeding,
Sweet raptures never felt before
Love's hopes fulfilled each heart pervading.

48
They gained the covert of a shade,
By lonely woods and rocks surrounded,
Where shepherd's steps had never strayed
Where woodman's axe had never sounded.

49
Alone with him who loved so dear,
So far from home, so late so lonely,

She knew no guilt, she felt no fear,
Absorbed in blissful feelings only.

50
Here first the enraptured Orwin dared,
To press her to his thrilling bosom,
While broken sighs repressed each word
She would have uttered to oppose him.

51
And then a kiss a long fond kiss,
While sparkling eyes and flitting blushes
Declared their deep their guiltless bliss
Beyond with love's most dreamy wishes.

52
And here they vow'd eternal truth,
And every solemn promise plighted,
That til the latest days of both,
Their fates henceforth shall be united.

53
The happy hours too quickly passed
The fainting stare but dimly burned,
And clouds slow purpling in the east
Announced the dawn as they returned.

54
Young Orwin reached his stormy home,
Sebana sought her lonely chamber,
Whence with fatigue and thought o'ercome
Long days of sickness did she number.

55
In vain sad Orwin watched the shore,
Each evening [?long] and lonely straying,
And many a longing look cast oer,
The restless waters round him playing.

56
Hours, days and weeks, had passed away,
No bounding boat came o'er the water,
More wretched each succeeding day,
He fickle and inconstant thought her.

57
Again of every hope bereft,
Each grief returned with deeper anguish,
One pang wakes many in the breast,
Where hope does her bright torch extinguish.

58
Careless of life he sadly roved,
His senses fled his vigour wasted,
Repeating oft the name he loved,
And wept for days too quickly blasted.

59
At length death's friendly hand set free,
A soul oppressed with hopeless sorrow,
Wash's by the surf supine he lay,
With none to shroud him on the morrow.

60
Nor knew Sebana half her woes,
When now (her convalescence over)
She sought the shore at evening's close,
To meet again her long lost lover.

61
The moon was up the air was chill
The moaning winds the dim woods sounded,
Dark night was low on every hill
The waves in hollow rocks resounded.

62

Lonely she wandered on the shore
And sung the songs, which Orwin taught her
And many a longing look cast o'er,
Across the darkly rolling waters.

63
When slow advancing o'er the strand,
Came Orwin, and stood close beside her,
Nor sigh'd nor spoke, nor took her hand,
Nor even sought by looks to chide her.

64
She sought his face twas wildly pale,
His dim eyes set in fixed glazing,
His locks far streaming in the gale,
And blue the lips, once sweetly pleasing.

65
"Orwin," she cried, "I faint in fear
O why so changed so sad, so gloomy,
Can you suspect, a heart so dear;
Alas I thought you better knew me!"

66
"Sebana ever dear," he said.
"Compose thy soul and patient hear me
Love bid me hope, dear faithful maid
That even in death you would not fear me.

67
For O! no more of earth I breath,
Cold lies my corpse in yonder tower,
Though now I've burst the seal of death,
To meet thee at this lonely hour.

68
For thee I died, and still for thee
My bosom feels its former fire,

Even now from human frailties free,
Love yet survives though life expire.

69
One favour at thy hands I ask,
And O forgive the fond desire;
That love will consecrate the task
The last poor Orwin will require.

70
To lay my corpse within the earth
In that loved spot where first you told me;
Your heart was mine which gave hopes birth,
That even in death's last pangs consoled me.

71
There lonely let me rest in death
By all but thee unknown unheeded
And lost alike to glory's breath,
From honour rank and fame degraded,

72
There too will thou ere long be laid,
And there will meet the village lovers:
And oft their solemn vows be paid,
To love like those that green turf covers.

73
And when some circling ages pass,
When yonder halls stand grey and hoary,
Then will the bard of Sheelin dress,
Our tragic fate in simple story.

74
The moon is low and I dare not wait,
The ruling powers now bid us sever,
No more on earth again we meet
Adieu dear love but not for ever.

75
Then slowly with the moaning wind,
The thin receding vision blending,
Left the bewildered maid behind,
Transfixed in grief and wonder standing.

76
Assisted by her faithful page,
Her wish fulfilled – his grave they cover,
Short was her tearful pilgrimage,
Short time survived his sleeping lover.

77
Her days were few upon the hill,
And long all those who knew, deplored them,
Now both one lowly grave do fill,
Each rolling year strews flowers o'er them.

78
And ofttimes in the pale moonlight,
Is seen the proud Black Baron's daughter
In Orwin's arms serenely bright,
Gliding o'er Lough Sheelin water.

The Minstrel's Grave, where they are buried, near Ross Co. Meath.

NOTE

In the traditionary records of my native hills the Castle of Ross is said to have been the residence of The Black Baron Nugent, the ancestor of the present Lord Westmeath. He is represented as a cruel tyrannical man and that he had a gallows always standing near the castle whereon he hung any of his serfs who were so unhappy as to fall under his displeasure. Nay the country people affirm that to this day no grass grows on the spot where it stood. The Black Baron is further said to be the person who destroyed the Abbey of Fore in the County of Westmeath.

Orwin is said to have been the last surviving son of Eman brí [sic, but mistake for 'buí'?] or swarthy Edmond O'Reilly and to have taken refuge in the old castle of Crover in Lough Sheelin after the defeat of Owen Roe O'Neill." [7]

Footnotes
1. James Carney, *A Genealogical History of the O'Reillys* (Dublin, 1959), p.109.

2. "The Baron and his wife are buried in the tombs of Fore."

(National Schools Folklore project UCD, Geraldine Aherne, Mountnugent, using information supplied by Henry Aherne of Mountnugent, p.122 and 123. The Aherne family are from Castlemartyr in County Cork from whence they came to run the quarry at Ross. They were also distinguished during the War of Independence in Ireland and one of them wrote a book, in New York, on Orwin and Sabina.) This refers to the Anchorite's Cell where you can still read the inscription placed on it by the 2nd Earl who used it as his tomb.

3. See the notes of Beryl Moore on Fore Abbey.

4. Westmeath was "in treaty" with the Cromwellian authorities from the 6th of May 1652 and Westmeath concluded his treaty, on behalf of the Leinster forces, on the 12th of May in Kilkenny. As early as the 14th of September there is talk of him going abroad and he was given a license to go abroad on the 19th of October 1652. But it doesn't seem that he actually went to the continent at that time because on the 29th of March 1654 Cromwell talks about a trip that Westmeath made into England to make representations against the authorities in Dublin.
(Robert Dunlop, *Ireland under the Commonwealth* (Manchester, 1913) vol 1, p.190, 197, 276, vol 2, p.vii, and p.414.)

The career of this Earl of Westmeath is summarised here by Robert Dunlop:
"Richard Nugent, second Earl of Westmeath, succeeded his grandfather, Richard, the first Earl, in 1642. Being in England at the time he returned to Ireland in 1644, took his seat in Parliament and in 1645 raised a regiment of foot for the King's service. He was instrumental in bringing about the Peace of 1648/9, and after Ormond's retirement co-operated with Clanricarde, being appointed general of all the forces in Leinster. He submitted to the Parliament on the Articles of Kilkenny in May 1652 and was allowed to transport himself abroad; but returning in 1659 he was arrested and imprisoned. He recovered his liberty and estates at the Restoration and died in 1684."
(Robert Dunlop, *Ireland under the Commonwealth* (Manchester, 1913) vol 1, p.71.)

Actually he wasn't completely under Cromwell's thumb as you can see from this letter by Cromwell. He wrote this on the 9th of August 1656 angry with the Earl of Westmeath who had prosecuted his officer Markham, "for discharging his duty", according to Cromwell:
"We understand by your letter of 8th September last that Col. Henry Markham, of whose constant fidelity and good service from the beginning, as well by our own knowledge as by your testimony, we are abundantly satisfied, hath been prosecuted at law by the Earl of Meath [i.e. Westmeath] for some acts by him done with other Commissioners of the Revenue in Ireland about the sequestration of the said Earl's estate, wherein they did only pursue the Orders and Instructions given them by the then Commissioners of Parliament for the

public service. We may well wonder that any person who hath been obnoxious should presume to molest a public officer, barely for discharging his duty and being faithful in his trust, and hold ourselves obliged to secure and indemnify such against such proceedings, which, should they be permitted, would be an ill requital to those who have deserved well and a discouragement to others for the future, and therefore we have thought fit to recommend the same unto your especial care. . . ."
(Robert Dunlop, *Ireland under the Commonwealth* (Manchester, 1913) vol 2, p.lix and 616.)

5. That Elizabeth Nugent was a daughter of the Black Baron who died young we know from: NLI Ms.122, previously Phillips Ms 15216, "Lindsay Papers", p.35.

Maybe the MacMahon involved was Collo:
"Col. Collo MacMahon of Balloghie in Co. Monaghan was one of the leaders in the Rebellion, being declared a traitor and a reward of £600 being placed on his head by the Lords Justices on 8 Feb. 1642. He served with distinction during the whole war and was one of those who adhered to the Peace of 1648 [-9] against the will of Owen O'Neill, for which he was expelled his property. Matters were made straight when O'Neill also gave in his adhesion, and he continued fighting till he surrendered with the rest of the Ulster leaders to Sir Theophilus Jones on 27 Ap. 1653. He died before the Restoration but his son Brian...was restored to his estate."
(Robert Dunlop, *Ireland under the Commonwealth* (Manchester, 1913) vol 1, p.246.)

6. PRONI D3975/B/8/15.

7. PRONI D3975/B/8/8. All punctuation was added in by this writer, Connell never uses any. This was first published in Philip Connell, *National Poems* (Monaghan, 1829), although there are great differences between the two texts.

In a later letter of his from Manchester of the 17th of December 1853 he states that:
"Orwin was one of the chieftains of Errigall in the County of Monaghan, he fled after the defeat of Own Roe to an old castle in a small island in Lough Sheelin near Crover."
He stated that Ross was built first by the Sheridans and then later the Nugents and also notes that:
"the old ruin is fast falling into decay, even within my own recollection two large masses of old grey walls fell to the ground."
He owned a house at one time called Auburn Cottage, as he describes in the same document:
"Old Kilnacrott Drumrora Green
And one forsaken spot between

Dear Auburn Cottage, mine no more
My last loved home on Erin's shore."
He also describes his father, who owned a small farm leased from Farnham in Kildorough which is near Kilnacrott, there saying that he "was considered "the best historian of the pensive plain.""
In the same document he describes how the Black Baron was said to have destroyed Fore in 1541 and that "entitles the present Marquis of Westmeath to the tithes of vast tracts of land in Westmeath and Cavan."
(All the quotes given above are from PRONI D3975/B/8/15.)

On the 5th of November 1853 he was back in Cavan, after 9 years of wandering – and then went back to Manchester it seems – and called himself "The last bard of Briefne" (PRONI D3975/B/8/14).
Here is an interesting extract from one of Connell's letters which show his keen knowledge and interest in housing:
"To the Right Honourable Lord Farnham
My Lord

In the Warder Newspaper of Jan 7 1834 [sic], containing an essay of mine on improvements in cottages sent by Sir William Young, the Editor dubbed me "The Rural Reformer" and unlike some Divines I practice my own precepts and Phill Reilly will assure your Lordship that Auburn Cottage was the neatest cleanest and most comfortable in that neighbourhood. I throw out these hints to give the more weight to what follows. It is hoped that poor old Ireland will now improve rapidly. I wish I could add my mite by improving the taste of my countrymen in cottage architecture wherein they are sadly deficient:-

In the first place when a petty farmer sets about building he is solely guided in his choice of a site by selecting the most sterile spot on his farm that he may not waste good soil – hence fifteen out of every twenty dwellings have one end half buried in the side of a hill making them damp within and unsightly in external appearance. The floor is seldom raised above the surrounding surface hence it can never be dry, the many discomforts arising from this neglect are indescribable.

He then begins with building walls often 24 generally 22 inches thick, being a worse than useless waste of stones, mortar, roofing, and thatch, while at the same time these thick walls are reservoirs for wet and damp. Nor can they be well built for the stones will not lap over each other so frequently as in narrow walls while the space within is filled up with small stones.

Again as to general appearance we have on every side wherever we look around still the same ugly unsightly blocks of houses all cast in the same mould. The long black roof, the low ragged door way and three small ratholes for windows.

These cottages are besides generally built too large rending them cold and bleak looking, they are usually filled with a confusion of useless furniture – The large dresser for the large kitchen, and that large dresser garnished with heaps of delph never used but like Goldsmith's teacups "wisely kept for show", then comes the settlebed, the Losset [a large flat wooden dish], the huge table and the never to be neglected "Black Oak Chest" which seldom contains anything necessary.

We next come to the "Parlour" where the most conspicuous object is the eternal two beds across the room. The cold damp floor seething and reeking under the fusty bottoms, and not unusual the milk and butter kept in the same apartment, a rather awkward mode of contending with the Dutch in the London Buttermarket. Then comes "the room behind the dresser" with another bed on one side and in the other side a promiscuous collection of implements of husbandry, which were much better stowed away in some of the half empty outhouses – in the erection of these outhouses the same want of taste and judgement is apparent, the cowhouse and consequently the dungheap constantly before the door oozing and steaming continually, the pigstye close by with all its circumambient [he is showing off here!] odours and the tenant stiffly insisting on his inherent right to "the run of the kitchen".."
(PRONI D3975/B/8/17.)

James Martin of Millbrook, another penniless farm labouring poet of the area who died in 1860, also wrote about Ross and the Black Baron:
"But here no more are heard the minstrel's strains,
Nor guest nor banquet in the Hall remains,
For time has laid this once strong fortress low;
But through its ruins we may plainly trace
The greatness, strength and grandeur of the place,
What marks of time and ruin now appear,
Since the Black Baron dwelt in splendour here!
– Whose chequered fortune and mysterious ways
Were oft the subject of both blame and praise;
Of Erin's friends and enemies the mule,
First Cromwell's foe, and then his hidden tool.
But, for the goodness of his daughter fair
I shall the father, for the present, spare:
The fame SABANNA, loveliest of her kind,
Still counted matchless in both shape and mind;
Her snowy bosom and her star-like eyes,
And cheeks that showed the rose and lily's dyes,
Soon charmed to love young Orwin's heart,
That warlike prince of the MacMahons brave
Who helped O'Neill Loughonter's town to save."
(Matthew Reilly TD, *James Martin of Millbrook*, in Ríocht na Midhe Vol II no. 1 (1959), p.68.)

APPENDIX E
19th century debate on the Registry of Deeds versus the Land Registry

While this book obviously deals with the almost uniquely Irish system of the Registry of Deeds – bearing in mind that the English version only extends over two counties, the various parts of Yorkshire and Middlesex, and never developed in the same way in practice – there is of course a competing system of land registry in Ireland which is modelled on similar systems around the world. This is known as the Land Registry (or 'Registry of Title') and its a place where, simply put, people can bring in deeds that prove their ownership over land and are then given a government guaranteed document which is taken as proof of this ownership (this used to be known incidentally as a 'Parliamentary Title' to land as opposed to traditional title deeds which may have been grounded originally on a royal grant or patent).

This might seem a better way of doing it in a sense, and so its adherents like to say, but in practice this can create a lot of problems, such as:

a) Since the government is now guaranteeing the land ownership via a document that it chooses to issue then of course the natural corollary is that it needs special court systems to cope with any problems that could arise. This is in contrast with the Registry of Deeds system which remember is simply a procedure whereby the state keeps a centralised register of summaries of land deeds. Hence the ROD is only claiming to be able to accurately keep a summary of the land transactions, which is not so difficult to do precisely, and any issue that arises within the deeds, such as land being sold that was not properly the seller's property etc etc, is not a problem for the ROD, they, and hence the state, are not dragged into the subsequent court case. As you can see this is not at all true of the Land Registry system which could easily drag the state into ruinous expensive court cases.

b) This then naturally gives rise to the second point which is the great expense and labour involved in registering under the Land Registry system. Clearly if the state is going to go to the step of guaranteeing land ownership then it will have to take its time examining carefully the deeds presented and will only issue the final document after exhaustative analysis of those deeds. Obviously it has to take much longer than the ROD system which only checks that the memorial is a proper summary of the original deed, they don't need to check anything else, and of course you will have to pay dearly for this extra time and labour.

c) Especially as it has in practice evolved in Ireland, the truth is that the Land Registry system has proven to be less open to public scrutiny and less transparent. In the ROD the general public can inspect whatever the ROD actually have in their possession as regards land ownership, the public copies of the memorials that you can inspect in the large volumes are exact copies of the memorials in their vaults, they don't have any documents that you cannot see. The Land Registry takes possession of the original deeds that are presented but the general public are not allowed to view them, you basically only get to see references to the final government decision as regards the land ownership, not the actual deeds. In otherwords it works on the basis that 'we are the government, trust us' which is pretty much the opposite way that the English Common Law system traditionally worked, where the legal system was supposed to always operate in public, a step which was always seen as a prerequisite component of a true justice system. Also that Common Law system in many ways saw itself as protecting the general public from the state, and the arbitrary power of politicians in general, so again it leaned against any concept of accepting the state's word at face value. So this then has proven to be another advantage of the ROD system, its great transparency.

But back in the mid 19th century some commentators were sure that a Land Registry system would be much better than the old ROD setup and in fact it generated some heated arguments at the time, as described here by James Maguire who worked in the ROD:

> "Registration of Title as compared with Registration of Deeds is modern in its origin. It was introduced in England in 1862 by Lord

Westbury's Act; in Ireland in 1865 by the Record of Title Act. Its advocates, including the then Council of this Society [Statistical and Social Inquiry Society of Ireland], were encouraged by the success that had attended its working in the Australian Colonies under Sir Robert Torrens, who introduced it there in 1858. It could not be regarded as a popular measure—popular opinion could not, or at least was not, so educated as to judge of its merits or demerits; but there was then current to a large extent a popular fallacy that land could be as easily transferred as stocks or shares or ships.

In furtherance of the principle a Registration of Title Association was formed in Ireland under the presidency of the Duke of Leinster, embracing a large and influential representation of the landed and mercantile interests of the country. Nothing that legal learning, speculative talent and the influence of high office could supply was wanting to promote the success of this movement. An ancillary measure, called the Land Debentures Act (1865), was passed to facilitate borrowing on the security of land, the title to which had been recorded under the Record of Title Act. But as the principal Act failed so also did the ancillary one. It is highly probable that many of the zealous advocates of registration in those days did not fully appreciate the difficulties attending the application in an old country like this of a system that had given marked satisfaction in the colonies, where the difficulties of first registration did not exist.

...

The Act had been thirteen years in existence when the Royal Commission in 1878 recommended that the Record should be closed and the titles remitted to the operation of the law for the registration of deeds. This was not done, and the Act continued a bare legal existence until 1892, when it was merged in the Local Registration of Title Act."

Another skirmish in the perennial Land Registry versus Registry of Deeds war occurred in 1892, which the latter successfully fought off:

"The failure of the Registration of Assurances Bill [which would have given extra powers to the Registry of Deeds] and the passing of the Local Registration of Title Act [which created the modern Irish Land Registry] created a situation unfavourable to the future prospects of the Registry of Deeds. Every title registered under the new Act in so far diminished the area under the operation of the older law. Men in high official position declared that the Deeds Office should be regarded as a moribund department. Happily, however, these gloomy forebodings have been falsified by results. In 1892, the first year in which the Local Registration of Title Act operated, 16,309 deeds or assurances were registered in the Registry of Deeds; in 1920 there were 26,377. In 1893 and in three years of the war period there was a drop in the number of deeds registered. In every other year there has been an increase, which in 1919, 1920 and 1921 amounted to an average yearly increase of 42 per cent, over the number of Deeds registered in 1892."

And Maguire then notes the only reason why the Land Register system got off the ground at all in 1892:

"The chief of these [changes between the two land register acts of 1865 and 1891] is the principle of compulsory registration, which was wholly wanting in the earlier Act, and the absence of which is commonly regarded as the cause of its absolute failure. Nor is it too much to say that the vitality of the Act of 1891 is mainly if not wholly due to its compulsory clauses. This is evidenced by the small number of owners who have voluntarily registered titles since the Act came into operation."

One criticism of the old system that the critics of the ROD made was in regard to the cost and labour of extensive searches through the ROD memorials, especially if you were trying to establish that there were no outstanding leases or mortgages on land that maybe you were going to buy or sell. But this constant criticism seems unfair, the fact that there were huge numbers of memorials in the ROD is simply a reflection of the importance and frequency of land transactions in Ireland, which was hardly under the control of the ROD, and after all right from the beginning they had compiled good quality indexes. In any case this is what follows underneath in this Appendix, what you read below is a long but fascinating debate on this subject in the Irish Law Times in 1867. Incidentally The Landed Estates Court and The Encumbered (or 'Incumbered', it seems both spellings were often used from the very beginning) Estates Court, mentioned below, are courts that were set up to expedite the sale of land whose owners in the post Famine period were encumbered with too much debt. The state compelled these owners to sell off their land rather than having the economy burdened by all this debt going forward, and these courts in turn began the process of introducing a Land Registry system to Ireland.

The amazing thing about it too is that this debate has never stopped in Ireland, we still have a Land Registry and the Registry of Deeds, both competing systems which still vie with one another for the title of the best system for registering land transactions! This simple quote from the website of Richard Black Solicitors of Clonee sets out the situation as it exists now in Ireland:

Registry of Deeds

Registration of a valid deed of purchase in the Registry of Deeds ensures that ownership appears upon a public register and renders it relatively indisputable.

The Registry of Deeds deals with the registration of documents, title passes when the deed is delivered and the purchase money is paid, however a solicitor must ensure the registration of a purchase deed or a mortgage deed in order to obtain priority over subsequent deeds. Each title deed records details of the vendor, purchaser and purchase price, providing you with a record of each change of ownership up to the present day. If a deed which has been registered becomes lost or mislaid, a summary of the document can be obtained from the Registry of Deeds.

Land Registry

The Land Registry, is a State-guaranteed system of title registration. With Land Registry title your ownership is recorded in a public register. The Land Registry will issue you with written evidence of ownership in the form of a Land Certificate if you request this. The Land Registry operates a website, www.landregistry.ie, which provides a host of information on this Registry.

Costs of Registration

It costs €44 to register a deed of purchase or mortgage in the Registry of Deeds. This is done by registering a brief summary of the deed called a Memorial. Once the registration is completed, the original deed of purchase is returned to the solicitor (with registration details marked upon it) and the Memorial remains in the Registry of Deeds. The cost of registering a deed of purchase in the Land Registry is more expensive and it depends on the purchase price of the property. The registration fee currently ranges from €125 to €816.

As you can see its still the case that the Registry of Deeds system is considerably cheaper, arguably quicker – especially with computerisation –, and more straight forward. But progressively over the last few years the Land Registry has taken advantage of legislation that compels landowners to register with them and this creeping compulsion has progressed quietly over the last few decades starting with Carlow, Meath and Laois in 1970 and ending with Dublin and Cork in 2011. It seems suspiciously true that only compulsion – as Maguire pointed out in 1925 – has put the Land Registry in front in this great debate!

To the Editor of the Irish Law Times

Sir – I propose to consider shortly the Registration of Title question – the circumstances which led to the creation of a permissive Register or Record of Indefeasible Title in Ireland (partly modelled on that existing since 1862 in England) the objections urged against the measure, and its probable effects as regards the profession and the public. Few persons are now indisposed to admit that it is a positive advantage to the owner of land to be able to sell any portion of it or to grant a valuable lease or annuity, or to procure a loan in a short time and at a slight expense. The impediments to dealings with land in the United Kingdom have for a long series of years been such as to diminish its value to the owners and to limit the number of persons bound by ties of property to the cause of order and loyalty. In this inquiry I will take it as an axiom that all artificial hindrances to dealings with land ought to be removed.

To Mr R. R. Torrens and to Mr Vincent Scully is chiefly due the credit of effectually calling public attention to this question. They demonstrated that existing systems might safely be applied to landed property in this country. Registration of Title is no new invention. In this country the title to Government Stock has been registered for more than a century; and there has been a perfect system as regards shipping property in operation for many years. Mr Torrens actually applied the method to landed property in our colonies. Lord Westbury and Sir H Cairns – the two greatest lawyers of our time – saw that the method was applicable to landed property at home and they framed measures for so applying it. The public mind was unprepared for compulsory measures and therefore permissive ones only were passed mainly through the influence of those two most eminent jurists. The English Act was passed in 1862, and the Irish Act in 1865; the latter applying only to titles conferred by the Landed or Incumbered Estates Court. Such is very briefly the history of the

Registration of Title question in this country. There are, however, intelligent critics who are in the habit of regarding the Registry of Deeds in Ireland as an institution calculated to accomplish every useful object. With more careful supervision, and a larger staff, the Registry might (they say) be kept free from arrear, the indexing and entering might be done every day, the searches might be completed in a short space of time. There is reason for supposing that the inherent defects of the Registry are such as to render those results impossible. The best Registry of Deeds that ever existed supplies but very partially the place of a Registry of Title. Could a "Registry Search" be obtained at a day's notice and at a trifling expense it would still as an evidence of title be unsatisfactory for the following reasons:- The search against names discloses acts by all other persons of the same name as the person searched against but even when limited to certain lands there remain the "general acts" or deeds not affecting a particular denomination of land. Thousands of deeds on the Registry affect in general terms all the lands of the grantor in the County of L___, or in Ireland, as the case may be. Even supposing all these acts to be satisfactorily explained (and this cannot be done without delay and additional expense) a search does not demonstrate a perfect title unless carried back to the coming of age of the person searched against – for before acquiring the property the person in question may possibly have covenanted to settle all his after acquired lands, or to charge all the lands he may die possessed of. And the ordinary search directed by counsel would not disclose a deed of this nature. When to these objections it is added that a search of the safest kind i.e., that against both names and lands, is very expensive and takes a long time to complete and that solicitors who wish to complete transactions speedily are every day obliged to rely on "hand searches" and "common searches," and thereby incur considerable risk which has not unfrequently led to their personally losing considerable sums of money; when to all this is added the remote position of the Registry Office at the northerly extremity of the city and the fact that other searches have also to be made in another office for judgments, recognizances, and Crown debts – when it is also remembered that all projected measures for improving and reforming the Registry of Deeds have failed by reason of the difficulty and complexity of the subject, and are likely to fail – it appears to me to have been a simpler and completer reform to withdraw, at least lands held under Parliamentary Title, from the old Registry of Deeds, and to register them *in such a way that a search shall disclose all that affects the estate, and nothing but what does affect the estate.* In these words is summed up the essence of the "Record of Title."

An incidental benefit, of no slight importance, is conferred by the existence and powers of the Landed Estates Court, which is enabled by the Act to correct any error that may happen to be discovered in the Record of Title. This power of rectification is one which does not exist as regards the Registry of Deeds; and one which perhaps could not exist conveniently excepting in the case of titles created by the Court, and remaining under the charge of its own officer. Other critics have objected that the Record of Title is not a register of simple ownership like that kept by the Bank as regards Government Stock but one that may be complicated by trusts and limitations. The objection if admitted as having some force can hardly be urged by the owner of land for the answer to him would be conclusive – "You are not required to encumber the Record with trusts in any case. The Act merely allows you to do so." As the measure was prepared in 1864, property could only have been recorded in the names of absolute owners, or of trustees having power of sale. The late Judge Hargreave, as is well known, strongly approved of this scheme; and he expressed his regret when a number of landowners procured the alteration of the measure in this particular, by representing to the Government their partiality for settlements and their wish to be able to record the interests under them. But the common sense of the proprietors of recorded estates may be trusted to, for telling them that a Record of Title can be of little use unless it enables a transfer or other dealing to be at once effected. And, in point of fact, nearly all the estates now placed on the Record (about 120 in number)[1] are recorded in the names of persons who are legally capable of transferring or mortgaging at once. So far little use has been made of the power of putting trusts on the Record; and therefore that objection to the measure practically falls to the ground. The first legal effect of recording an estate, is to withdraw it completely from the operation of the Registry Acts, which no longer affect it. Consequently no act by the recorded owner of an estate is registered in Henrietta street and no search need be made against him.

The next effect is, that no judgment recognizance or Crown debt of any kind affects the estate unless specifically entered on the Record under the title. If a person possessed of some common name (as Wilson, Johnson, Murphy, &c) wishes to show title under the old system, he must furnish a Judgment Search on which, probably, one hundred or more items may appear, as to all of which he has to show that they are satisfied or paid off, or that they are against other persons similarly named. Where the name is a more unusual one the inconvenience is less heavily felt. In all cases the necessity of *preserving* the various Searches in safe custody, so that they may be available in case of a future transaction, and that their loss may not involve the expense of making them over again, is a minor grievance of which few professional men have not experience. Another incidental advantage, therefore, that no documents have to be preserved excepting one – the Duplicate or Certificate of Title – which is, by the Acts, rendered perfect evidence of the title as of its date. This instrument, although its issue is not compulsory, is, in point of fact, taken out by all owners of recorded property, for their own satisfaction. Its production is called for whenever any act or dealing by the owner is to be put on record; and a note of every act or dealing is entered (in precisely similar terms) on it, and on the original Record, before it is handed out. This is the machinery by which a Record of Title is maintained.

I am Sir
Your obedient servant
Leguleius
9 Feb 1867

Sir – Observing in the Solicitor's Journal of 9th instant an appeal for that support hitherto denied to "the Record of Title" by the Irish solicitors, it appears but proper that a profession which rarely takes, or omits to take, action, on legal changes without good reason, should have a few words to say in explanation of that neglect under which this Registration Office pines, as does its English sister, Lord Westbury's pet, of 1862.

Those who considered the observations of the Law Society by its Council, dated 16th May, 1865, could have little doubt that the prediction of failure would be fulfilled, and those who did not see that print need only to read the elaborate anatomy therein, to learn how disregard of professional suggestions produced its usual result – when on the Shipping Acts and Mr Torrens' Australian experience was founded an Irish Land Act.

Ask any eminent solicitor in the hall whether he "records" his client's conveyances, and the answer will be almost invariably that he has never done so; and, although each may give a different reason, the result is the same.

It may be asked, whence comes it that any titles have been recorded, and the answer is supplied by the 7th Section of the Act, taken with the General Order, that unless within a very short time registration of a conveyance is stopped, it must be impounded to be recorded, and every mistake thereafter becomes indefeasible, which being unknown to many of us, and especially of our country brethren, several deeds were caught in the meshes of the Act before the practice was adopted of lodging the prohibitory notice at once on execution by the Court; but so careful have been some of our ablest members in this matter that the execution of a conveyance has been known to be delayed for six months, while the purchaser from absence or ill health was unable to sign this "stop" notice.

I need not dwell on "the meddling and muddling" of inexperience which produced a statute uncalled for while we possess a system of registry in Henrietta-street so perfect now as to leave little to desire, nor the additional expense occasioned by having to register there an entire conveyance with its schedule of tenants, running to the same or even a greater length than the deed itself, besides the trouble entailed by that strange direction for compulsory record unless stayed by the party, but leaving those who wish to learn wherefore the twin offices have failed in London and here to the solicitor's reasons of May, 1865.

I am, Sir,

Your obedient Servant,
A Solicitor
12th February 1867.

Sir – As you have opened your columns to free discussion upon the above subject, I avail myself of the opportunity thus afforded to make a few observations upon the letter of your correspondent "Leguleius" which appeared in your second number.

The first part of his letter is, I may say, in the nature of a "preamble" to an Act of Parliament; and is intended to lay a foundation for the measure of which your correspondent is so warm an advocate. His first proposition, that every owner of land desires to deal with it by sale or mortgage with economy and rapidity is, I take it, a self evident one, and needs no argument to support it. Whether this great facility in dealing with land which is the *desideratum* of supporters of the Record of Title system, would be a benefit to the landed and agricultural interests of the country is another question. It may be sought to establish an analogy between Government Stock, or even between ships and landed property, but a little consideration will show that it fails in most essential particulars, one of which however is sufficiently important to destroy the fabric built upon this uncertain foundation. The relation of landlord and tenant, which has been of late absorbing so much public attention both in and out of Parliament, and on the right condition of which hangs the welfare not only of the agricultural interests but of society itself in this country, has no counterpart in the funds or in shipping property. The man who buys Government Stock takes it with no obligation, legal or moral. What Iago says of cash in currency maybe as truly said of money in the funds – "'Twas mine, 'tis his, and has been slave to thousands." Not so the purchaser of land. He takes his purchase not only burdened with more duties, which he must be insensible to all principle to neglect, but also with legal obligations which he cannot evade. What, I would ask, Sir, would be the condition of a country in which land in the hands of occupying tenants was transferred from one person to another with the frequency of transfer of Government Stock, and in which a tenant might have a dozen different landlords between May and November? Nor has the relation of landlord and tenant any counterpart in the shipping interest. The ship's crew are seldom the same for two voyages; and the sailor has no tie binding him to any ship longer than the voyage for which he is engaged. Another distinction between funded and landed property is, that the latter is subject to the creation of various interests which are unknown in the former. Land may be held in fee by one man, subject to a contingent jointure to his wife, a charge for younger children, mortgages, annuities redeemable and perpetual, and be also subject to leases for lives renewable for ever, or long terms of years, which in their turn are subject to like incumbrances, or it may be also to sub-leases. Now what analogy has property capable of being made the subject of such varieties of interests to Government stock, which is in fact but security equivalent in value to a variable market price, and therefore capable of the most simple transfer.

The second part of your correspondent's "preamble" is certainly rather strong in statement. He says that the impediments to dealings with land for a long series of years have been such as *to diminish its value to the owners,* and to *limit* the number of persons bound by ties of property to the cause of *order* and *loyalty*. Now I would like to know how your correspondent proposes to prove this very strong proposition. Does he mean to contend that if the "artificial hindrances" and impediments he refers to were totally removed, and land could be as easily bought and sold in the market as Government Stock, that the *price* of land would be increased? Common experience teaches us otherwise, and tells us that the greater facility of transfer would affect the land market, by thrusting a quantity of property into it, and that the price of land would thus be depreciated rather than enhanced. But by what principle of ratiocination [sic] can "Leguleius" prove that the absence of such facility "limits the number of persons bound by ties of property to the cause of order and loyalty." If the tie of property binds to the cause of order and loyalty, then are the present proprietors land so bound, and if by the greater facility of transfer their estates are sold to others, the *number* of persons bound to the cause of order and loyalty remains the same. If the facility of transfer has any affect upon the cause of law and order, I would say it would be to make the proprietor sit looser to the land, and view it rather as a mercantile commodity which he could readily dispose of to a purchaser in the market. Perhaps (and I really see no other solution of his meaning) your correspondent intends that by this greater facility the land is capable of being cut up into *small* parts and that thus a numerous proprietary may be attained. If this is his meaning I think he will find few of the gentry, at least, to agree with him, or to believe that such sub-division of property would be a national benefit.

So much for your correspondent's "preamble." Had he made it a little more moderate, and merely stated that it was desirable, so far as practicable, to reduce the expenses and delays in connexion with the transfer of landed property, I for one could not have differed from him; but when he makes such very startling assertions one is disposed to question them, and to declare his "preamble" as not proved.

Passing by his historical sketch of the Registration of Title – upon which however I think some cross lights might be thrown – I now come to his strictures upon the Registry of Deeds in Ireland, and the "inherent defects" in that system, which render it "impossible" that searches could be completed in a short space time, or the useful objects of that institution be carried out. The first of these defects is what is known by the profession as "general charges," that is, deeds in which the lands intended to be affected are described in general terms, as, for instance – "All the lands of the grantor in the County of Leitrim." Now any one who will take the trouble to read the Act of 2nd and 3rd Wm. IV., cap. 87, will, I think, see that it was never contemplated that such deeds should be received in the Registry Office, and that, on the contrary, it was intended that every deed to be registered there should state the barony or parish in which the land comprised in it are situated. The practice of receiving such general charges has been adopted; but were conformity to the Act enforced, or a new stature passed, forbidding the reception of such deeds, this difficulty would be overcome, and I cannot, therefore, consider it an "inherent defect" in the Registry of Deeds. The real objection, namely, that you have to search from the coming of age of the person searched against, seems to me scarcely worth referring to, as it merely makes the search a few years longer, which, if the Registry of Deeds system were properly carried out would be comparatively nothing in the way of trouble. As to the ordinary search directed by counsel not disclosing "post obit" deeds, I must beg to differ from your correspondent and can appeal to the experience of your numerous professional readers, who, I am sure, are quite familiar with direction of search from the attaining of age of the party searched against. I apprehend the counsel must be a novice in "title" who omit such a necessary direction. I cannot look upon this objection of your correspondent as disclosing an inherent defect in the registry system. The delay obtaining searches I believe to be capable of removal, at all events, as regards modern searches, i.e. for more recent periods. I made suggestions to this end in a paper I read at the Social Science Congress here, in 1861; but of course, any reform in the registry system should be fully carried out, and a liberal expenditure allowed for that purpose, to bring it at all near perfection. Your correspondent's last objection to the Registry of Deeds, if novel, is not certainly very weighty, namely, that it is situated at the northerly extremity of the city, this "northerly extremity" being about ten minutes walk from the Record of Title Office. It seems to me, then, upon the whole, that if there be "inherent defects" in the Registry of Deeds system, your correspondent has failed to expose them.

Having trespassed so much on your space, I must reserve the discussion of the Record of Title, which your correspondent "Leguleius" would substitute for the Registry of Deeds, to another letter, and
Remain Sir
Yours faithfully
Henry T Dix
9 Upper Gardiner street
23rd February 1867

(Second Letter)
Sir, – In my last I traced briefly the history of Registration of

Title up to the time when, under the auspices of some of the most eminent of living lawyers, permissive Acts came into operation in England and in Ireland. In England the system has been in operation for four years, and about 500 applications to register titles under it have been received. In Ireland it has been in operation for a much shorter period; but here, as in England, several of the many estates recorded are those of members of the legal profession – a weighty fact which the most flippant and reckless assailant of the system cannot displace.

Proceeding to the actual working of the system in this country, we find that a Parliamentary Title, granted by the Landed Estates Court, must form the groundwork of every recorded title. Every conveyance or declaration now issued by the Court passes into the Record of Title Office, *unless* the new owner, by a written requisition, lodged during the period of seven days, allowed him for exercising his option, declines to come under the Act. That form of requisition is not so worded as to give much information to a nonprofessional reader of it; and there have been instances of it having been signed by persons who were desirous of coming under the Act, but appended their signatures to a printed document emanating from the Court without observing that its effect was to *exclude* them from the Act. No blame can, of course, be given to professional men who know little about a new system, and are indisposed to try experiments. Still I submit that where the Solicitor sends the form of requisition to be signed, the client ought to be supplied with well-defined, tangible objections against a measure which became law with the concurrence and by the aid of eminent men of all parties, and was opposed in its progress through Parliament by only one voice.

Usually a solicitor, while preparing a conveyance, ascertains at an early stage whether his client is to "record" it; and by this he is guided as to the preparation of one or of two originals on parchment for the signature of the judge. In practice, when the deed is not to be recorded, one original and a printed memorial are bespoken; and where the deed is to be recorded, two originals are bespoken and no printed memorial. The duplicate is stamped as such, and involves no extra expense beyond that stamp. In point of fact, in most cases it is much cheaper to have the deed recorded, for the following reason :- The memorial for registry, under the 16th section of the Record of Title Act, is invariably a very short one, containing no schedule of tenancies, and the deeds registry fund stamp on it rarely exceeds eleven shillings. The full printed memorial of a deed which is not recorded is, on the other hand, an exact transcript of the deed, whatever be the length of the latter; and the deeds registry fee frequently amounts to two or three pounds or more; and in a well-known case actually amounted to over forty pounds, owing to the number of leases and tenancies.

Now, as duplicates of the deeds are bespoken when the deed is intended to be recorded, and are not bespoken when the deed is not to be recorded, it follows that the duplicates furnish distinct and incontrovertible evidence of a deliberate intention to take advantage the Act. Any person who is willing to receive demonstration on this point has only to inquire "what proportion of the recorded estates were conveyed to the new owners by deeds in duplicate," and he will, as I am informed, learn beyond question that about one hundred of such cases have occurred representing property of the value of £300,000. It is possible that in a very few other cases, perhaps in ten or a dozen, the deeds have passed into the Record of Title Office, without the wish, or even against the wish, of the proprietors; but they seem to have become reconciled to the system, for no application has been made under the 32nd of the Act, to *remove* a property from the Record of Title, although the process is simple, and the expense of so doing could hardly exceed fifty shillings.

While the Act was in progress objections against it, of various kinds, were suggested by professional men; but, discarding such as were merely grounded on the supposed danger of a new system, and the imaginary perfectness of the deeds registry, the objections which usually had weight and were worthy of serious consideration resolved themselves into this – that a transfer or charge, if fraudulently placed on the record, might be ruinous to the recorded owner of the property. Hence, Parliament was careful to introduce numerous and cumulative safeguards against fraud or forgery; and the practice of the new office embraces other safeguards of an important character. The recorded owner must have *notice* of every attempted dealing with his property, and his duplicate or certificate of title must also be produced on every such dealing. As transfers, &c., are accepted in writing, the officer has, moreover, the means of comparing the handwriting on such occasions; and, again, every transfer in the office must be in the presence of a solicitor, and every deed executed elsewhere must be proved to have been duly executed, by the affidavit of a solicitor. Would it not require more than the ingenuity of a Sadleir and a Stephens combined to evade all these safeguards, and by a network of personation, robbery, and forgery to falsify the record of title? And, be it remembered, that no person but an innocent mortgagee or purchaser for value could take advantage of the fraud, even were it accomplished. Another preventive against fraud, although one of minor value, was the withdrawal of the Record of Title, which contains all the particulars of the property, charges, ownership, &c., from public inspection. By the Act, it can only be seen by some person directly interested, or by his solicitor. The Law Society objected, that the Record of Title ought to be regarded as a public document; but the legislature affirmed the opposite view taken by the framers of the measure, and by keeping the Record closed against strangers diminished the temptation to fraud and increased the probability of detection in the event of a forged deed being presented. This suggests a question concerning the registry of deeds, the utility of which is much impaired through the natural unwillingness of owners of property that their family arrangements should be open to general inspection. What has been the result of a registry of deeds which is open to inspection by any person who is willing to pay a small fee? Simply this – that it has been usual in memorials to *suppress* the trusts of settlements and other deeds, thus neutralizing, to a great degree, the object and purpose of the registry, and in several recent instances, where the deeds themselves have been lost, rendering titles, at least during many years, hopelessly bad.

To resume our review of the mechanism of the Record of Title. The conveyance or declaration of title gives a perfectly new root of title, and declares in almost every case an absolute ownership. When the recorded owner desires to sell or mortgage, his title appears at once on production of his duplicate or certificate of title, which can at any time be brought down and re-dated. Or the intending purchaser or mortgagee may, by permission of the owner, satisfy himself of the title by an inspection of the record, in which every act affecting the property will be found entered under the proper heading. The mode of entry is by an "official note," or summary of the purport of every deed. It is, of course, easy to frame a short "official note" of a simple transaction. Of a complicated one the official note may be longer; and it remains to be seen whether such notes will in that case attempt a summary of the deed, or will merely *refer* to the deed, the original or a copy of which must in every case be deposited in the office. In the English office it is understood to be the practice to make a note of reference only to any instrument which is not a simple transfer or charge. Where an estate is put in settlement by deed or will, the simplest and most effective mode of recording will be to enter the names of the trustees, supposing that they have a power of sale. Modern settlements usually contain such a power.

If, however (as in the case of a great family mansion) it is *not* intended that the property should, under any circumstances, be sold, probably the best course would be to remove the estate from the operation of the Act, under the 32nd section. Evidently the object of the Act is to facilitate sales and transfers by condensing the evidence of title; it is intended to apply to land legally capable of being sold or mortgaged; and therefore strictly settled estates, incapable of being sold, do not fall properly within its scope. Nothing is gained by claiming for any system more than it is well fitted for accomplishing; and it may be that some advocates of this system have gone too far in predicting that it will supersede the deeds registry, and absorb into itself, some day or other, all the landed property of the country. It can only claim to facilitate very greatly all transfers, charges, leases, and other usual dealings with property which is not in settlement, or which, being in settlement, is intended to be capable of being sold.

I am, Sir,
Your obedient Servant,
Leguleius
2 March 1867

Sir, – Having dealt with that part of the letter of "Leguleius," which is in the nature of a "preamble" to measure which he would commend to your professional readers, I will now, with your permission, enter upon discussion of the system which is the subject of his laudatory remarks.

I think I can scarcely be mistaken if I take your correspondent as a high authority upon the subject on which writes. He has evidently made it his particular study, and I am sure is most competent, from his ability and experience, to become an apologist of the measure. I may say further that one who is so enamoured of the system will, no doubt, be best authority upon its charms and virtues. First among these, in your correspondent's opinion, is the separate account, as it were, opened in the Record for each Title, so that, in the words of your correspondent, which he has italicised to give them greater importance, *"a search shall disclose all that affects the Estate, and nothing but what does affect the Estate."* "In these words," he tells us, "are summed up the essence of the Record of Title." We may therefore fairly assume that this peculiarity constitutes its chief attraction. Now, what is the great merit of this plan as contrasted with the present system of Title? In the present system an abstract of Title is presented to the solicitor for purchaser or lender, which contains nothing but what affects the estate to be sold or mortgaged, and this is offered as the true history of the dealings with the lands. To test its accuracy, searches are made in the Registry Deeds Office, and if the abstract has been accurately prepared, nothing appears upon the search beyond what is found in the abstract, save some few "general charges," which, on being examined, are at once seen not to affect the lands. Your professional readers know that the routine I have mentioned is part of their every-day experience, and that the mountain of difficulties which the advocates of Record of Title speak of are chiefly in their own imagination.

The great simplicity of the Record of Title, which your correspondent seems to attach so much weight to, will just continue so long as the transactions and dealings of the estate remain simple; but once they depart from that simplicity, the Record will become as complicated as the same title would become under the Registry of Deeds system, and will completely baffle unprofessional intelligence to unravel or explain it. Let any one examine the "Model Records" contained in the "Report of the Legal Sub-Committee of the Registration of Title Association," in which, of course, any really knotty and difficult titles are avoided, and he will readily see that the Record of Title may become as difficult to understand as a complicated abstract of title under the old system. In fact, the unfitness of the system for everything but the very simplest transactions is evidenced by the letter of your correspondent; for he meets the objection that it becomes "complicated by trusts and limitations," by saying to the owner of land so objecting, "You are not required to encumber the Record with trusts in any case. The Act merely allows you to do so." This may seem to your correspondent a highly satisfactory answer, but I doubt exceedingly if, to an owner intending matrimony, and desirous to make a provision by settlement for his wife and the children of the marriage, it would be considered equally so. However, it is an admission of a fact which is of the greatest importance in respect to this Record of Title system, namely, that it is *totally unfit for lands, or charges upon lands, which are ever to be put into settlement.* This was the opinion, as Leguleius admits, of one of the ablest real property lawyers we ever had in this country, namely, the late Judge Hargreave, and who would have excluded all trusts from the Record. The landowners, however, as your correspondent states, and who knew their own requirements, very naturally objected to this arrangement, which would have had the effect of destroying one of the greatest advantages of landed, over funded property, namely, its safety as a security for trust purposes. This unsuitability of the Record of Title for property, that is ever to be the subject of settlement (and let any one of experience in title say what property is not so subject in the course of time), is so candidly admitted in the last paragraph of your correspondent's second letter, that it is unnecessary for me to dwell longer on that branch of the subject. The Record of Title, he says, "can *only* claim to facilitate very greatly all transfers, charges, leases, and other usual dealings with property, *which is not in settlement,* or which, being in settlement, is intended to be capable of being sold." If, therefore, you want the property you have settled for the benefit of your children to be kept for them, and not sold, you will, of course, not have it recorded.

The next ground of objection to the Record of Title, and which was very strongly pressed by the Council of the Law Society in their memorial against the measure, is the danger of clothing every act under its provisions with an indefeasible character. This principle of indefeasibility applies to erroneous as well as to correct entries upon the Record. That errors of importance may occur is evident, as in your correspondent's first letter he says :- "An incidental benefit of *no slight importance* is conferred by the existence and powers of the Landed Estates Court, which is enabled by the Act to correct any error that *may happen to be discovered* in the Record of Title." But suppose this error did not "happen to be discovered" until after the mischief had been done, and it had been acted on as an infallible Record, and the property dealt with accordingly, what would be the use of correcting the Record then! In the present system there is no necessity for correcting any mistake of the kind, as the deeds registered in the Registry of Deeds Office have not an indefeasible character, and consequently if the mortgage or judgment of A is registered against the estate of B, the latter is nothing the worse for it, as it is not a bit more a charge upon his estate on that account. Not so in the Record of Title. There, a similar registry or recording would saddle B's estate with an indefeasible charge which may not "happen to be discovered" to be erroneous, until after it has been assigned to a "bona fide" purchaser for value, who, under the Act, must be protected at the expense of the unfortunate owner whose estate is thus erroneously charged.

Another objection felt by many to the Record of Title system is, that once a proprietor puts his estate into it, it is practically in the Landed Estates' Court as much as if it were going to be sold. It is subject to the rules and orders of the Court for the Record of Title, and every step taken is liable, should there be any difficulty in it, to be brought before a Judge of the Court for adjudication. In the case of deaths, too, public notices are required, and proceedings have to be taken, which are quite unnecessary and unknown in ordinary dealings with real estate, so that if a recorded owner really appreciates his position, he must have the uncomfortable consciousness that he is always a suitor "in Court."

Admittedly there have been comparatively few purchases recorded, but how are we to account for even those few having been put on the record! Simply by the exceedingly unfair clause in the Act which declares every purchase in the Landed Estates Court recorded unless the purchaser shall, *within seven days* from the date of his conveyance, protest against being put on the Record. There could not be stronger proof of the infirmity of the whole system, and the consciousness of the promoters of such infirmity, than the insertion in the statute of this trap to catch purchasers. If they could trust to the merits of the system why not leave it to those who desire to be recorded to say so. Your correspondent's second letter contains, it seems to me, an exceedingly unfair charge against solicitors in respect to this matter, and one which it is very easy to displace. He says that when purchasers intend to record their estates they take out duplicate conveyances, and hence that the fact of about one hundred duplicate conveyances having been taken out is "incontrovertible evidence" of a deliberate intention on the part of purchasers to take advantage of the Act. The insinuation here is evidently that purchasers so intending have been dissuaded by their solicitors, who ought, in that case, your correspondent reprovingly tells us, to supply their clients with well-defined tangible objections against the system. Now the fact is perfectly well known to every solicitor of experience that duplicate conveyances were frequently taken out of the Landed Estates' Court before the Record of Title had existence, being required for various purposes, but most commonly to hand to a mortgagee who may be lending part of the amount with which the estate is purchased. So much for your correspondent's "incontrovertible evidence." As to the insinuation that solicitors, who advise their clients against recording, do not give well-defined, tangible reasons for such advice, I can only say that it is a gratuitous assumption on the part of your correspondent, for which I am not aware of any foundation. May I not as justly say that those who advise their clients to record, should give equally good reasons for that advice. The truth is, that many of the cases recorded are put upon the Record because the solicitor for the purchaser, not having looked into the question, hesitates to pass an opinion *pro* or *con,* and meantime the client is recorded by operation of the trap clause I have referred to. With the assistance of this very ingenious contrivance, I have no doubt that for some time to come there will be occasional purchasers caught and caged in the Record of Title, but I do not believe that a system of registry of real property, which admittedly fails when applied to trusts and limitations, and which is unequal to transactions of a complicated nature, while it is dangerous in those of a more simple character, will ever be accepted by the Solicitors of Ireland, the friendly recommendations of your clever notwithstanding.

I remain, Sir, your obedient Servant,
Henry T. Dix.
13th April 1867

(Third Letter)

Sir – When I undertook, at your request, to furnish, for the information of your readers, some account of the Record of Title Act of 1865, and of the practice under it, I had no intention of engaging in controversy. My object is not to wrangle about collateral points; and to the objections of your correspondent, Mr H. T. Dix, I shall reply in the briefest manner that the case will admit of. First, let me thank him for completing the proof of my assertion that there are inherent defects in the registry of deeds. He shows that an Act of Parliament, passed more than thirty years since, has proved wholly inadequate to prevent the incumbering of the Registry with those "general charges" which are productive of so much trouble and expense. He further shows, that his own suggestions, publicly made six years since, for remedying some of the defects complained of, have received no attention. A report of a committee of the Law Society (to which are appended, amongst others, the esteemed names of the president and vice-president), thus forcibly summed up the question in 1862:- "The present system is so tedious and embarrassing that in practice it imposes undue responsibility on the profession, without giving to the public the protection and security it was originally intended to afford." A Bill was, I believe, brought in several years since by the Government of the day for reforming the system of the registry of deeds; but it broke down, so to speak, from its own weight. So much for improving the deeds registry. Your readers will have observed that Mr Dix's zeal in defence of a system which he ably attacked in 1861, and which remains unchanged, has led him into the error of stating that a search, as usually made, is a sufficient evidence of title. Now let A B, aged sixty years, be supposed to have purchased an estate with a parliamentary title ten years since, and to be now obtaining a loan on mortgage. The search to be procured and furnished on such an occasion will be a search against A B from the date of his purchase in the Court to the present time. If Mr Dix, in a case like this, insists on any more extensive search, he is singular, and he does that which is not only contrary to usual custom, but which adds very considerably to the expense of the search. But it will be admitted by any lawyer that A B, at any time after attaining age, may have covenanted to charge all his after acquired lands, and that such a covenant is considered to be binding if duly registered. Therefore the title in the case supposed is not complete without a search, carried back for nearly forty years, against A B. Again, Mr Dix airily disposes of all the acts appearing on a search, by saying that they "are at once seen not to affect." He may possess the secret of some mode of enchantment which shall discover in a moment that all the "acts" relate to other matters; but ordinary mortals are compelled carefully to peruse and tediously to scrutinize for fear of mistakes. Examples are valuable in this discussion; and I shall now adduce, from my own recent experience, some examples of the difficulty of making out title under the present system. A search lately made against a Mr Kennedy disclosed 85 acts on the registry, which were only shown after a patient and minute investigation, not to affect the property in question. Still greater embarrassment was caused in the same case by the return of 95 acts on one judgment search, many of which appeared very doubtful, and some of which to this day, I believe, have not been satisfactorily proved "not to affect." A recent search against "William Kelly," in the judgment office, disclosed 134 acts, many of them against a person whose place of abode is not stated. Among them appears a judgment against "____ Kelly, gentleman," which I recognized as an old friend, for it, of course, turns up on every judgment search made against any male person of the name of Kelly. A recent search against the name of Wm. McDermott discloses 84 acts. A recent search against the name of John Wilson discloses 181 acts. A recent search against the name of John Johnston discloses 199 acts.

Such instances naturally lead one to appreciate a registry from which, to use the words of Lord Westbury, "a landowner can at any time procure a certificate showing the exact state of his title." Such a document Mr Dix can hardly be serious in comparing with an abstract of title, which is of infinitely inferior value as an evidence of title for many reasons. Among them the following:- An abstract must be fortified by searches, certificates of birth and burial, affidavits, and other evidence; and it must contain the particulars of transactions which are now at an end and have ceased to affect the title. For example A B, some years since, we will suppose, mortgaged to C, who assigned the mortgage to D, on whose decease the mortgage money was paid off by A B, and a release and reconveyance obtained from E, the heir at law, and from F, the executor of D. Now all these persons must figure on the abstract, and the deeds executed by them must be set out; and, in short, it is necessary for the security of any intending mortgagee or purchaser that all these bygone transactions should be carefully and thoroughly investigated. A certificate of title, on the one hand, is silent as to paid off mortgages and all other completed transactions, which no longer affect the title; for mortgages and other matters, as soon as they are satisfactorily shown to be paid off and put an end to, are treated as things of the past, into which no further examination is in any sense necessary. In my last letter I admitted that the utility of a Registry or Record of Title was chiefly shown in simple transactions; and that property which is not intended, under any circumstances, to be capable of sale, &c., is not likely to derive much benefit from the new system. Mr Dix is, however, quite in error in supposing that the system is not adapted for the great majority of settled estates. He will find that all standard conveyancing books of modern date suggest a power of sale as a convenient, a usual, and a proper clause in any marriage settlement; and that nearly all modern settlements, if well drawn, contain that power. He will find, also, that all the eminent lawyers who have expressed themselves as in favour of a Registry of Title, have contemplated the entry of trustees of settled estates having a power of sale, as owners, for the purpose of transfer, &c. Any owner of a recorded estate who makes a settlement of it, should, therefore, have the trustees entered ("without survivorship") as owners, and should have his own name entered as that of a person whose consent is required, or who must have notice before any sale can be effected. This is all provided for by the Act.

Mr Dix, whose experience of Parliamentary titles will extend over a course of years, during which the I.[ncumbered] E.[states] Court has never exercised, even if it ever claimed, the power to rectify errors in its own conveyances, seems alarmed such power is at last conferred; but it will be seen at once that this power of amending the record is fraught not with danger, but with safety. For there is the same probability as ever that mistakes will *not* be committed, while there is a strong probability that if there should be a mistake it will be discovered and rectified, before mischief has been done. And in the extreme case of a loss of property occurring (though how such an occurrence could take place, I am unable to imagine), its owner will derive some consolation from the reflection that Lieutenant Colonel J. H. Keogh, who was the victim of the most important error made throughout the long history of the Incumbered or Landed Estates' Court, was fully recompensed by the Legislature.

Mr Dix is also in error in saying that "few purchases have been recorded." Duplicate conveyances are not in practice bespoken for any purpose, except for the Record of Title; and the fact that they have been taken out in more than a hundred instances, where the conveyance has afterwards been recorded, furnishes as incontestable evidence on the point, as the previous taking out of a ticket can do of the intention of a passenger to proceed by a railway train. Mr Dix's supposition that the passengers have been carried off against their will, is, therefore, unfounded; perhaps equally so is his anticipation that other passengers will, when they understand the subject, prefer the old stage coach to the railway. There have been more than a hundred purchases deliberately recorded, not by mistake or inadvertence, but with a clear intention of taking advantage of a measure which is the rational corollary of the Landed Estates' Act. The objection to the 7th section falls to the ground, now that every solicitor knows, or ought to know its effect: and I venture to express an opinion that a solicitor should not content himself with writing a mandatory note, like one I lately saw, merely desiring the client "to sign the enclosed requisition [against recording a conveyance] and return it immediately." If the clients had been informed of the nature of the measure, there is every reason to conclude that their conveyances would have been entered on record in still greater numbers. The requisition against recording has in fact been signed by numerous persons in entire ignorance of its nature and effect.

It is difficult to understand why any proprietor should feel uneasy (as Mr Dix intimates) because the Registry of Parliamentary Titles is under the control of a court usually supposed to possess the confidence of the profession and of the public. I never heard that any tenant-in-tail felt it objectionable that his deed to open the estate is required to be enrolled in Chancery; nor are married women alarmed at the jurisdiction of the Court of Common Pleas over their legal transactions. Fines and recoveries, bills of sale, probates and administrations and fifty other common incidents, are or were, more or less, under the control of courts of justice. Nearly all dealings with property are in some way liable to judicial control. Mr Dix also objects to a public notice, forgetting that it has lately become the established custom for executors and administrators to advertise for claimants, as inspection of the columns of any newspaper will show. An advertisement, will, it is true, be required before any dealing by an heir at law with the recorded estate of his ancestor. And I mistake much if an experienced and cautious solicitor would recommend a client to lend on mortgage to an heir at law immediately after the decease of the ancestor, unless after an interval had elapsed, and publicity given to the claim founded on an alleged intestacy.

On this point it is worthy of remark, that an heir at law, who has lately experienced difficulty in procuring a loan (for it is proverbially hard to prove a negative, such as the nonexistence of a will) has actually applied to have his estates entered on the

Record of Title, in order to facilitate dealings with them. Such an instance proves the utility of enabling the heir at law, after public notices, to obtain a formal recognition of his title; and it is almost incredible that any person should object to publicity in such [a] case.

In concluding this letter, I venture to recommend Mr Dix and other gentlemen, who are prejudiced against this method of preserving the indefeasible character of Parliamentary titles, to satisfy themselves as to its nature and capabilities, by actual inquiry and investigation. As the carefully considered initiation of an important law reform, the Record of Title commends itself to the attention of solicitors. As a reform in real property law, I hold it to be as valuable, as it is full of public interest; but beyond this it is, let me add, a matter of indifference to me whether the majority of the past and future purchasers of estates in the Court avail themselves of it or not. If they and their legal advisers, through prejudice or through inadvertence, neglect to obtain, by means of this Act, the clear and substantial advantages which it is calculated to afford them, the loss is their own. Of this I am certain, that before many years have elapsed there will be a general adoption of conclusions resembling those to which a long and careful study of the subject has brought your obedient servant,
Leguleius.
4th May 1867

Sir, – I can readily imagine that when your correspondent, "Leguleius," began this subject in your columns, "he had no intention of engaging in controversy." Still less, I am sure, did he anticipate that his letter, so eulogistic of the "Record of Title," should be the means of exposing the faults and infirmities of the system which it was his purpose to commend to your professional readers. However, sir, he must have been fully aware that the correspondence in every respectable journal is subject to the principle, "*audi alteram partem*," and that in that column, at least, no one is allowed an immunity from contradiction. In his last letter he charges me with inconsistency in having (he says) attacked the system of registry of deeds in my paper read at the

Social Science Congress here in 1861, and being now zealous in its defence. In this your correspondent overstates his case. I am not, and never was, a partisan either for or against the registry of deeds. I made some suggestions, which I believed, whether rightly or wrongly, would, if adopted, have facilitated the transaction of the vast amount of business in the Registry Office, but I never found fault with the registry of deeds as a system. The improvements I suggested could not have been made without legislation, and therefore the heads of the office are in no way answerable for not acting upon my suggestions. On the other hand, I do not now assert that the system, as worked at present, is perfect, but I believe it much preferable to the Record of Title system, and my defence of it "hath this extent, no more."

As to the suppositious case which your correspondent puts, of a covenant to charge real estate, binding land purchased in Landed Estates Court and conveyed by Parliamentary conveyance. I venture entirely to differ from him. I do not believe that any such covenant would bind property derived by Parliamentary title; but if he be right in his view of the law, then the error lies in counsel not directing searches from the time the purchaser came of age. But searches are not directed against purchasers from Landed Estates' Court further than the date of the sale, simply because no Act before the sale would affect the estate conveyed by the conveyance of the Court, which is good against all the world. If such covenants would bind land purchased in the Landed Estates' Court, then counsel are wrong not to direct searches accordingly. But this is a question between your correspondent and the Irish Bar, who are well able to defend themselves, and does not affect the discussion in which I am engaged with him, save that if he is right in his opinion it seems to me very questionable whether such covenants would not bind recorded land, in which case the indefeasibility of the Record is extinguished.

"Leguleius" says:- "Examples are valuable in *this discussion*," and thereupon exhibits a number of judgment searches, some with as many as 181 acts upon them, which, he says it is necessary "carefully to peruse and tediously to scrutinize," in order to determine whether they affect the lands in relation to which they were directed. Now the present "discussion" has reference only to land purchased in the Incumbered or Landed Estates Court, to which alone the Record of Title applies; and I am, therefore, at a loss to know for what purpose the searches for judgments were directed, as under the Act 13 and 14 Vic., cap. 29, no judgments affect property purchased since 15th July, 1850 unless registered as a mortgagee in the Registry of Deeds Office. So much for these "valuable examples."

Your correspondent, in his last letter, endeavours to qualify, if not to retract, the admissions of his preceding one, in which he acknowledged frankly the inadequacy of the Record of Title for property which is likely to be put in settlement. All can be made perfectly safe, it seems, according to his last letter, by the wonderful contrivance of entering the trustees on the record as owners, "without survivorship," and the tenant for life taking special care to have his own name entered as that of a person whose consent is required, or who must have notice before any sale can be effected. This is all very well for the tenants for life; but what about the poor remainderman, who may not have taken this precaution to prevent his estate being sold to some one else without his knowledge? Unfortunately, too, infants and minors cannot (unless some next friend interferes) take this prudent precaution against the rapidity of transfer and indefeasible action of the Record of Title, and which has ever been its greatest merits in the eyes of the promoters of the system.

As to the correction of the Record, I am quite at a loss, I confess, to understand your correspondent's argument. He says, in terms, that over the course of years in which the Incumbered Estates' Court existed, it never made any mistake; that there is every reason to expect the same infallibility in the "Record of Title," and yet that the power of amending the record is "fraught with safety." Surely when we speak of any plan being "fraught with safety" we mean that the absence of it would be fraught with danger. If there are no mistakes to be corrected, where is the danger? Yet he must contemplate *some* mistakes, for he adds, "There is a strong probability that if there be a mistake it will be discovered and rectified before mischief has been done." Now, I am at a loss to know what is the ground for this "probability." For my part, I believe the probability to be exactly the other way, and that every act in the record being of a conclusive character, the mistake will *not* be found out until it is too late to rectify it without injury to some one. The Incumbered Estates Court has never, it is true, either exercised or claimed the power to rectify the errors in its conveyances, because such power is entirely inconsistent with their indefeasible character, and the power given to correct the errors in the Record of Title is equally inconsistent, indefeasibility being the very essence of that system. How do I know, if I purchase a recorded estate from a recorded owner, that, after I have paid my money for it, the Recorder of Titles may not find a mistake in the record, and correct it. Where, then, is the indefeasibility of my certificate, which, in the words of Lord Westbury, is to show "the exact state of my title"? The indefeasible record has proved fallible, and now it is to be corrected, and the correction will be indefeasible until it, too, is found to be wrong, and is corrected by this power to alter what is "fraught with safety" to the public.

Admitting your correspondent's assertion that one hundred duplicate conveyances having been taken out is evidence of that number of purchasers desiring to be recorded, then we must assume, for the same reason, that those who do not take out duplicate conveyances have no such desire, in which case it is quite plain that of the number of cases recorded only one hundred, or thereabouts, represent those who really desire to be so, and that the rest were caught in the trap, or, to adopt your correspondent's illustration, have been carried off in this indefeasible express train, at considerable risk, by accident.

Although to "Leguleius" this may appear the very best thing that can happen to them, the purchasers themselves may not be quite of that opinion. An instance of this kind came under my notice lately. A gentleman of large property had purchased a small estate in the Landed Estates Court which had been recorded, he not having resisted. Subsequently to being recorded he married in England, and the recorded lands, with a considerable amount of other property, was put into settlement, the deed being necessarily a very voluminous one. So far as the recorded estate went, the settlement had no operation, because it was not recorded, and how to record it was the question. The anomaly and inconvenience which was pointed out in the observations of the Incorporated Law Society actually arose in this case, for part of the settled property was under one law and part under another. The law advisers of the party interested under the settlement have, after much consideration, advised their client to take the only safe course under the circumstances – namely, to withdraw the lands out of Record of Title and bring them under the ordinary law.

And now allow me to protest against the charge which your correspondent has made against the members of my profession, and which he repeats in his last letter – namely, that they purposely keep their clients in ignorance of the benefits and advantages of the Record of Title. I think the most prejudiced in favour of the system must admit that there are ample reasons to justify a solicitor in hesitating to advise his client to record, and yet, because the profession do not surrender their opinions as practical men to those of your correspondent, he charges them with a wilful suppression of facts from their clients. As to informing their clients of the nature of the Record of Title, I suppose, in many instances, they might as easily be informed of, and as readily understand, the nature of the differential calculus. No doubt it would be easy to describe, in general terms, what the promoters *say* of it; but it would be utterly impossible to explain to an unprofessional person the objections to the system. In such matters the public in general, who have confidence in their solicitors, will act on their advice, believing as they do that it is honestly given.

To meet my objection to keeping my client still a suitor in the Landed Estates' Court, as I maintain is done by recording his estate, "Leguleius" endeavours to prove an analogy between that step and enrolling a deed in Chancery, or examining a married woman separately in the Court of Common Pleas. I am really surprised at any one of your correspondent's intelligence and experience offering such an argument to your professional readers, all of whom must be perfectly aware that there is no analogy whatever in these proceedings to the recording of an estate. A deed once enrolled, you have never any occasion to come near the Court of Chancery again respecting it, nor is there anything to bring you back to the Court of Common Pleas after you have filed the acknowledgement of a married woman. Not so with the Record of Title. It is absolutely part of the Landed Estates Court, and every difficulty in respect to any transactions with recorded land (and if the business increases there will be plenty of them), must be brought before the Judge of that Court for adjudication, for which purpose regular rules and orders have been made and published. My objection is not to the Landed Estates' Court. If I must be in Court, I would as soon be there as in any other Court, but what I do object to is being kept in Court at all.

Your correspondent does not seem happy in analogies, for the instance of an executor or administrator for his own *protection* publishing a statutory notice to creditors, has no analogy whatever to the case of an heir at law, or devizee being obliged to give notice before he can exercise ownership respecting a real estate to which he succeeds by descent or devize. As to the difficulty of showing that you are an heir at law, from not being able to prove the negative fact that there was no will, it is certainly a new one and one which I do not believe real property lawyers have hitherto experienced; large estates in Ireland are constantly passing by descent to heirs at law, but I never heard of this fact embarrassing any one until your correspondent mentioned this extraordinary case of an heir at law, who cannot make title to his estate because no one will believe that his predecessor died intestate. I do not see, for my part, the "utility" of enabling the heir at law to have himself *indefeasibly* recorded to the absolute exclusion of a devizee deriving under a will which may be afterwards found, although such is the law in recorded estates. The Court of Probate may recall letters of administration, if a will turn up after they have been granted, and I see no reason why a different rule should prevail respecting real estate.

I am not aware that anything I have written in this discussion betrays such ignorance of the subject as to warrant the patronizing rebuke contained in your correspondent's last paragraph, but of this your readers will be better judges. I hope I am not in the habit of writing upon subjects of this kind without "investigation and inquiry," and that I have a sufficient acquaintance with the Record of Title system to be allowed to express an opinion upon it, without drawing down upon me the kind "recommendation," of your correspondent, to prejudiced persons. It may be that as he prophecies before many years have elapsed conclusions resembling those which he has arrived at may be generally adopted, and that his Indefeasible Express Railway Train (to follow his own illustration), may have effectually driven the old slow-coach system of Registry of deeds off the real property road. Perhaps so; but it seems to me quite as probable that when a few "dreadful accidents" have occurred on this indefeasible line, the public may decline to trust their property upon it, or that the danger of such casualties may occasion the formation of a Record of Title Accident Assurance Company, to provide compensation for the sufferers.

I remain, Sir, your obedient servant,
Henry T. Dix
25th May 1867

(Fourth Letter)
A living philosopher has said, "whoever points out the rocks and shoals with which our course is beset, does us a service which may be all the greater because we are not terrified thereby into renouncing the voyage." Fair and well-reasoned criticism is especially admissible in the case of new legislation; for its dangers, if hasty and ill considered may be considerable. But our gratitude to the timorous navigator will be vastly lessened if we find that he is uttering alarming warnings of rocks and shoals which only exist in his own imagination.

When we call to mind the fact that, with few exceptions, all past and present measures of law reform, however supported by reason or justified by experience, have been strenuously objected to by a proportion of the really well informed in legal matters, we can hardly wonder that the public out of doors entertain a belief that the legal world has what the above quoted philosopher describes as "a professional interest in the expensiveness and unintelligibility of the law." Did I concur in this view, I should not further seek to occupy the columns of your valuable journal with the subject; but as I firmly believe that while the profession are not to any great extent acquainted with it, they are, for the most part, quite open to conviction, I am induced to prolong the correspondence. Little remains to be said on the points put forward by Mr Dix. The well meant recommendation contained in my last letter that those who dislike the method of recording or perpetuating Parliamentary Titles should acquaint themselves with its details, has failed of effect so far as he is concerned. Were he as anxious to understand, as he is to find fault with, the system, he could hardly have used words conveying the idea that the Recorder of Titles has authority to correct any error which may be discovered on the Record. Under section 17 of the Act (28 & 29 Vic., c. 88) every amendment, or correction, must be made by direction of Court. It is not to be expected that a judicial act of this importance should be done without ample notice to any person interested, or that the rights of any *bona fide* purchaser for value should be disregarded. Again, in the case quoted of a small portion of a large property being removed from the Record of Title, on the occasion of being put in settlement, there is not a shadow of pretence for the statement of Mr Dix that this was the "only safe course" to take; for, as I have before shown, the property, although in settlement, might have been recorded in the names of the trustees. Nor is there any reason to doubt that the Court, on an application by any party interested under the settlement, would, whether the trustees were recorded or not, by stop-order, or in some other mode, take steps to prevent any improper dealing with the property by the limited owner. Mr Dix might have been justified in saying that, under the circumstances, to record a small portion of a settled estate would be inconvenient, but he not justified in stating that to do so would be unsafe. I might also complain of Mr Dix's habit of taking some one illustration brought forward in support of a general maxim or proposition, and limiting his argument to it while ignoring the proposition which it supports, as though a rule might not be supported by examples varying in detail. Thus where he objected that publicity is required in certain cases before a transmission of real estate can be recorded, and in reply I referred him to the growing usage of advertising for claimants where there is a devolution of personal estate, he rejoins that the advertisement is of a different kind – forgetting that the point at issue is the publicity, and not the form, of an advertisement. Again, in reply to the imaginary grievance of a recorded owner being in the position of a suitor, merely because his acts are recorded by an officer who is under the control of a Court, I pointed to numerous dealings with property which are registered in Courts. Mr Dix thereupon makes the discovery that an enrolment in Chancery, or in the C. P., is distinguishable; further, that it is unobjectionable, because once done it is done for ever. Here, again, he is wrong – for the law Reports contain numberless decisions as to the amending and vacating of these enrolments and other entries. But I may, with even greater justice, complain of Mr Dix's attempt to put me in conflict, so to speak, with both branches of the profession. This rhetorical artifice will hardly succeed; for I have not in my former letters written one word implying any doubt either of the learning of the bar or of the honour of the solicitors, and I have the highest possible appreciation of both.[2]

So much for the objections of Mr Dix; and perhaps I have considered them at unnecessary length, having regard to this fact, that they do not touch the essential and distinguishing merit of a Registry of Title. Difficulties will be met with (and overcome) in working out the system; but its great result of collecting together under one folio, all the acts relating to one title remains unassailed. When the Incumbered Estates' Act was passed there were objections precisely similar urged against it. Parliamentary title was, we were told, new-fangled and unsafe – existing systems (if a good deal amended) were sufficient – the "poor remaindermen" and the absentees would be injured. All this many of us will remember; but we have seen that with caution and with publicity the system has worked with remarkable freedom from error, and with great public advantage. The Record of Title may be described as its natural development rather than as anything new – for it is conducted on similar principles, and under similar control. If complications of title can be safely cleared off, it is reasonable to conclude that they can be safely prevented from arising. So long as the title is straightforward, the mechanism of the new office will suffice, without recourse to the Court. When something occurs which that mechanism is not adapted to deal with, or in other words, when a difficulty begins to arise on the title, then, and not till then, there will be a reference to the Court which is familiar with all questions that can arise on titles, and can exercise all the powers of a Court of Equity in disposing of them. A very eminent London conveyancer, while discussing the various plans for registering titles, aptly compared this power of reference to the Court to a "safety valve." The Court is not, it is true, bound to decide every question that arises, but may, under section 11 of the Act, reserve any question by putting a "caveat" or a "qualification" on the Record. In this way the rights of absent and unrepresented persons will be saved. Under the present system a lender or purchaser will most probably be unaware of a flaw until it is too late. But whoever deals with a recorded owner, on the contrary, will have distinct notice, not only of the existence, but of the exact nature of any flaw or "qualification." His position is, therefore, assured. So far as experience of the system has gone, both in England and Ireland, a "qualification" is a very rare thing – absolute and unqualified, as well as indefeasible ownership existing in almost every instance.

Questions are frequently put as to (1) Custody of Deeds, (2) Practice of Conveyancing under the Record of Title Act. I shall proceed to explain both these points.

(1) The Original Conveyance from the Court is entered on the Record of Title, under section 8; but it is usual to have conveyances executed in duplicate. The extra expense of a duplicate conveyance does not, exclusive of the cost of a map, if any, exceed a few shillings, and in fact amounts to less than the expense of a Certificate of Title, inasmuch as the latter is not printed. The duplicate is duly stamped as such, and is retained by the purchaser, who must, however (sec 19), produce it at the office whenever the estate is dealt with. Where no duplicate has been executed to him, the owner may at any time obtain from the office a sealed certificate, which is (Section 21) conclusive evidence of his title. If any instrument of title should be lost, an application to the Court on affidavit will be necessary before a new one can be obtained.

With regard to all subsequent deeds affecting the title, they should, immediately after their execution, be produced in the office, in order that an entry may be made on Record. It is not required that the originals of such deeds should be deposited in the office. If required, or likely to be required elsewhere, or if relating to other property, the proper course will be to have them executed in duplicate, or else to have a printed copy made for lodgement in lieu of the original. No memorial or abstract of any deed is required to be made by any person who brings in a deed to be entered on the Record. On production of original instrument, a note of its date, contents, &c., is made by the officer and entered on the Record. As far as recorded land is concerned it is absolutely useless to any such deed in the Registry of Deeds. If the deed, however relates to property *not* on the Record of Title, it will, of course, be proper to register it in the usual way.

(2) Some persons have supposed that all deeds affecting recorded estates must be in the extremely brief form appended to the Act. This is not the case, the forms being (like that appended to the Landed Estates' Court Act), apparently intended as suggestions or models suitable only for the simplest possible cases. Persons who prefer short deeds, and are transferring or charging fee simple estates, may use the forms, for they are effectual and sufficient. In any case of a charge or mortgage, however, it will be advisable to add a short covenant for repayment; and in the case of house property, a covenant to insure against fire may also with advantage be added. The use of the short forms appended to the Act is, it seems, optional; for any deed or instrument whatever, and in whatever form prepared, may be presented at the office; and if the officer is satisfied as to its due execution, he (after giving notice to the owner, unless the latter be represented by a solicitor) will proceed to enter it on the Record, under the proper folio. The officer is entitled to call for the fiat of a judge, if the instrument be not one which he considers properly receivable without such direction.

It seems that a very small proportion of the deeds hitherto executed have been executed at the office under sec 27. The owners usually execute instruments at own homes, or at least in their own localities, and in presence of their own solicitors. The solicitor who witnesses the deed endorses an affidavit of due execution, which is sworn in the usual manner, and the deed is sent up to office (by registered letter or by hand) to be entered on the Record of Title. For obvious reasons these deeds relate to the recorded property only; and there is, therefore, no objection to their being permanently deposited in the office, as they can hardly be wanted elsewhere for any purpose. There have been instances of mortgagees insisting on the retention in their own hands of the original deed of charge, and in such case the deed of charge has been executed in duplicate. The deed of charge is, beyond doubt, of no greater legal value to its holder than the "certificate of charge" provided by sec. 18 of the Act; but the intention of the Act in this, as in other points, seems to be rather that the most simple and effectual methods of carrying out dealings should be provided, than that their use should be made compulsory. It was evidently not intended by the Legislature that the practice of conveyancing should be revolutionized; for the novelties in conveyancing, either as regards form or manner of completion, are optional. There is considerable latitude allowed in all such matters, while there is, on the other hand, the utmost strictness required as to the essential point of the whole system, viz. – that every act or dealing shall be recorded in the folio of the record allotted to the particular estate.

I am, Sir,
Your obedient servant
LEGULEIUS.
15th June 1867

Footnotes
The quote from Robert Black Solicitors is from http://www.rblacksolrs.ie/registration.html and the 1867 debate is from the *Irish Law Times and Solicitor's Journal,* vol 1 (Dublin, 1868), p.30-31, 49-50, 67-68, 86-87, 196-197, 248-249, 303-304, 356-357. The description of the 1892 situation and the quotes from Joseph Maguire are from: Joseph Maguire, *Land Transfer, Registration of Deeds and Title,* read 17th Feb 1922 and published in the *Journal of the Statistical and Social Inquiry Society of Ireland,* vol XIV, p.167-168.

1. It is worthy of mention that of the recorded owners, nine are solicitors who have placed their own property under the Act.

2. Mr Dix is welcome to any amusement which the prospect of loss to others, caused by mistakes in the new system, may afford him; and he certainly deserves the appointment of solicitor to his projected Company (Limited) for assurance against them; perhaps he will accept a hint that the prospectus of his new Company might usefully be enlarged by assuring against other casual injuries which might befall owners of property, such as loss of title deeds, defaults of agents, etc.

APPENDIX F
Mr Dillon's Invention of a Mechanical Index in the Registry

On the 13th of April 1877 a mysterious question was asked in the House of Commons in London by 'Mr Meldon':

"asked the Secretary to the Treasury, For what period has Mr. Dillon, one of the clerks in the Registry of Deeds Office, Ireland, been absent from duty during the past four years; whether such absence was on leave, and if he has, during such absence, been in receipt of full pay; what amount of money has been paid to him during the period of such leave; and, whether the office has been short-handed during a considerable part of such period of absence?"

The government reply, from Mr W. H. Smith, was:

"I beg to inform the hon. Gentleman that Mr. Dillon was detached from the Irish Registry of Deeds Office in the summer of 1874, in order to assist the Commission appointed by the Treasury to test the value of his invention. He continued working under the Commission until the summer of 1875, and that body finally reported favourably on it about Christmas. It was believed to be more advantageous to the public service to allow Mr. Dillon a further increase of time to improve his system of indexing, which was thought to be very valuable. Since Mr. Dillon was detached he has been in receipt of his ordinary salary, now about £300 a-year. A writer was employed during Mr. Dillon's absence. I am not aware that the staff of clerks has been insufficient during Mr. Dillon's absence. I believe that the contrary is the fact."

'His invention'? Indeed, it turns out that in 1874 this enthusiastic member of staff – we never find out his first name, he is always 'Mr Dillon' – in the Registry of Deeds was commissioned to make a mechanical index and printing system for the ROD which would automate most of the workings of the

Registry. In theory he was working in the office and came up with a small wooden working prototype. Then a high powered committee was funded by the Treasury to aid his work and he perfected his apparatus, over 3 months, initially in the ROD and it seems was still working on it years later.

I say 'seems' because there is a lot that's mysterious about this. It seems quite an ambitious and exciting invention but really a step too far for the ROD you would have thought, and the Registrar certainly thought so. But why did the Treasury back it so quickly, up to the 3rd of September 1874 they had expended £180 6s. on the scheme and they allowed Dillon to patent it under his own name but funded by the Treasury. Its mentioned in the report too how some of the metal came via the Admiralty and I notice that one of the members of the committee was a Lieutenant Colonel in the Royal Engineers. You see this kind of very advanced technology, photography and printing on carbon paper etc, seems out of place in the ROD for 1874 but it doesn't look as bad a fit if you think about Dublin Castle in the period and the advanced photography that they rolled out in spying on the Fenians. My guess is that the powers that be saw great advantages in a mechanical index for those kind of files and maybe Dillon was in fact employed in building such a machine for some discreet government department from which we have little information. They certainly could have put to use such an invention and it might have suited them to give our Mr Dillon the cover story of just working on the ROD files.

In any case what follows first is an enthusiastic description by the committee which was backing Dillon's invention of an automated index machine, replacing the names and lands indexes, combined with a printing machine which automatically printed out an abstract of the deed found in the index (by the way that practice of the office preparing an abstract of the memorial came in in 1833 and is not available for the 18th century deeds):

"1. The objects which Mr. Dillon proposes to arrive at by his index are—

2. First: *Rapidity and accuracy of registry*, so that within 48 hours after each deed has been deposited in the office it will be

found registered in a legible type, in its proper dictionary position on the index.

3. Secondly: *Rapidity of searching.* The index is so constructed that by the simple operation of turning a handle, the whole of the information registered on a roll containing the acts done during a known period will be quickly brought under the searcher's inspection.

It has been found by trial that what now takes hours, and sometimes days, can be effected by Mr Dillon's index in a very much shorter period.

Construction of the Index.

4– The index is composed of a continuous band of thin rolled brass 10 inches wide, and which can be added to when necessary and which has a prepared paper or linen surface, suitable to receive deeply indented type printing. This long roll of brass is coiled on two cylinders or cores, the one vertically over the other, at a suitable distance from it. These cylinders revolve freely on bearings, and when set in motion by a handle and multiplying wheel, the one receives what the other discharges from the coil, the handle moving but one cylinder at a time, the other revolving only as the tension of the band in process of uncoiling causes it to do so, and thus the conflict of velocities which would otherwise arise between the two cylinders revolving at the same rate, but the coils contained on which, when in action, would always be of different and varying circumferences, will be avoided. The whole roll can thus be reeled off one cylinder on to the other in a short space of time, allowing each portion to pass under the eye of the observer.

5. Great rapidity of motion is essential to facilitate searching, and any possibility of inconvenience arising from the too rapid passing of the index before the eyes of the observer is ingeniously met by Mr. Dillon's adaptation of an indicator, which travelling along an endless screw by the motion of the machine tells on a dial-board the exact position of the index which at that moment is passing under the plate glass which forms the reading desk of the

searcher, so that he, keeping his eye on the indicator, may allow the roll to run at its full velocity checking it only when he sees the pointer approaching that part of the dial which tells him that the letter or county (as the case may he) is coming up and close at hand for his inspection.

We have thus secured the means of using a long band, and a vast mass of matter with great rapidity, and yet by the aid of the self-acting indicator, which moves very slowly, with safety.

Mode of Registering by Mr. Dillon's Index.

6. This may be concisely described as follows :

1st Step. To photograph the abstracts [remember these 'abstracts' are not the memorials, they are short abstracts of the memorials that were prepared in the ROD from the early 19th century on] when handed into the office, if sufficiently long to require it.

2nd Step.—The duplicate of the abstract, –which it is proposed to substitute for the old memorial, or its photograph is given to compositors to set up in type.

3rd Step. —Ordinary papier mache moulds are taken which are required for stereotyping, and which when used can be stored as matrixes for future reproduction if necessary.

4th Step.—The stereotypes having been taken in blocks containing all the abstracts of the deeds registered during that day, are then cut by a circular saw into separate portions, each containing one abstract.

5th Step.—Each of these separate blocks above mentioned is then placed in a powerful press, and the type having been treated with ink, a deeply indented impression is forced into the brass, leaving a perfect print on its white surface, each abstract being stamped on the roll in its proper place in dictionary order.

When it becomes necessary to interpolate, the brass band can be cut, and portions introduced. A means of uniting these portions has been devised, the strength and permanency of which is beyond dispute. On examining the junctions of a composite band (the junctions being at every two or three inches) which was subjected to about 13,000 revolutions on the shaft of a steam-engine, no tendency to fractures could be discovered, though a powerful magnifying glass was used.

Mode of Applying Index to Office Work.

7– The arrangement of the index is in chronological and dictionary order. Suppose a search is to be made against the name of Alexander Hamilton (as that is the surname on the specimen forwarded), and that the searcher is at the commencement of the index.

He turns the handle rapidly until he arrives at Ha. Once the indicator shows he is there, he seeks the sub-index or tabulated portion (printed in red ink in specimen) at the commencement of the required year. He is among the Hamiltons. Having found the required year, and Alexander being the christian name of the individual he is searching against, he consults the sub-index under letter A, to see where, if anywhere, Alexander appears. If the sub-index of the year discloses no Alexander, his search for that year is over. Hamiltons have done (in the technical language of the office) certain acts in that year, but Alexander Hamilton has not. If, on the other hand Alexander, does appear on the sub-index, it is followed by certain figures, say 3, 56, 100, 180, and so on; which correspond with the figures attached to the abstracts in which the Alexander Hamiltons have done acts, and by reference to them in connexion with the locality in question, it will appear whether his Alexander Hamilton has done the act he is in search of, the nature of the transaction, and the lands affected by it being disclosed in each entry. Should the searcher desire to check his search a figure or figures on the entry he has found refer him to the entry on the lands index where the similar information is registered, and without searching he can go direct to it, and vice versa, since the lands index discloses the same information as the names index. The entries are in fact identical as to contents, but differently arranged, the object of the names index being to show the acts of an individual against lands, that of the lands index being to disclose the names of all parties who have dealt with the denominations of land, the object of the search; each, however, tallies exactly with the other.

8. Again searching on a lands index the same facilities are given by a sub-index, with this difference, that the barony, a well-defined and unchangeable geographical division, is treated as the surname, while the lands figure according to their initial letter in lieu of the christian name. The initial letter is the present mode by which lands are arranged in the books of the office, and it is a necessary arrangement so long as the registration of "aliases" is continued, or until the ordnance townland is made the basis of the lands registration; in the latter case the ordnance townland names will be treated as the christian names to a barony. If these observations are attended to, a search on a small scale can be made on the specimens sent.

9. The characteristic of the index is, that though a searcher may have to manipulate large masses of matter he need not investigate them, its appliances accurately designating the isolated points where that process becomes necessary.

To take prints from the Index

10. In order to do away with the necessity of making manuscript copies (or extracts) by searchers, Mr. Dillon has proposed that imprints shall be taken from the underside of the brass index itself (the printing having been indented sufficiently to enable a satisfactory impression to be taken from it), by allowing the band to pass between the rollers of a small specially adapted press, and using carbon paper. He has also tried another process of printing, which depending on the action of metal on a chemical prepared paper or linen, produces a distinct impression of indelible blackness; this latter process requires further development.

11. It is suggested that should it be contemplated to give Mr. Dillon's invention a trial, the rolls on their cylinders should be set in cast-iron stands of suitable form, and be ranged in an apartment separated from the searching room by a partition; thus the outside searcher would have no access to the rolls, but simply have the

power of bringing any part of the index under his glance by the motion of the handle (vide Sketch No. 1 in Appendix). The apartment in which the rolls are placed should only be accessible to officers and employees of the establishment.

12. Sketch No. 2 exhibits a form of cast-iron stand, which appears to combine all that is required, but which could be modified according to circumstances, retaining always this principle, viz., the power of being able to ship and unship the rolls, so that the proposal of having duplicate index rolls, one in use, whilst the other is in the hand of the mechanical registrars, can the more readily be carried out.

13. The portions of the sketch shaded represent a cast-iron frame, one of two in which the index is to work; these frames to be set up in pairs for as many indexes as may be required. The projections on the back of the frame are bearings on which the axles of the cylinders are to revolve, and they admit of the index being removed, and of its duplicate, made up to the last entry, being inserted in lieu of it, each counterpart undergoing a similar process in its turn.

Several of these projections appear as provision for moving the index, in the event of its outgrowing the space allotted to it. A and B represent the index itself coiled on its cylinder; the line marked throughout C is the index in its transit from one cylinder to the other, C C to C C representing the portion the searcher examines, D and B are two movable guiding rollers.

14. As regards the lasting properties of Mr. Dillon's proposed appliances, we are of opinion that if the machinery is properly constructed the amount of friction will be much less than would be supposed, for it should be observed that, the band being coiled in compact masses round the two cylinders, the only portion exposed to friction is (say) the three feet or so between the cylinders, and that only during its transit from one of them to the other, since when on either, though it revolves rapidly, it does so in a compact, and save that it does revolve, in a quiescent mass; the portion liable to injury being only that which is in process of leaving one cylinder to reach the other, and when once there it relapses, save as above stated, into quietude until again disturbed.

15. It must also be remembered, that so long as the office

retains the original moulds, or indented brass, or reproductions of them, they have the means of reproducing the index as often as necessary."

These proponents of a mechanised system then took time to emphasise the bureaucratic nature of the office at that time, to emphasise their point of view of course but its interesting to see how the ROD actually operated then:

"9. The practice which at present prevails for the registry of deeds may be generally stated to be as follows, viz.; the engrossment of the deed having been made from its draft, the latter is handed over by the solicitor to a clerk, for the purpose of preparing the memorial, the document to be put on record. There are special statutory provisions with regard to the contents of a memorial, which may be stated in general terms. It should contain the date of the deed, the parties' names, the lands affected by it, the barony and county in which they are situated, and the fact of its execution. In practice, however, memorials set out the contents of deeds at much greater length. The clerk to whom the draft has been handed, and who may be, and probably often is, an unskilled person, strikes out with a pencil such portions of it as in his judgment should be excluded, and attempts a condensation, often a difficult task to a skilled draftsman. There are frequently included matters altogether outside the statutable requirements, unskillfully and inartistically selected and arranged, and tending to unsatisfactory results. It is not the duty of the registrar to compare with the deed any of the statements contained in the memorial except such as are required by statute, and hence arises a possibility that there may be introduced into it matters not contained in the deed, and at variance with truth. In fact, a memorial may misrepresent the contents of the deed in most important particulars, without in any way invalidating its right to registration, and a door is thus left open to fraud. This appears to be a very important defect in the existing system.

10. The execution of a deed and memorial having been perfected, they are taken to the Registry Office, and presented for registration. The first step in the process is their receipt and

examination by two clerks, who having examined and compared the deed and memorial against each other, and satisfied themselves that the statutable requirements have been complied with, a duty apparently involving a considerable amount of technical skill, they mark their initials on each, and having done so they return them to the party registering, whose duty then is to take them to the local stamp department to have affixed to the memorial the stamp duty to cover the fees for registry. The documents are thus for a time left in the power and control of a person who may have an object of altering or tampering with them before registry; under a practice which previously prevailed, the deed and memorial having been accepted for registry, did not leave official custody. The stamp duty having been affixed, the deed and memorial are handed by the person registering to the registrar, who having examined the stamps, and satisfied himself that the documents are in form for registry, administers the oath to the party verifying the execution. He then, in what may be described as a rough book, writes down the serial number of the deed (which practically indicates the priority of its registry), the name of the solicitor by whom it is registered, and the fee for registry. On the deed and memorial he notes the same information; a docket is given to the person registering, to be returned on getting up the deed, which is usually ready within a day or two. On its return an acknowledgment is taken for it in a duplicate copy of the day-book mentioned further on, and the duty of the person registering an instrument is then discharged.

11. The next official step is the entry of the registration in the "Day Book," in which are given the day, hour, and minute of registration, the names of the grantors and grantees, the county, city, or town in which the lands or premises are situated, the nature of the deed, and the number of reference to the memorial, with the name of the solicitor by whom it was lodged for registration. A duplicate of this book is kept, which serves the purpose of a receipt book to be signed by the person to whom the deed is returned when its registration is completed.

12. The next process is the compilation of the "Index of Names" or "Sectional Index" from the day book. The names of the grantors are arranged alphabetically according to the two first

letters of each surname, opposite to each being the name of one or more of the grantees, the county, city, or town where the lands or premises are situated, and the number of reference to the memorial. Formerly this book was kept in duplicate. The practice has been to some extent altered; instead of an actual duplicate, a paper copy, called the "Consolidated Names Index," is made, with spaces with a view to a dictionary arrangement. This book is not open to the public. It is from it the decennial index referred to further on is to be prepared.

13. An "Abstract Book" is compiled, which shows again the date of registration, the number of reference to the memorial, the date of the deed; the names of the grantors and one or more of the grantees, the consideration, the name, description, and situation of the lands, and the general nature of the instrument. A duplicate of this book is required to be kept, but the practice has been discontinued. As stated in a previous part of this Report, there exists in the office the duplicates of these books for very many years, which, owing to their never having been compared, are for all practical purposes utterly valueless.

14. Concurrently the "Lands Index" is prepared. It shows the name of every denomination mentioned in the deed, arranged alphabetically by baronies and counties, opposite to each being the name of the parish, the name of one of the grantors and one of the grantees, and the number of reference to the memorial. The duplicate of this book, under the present management, is not compiled until the end of each quinquennial period.

15. It sometimes happens that the deed does not contain the name of the barony in which the lands are situated. To meet this omission another book called the "No Barony Book" is kept. In some cases the deed omits to give the name of either parish, barony, or county; to provide for this another index is kept, simply of denominations, and called "The General Index." All the books lastly referred to are kept in duplicate. Again, there are the quinquennial and decennial parties' names indexes re-compiled in dictionary order, the latter called "The Consolidated Parties' Names Index," likewise kept in duplicate.

...

Independent altogether of the numerous volumes referred to,

there are the "Transcript Books," into which are copied all the memorials deposited for registry. There are likewise books which contain copies of negative searches, and names and lands indexes to these searches, likewise in duplicate. It is obvious the multitude of operations described must involve a very considerable amount of risk, responsibility, labour, and consequent expense; the cost of books alone represents a serious item of expenditure; the number required for a decennial period, including the transcript books mentioned afterwards may be approximately stated as costing 600 L a year.

...

20. It appears to the Committee that the value and importance of the adoption of the Ordnance maps and survey of Ireland as a basis for a system of land registry can hardly be over-estimated. There now exists a complete set of Ordnance maps on a scale perfectly clear and easy of reference, on which is delineated every county, barony, parish, and townland (the latter the smallest fiscal division recognised) in Ireland, in the case of a city or town, the parish and street being shown. To these maps there is a well-arranged index. As matter of fact, it is as easy to find by reference to it the sheet on the Ordnance map at which a particular denomination of land will appear as it is to ascertain a name or address in an ordinary directory. Already these maps are easy of access and reference; they are capable of being made so to any extent. The townland denominations, as ascertained, are the result of a Government inquiry carefully and systematically conducted, neither trouble nor expense having been spared to secure accuracy. The index to these maps is published under authority, and can be purchased for a few shillings; it returns Ireland as containing 63,000 townlands the boundaries of which are distinctly and accurately defined.

21. There is scarcely a denomination of land in Ireland which has not from one to five or six or more alias denominations. A leading, and one of the most important results of the Ordnance survey, is the elimination which it has effected of an enormous majority of them without interfering with identification or any other practical or useful purpose. In the county of Londonderry, for example, the townland denominations, as they appear from the

Ordnance survey, number 1,306, the number of aliases being 3,705 (the average would be larger in any of the southern or western counties). If it be remembered that in the registry of a deed a separate entry is made of each denomination of land, the benefits which would arise by the elimination of alias denominations become at once apparent. For example, if it be assumed that each day 50 deeds are registered, that each deed contains five denominations of land, each denomination having three aliases, that in the working year, composed of 311 days, the gross number of deeds registered is 15,600, each deed containing 15 (3 x 5) alias denominations, the result is a total of 232,500 names, each of which must be separately entered in the lands index book, the abstract book, the transcript book, as well as in their respective duplicates.

22. Transcribing in ordinary words conveys no accurate idea of the trouble and difficulty involved in copying out such names as, for example: Farrandahdoremore, Ardmanningmore, Killeenreendowne, or Doughcloyne. If to this consideration be added the difficulty and responsibility of comparison, regard being had to the necessity for extreme accuracy, a strong case is made out for the adoption of the Ordnance survey, legalising for the purpose of registry the townland denominations given in it, and excluding from the indices of the Registry of Deeds all others. The utility of the survey was recognised by the Act of the 13 & 14 Vict. c. 72, already referred to. Over and over again the desirability of its adoption has been urged and advised by the most eminent authorities; and in the Landed Estates Court for many years back, and with immense advantage, the facilities it offers have been availed of."

This enthusiastic new broom of a report was then signed by the committee, who were:

M Longfield, LL.D,
Herbert Murray, Treasury Rembrancer for Ireland,
R O Armstrong, Chief Clerk to the Lord Chancellor of Ireland,
S J Lynch, Registrar of the Landed Estates Court,
Berdoe A Wilkinson, Lieu. Col., R. E., Ordnance Survey,

M Keatinge, A Principal Registrar, Court of Probate.

Except that is for the following member:

Not being able to agree in the portions of the above Report which relate to Mr. Dillon's mechanical index, and other matters incidental thereto, I cannot sign it, and shall forward a separate report.
(signed) M. F. Dwyer,
Registrar of Deeds.

Which is how the fight back begins, this old hand of the ROD then proceeded to lay it on the line as to the whys and wherefores of their current practices and the hopelessness of these new fangled inventions!

Sir,
The main principle of Mr. Dillon's invention is to substitute printing for manuscript in all the operations of recording and indexing in the Registry of Deeds Office, and to substitute an index to be worked by machinery for the present index books.

In May last he exhibited to some gentlemen, now members of the Committee appointed to examine his plans, and to other gentlemen, a mahogany box about two feet long and a foot broad, and some inches deep, sufficient to hold rollers turned by handles, and carrying bands composed of sheets of brass, about as thick as Bristol board, attached to each other by the description of brass pins called "paper fasteners," and sufficiently flexible to admit of being wound round the spindles.

Upon these sheets of brass he had pasted slips, about three-fourths of an inch broad, of paper, each slip having a name printed upon it in type; and to provide for names coming in after the space left for them upon the band should happen to be closed, he had a contrivance to detach the band at the place and insert a new piece of sheet brass to receive the additional names. This was to be done by means of holes punched in the brass to receive the brass pins by which the junction was to be effected.

Some of the gentlemen present saw such objections to this plan that they did not think it could work, and one of them suggested that linen or calico bands, upon which the slips forming the index entries could be pasted, would be a more simple arrangement. Mr. Dillon seemed to catch up this idea, and said he would adopt it.

After he had obtained his patent, the Committee were called together to witness the completion of his machine index.

On this occasion he exhibited a mahogany box, nicely made and polished, about the size of an ordinary writing desk, breast high, at which the writer or searcher stands; within it were two rollers of linen, upon which printed slips, with the entries for the indexes, were pasted. It had a sloping lop of plate glass, through which the printed slips could be seen. When sufficient room had not been left for the entries, he proposed to have the bands cut across and pieces of linen stitched in.

The box was divided in the middle, having the lands index on the right and the names index on the left, each being about one foot wide.

He stated that he had the entries required for about 270 abstracts on the names index and about 300 on the lands, spaces being left for incoming entries as the index would go on. That quantity, when wound, formed a roll, which he wound and unwound by means of cog-wheels and chains according as a name or land was required to be found; the wheels should be wound by the hand. This he did very rapidly, to show what little time it would take to wind the whole length of band; but so rapidly, that one might as well try to count the spokes of a carriage wheel in rapid motion as to catch an entry. It was evident that in practice of searching, the winding should be carried on much more slowly, and would therefore take more time.

The number of slips (i.e. abstracts) necessary for both lands and names indexes were printed off, cut across, and pasted in their proper places down upon the bands. These slips were stated to be set up in type from photographed copies of the abstracts; the arrangement and transposition of the names and lands being done by the printers.

I was under the impression that Mr. Dillon had adopted the linen bands finally as his plan, and had so exhibited them; but it now appears he has abandoned that design, and means to use metallic bands, such as he exhibited to me and other members of the Committee at a recent meeting, and which appeared to consist of a series of thin brass plates, each about 10 or 12 inches long, joined together by laps of the metal on each other, or by some other means, and supposed capable of resisting a strong tension. Upon these bands some white composition was to be spread, and upon this the entries are to be printed from the type, instead of being printed on slips of tape or paper to be pasted down, as in the other specimen index as above mentioned.

Mr. Dillon prints the full abstract for the names index for each grantor, and the full abstract for the lands index for each denomination of land; suppose there are three grantors in a memorial, A., B. and C., and 10 townlands, Blackacre, Whiteacre, Redacre, Greenacre, Yellowacre, Kingstown, Lurgan, Tara, Dalkey, Aughrim, the whole abstract is printed against A., again against B., again against C., and again against each of the ten denominations of land respectively; that is thirteen different times. For each of these operations the type must be transposed; that is thirteen transpositions, three of the names and ten of the lands. The greater the number of names and lands in a memorial, the greater the number of transpositions and operations. There are then 13 slips to be pasted on linen or printed on brass on the index rollers. All these slips should be carefully checked against the original abstract or photographed copy; in the first place, to see that the several transpositions had been correctly made, and again each slip should be carefully checked against the index roller to prove that it was put in its right place. Without these several checks there is no way of guarding against fatal errors. It would certainly be tedious and troublesome to carry out this checking, but it could not be dispensed with, and it could not be left to printers. Many more comparing clerks than we at present employ would be necessary for the supervision of these arrangements. Mr. Dillon (as after mentioned) did not seem to contemplate this check against the rollers as to the proper place of the entries. Our present indexes contain every entry in its regular order, no adding to nor taking from without a perfect check, every entry having its check mark before it or on it corresponding to a like check mark in the day book or abstract book, so that the responsibility as regards correctness is permanently fixed. In this alone is there real security. In our books a mistake can be set right in a minute by the pen. Who could be responsible that in all these cuttings, and shiftings, and junctions, entries might not be shifted or left out, involving interests, perhaps, to a vast amount? Such risks could not occur with books.

Such is an outline of what appeared to be Mr. Dillon's plan.

The operations of the registry, as practically carried out in the office, are as follow:—

A memorial, which must be upon parchment, is presented with the deed. It is a duly executed instrument under hand and seal by the parties registering, and must be witnessed by two persons at least, one of whom must prove its execution by affidavit of record. It is an abstract of the deed, more or less full, according to the desire of the parties, and is required by law to be a true statement from the deed of certain particulars necessary for forming the abstracts. Every memorial is first compared by officers of the department with its deed, and if material discrepancies be perceived, it is returned to the party to be set right. Sometimes the affidavit has to be re-sworn; sometimes a new memorial becomes necessary, &c. The deed and memorial are then presented to the registrar, who passes them through the several processes required by law for the registry. The memorial is then immediately delivered to the officer who makes out the day book.

The day book is always written up as the deeds come in.

The names index is posted from it forthwith so that the memorials presented for registry are entered upon the names index without delay or cessation. The lands index which is required generally in tracing title cannot be entered so promptly, because many abstracts contain large numbers of lands which have to be entered on several baronies and counties; nor has this been found necessary. Provision is accordingly made by law for the delay. The names index is sufficient for disclosing immediate dealings with land and incumbrances.

The compiling of the day book is usually the work of one clerk.

Being the root of the names indexes, a duplicate of it is kept, as it enables searches to be carried up by the public to the latest moment.

There are two kinds of names indexes now kept, one called "quinquennial," for a period of five years. This set is also called "sectional; " that is arranged in the letters of the alphabet by the two first letters of each surname; it is the most safe for the public use from its simplicity, but is necessarily more slow than the other index, "decennial" or "consolidated," which is in strict dictionary order of the surnames, and is of rapid reference. It is also posted hourly, concurrently with the quinquennial or sectional index.

...

Now when the plain and simple entries as above are found to answer every purpose, I am not able to see any benefit, economic or otherwise, that can be attained by the roundabout processes of photographing, setting up type, transposing, printing and correcting revises, pastings, fixings, &c., &c. I am satisfied that the entries would be made with the pen, over and over again, in much less time, by merely opening a book and writing eight or nine words, than by winding a long roll, pausing to catch the place, taking up the slip, cementing it, putting it down in its place (or in printing it upon a metal band, if that be possible), all to be done with the care and precision that should be observed. It is suggested, no doubt, that these operations will take but little time. This I consider to be a miscalculation; they could not be done, if done properly, without time, and much time.

...

The public and the official searchers could not work at the same set of boxes, and so there should be at least three sets of boxes. Where are they to be kept? About a dozen of such as I have seen would occupy a room 20 feet square, for there should be space to pass round each, and there should be desks or tables at convenient distances for the searchers to use their papers, they could not take down their notes and references upon the glass lids of the boxes, for they have to look through these to see the index. Their hands will be engaged turning the wheels and working the machine, so they must turn from it to the desk or table to write down the note on their reference papers, and taking off their eye even for an instant will cause them to hesitate, and delay, and mistake. What is to be done with these sets of boxes while one set is in use being pasted or printed, another in use by the public, and a third in use by the official searchers? Where are they to be moved to? How many apartments will be required to hold them?

Another objection to the machine indexes is, that from their weight and structure they cannot be moved about like books, to suit the convenience of the reader and catch the varying shades of light.

There is very little doubt that Mr. Dillon's machine index would be found in practice not merely more complicated, but less lasting than the parchment books. What, then, is the use of it? The wear and tear of the perpetual rolling and unrolling would speedily damage it and obliterate the entries; the machinery would be constantly getting out of order, more or less, perhaps to the entire stoppage of the work, as is liable to happen with every machine which is in constant use. It seems plain, then, that machine indexes would be uncertain, dangerous, and clumsy. They are uncalled for, too, because in no way more facile than those in use. They are unsuited to the purposes of this office, and would soon, in my opinion, be found unworkable.

But the question is, do we want printed books? The registry has gone forward for more than 150 years without such. However, if desired for any object it is easy to have them; it is only a question of expense; there is no objection to printing as printing; it has frequently been proposed. But unless a number of copies of the books and document were required, which they are not, printing would be a wasteful expense; for a single copy it would be four or five times as costly as manuscript. It would involve the necessity of a printing office and staff of printers with plant, &c. being kept up in the department, as the original documents could not be subjected to risk by removal, nor would the landed proprietors and others interested in land be satisfied with the notoriety as to all their affairs, which printing elsewhere with all its facilities for multiplying information, would involve.

...

The idea that Mr. Dillon's plan could be carried out with more economy than the present system I consider fallacious. To render its working equal to the present mode would require as many hands, if not many more, printers, comparers, &c. To do the small specimen portion of the index which Mr. Dillon completed (the work of 270 abstracts on the names index and about 300 on the lands), he had four printers, one paster, and one stitcher engaged, and himself revising. I do not know what exact time these persons took, but three months were taken to produce the above result of his machine index.

...

To show that Mr. Dillon's plan is of any use, he must prove that he can photograph, set up in type, transpose, print or paste, dry and check, in accurate and reliable dictionary order easily and economically and satisfactorily, the work of 50 abstracts per day, on a moderate average, to be placed punctually upon workable and easily used indexes; otherwise, his scheme is not worthy of serious notice, for our simple system, which everyone can understand actually does all that.

Many other objections may be expected to arise to a design so complex in principle. I would welcome any plan really better than the present that could be found to perform the work of the Registry Office, but I do not consider the one now under notice to be such. Indeed, though many schemes have from time to time been suggested, all of them have been abandoned because conceived by persons ignorant of the practical details, the legal bearings, and the rigid precision with which every operation of a land registry must be carried out.

...

In reference to the Registration of Assurances (Ireland) Bill, brought into the House of Commons in 1882, in the petition presented against that Bill by the Incorporated Society of Attornies and Solicitors of Ireland, they bear this testimony towards the office. That it

> "has been conducted so as to secure public confidence, and that any instances of errors or omissions in the certificates on the searches issued from that office, whereby any individual purchaser or creditor has sustained loss or injury, are unknown to your petitioners, either personally or as matters of repute....

> That any changes in the system so long established should be made with 'every degree of caution and certainty, and not loosely and speculatively."

In the debate upon the Assurances Registration (Ireland) Bill in the House of Commons in 1863, Mr. Whiteside, now Chief Justice for Ireland, deprecating the introduction of such a Bill, stated that,

> "during the 15 years that the Incumbered Estates Court and Landed Estates Court were in existence, the registry office succeeded in accomplishing the duty imposed upon it, though the labour cast upon it was enormous. Its business was conducted with the greatest care and precision, the work was performed with a degree of mathematical accuracy which he never saw rivaled, and he was at a loss to conceive how it was possible by any scheme or contrivance to construct an office in which the work could be better or more securely done."

[To] The Secretary to the Treasury,
London.

(signed)
M. F. Dwyer
Registrar of Deeds, Ireland."

Sometime later he followed this up with another broadside against the scheme but in this case he also added in a defence and outline of the normal practices of the ROD which needless to say are of great interest to us now. He also stoutly defended the accuracy of the ROD against the pretences of Dillon's infernal machine, as you can see here:

"The present system of records, including indexes as directed by the 2 & 3 Will. 4, c. 87, has been in use since the year 1833, and during that long period I am not aware, and I have not heard, of a single instance in which material error of any kind in its operations or results has come to light. Landed property to the amount of millions has been sold by the Incumbered and Landed Estates Courts alone, and those millions duly distributed on the faith of its searches, without a single instance of loss having occurred through inaccuracies in them. If losses had occurred through mistakes or omissions in the searches, my predecessors in the office of Registrar, and I myself would have heard of it, as being personally responsible in heavy securities for their absolute immunity from error. The accuracy of the present system of registry is, therefore, placed in the strongest light by experience, the most unexceptionable of tests, for the searches could not be as correct as they have been if the indexes, and other records from which they are taken, were not equally so. In the Report, at page 10 of this Paper, credit is claimed for accuracy as a special merit of Mr. Dillon's plan, as if his plan, or any plan, admitted of higher excellence in that respect than the existing system, which by the evidence of fact has attained the very maximum of accuracy. If Mr. Dillon's system be capable of the highest accuracy, which I believe it is not, it cannot be said to be so far at least "a great improvement" upon the present system, which, not as a matter of opinion, but as a proven fact, has already attained a degree of accuracy upon which there can be no advance or improvement. With respect to the experimental searches which have been made on both indexes, the result in the matter of accuracy, which is really the only point determined by them, is just what I should have expected. Of the eight searches made in the office, five by Mr. Taylor (a third class clerk in the office) and three by Mr. Caicy (an unofficial searcher), *all were correct* (the mistake in copying one of these searches after it had been made, not affecting the accuracy of the indexes, or of the searcher, as appears by note (in 2nd Report of the Committee) at foot of page 7 of this Paper in these words: "*This mistake was made in the office copy, and not in the search*";[)] while of the five searches made on the mechanical index, two only were correct, and of the two searches made a second time upon it by the same searcher, one was correct and another incorrect. There is said to have been only one mistake in the last mentioned search, from which, having regard to the reticence of the Report as to the mistakes in the other incorrect searches, it is not too much to infer that the mistakes in them were considerable. Somewhat more of detail upon this point would have been desirable. So far, therefore, as *accuracy* is concerned, the test, whatever be its value, is as unfavourable as it could well be, to the mechanical index. But then it is said to be otherwise in respect to time. The apparent advantage, however, in this is easily explained; but even if it were not it must be admitted that time is a secondary consideration in a matter of the kind, as compared with accuracy, which is of its very essence. An accurate search is a warranty of title, an inaccurate search is a misrepresentation of the title. The difference, therefore, between a correct search and an incorrect search is just the difference between a good title to an estate and a bad one. It follows that an incorrect search, which is really not a search at all for the purposes of the test in question, or indeed of any other test, is something worse than useless, and it is little better than trifling with a serious subject to talk of the time occupied in making it as against the time required for producing correct and reliable returns.

...

In simplicity of construction and facility of reference I consider the present system will contrast quite as favourably, as in the matter of accuracy, with Mr. Dillon's plan. The office indexes are expeditiously constructed in books by the simple use of the pen, and are carefully checked and compared without either difficulty or confusion.

The Index of Names and the Index of Lands are both dictionaries of reference to the abstract book, which is common to both these indexes, and is a carefully and skilfully prepared epitome of the principal particulars of the memorial. The "Year, Book, and Number" in either index refer at once and readily to the particular abstract required, and the consulting of these abstract books, i. e., taking the light and handy volume down from the shelf, and reading the abstract referred to, can be done in a much shorter time than the manipulation and adjustment of the mechanical index would require. Should further information be wanted than the abstract book discloses, the same references, i. e., "Year, Book, and Number," refer to the original memorial, or its transcript, which can be consulted with great ease. One abstract may supply the usual particulars as regards a number of surnames or a number of denominations of land. Mr. Dillon's system needlessly and uselessly reproduces on his mechanical indexes the whole abstract in full on each grantor's name, and if the lands be in different baronies or counties, on the lands index. There may be 10 names and 50 lands in one abstract. A person may require to search after only one grantor or one denomination of land. On the office indexes he can do this, but Mr. Dillon's indexes give him the full abstract in connection with each particular grantor, and there may be several grantors in each abstract. Mr. Dillon's indexes also give the full abstract for each parcel of land; a great deal more than the searcher requires, and consequently an irrelevant and confusing superfluity of information; therefore, in simplicity of construction and facility of reference, the present system of book indexes appears to me to have a most decided superiority.

An index upon rollers may look well and simple prima facie, but unless it can be made to contain all the particulars and all the information that is to be found in our books, and in as reliable and well arranged a form, it will be defective, and, if so, cannot be worked with the same security to the public. It must be capable of all the care and checking which our books undergo. This is as necessary on one system as on the other. If it be as perfect in these particulars as our indexes are, it cannot be made with less expense or more expedition, and under no circumstances can it afford such facilities to the public for the purposes of searching.

...

The abstracts on searches are generally brief extracts containing three or four lines (see below); seven or eight of them usually fit on a folio page of paper used for searches. In the last volume of recorded negative searches (vol. 112), containing 288 searches, of those which exceeded the length in this example, nine occupied about half a page, 14 about a quarter, while few only occupied full pages. Now by the time that the machine would have been opened, the roll unwound to come to the abstract, the machine by which the impression is to be made, the paper laid on which it is to appear, the carbon paper placed, the impression made, the whole apparatus then removed, and the index case closed, as I suppose all these processes would be necessary, I think it is evident that any ordinary abstract would be copied from the abstract book with the pen sooner than it would be obtained by printing from the band.

...

The Memorial.

Under the present registry code, the memorial which is the basis of the entire system, besides supplying materials for the entries in the day book, abstract book, and the names and lands indexes, was designed to serve other important legal purposes. Being an epitome, verified upon oath, of the deed, the memorial is good secondary evidence of the existence and contents of the deed, as against the parties signing such memorial, being an admission under their hand and seal of the facts stated therein, and, so far, is a permanent public record of the transaction to which it relates. It remains in official custody in the Registry Office, where it is available at all times for public or private use, and in judicial or other legal inquiries is procurable either by the production of the original instrument or by certified copies, as the case may be. The constant use made of the memorials in the investigation and proof of title, or for other purposes of evidence in legal inquiries, is shown by the large demand for office copies of those instruments, and by the number of instances every year in which the original memorials themselves have to be produced in courts of justice, both in Dublin and throughout the country at large during the assizes and sessions. If the convenience and practical value of the memorial are to be estimated by the use made of it, it must be regarded as very considerable indeed. Nor, bearing in mind how very liable deeds are to be lost or destroyed, or from other causes rendered inaccessible or unavailable when most required, is it surprising that the memorial should be found so useful in practice.

The memorial contains the following most useful particulars, which the abstract does not:—Descriptions, residences, and signatures of parties and witnesses, acreable contents, and boundaries of lands and tenements; particulars of great importance, which are constantly made use of. When different parties deal with different lands in the same deed, as in the case, for instance, of marriage settlements, the memorial shows, as in the deed, the parties, as they affect the particular lands, and the lands as they are dealt with by the particular parties. The abstract, necessarily, cannot discriminate in such cases. The memorials are daily referred to by solicitors, by our searchers, and by other persons, for these particulars.

I extract the following from the Report of the Committee of the House of Commons of 1833 preparatory to.the passing of the 2 & 3 Will. 4, c. 87, the present Registry Act: —

> "As original deeds are frequently lost or rendered illegible through neglect, or may be in the hands of parties who are not willing to give up possession of them, their memorials are occasionally admitted in courts of justice as evidence of the existence and contents of the original documents. It is obvious, therefore, how essential it must be to the landed proprietors of Ireland that these memorials should be placed in a situation the least liable to be defaced or fraudulently used."

For several important purposes the memorial discharges the functions of a duplicate deed, without a third part of the expense to the public and of labour to the office. From the necessary length of deeds affecting lands, the lodgment of duplicates engrossed on parchment would involve very considerable increase of expense to the parties as would copies of these afterwards entail proportionate increase of charge to the public, while to the office the additional labour caused would be very great indeed. It would be the difference, in the first place, between reading two long deeds against one another, instead of a comparatively short memorial against certain portions of a single deed; and in the next, the reading of the duplicate deed in full against the abstract.

The discontinuance of the memorial would reduce to a *minimum* the information which the office could afford the public with respect to the contents and nature of the deeds to be hereafter registered. It would be confined, in fact, to the few particulars to be found in the abstract, and without any of the explanatory circumstances or recitals in the memorial which throw light upon the subject of each particular transaction, and make the scanty particulars in the abstract clear and intelligible. So useful is the memorial in the interpretation of the abstract book that both the public and official searchers are in the constant habit of resorting to the former for explanation of entries in the latter; nor would an official searcher feel himself warranted in returning or in omitting certain acts from his returns without consulting the memorials in cases of any doubt or apparent ambiguity. I need scarcely say that in my opinion the suppression of the memorial now so constantly availed of by courts of justice as secondary evidence would be a public disadvantage, for which no compensation would be found in a duplicate abstract, a skeleton document that would be comparatively, if not absolutely, worthless for such a purpose. The Report, Part 3, page 13 of this Paper, sec. 9, complains that there is a possibility that there may be introduced into the memorial "matters not contained in the deed, and at variance with the truth."

I can only say that the memorial is a document as formal as the deed to which it relates. It is under hand and seal of the parties to the deed, or some or one of them, verified on oath; and this is as good a guarantee of its integrity as the affidavit of execution is that the deed to which it relates is not a forgery. I never heard of a case such as the above, where matter not in the deed was introduced into the memorial; but if the possibility of its occurrence is worth guarding against, it could be provided for by a slight modification in the verifying affidavit to the effect that the memorial contained no matter or statement not in the deed.

The 2 & 3 Geo. 4, c. 116, which, according to the Report (par. 32, page 18 of this Paper, Part 3) "provides a very complicated method of registering deeds" executed in England, and which appears cumbrous and out of date," was passed at the instance of English solicitors, for their accommodation and the safety of deeds belonging to their clients. Under that Act it is not necessary, as in all other cases, to exhibit the deed to the registrar for inspection at the time of registration, the production in its place of a certified memorial and copy being made sufficient. So far from being "cumbrous and out of date," most, indeed nearly all, the deeds executed in England are registered by means of the certified memorial, a pretty good evidence, surely, that in the opinion of English solicitors the "method" is not very "complicated" or inconvenient, when they habitually prefer it to the other course of registry by production of the deed itself. This statement is made, I presume, in the Report, not so much in the interest of English solicitors or English clients, as in the interest of the suggestion that all memorials should be done away with, for the purpose of trying the mechanical index. But then the practice referred to should not be represented as "complicated," when it is evidently considered quite the contrary by English solicitors, who ought to know best what is or is not for their convenience.

The fiscal consequences of suppressing the memorial, though not noticed in the Report forwarded by the Treasury Remembrancer, are nevertheless well worth consideration. There were 15,170 memorials filed in the office from the 1st January 1874 to the 31st December following. The general stamp duty on these memorials may he stated approximately as averaging 5s. each, and the fee stamps as averaging 10s. each, giving an estimated total from both sources of £1,377. The abolition of the memorial would therefore involve in the first instance a large sacrifice of revenue, and it is quite possible that much difficulty might be experienced subsequently in recouping the loss when the new scale of duties and fees came to be adjusted. I am apprehensive that the legal public would not be easily reconciled to the imposition of the same charges upon a meagre memorandum such as an abstract, sometimes not exceeding three lines, as upon a formal legal document and record like a memorial, which is always evidence of the deed and of its contents to a large extent, and answers such a variety of official and judicial purposes."

Here he tackles what must have seemed to outsiders as the most common sense proposal of the reformers, and indeed of the casual observer, the idea of linking the deeds to the Ordnance Survey maps. As he describes its not as simple as it sounded at first.

The Ordnance Survey.

The feasibility of making the ordnance survey the basis of the land registry in Ireland has been repeatedly discussed, and has provoked much diversity of opinion. The most competent authorities differ about it, but the preponderance of professional judgment is strongly opposed to its adoption. The difficulties which beset the question are entirely overlooked in the report as if they had no existence. This is not judicious in the public interest. At page 15 of this Paper, Part 3, section 20, it is said:—

> "It appears to the Committee that the value and importance of the adoption of the Ordnance maps and survey of Ireland as a basis for a system of land registry, can hardly be over-estimated."

For my own part, I can have no objection to the registry being based upon the Ordnance survey. It would very materially shorten and simplify the work of the land registry in the Deeds Registry Office. The question is, can it be effected.

This subject was very much discussed some 10 years ago, and some of the objections to Mr. Torrens's proposal to base the registry on the Ordnance survey in his Bill introduced in 1864, are stated in the following extract from a work published at that time :

> "It is a well-known fact that the Ordnance maps of Ireland are not legal evidence at present of any single fact which is recorded upon them. No one who has examined them but will admit their artistic finish, and acknowledge their general accuracy, but no attempt has ever yet been made to declare the boundaries shown upon them or the names entered on them, binding and conclusive evidence before any legal tribunal of the country. In many hundreds of instances this could not be done, as that survey at present stands, without the greatest injustice being inflicted upon landed proprietors. Some cases of great inaccuracy existing on these maps have come under my own

notice during the past few years, and I cannot do better than illustrate my argument by reference to two of them.

A. B. was entitled in fee simple to lands called 'Ballynagowan' which appeared by the Ordnance maps to contain only 83 acres, 3 roods, 6 perches, statute measure. On inquiry, however, it turned out that the townland boundary as given on that map, excluded portions of ground which were in reality parts of Ballynagowan, and were in the occupation of the owner's tenants, and had been dealt with by all his family deeds as his property, under the name of Ballmagowan, while the same map gave to those excluded portions wholly different names, one being mapped as part of Richhill, and another as part of Mount Shannon, townlands to no part of which under these names was A. B. entitled.

In the other case the townland boundary on the Ordnance map of Ballysallagh lands, excluded a field which in truth belonged to that townland, while in another place it included as part of those lands that which in reality belonged to another townland altogether. These two instances are sufficient to show that even the outlines and designations of lands as shewn upon the Ordnance maps of Ireland, cannot be relied on as accurate, and should not, without further inquiry, be made the basis of any judicial proceedings to bind the world [sic].

Every landed proprietor in Ireland knows that even where the boundaries are correct, in very many instances the names given to the townlands upon the Ordnance maps, materially differ from those by which they are known in the neighbourhood, or *dealt with by the title deeds.*

And if any other proof was needed of the impossibility of dealing with that survey as it stands as absolutely correct, it is to be found in the fact that the judges of the Landed Estates Court refuse to adopt it, even when the boundaries of the particular property have been marked upon it by the officials of the Government Valuation Office; and verified by the owner, or his agent, as correct, without a special survey which is now made by the Ordnance Department after much delay and at great expense. One of the judges refuses to act without such a special survey in any case; except where the property to be sold is a short leasehold interest; the other two sometimes dispense with it, but only in very exceptional cases.

One of two courses will have to be adopted, either to have the entire survey of Ireland reviewed on proper notice to all landed proprietors and their tenants, so as to bind all parties by its outlines and designations, or in every case to require a special survey to be made before the conveyance or declaration of title is executed."

On this subject the present Lord Chief Justice of the Queen's Bench, Ireland, expressed himself in the House of Commons in 1863, to the following effect: —

"On that matter which went to the whole root of the Bill, namely, the townland basis on which the proposed system of registration was to proceed, the Bill was in diametrical opposition to the opinion of the gentleman who, under the directions of the Government, made the report on which the Bill was founded. That gentleman rejected as impracticable the townland or Ordnance survey as a basis of registration. The names of the townlands in the Ordnance survey did not correspond with the names in the deeds. The Bill before the House not only recommended, but enforced a compulsory alteration of the present survey. He contended that the clause of the Bill which had reference to the boundaries of the townland, was altogether wrong, illusory, and he ventured to say impracticable, and he submitted that it ought not to be sanctioned by the House."

I may here observe that Messrs. Law and Chisholm, in their Report, page 19, state that "Mr. Lane agrees in opinion with the practical men in the office that the Ordnance Map Registry, such as contemplated in the Act 11 & 12 Vict. c. 120, could not be effectually worked."

It is also a difficulty in the way of adopting the Ordnance survey that it is subject to revision and alteration, if the Act to enforce it be passed, say in 1876, and conveyances made according to it in that year, the descriptions from it may not apply to the same lands conveyed in 1886. What, then, is to be done? Must the maps as they were in 1876 be perpetuated, and conveyances in 1886 follow their designations and boundaries although known to be wrong at the time?

However desirable it might be to have the Ordnance survey established for Mr. Dillon's registry, I apprehend it cannot be done and that lands in Ireland must continue to pass by the old verbal descriptions in the deeds and conveyances by which they have passed and are popularly recognised.

This view appears to have been taken by the Legislature at the time of the passing of the Record of Title Act, 28 & 29 Vict c. 88, although the original intention was to make the Ordnance survey a basis of this Act.

The plurality of alias names of the same land is no doubt a inconvenience (Report, Part 3, page 16 of this Paper, sec. 21), but it amounts only to a somewhat more scrivenery work in the documents, a matter after all of no great moment. It will not embarrass a searcher for a land; Moneymore, for instance, will always have its alias names in connection with it in the memorial and the abstract book as we have it: Moneymore alias Moneybeg, alias Carnogue, alias Drumglas, &c. (Report, Part 3, secs. 4 and 22, pages 13 and 16 of this Paper). As I have said, the question as to the advantage of the Ordnance survey is, can it be brought into use? The circumstance that the proper authorities did not give the notice required to bring the Act 11 and 12 Vict. c. 120, into force, seems rather to imply a well-considered doubt than a certainty of its utility."

Dwyer finished his report by giving some details on the 1833 Act that regulated the ROD at that time

"The codification of the Registry Acts recommended at page 21 of this Paper, Part 4, of the Report is unobjectionable, of course, and is desirable in every case alike, where there are several detached enactments dealing with one and the same subject. No practical inconvenience, however, occurs in the present case, owing to the fact that there are no discrepancies between the several Acts which appear to have been all pretty carefully adapted to one another. The practice of the department is regulated by the 2 & 3 Will, 4, c. 87, and the codification and amendments suggested have, I apprehend, for their real object the repeal of this Act, which is referred to in paragraph 44, page 21, wherein it is stated that

> "many of the defects in the operative system of the Registry of Deeds Office would doubtless 'have been the subject of official reform had not the inflexible and inelastic letter of the law precluded such action."

A very different estimate from the above has hitherto prevailed among legal and professional people of this enactment which it is now proposed to get rid of summarily, in the whole or in part, and, apparently for no other immediate necessity than as a prelude to further experiments with the mechanical index.

Few legal measures have been better considered than the 2 & 3 Will 4, c. 87, by which the present working processes of the Registry of Deeds Office are regulated, and which it is proposed forthwith to repeal. It was passed in accordance with a long and very elaborate report prepared by a Special Committee of the House of Commons from evidence given before it by Mr. Moore, an eminent barrister and King's Counsel, who was then registrar and had had long previous official experience of the department, as well as from the evidence of some attorneys and solicitors, in leading practice at that time in Dublin, whose suggestions subsequently incorporated with the report show their minute and practical knowledge of the subject on which they were examined, and their competency to advise upon it.

The Act, prepared and passed under these circumstances, has now been in operation for more than 40 years, and its working capabilities severely tried, especially in connection with the enormous sales of land carried out by the Incumbered Estates Court and the Landed Estates Court respectively extending over a series of years. The rapidity, amounting almost to precipitancy, of these sales is as well known as their extent, and as they must have been in every case preceded by searches, it is hard to conceive how the latter could have kept pace with the former, if the system established by the 2 & 3 Will. 4, c. 87 be so cumbrous and unwieldy as it has been represented. I am sure that such is not the opinion generally of practical men having business relations with the office, and I believe that the attorneys and solicitors for the most part would incline to say that if anything were wanted for its improvement it would be, not a change in the system itself, but an addition to the staff engaged upon it. The business has increased, as already stated, by fully one-third since the year 1866, when the staff was fixed in conformity with the full and able report of Messrs. Law and Chisholm; and this fact explains why the lands index is somewhat behind hand. If the business had fallen off during the interval in the same proportion as it has increased grounds would be established for the reduction of the clerks but the fact being otherwise, the opposite inference would be equally obvious, if the increase could be regarded as certain to continue. I incline to think, however, that it is not, being attributable chiefly, in my opinion, to temporary causes connected with the Church Act, and therefore I have not felt it my duty to bring the subject before the Treasury, more especially as the slight arrears referred to in the report do not interfere with the requirements of the public, which, to use the language of Lord Percy's Report, are "adequately and faithfully met," as matters at present stand.

It is quite a mistake to represent as "inelastic" and prohibitory of well-considered modifications an Act of Parliament which provides, as the 2 & 3 Will. 4, c. 87, does, by the 35th Section, expressly for such modifications, and prescribes a suitable mode for effectuating them. Too much facility for tampering with and disturbing a system which requires so much uniformity, precision, and continuity of practice as a land registry, is not, I submit, desirable in any point of view, and not the least among the merits of 2 & 3 Will. 4, c. 87, is the comparative security it has hitherto afforded against hasty and unnecessary changes of more than doubtful expediency.

(signed) M. F. Dwyer"

Unfortunately we are told in a letter to the Freeman's Journal of 6th July 1877, p.6, that:
> "As to what is called Mr Dillon's system: its fate, from the day when the reports of the Registrar of Deeds were given to the public, was a foregone conclusion, and the action of the Law Society must render its adoption an impossibility. I may state here that the mechanical index, or any other portion of Mr Dillon's system, is not, and never has been, in operation in the Registry of Deeds Office, nor even imported into any place in the King's Inns."

But confusingly on the 19th of January 1878 we are told, in the Nation p.11,:
> "A commission has been appointed to inquire into the working of the Registry of Deeds Office, and the proposed changes contemplated by the adoption of Mr Dillon's patent. The commission consists of the Lord Chief Justice, the Chief Baron, Vice Chancellor Chatterton, Judge Flanagan, Judge Ormsby, Frederick Walsh, Q.C.; Dr Elrington Q.C.; C. H. Meldon, Q.C. M.P.; D. H. Madden, Richard Owen Armstrong, Esqrs."

Actually Dillon, and this is Thomas Arthur Dillon,[1] was a really talented inventor who put his ideas into practice in many areas with notable success. As early as the 1850s he attempted to address the question of ship's compasses deviating because of local magnetic attractions,[2] and in the same decade he worked on improving the signalling systems on train networks.[3] In the 1870s he invented a new type of safety lamp,[4] *and figured out a way of utilising excess exhaust gases on trains to boost fuel consumption,*[5] *which in fact was fitted on and used with success on some trains.*[6]

This following quote describes his method of raising ships using a 'bell', a 'tent like' construction or 'sail', which is placed over the sunken ship and then the water captured by the bell is pumped out and so the ship rises. He particularly felt that this system could be used to raise the 'Vanguard' which had sunk off the coast of Wicklow as he explained to the Duke of Edinburgh and other interested parties:

"**The Dillon System Of Raising Sunken Vessels.**

On Thursday the Duke of Edinburgh honoured Mr. Thomas A. Dillon with a visit at his rooms, at the Westminster Palace Hotel, to inspect the latest development in his system of raising sunken vessels by the aid of compressed air. There were present on the part of the Admiralty, Admiral Sir Houston Stewart, K.C.B., Controller of the Navy, and Mr. Barnaby, C. B., Director of Naval Construction. The First Lord was unavoidably absent, having been summoned to attend a Cabinet Council. The French Government was represented by Count de Montebello, Minister Plenipotentiary, and principal secretary of the French Embassy, the Marquis de la Ferronays, French Military Attache, M. Shilling, French Naval Attache, and M. de Kergolay and M. de Savigoy, secretaries to the French Embassy. The Dutch Government was represented by the Count de Bylandt, the Dutch Ambassador, and Mr. May, Consul-General for Holland. There were also present Dr. Siemens, F.R.S., Mr. Edge, M.P., Major O'Gorman, M.P., Mr. Gray of the Board of Trade, and Mr. G. Lindo, as well as Mr. Robert P. Spice, the President, and Mr. Perry F. Norsey, the secretary of the Society of Engineers, of which Mr. Dillon is a member. The invention consists in a method of causing sunken vessels to rise and float without the aid of divers, and without in any way touching the ship. This is effected by the adaptation of certain pneumatic and hydrostatic laws, which have hitherto been either unobserved or neglected, but which Mr. Dillon has laid under contribution in the attainment of his desired end. The principle consists in surrounding the vessel to be raised by an air-tight bell of tent-like construction, which is floated and lowered over the vessel by means of simple mechanical appliances. The water is then displaced from beneath this bell, and at the same time from out of the ship, by means of compressed air. When a sufficient amount of water has been displaced the bell rises to the surface, and with it, strange to say, comes the ship, although not in any way supported or touched by the bell. This is the essential and distinguishing feature of the latest development of a system of ship-raising upon which Mr. Dillon has been engaged for several years past. The system was explained in detail, and its working illustrated by a number of experiments by the inventor to his royal and distinguished visitors, who, on taking their leave, expressed themselves highly gratified with this ingenious and promising invention. Mr. Dillon pointed out the desirability of applying his system to the raising of the Vanguard without loss of time. It was conceded that the experiment would be one of national and universal importance, and it was stated that the Admiralty intended removing the masts of the vessel." [7]

This ship raising invention was actually put into practice, as you can read here in the Irish newspapers of the time:

"On Saturday Mr Dillon made his first real attempt at Waterford on the Avena, a 500 tons barque. The sail was lowered, well tightened around the wreck with perfect ease, without the aid of divers, in forty minutes or so, and in twenty minutes the air pumped into the sail caused the ship to surge, lift, and slip, and volumes of mud appeared. The strain on the wire cables on shore grew alarming as the vessel was gliding away without any steam-tug to hold her. She is now free out of her mud berth, and will be hauled out next neap tide. Although in her struggles she injured part of her sail on the port quarter, the sail forward retains its air. The ship is all alive and moving, extra cables being put on to keep her steady." [8]

He was also central to the invention of the fax machine as you can read here in the Electrical Journal of 1879:

"Nonsense.—The following is a fair specimen of how the non-scientific reader is filled with wonderment, and the expectation of what is in the eyes of the electrician mere dreaming. A contemporary thus writes:—"Will wonders ever cease? Certain it is that marvels in scientific discovery are following one another in rapid succession. The most recent and the most wonderful appears simply incredible. A New York cable company has secured the exclusive right to the use of an electrical discovery wherewith at least two hundred and as many as two thousand words a minute can be signalled through a submarine wire! It is said that what could at the maximum speed be sent through the conducting wire between London or Paris and New York would be equal to the number of words contained in one number of The Times or the New York Herald, and it is also asserted that, by this process, an entire number of either of the above-named journals could be despatched through the cable from New York to London or Paris, or from London to New York, and be reproduced at those points in facsimile on a stereotyped block or plate, complete and ready to be printed from, in thirty minutes, and at a trifling expense. Not only is it possible to do all this, we are assured, but, furthermore, secresy and despatch may be obtained in this wise:— The sender writes on a piece of prepared paper, places it in a box, a handle is turned, the message returns to the sender, and at the end of the wire a blank sheet is sent to the person addressed. When the paper is heated the message appears on the blank sheet. To a Dublin gentleman whose name is well known in the scientific world— Mr. Thomas A. Dillon—belongs the credit of the invention, certain improved electric batteries controlled by the American Cable Company serving as the basis of a new discovery. With the combined use of these two inventions it is believed that the Company will be enabled to reduce the tariff for cable messages between New York and the five different countries to be directly connected with its cables, to the extent of from three to five cents per word. We have the further statement that the Anglo-American Company offered to buy the invention for £400,000; and that, as that Company lacked the proper electric instruments for giving effect to the new process, it would have been lost to the public world." We are extremely sorry to say that Mr. Dillon is not well known to us, but this is our misfortune." [9]

This 'scientific discovery' of his is so important its mentioned in a history of the invention of television,[10] and he is even acknowledged in a history of the microfilm machine.[11]

What follows is an interview he gave on the 1st of April 1879 to the Select Committee on Land Titles and Transfer in the House of Commons in London. This long text is not strictly necessary to read of course in understanding the ROD but it does explore quite a lot of the issues raised in this book and as such should clarify some points for you, the committee consisted of:

"Mr Gregory, Sir Harcourt Johnstone, Mr Shaw Lefevre, Mr Patrick Martin, The O'Conor Don, Sir Sydney Waterlow, and chaired by George Osborne Morgan, esq.

The O'Conor Don.

You are one of the officers of the Registry of Deeds Department in Ireland, I believe?—I am.

How long have you been in the service of that department?—Something over 32 years.

Are you also an engineer?—I am a member of the Society of Engineers.

Is it the fact that you have given considerable attention to the working of the Irish system of registration, and that you have invented some mechanical appliances for its improvement?—Yes, mechanical and scientific appliances.

I see Colonel Leach's pamphlet, issued in 1861, mentions your having then given suggestions to him; were you associated with him in his investigations into the Irish registration system?—We were associated, but not officially.

Were the suggestions contained in his pamphlet mainly made by you?—Altogether.

You suggested at that time the use of photography and printing, in connection with the registry, did you not?—Yes, I first suggested it.

And, I believe, you have carried on a series of experiments with the view of ascertaining whether some mechanical appliances might not be substituted for the book indices?—Yes.

I believe that the Treasury in 1874, appointed a Committee to inquire into your invention?—They did on the recommendation of the Percy Committee, which was the precursor of it.

Will you give the names of the leading Treasury Commissioners?— Judge Longfield, Mr. R. O. Armstrong, the Lord Chancellor's Clerk, Mr. Herbert Murray, the Treasury Remembrancer, Mr. Lynch, the Registrar of the Landed Estates Court, Colonel Berdoe Wilkinson, of the Royal Engineers, commanding the Ordnance Survey in Ireland, Mr. Maurice Keating, the Registrar of the Court of Probate, and Mr. Dwyer, Registrar of Deeds.

Did they report in favour of your proposal?—They reported very strongly in favour of it, with the exception of the Registrar of Deeds.

The Report of that Committee has been issued as a Parliamentary Paper?—Yes.

Before entering upon your proposed improvement, I would wish to ask you to describe as briefly as you can the system of registry adopted in Ireland; it is a system of registry by memorials, is it not?—It is a system of registry by memorials.

What is the memorial bound to contain?— Certain statutory requirements, such as the names of the parties, the names of all the parcels, the names of the counties and baronies, and the names of the witnesses.

Chairman.
Does it give nothing more; does not it give the operative part of the deed?—It gives the nature of the deed, but not necessarily the consideration.

I understand that you could tell from the memorial whether the deed was a conveyance, or mortgage, or a re-settlement?—Yes, the solicitor states what it is.

The O'Conor Don.
That is one of the statutory requirements?—Yes.

When a person is desirous of registering a deed in Ireland, what is the first step that he must take?—He brings the deed and memorial up to the Registry of Deeds Office, and presents it to two of the sub-officers for comparison, and if the deed and memorial coincide in every respect, with reference to the statutory requirements, the sub-officers initial it; the solicitor or person coming to the Registry of Deeds Office then takes the verified deed and memorial to the registrar or assistant registrar, who examines them and asks questions, and sees in fact that the stamp duty is correct. If that is satisfactory, he administers an oath to the person presenting the deed and memorial as to its being a true memorial of that deed; the registrar then enters in a little "fee book," which runs from No. 1 in the morning to a number, whatever it may be, in the evening, the name of the solicitor, and the fees paid, and puts a number corresponding to that in his book on the deed and on the memorial; if he enters in his book No. 5, he puts No. 5 on the deed, and he puts No. 5 on the memorial.

What does he enter in this Day book as to the contents of the memorial?—That is a subsequent transaction, transaction No. 2. The deed and memorial having passed from the registrar, are manipulated by the clerks in the office; the first clerk who takes charge of them is the "Day" book clerk, who extracts certain particulars, such as all the grantors and all the grantees, and the name of the county, and so on, but he does not take the lands from the memorial.

In the Day book he enters the names of all the grantors and grantees, and the county or barony?—Yes, he enters the names of the grantors and grantees, and the county or barony, but not the parcels.

Does he also enter the number of the memorial?—Yes, that corresponds with what the registrar puts on.

And the date at which it was registered? —Yes, the date is taken from the affidavit.

From the Day book, is not what is called the names' index composed?—The names' index is composed from that Day book only.

Would you explain to the Committee in what way the indices are made up; are they alphabetical, or are they in regular dictionary order; will you explain the index of names first of all? —They are made in two forms; one is a rapid but very imperfect alphabetical form, and the other is an attempted dictionary order.

Is what you call a very rapid imperfect alphabetical order, arranged under the letters of the alphabet, but not in dictionary order?— By the two first letters of the name, so that all the Ma's would be together, and all the Mu's would be together, but then you would have all the Martin's and Marables mixed up, and you must look through all the Ma's for your name, and so in the case of the Murphy's, if you are looking at the Mu's. That book is entrusted to the public, and the second book which I am about to describe, is not entrusted to the public; it is an attempt to make a dictionary index day by day, so that you would find all the Brown's together, which by the first index could not be the case. That is made upon paper, and the other book is on parchment. The second book is an experimental book, never given to the public; it is only used by the establishment.

This book has been only a short time in use, has it?—Ten years or so.

And in this second book the names are arranged, as far as it has been found practicable, in dictionary order?—Yes, as far as practicable in dictionary order.

Chairman.
Is not that first book very confusing as an index?—It is dangerous and confusing to the last degree, after a certain time has elapsed. The difference of time in searching in that parchment book by the two first letters, and the one which is a dictionary index, is as hours to minutes, and I consider the danger very serious.

Do not you think that a good index is the real secret of the success of any scheme for the registration of deeds?—I have given 30 years to that consideration, and after 30 years I say it all turns upon that.

The O'Conor Don.
The next step after the index is made out from the Day book, is entering in what is called the abstract book, is it not?—Yes.

Does not the abstract book contain, in addition to the information given in the Day book, the nature of the deed?—It contains the nature of the deed, all the grantors and grantees, and all the lands.

And the names of the lands?—Yes, the names of the lands, the situation of the land, the date of the instrument, and the consideration.

From this abstract book, what is called the land index is made out, is it not?—Necessarily so.

Would you explain to the Committee how the land index is arranged; is it arranged by counties and baronies?—It is divided into counties, and sub-divided into baronies.

In what way are the names of the lands arranged under the baronies?—I come upon a very great difficulty, and I may be pardoned if I explain it; they are compelled to be arranged by only the first letter; all the A's go together, all the B's go together, and so on; if you have a search, and there are a thousand lands, every one commencing with the letter A, you must read every one of them down, though you are morally certain that you have already got your own lands down: that is because of the bad system of "alias" names.

Is it not the fact that, in Ireland, these denominations of land very often have several names, the same denomination has several names, which have all to be entered in this book?—That is quite true.

What are called "alias denominations"? —Yes; they shift round from one to six; the average number of alias names is three; but I counted 16 upon one occasion.

You have suggested as one improvement, that the ordnance names ought to be taken in all cases, as the names that would be found in the registry?—Yes, I have written upon that subject, and I am in accord with every man who has thought upon the subject.

Then in Ireland we have the names and land index which you have described?— Yes.

Besides this, are not the memorials copied into books?—Yes, they are copied into books for the convenience both of the inside searchers, outside searchers, and the public generally, to whom we would not give the original document.

If the memorial comprises what is called the statutory requirements of the deed, the officers need not look any further as to its correctness, I believe?—They have no right to do so, and are not compelled to do so.

Do you consider that any disadvantage arises from this?—A most serious disadvantage, and most serious danger.

And you would propose, as an improvement, that the full deed should be registered?—Most decidedly and unquestionably.

As you stated in the commencement, you have given your attention to certain improvements of a mechanical character in connection with this registry; what would you do under your proposed system with a deed when it was lodged at the office?—The moment the deed was lodged in the office, I should produce a facsimile copy of such deed in miniature.

By photography?—By a system of photography; as soon as I had produced the miniature copy, I should transfer it on to a thin brass sheet, and from which it subsequently could be enlarged at will, and facsimile copies given at discretion.

And you would preserve this brass sheet, from which you have the contents of the deed transferred from the photograph in the office, as a record?—Yes, and give back the original deed almost immediately.

Would this system of photographing and transferring to brass the full contents of the deeds be a tedious or an expensive one?—It would be both very cheap and very rapid; inconceivably so to a man who had never seen the process.

What would be the average cost of a page?—After four or five years' trial, I should say, including labour and material, it would cost 1s. per page.

What length of time would it take you to treat a deed in this manner, taking a deed of average length?—I must ask you to state how many pages to the deed, say a deed of one page, or a deed of two pages.

Say a couple of pages?—The size of the page is perfectly immaterial; the London "Times" can be done as cheaply as "I remain, yours truly."

Chairman.

Your deeds in Ireland are shorter than ours in England, are they not?—I have seen yours in England; I do not know that ours are shorter.

Take an ordinary conveyance of two pages, how long would it take?—It would take, I should think, about 50 seconds, that is 25 seconds for each page. I am going over it rather than under it; but if you like to do it as a scientific experiment, I will do it in four seconds, but I will guard myself as to the time by taking a margin.

The O'Conor Don.

You give merely the time that it will take to photograph it?—Merely doing the photographic part.

What length of time would it take to complete the transfer and transfer it to the brass?—All the deeds having been photographed and ready, it will take about nine seconds to put them into the brass. I can do it before the Committee if you would fix a day. I have brought the things to London on purpose.

Having transferred the whole of the original deed, as you have explained, to the brass, do you propose to return the original deed to the solicitor, who brought it in?—Of course I should return the original deed to the solicitor, and he would know he had a facsimile copy indestructible, on the record.

What would you next do for the purpose of compiling your indices?—I assume that the abstract of the deed is furnished by the solicitor or made in the office.

You would propose that the abstract should be made out either by the solicitor or in the office, containing what is called the statutable requirements?—Yes.

That is to say, the names of the grantors, the nature of the instrument, and those particulars which you have already described?—Yes, in fact a complete abstract; I would take the liberty of suggesting also that the names and residences of the witnesses might be added.

The parties who witnessed the deed?—I would take the residence of the parties, and the names of the witnesses; my experience goes to that; it would save a vast deal of trouble, and asking perpetually for the original deed.

Having got this abstract, what do you propose to do with it under your system in Ireland?—In Ireland, we have thousands and thousands of townlands commencing with the same prefix; those I should have all logotyped.

You would set up the contents of the abstract in logotype printing?—Yes.

Do you not propose subsequently to stereotype it?—Having

logotyped the day's work and having set it all up, I should take a stereotyped plate of the day's work, for this reason; when once a thing is stereotyped, no bribery could prevail with the printer; if there was a mortgage for 5,000 l., he could not drop a nought to make it 500 l.; being stereotyped, there is no longer any control over it.

What would you next do with the stereotyped plate?—I would take the stereotyped plate and divide it up, as you would with postage stamps, and divide the 10 Browns, and get them all together; if there were 10 O'Connor's I would put them all together, and arrange them according to their different books. I then should put them into the machine and stamp them into the book first. When they were-printed into books, I should take the same stereotyped plate and bring it to the mechanical index, which consists of metal paper, and indent it into that; so that I should have books to read from, and an indestructible index to fall back upon if the books were injured or lost, which could not be acted upon by heat, damp, insects, or vermin, which would reproduce books to any amount afterwards, and would also give copies ad infinitum when required.

Are you now referring to what is called your mechanical index?—To both.

We had better keep them distinct; with regard to the mechanical index, it is an index consisting of a brass band upon two rollers, is it not?—A feeding and receiving roller.

It has been very accurately described, has it not, in the Report of the Treasury Committee?—It has been substantially described, but I must say there are a great many improvements which I have brought in since then.

Have you this instrument in London?—I have had no orders to bring it over, but on chance I have ordered it to come over, assuming that the Committee might like personally to inspect it at the hotel.

This brass band is really to constitute the index itself, is it not? —It does constitute the index.

And it is covered with some white substance, either paper or linen, in order that the printing ink may show upon it?—By preference, but not necessarily.

But that is what you have adopted?—I have adopted common paper.

And by turning the handle, you unroll this brass band to any point that you desire to come to?—Yes, quite so; by suitable mechanical appliances any particular entry comes under one's eye directly.

One of the advantages that you expect to derive from the adoption of this system, would be, not alone the facility in making the search, but in being able to print from this band itself, is it not?—That is one of them. Supposing a man is dealing with, say, 400, 500, or 600 lands, it is a long time before he can copy it out by hand; and the question is, will he copy it correctly from the abstract, but by turning the handle he gets in four seconds a printed copy of the brass band, which is a facsimile copy.

I will not ask you for any further explanation of the machine, because it cannot be understood without being seen; but was it not the fact that you found a very strong prejudice existed against the use of any mechanical contrivance as compared with the use of books?—Yes, very much so; there was a very strong objection with certain persons.

In consequence of this, have you not devised another means by which you can print in books, in their proper dictionary order, from day to day, every record that has been furnished to the office?—I have.

You have that instrument on the table before you?—Yes.

What is the average number of deeds registered in Ireland each day?—Sixty at present; it was 18 when I went into the office.

Therefore it would seem that the daily average number of deeds registered has very much increased?—Enormously; it was about one a week in the beginning of the office days. When I went in in 1847 it was 18, and now it is 60.

Taking 60 as a standard, how long would it take you to have the abstracts which you have referred to printed in their proper places in books, in dictionary order, both as to lands and names?—It depends upon the number of men you give me to do it with; that is a geometrical proportion very easily understood; 10 men will do 60 deeds in three hours and a half. At 4 o'clock to-day, when the official attendance ceases, with 10 men and my appliances, I shall have everything ready for you, at the ordinary hour of ceasing work in any printer's establishment, which is 7 o'clock. (*The Witness explained the working of the printing machine to the Committee.*) This was a handsomely finished mahogany frame, containing platten press, elastic frisket, blanket, and a moving tray wherein the bound book was held, the page grasped, and the printing executed with unerring precision.

Having seen your instrument, may I ask whether you could undertake with 10 men to have printed within a reasonable time, say 3 1/2 hours, the 60 deeds which are recorded daily in Ireland?—Yes, from 4 to 7 o'clock, ordinary printers' hours.

And you could supply every day two indices, one for lands, and one for names in dictionary order?—With 10 men, 60 deeds, and in geometrical proportion.

If registry by means of the Ordnance denomination of townlands in Ireland, were adopted, might not there be a sort of folio opened for each townland, showing all the different deeds relating to that particular townland?—Quite so; it would be the converse of the proposition I have given you, and the folio would refer to the land, instead of the generic surname.

It would be a record of title in connection with that particular denomination?—It would afford such facilities for clearing titles as it is impossible to describe in words.

I believe several of the books of the Registry of Deeds Office in Dublin are in arrear, are they not?—The land index is always in arrear.

To what extent?—The average time as shown by the Parliamentary Return, ordered by Mr. W. H. Smith and the O'Conor Don, was three months or so; therefore you could never make land search closer up than three months. Lately pressure has been put on, and it is kept somewhat closer up.

Could you under your proposed system very quickly make up the arrears, and bring the existing books down to the present date?—Yes; that is an equation quite easily understood; if 10 men at the present Registry of Deeds can do all the index work, you will have either 40 or 50 men to do the arrears; but with 10 men I could not do more work than the work I have stated; I could not touch the arrears.

Do you consider that a good system of registration of deeds would have a tendency to lead up to record of title?—My experience and theory both coincide that a good system of registration of deeds necessarily leads up to clearing the title.

Chairman.

Do you think that a proper registry of deeds, with a proper index, would in themselves constitute a record of title without anything more; that is, they would give you the evidence of which the registration of title would be the net result?—The registration of title would be a work of supererogation; I think that the other would be so perfect that you would not require registration of title.

A record of title in such a case would be like adding up a simple sum, would it not?—It would be like adding up a simple sum. My views on the record of title question are, that in Ireland it would be rather a dangerous thing to insist upon. Mr. Joshua Williams and Mr. McDonnell, of the Landed Estates Court, are in perfect accord with me, and whatever they have said I agree to.

The O'Conor Don.

Returning to the question I was asking you a moment ago; in a country like England, not divided into townlands, what method would you propose as an alternative for registering deeds?—What we want is to get a unit, the smallest unit possible. I have got a plan which I will now submit to the Committee, it is to divide up a standard map into squares and subsquares; first, by numbers, and secondly, by letters, supposing you want to identify a property in square 7; that is the square map of Kingstown, Dublin (producing a plan).

You propose the Ordnance survey?—A standard map.

And to divide it into squares?—Yes, as you are aware, there has been a signal failure in attempting to make a standard map do; when you identify a man's property upon a standard map, it is all right to-day, but when he sells it to-morrow you write another name over it, and when it is sold again you write another; in fact, it is impossible to record it; it is practically obliterated. This is my plan: I take square 7 on that map, and apply one of these metal squares to it. Now one part of that No. 7 is registered by the Crown, and the other part is preserved by the owner; they are both stamped with a single die; I keep one square, and you keep the other.

You cut out on brass a particular portion of the property belonging to A.B.?—I first lay down a piece of tracing-paper upon the map, and having traced on the tracing-paper the terminal points, I put the tracing-paper upon the two bits of brass, and cut them out into counterpart stencils; and the die of the Crown is affixed to both; you keep one, and the other party keeps the other; supposing he sub-lets, it does not matter at all. Here is another square, but that is a sub-square (producing the same, and explaining the system to the Committee). The suggestion that I have made has reference to Ireland; there you would have a folio for each name; but what are you to do in England? Then I say, let the unit be the map; let it be divided into squares, and, inasmuch as your property must exist there, it gets over the mechanical difficulty which existed before.

Chairman.

That presupposes an Ordnance survey of the whole country?—Yes, unless you have a recognised authenticated survey of the whole country, I cannot do it.

The whole of Ireland is surveyed upon a scale of 6 inches to the mile, is it not?— Yes.

Do you find that that is sufficient?—Yes, because we have the power of enlarging this; supposing anyone says it is a little bit too small for me; it does not matter, you can enlarge it by the photographic process.

The O'Conor Don.
This is a map of Kingstown, of 6 inches to the mile?—Yes.

Chairman.
Have you the 25 inches to a mile map in Ireland?—I think there is nothing larger than the 6-inch scale.

Mr. Shaw Lefevre.

Are towns given on a larger scale?—The towns are given on a larger scale.

The O'Conor Don.
What you would propose in England is to take a map register, and have a unit, one of the squares of the map?—Yes, I would take square 7, No. so-and-so, and I would get an entire record of every event occurring within that square or sub-square; there could be no error, because the Government could keep one part, and the owner the other.

Chairman.
What you propose is, to take the map and divide it into squares, and then make it the basis of your registration?—The basis of my land registration, having a nominal registration also.

Supposing that every deed was registered as you propose, with a perfect index which would make the labour of search very small indeed; might not you dispense altogether with any system of record of title; would not a registration of deeds amount to a registration of title; or would you propose to superadd to the registration of deeds the registration of titles?—No; I answer distinctly from my experience of 30 years, that a good system of registration of deeds does everything that is practically required.

Supposing all dealings with land consisted simply of transfers of land from one hand to another, in that case I presume you would consider that registration of title would be exceedingly easy?—Yes.

It would be as easy as the title itself would be simple?—Yes, they correspond; if one is simple the other is easy.

The moment you come to split up the ownership of property amongst different persons, that is to say, the moment you settle property or lease it, or charge it in favour of unborn or unascertained persons, or load it with easements, chief rents, or servitudes, in favour of strangers, you get into one of two difficulties in the registration of title; either you must put all the interests carved out of the fee on to the register; in which case you defeat the object of registration, namely, simplicity of transfer; or you must have plus the registration of title, and outside the registry another record of unregistered dealings; is not that so?—Yes; you have described it most accurately. I was much taken with the registration of title. Sir Robert Torrens was kind enough to instruct me; but I have changed my views at a more recent stage.

Registration of title has been tried in Ireland under most favourable circumstances; you started there through the medium of the Incumbered Estates Court, with a statutory title?—Yes.

Yet it appears from the evidence that has been given before us, that very little use has been made of the Record of Title Act, 1865; to what do you attribute that?—I attribute it, after long conversation with Mr. McDonnell, to this: I say you should either abolish it altogether, or make it compulsory; you are upon the horns of a dilemma.

Could it be accounted for in this way, that people find, that although their title is for the present clear, still their property may be settled and leased, and so forth; and loaded with these different charges, and in that way the difficulty of registration may in course of time become great; is that so?—I believe the most experienced solicitors anticipated something of that, but they have superadded other reasons that the mechanism has proved to be more theoretical mechanism than a practical one.

Applicable, you would say, to such a state of things as is almost universal in the Colonies, that of lands simply passing from hand to hand, either by way of sale or mortgage?—That is the reason; and perhaps I may venture to state another reason. In old countries it resolves itself into what was instinctively thought, and positively stated by experienced conveyancers at the outset, that it would do very well for a new country but not for an old country, and it is coming to that.

May I put it in this way, that registration implies simplicity of transfer, and simplicity of transfer presupposes simplicity of tenure, and that you cannot have in an old country?—You have put my views and the views of every man with whom I have had conversation, into a sentence; that is what it means.

You said that the land index of the Irish Registry Court was in arrear sometimes for three months; surely that must make searching exceedingly unsatisfactory; is it not so?—Both unsatisfactory and very dangerous; most seriously dangerous.

Can you conceive registration being of any use, unless the means of getting at the result of the registry were brought up to the date at which you searched?—In that case you have to trust to an unreliable method; that is to go upon names alone; the lands record is a check upon the other in all cases.

Have you no provisional registration in Ireland?—No, we have nothing of that kind; you register straight off.

Could you give me any idea of the cost of registering a deed, according to the present system in Ireland?—I should rather refer you to Mr. Littledale, now present, for that. Solicitors know a great deal more about that. I confine myself to mechanical details.

You never register the whole deed, do you?—There are cases in which the whole deed is practically registered; as when you have a printed deed you may register the memorial, which is a copy of the deed.

You, I understand, very much prefer registering the whole deed to registering the memorial?—Certainly.

Another advantage, I presume, of any system of registration is, that it compels people to pay stamp duty; is not that so?—Your first question necessitates an answer to your second question. You asked me about the whole deed. There is a prevailing idea in the public mind that the act of registration is an all important question, whether the original deed is lost or not; 60 deeds a day are now registered, where but 18 were registered; this is going on, because registration is really believed in; but thousands of people believe that, when a solicitor registers a deed, it is of very little consequence whether the deed is lost or not; they say, put it on the register, and there is an end of it.

One advantage of registering the whole deed is, that the register would preserve evidence of a lost deed?—Yes; that is very material. Very serious consequences have occurred through the loss of a deed. I may mention an extraordinary case, the case of Scully v. Scully, in which a law suit prevailed 40 years. A man came into the office, got at the original document, and cut out the word "third" from the memorial.

Have you considered the question of having more than one registry in Ireland?—I have thought of it seriously and conferred with the best authorities, and I am at a loss to discover the utility of it. I do not think there is any necessity for it. I think it would lead to confusion.

Mr. Patrick Martin.

I understand that you are anxious that the area of the search should be confined as much as possible?—I am anxious that it should be confined as much as possible.

Do you think it would be possible to frame an index having sub-divisions, so far as the index of places is concerned, so as to limit the area of the search?—If you once adopt the Ordnance map as the basis for your registry, you can sub-divide it ad infinitum with mathematical certainty. I must guard myself by saying this, that unless the Ordnance survey is used it is an impossibility.

As a practical matter, in the Irish Register Office at present, considerable difficulty is experienced from the great number of deeds being registered that have no names of counties even, or baronies in them, is not that so?—That is one of the most disastrous features, and it should never be permitted in any registry.

In what mode are those deeds indexed?—A special book is provided for them where a deed is registered that has a county but not a barony; it is entered upon that county, but entered upon what is called a "No Barony Book;" when the county is omitted, it is entered in a book called "General Index" or "No Situation Book." Consequently every time a man makes a search he has to search those books.

To a certain extent that increases the difficulty and expense of the search?—Naturally, it does.

So far as searches are concerned, as I understand, one of the main expenses of searches arises from explanation of Acts in Ireland, more than from any fees charged in the Registry Office? —I have always understood so, but being disabled I was never a practical searcher myself, but I have heard it from gentlemen.

What you speak of at present is as to the registering of memorials; are there many memorials registered in Ireland containing simply the statement of the lands alone, without any reference to limitations in the deed, or anything further than showing generally the nature of the deed?—Yes, as a rule, the memorials give as little information as they possibly can.

Under the provisions of the Act, all that would be required would be the grantor and the grantee, and the description of the land?—Yes.

Chairman.

Would a memorial of settlement contain no mention of a trust? —It would conceal as much as possible.

Mr. Patrick Martin.

As a general rule, speaking from your experience, the memorials that have been brought into the office would simply contain that the lands were settled upon certain uses and trusts, set forth in the deed; is not that so?—Yes, upon considerations therein mentioned.

So that practically, under the present system the memorial is but of little avail, as evidence, in the case of a lost deed?—Of very little avail, and worse than useless in many cases; sometimes it is misleading.

So far as the question of district registries is concerned, I believe your simple objection to registries in Ireland arises more from your conceiving that one general registry is sufficient from the number of registrations passing through it?—Only a certain number of people would have property in the same district, but in the case of a large landowner he may have property in one place, two places, or three places; if you are lending such a man money, you would like to search through the registries and see whether he had property in other counties, whereas if you come to the local registry you have only to send up and make a search, and you have everything at once.

Chairman.

From my experience as a conveyancer, the case of a man mortgaging properties at the same time in different counties is very rare.

Mr. Patrick Martin.

Is it part of your duty to examine memorials?—Yes.

Are you able to state that in Ireland many deeds refer to properties in several counties—I have frequently seen them, and there is what is called a general charge, which says, "All my property of all kinds, in every part of Ireland." I have not had the Chairman's experience of English conveyancing, but in Ireland have been 30 years at that work.

Chairman.

Does a man often mortgage in general terms the whole of the property to which he is entitled, wherever situate?—Yes, and he is very glad to get any one to lend him money on it.

Mr. Patrick Martin.

It is not uncommon, I believe, in the memorials of settlements, that a man agrees to charge all the property he may have?—He will agree to anything when he is hard up, particularly in the Incumbered Estates days, and in the famine times, he would agree to anything.

With reference to the objection stated by some of the witnesses as to the publicity, will you tell me from your experience in the Registry Office, whether you would conceive that any persons go up there to search for the mere purpose of curiosity?—Unquestionably; I know it, and nobody knows it better than I do; I will give you an instance, there are seven men searching for banks daily.

I mean for the mere purpose of idle curiosity?—I will not say it is idle curiosity; for such curiosity I do not think any man would go up and search frouzty [sic] documents for that purpose; nothing is commoner than for farmers, graziers, and such people, possessed, as they think, of immense wisdom, but really of low cunning, to come on the quiet to make these searches and to get it cheaper done, than letting it go through their attorney's hands, to dodge the solicitor's fees.

But they have an object?—It is not an idle object: I never knew a case yet where there was no object, but idle curiosity; but there is no doubt, if you made the Registry Office brighter and cleaner, and the books neater, that you might have a great many persons going there.

Chairman.

Are you aware that one of the objections raised against registration generally is the publicity of it; that it would give people acting from idle curiosity or worse motives, the opportunity for finding out all about their neighbour's concerns; have you found from your experience that people come to your registry from idle curiosity, or to find out something against their neighbours?—As to "idle curiosity," there is no case of that kind.

Mr. Patrick Martin.

Your experience is this, there would be the same searching in the Registry of Deeds Office as there would be in the Probate Office to see wills?—Yes, you have exactly hit it; they want to see a will; they go and pay one shilling; they go to the Probate Court oftener than they come to us. We charge 2 s. 6d.

But in addition to what you spoke about, I assume there are searchers, who for the purpose of the black list, circulated for mercantile purposes, go and search the Registry of Deeds Office, at the present moment?—Yes, and it is upon that point I would like to explain particularly; I have thought of that for 20 years; many a man has been ruined by it; it is very cruel; it is one of the objections to the registration, and it is an objection to the putting of the whole deed upon the registry.

Chairman.

Do you propose to obviate that?—Yes; by putting the whole deed upon the register; having eliminated the mechanical objections which hitherto have obtained in the case you cut the root at once, from the publication of the black list and the objections to registration. From my knowledge of the matter, I believe that you would increase the registration enormously, if when a facsimile deed is lodged and you had only an abstract of it, the owner of the title deed was aware that his deed never would be shown, except upon his own order, or upon the order of the court, for certain purposes. At present you are asked no questions, you pay 2 s. 6 d., and you see everything that is to be seen.

You would not have the registry open to the public?—I would have abstracts open to the public, but the trusts in the deed, and the private history of the family, I should never publish; I should keep it on our metallic tablets, only to be shewn to an authorised person, only to the owner of the deed or his authorised solicitor, and so on.

Mr. Patrick Martin.

In point of fact, you would have a short abstract open to the public inspection, and the entire deed preserved simply for the purposes of those who have some right or interest in it?—Yes, or in the case of the loss of the original deed, or the production of its facsimile copy in court.

Now about the search sheets; the search sheet is handed out from the Registrar's Office in Dublin?—Yes; the negative search or the other search, called "common search."

That search is signed by the registrar?—Yes, or by the assistant registrar.

Is not there a book kept in the office on which, when that search sheet has been thus signed by the officer, there is an entry made stating the fact of that search?—A full copy of that search is made in that book; it is under the Act of Mr. Pierce Mahoney.

What is the name of that book?—The Record of Negative Search Book.

So that if a subsequent search be taken, it is only required to have reference to that book, and you proceed by search for further acts from that date?—That is the principle of it, but the search varies occasionally.

But if the same search against the same names and lands be required, you get a copy?—Yes.

And that copy is of equal validity with the search which has been previously transmitted?—Yes; it is compared with the book, and is of equal validity as far as theory goes.

Chairman.

That is handed to the purchaser or mortgagee; all depends upon that; does he transmit it, and does it form part of the title deeds, as in Scotland?—It is submitted to the inspection of counsel, and he accepts it.

Mr. Patrick Martin.
It is handed to the solicitor, and becomes afterwards a portion of the evidence in the case of the mortgage or purchase?—Yes.

Mr. Shaw Lefevre.
I understand you to say that you considered that registration of title becomes very advisable and desirable in a new country, but not in an old one?—Yes.

What is the difference in that respect?—The Chairman has put it much better than I could possibly put it; he formulated all my views in one moment

What is your own view upon the subject; take Melbourne and compare it with Belfast, what distinction is there in the nature of the property, or in the method in which people deal with their property, which would make the registration of titles advisable in one country and not in the other?—Melbourne is a new country, and Belfast is a very old place.

The houses in Melbourne, I presume, are not dissimilar from Belfast; and the mode of living must be very much the same there, and the people use their houses for much the same purpose?—Just imagine that there was a revolution to take place in Melbourne, which has not yet taken place; in Belfast we have had many rebellions and revolutions.

I cannot see what rebellions have to do with it; what distinction is there in the method of tenure in the case of house property in the one country compared with the other, that would make one system advisable in the one and not in the other?—Melbourne being a new country, has not gone through the phases of the old one; and the principle is a very different one after a certain time has elapsed in a country.

Chairman.
Are you acquainted with the tenure of land in Melbourne?—Only from what Sir Robert Torrens told me of Australia.

Mr. Shaw Lefevre.

On what do you ground your opinion that there is a difference in the tenure of land in Melbourne as compared with an Irish town; which makes you think the system is advisable in one and not in the other?—My answer is that I do not know.

Supposing you were informed upon that point, and you found that practically there is no distinction as to tenure of land in Melbourne and in a town like Belfast; do not you think then that a system which has worked so well for people there might be advisable, even in Ireland?—It is a question I might write a long paper upon, because I say with great respect, I am placed in a difficult position; it is assuming what I am not prepared to grant, that the Melbourne system is perfect.

I thought you said that a particular system might be very advisable in one country and not in the other; I want to know upon what you base that opinion; it seems you do not know the system of tenure in Melbourne?—I must take the liberty of asking what is the supposed difference; because I am somewhat in the dark; I am not aware what the system in Melbourne is; is it the ordinary title system?

Chairman.

Are not small properties, as well as large ones, frequently settled in Ireland?—Yes.

Mr. Shaw Lefevre.

Are they not usually settled by way of marriage settlement with trustees; is not it the usual mode of settling either small houses or small properties?—I am speaking in presence of counsel. I believe that is so.

Is not it the usual way of settling both small and large house properties?—I cannot give an opinion upon that.

Could you get from the registry of deeds an analysis of the number of deeds registered showing how many are mortgages, how many are leases, how many are transfers, and how many are settlements in the sense of entails?—It is a curious thing that I at one time took those down, and I made a most diligent search before coming over here to find the manuscript, but I recollect perfectly well that one deed mastered all the others.

Could you get the Committee an analysis for a week, showing the number of transactions registered?—It could be done in a few moments, by writing to the registry of deeds.

I understand there are 60,000 deeds registered in Ireland in the course of a year, that would be about 200 a day, therefore for a week it would be about 1,200?—You could obtain an answer to that in seven minutes if you were to write to the registry of deeds.

Can you give the Committee an idea what the bulk of the cases are; are they mortgages, or leases, or what?—Leases are not all registered; not necessarily.

Is it merely permissive in case of leases?—A great number of leases are not registered.

Any lease beyond 20 years would necessarily be registered?—Yes.

Would mortgages form a very large proportion of the deeds registered?—Yes.

I presume they are not only simple transactions themselves, but must be in respect of property held under simple tenure; you could not mortgage a settled property?—No.

Mortgages of landed estates must be comparatively rare, are they not?—I cannot say that.

Would not the great bulk of transactions be very simple ones and in respect of property held in a simple manner; are not the great bulk of the transactions registered in the registry of deeds in Ireland, very simple transactions; and in respect of property held under very simple tenure, namely, freehold or leasehold?—That is more a question for counsel." [12]

Footnotes
The reference to the House of Commons question is from HC Deb 13 April 1877 vol 233 c1072 available at
http://hansard.millbanksystems.com/commons/1877/apr/13/registry-of-deeds-office-ireland-mr , and the report itself is William Henry Smith, *Registration of Deeds (Ireland)* (London, 1876), p.10-12, 13, 23, 33 available at http://pdf.library.soton.ac.uk/EPPI/194.pdf .
1. It seems he lived at a number of addresses in Dublin including for the year: 1854 Upper Buckingham Street, 1875 19 Lower Sherard Street, 1893 55 Chancery Land in London, and 1900 Kingstown.

2. PRIA vol 6 (1853-7), p.157-160.

3. *London Gazette*, 4th Nov 1856.

4. *English mechanics and the mirror of science,* vol 11, 1st April 1870, p.48.

5. *The Mechanics' magazine and journal of science, arts, and manufactures,* volume 97 (1872), p.198.

6. *The Freeman's Journal* of 3rd August 1870.

7. *Capital and Labour,* vol vi, p.331, and see also *English mechanic and world of science,* Vol 29, (1879), p.286, and the *Nation,* 2 Oct 1875, p.1.

8. *Freeman's Journal* 25th June 1877, p.11.

9. *The Electrical Journal*, vol iii, p.14.

10. R W Burns, *Television: an international history of the formative years* (London, 1986), p.26.

11. For which he took out a patent in 1874: Peter Hernon, *Microforms and government information* (London, 1981), p.111.

12. *Reports from Committees* (London, 1878-9) vol xi, p.129-138.

APPENDIX G
Fraud in 18th century Ireland, the examples of Hugh Maguire, Kedagh Geoghegan and Robert Nugent

While the integrity of the 18th century ROD and its successive registrars has never been questioned, as far as I know, and we can absolutely rely on the basic facts outlined in the memorials within, nonetheless there is an element that has to be explored here in 18th century Irish land transactions: and that is frankly fraud. Fraud not in the basic facts in the deeds, i.e. the fact that X or Y signed away this or that lands, but rather it might lurk in the background to the signing of the deeds. Sometimes undue pressure or other details might be lacking which could put a different gloss on the proceeding and this possibility in 18th century land deeds is definitely something that it is not healthy to ignore.

This appendix then is an attempt to address that. We will present a number of facts relating to three different characters from 18th century Ireland to give readers a glimpse of the dark side, as it were, of these kind of legal transactions in order for you to get an overall picture in your mind of what, in some cases, could be unsaid in the deeds you are reading. That said there are very few specific facts relating to the ROD in this appendix, as I say only an overall picture of this kind of legal abuse, so you can skip this section if time presses you.

Its interesting that these three characters are all representative of a basic type of 18th century Irish 'squire'. They are each of them directly descended from the great families of 16th century Ireland, the Maguires lords of Fermanagh, the Geoghegans, the original pre-Norman rulers of Meath, the remains of the Southern Uí Neills who ruled over that area almost from pre-Christian times, and the Nugents, the great Norman lords of Westmeath. But all three of them either conformed to the Established Faith or at least associated mostly in that milieu, doubtless at least in part to protect their financial interests, and maybe the latter fact tended to breed a kind of cynicism in them about the law which may partly account for the colourful activities you will read below.

Colonel Hugh Maguire

He is possibly the best example of an Irish Catholic gentleman who seems to have gone almost mad – a kind of madness that you can see described infra by Andrew O'Reilly in his account of what happened to some people who conformed under the penal laws – as he turned from his religion and political allegiance in order to secure lands and money. He started off as a proud member of the Wild Geese, an officer in the Austrian service, who came back, conformed, and received a commission as a Colonel in the British army. He then got married to the wealthy Lady Cathcart in circumstances that you can see related here by Revd Edward Young (1681-1765) writing in October 1746:

"The following pretty tale for a tragedy may perhaps be new to your grace. Ly C____ at 59 is smitten with ye gay feathers of 33, and after short ceremony of Billing and Pruning, takes him into her Nest. 33 finds it very well feathered, and had a great mind to pluck some plumes of it for his private use. This made Dame Partlet bristle against him, at this the cocks-comb rose and could not bear it. It came to a little sparing, war was declared, and 33 must show all his generalship on this occasion. To this end he thought it prudent to strengthen himself by allies. And it happened very fortunately for him, that there was a young Princess in ye family of 18, whom 59 took from ye dunghill, and tossed her into a tub of soapsuds, out of which, she soon rose, like Venus out of ye sea, the delight of her Ladyship's eyes, and ye confident of her heart. This Venus fell in love with Mars, who was very happy for him, for she returned ye favours she received from him with ye key of her Ladyship's scritore, where he found ye will, which has made him run mad. In his distraction he snatches both away to Ireland, where the young princess personates her Ladyship, who is kept out of eyesight, for fear of telling tales. And as she before discovered the undutifullness of her husband, so very lately are her eyes open as to ye treachery of her bosom-friend. And yet none but these two are ever suffered to come near her. Can your grace easily feign a greater picture of distress? I own I can not. And yet for this terrible sore, she neither has, nor is likely to have, any other plaister that potatoes and milk." [1]

Lady Cathcart was to remain as a prisoner of her husband from 1746 until his death in 1766, as recounted by Maria Edgeworth, thinly disguised as fiction, in Castle Rackrent.[2]

We might then read with some suspicion some of his land dealings in the Registry of Deeds. As an example of this we find that Colonel Hugh Maguire in 1750 purchased from the sons of the late John Nugent's – of Castlenugent, pictured below – sister Frances Nugent, i.e. Garrett, James and John Nugent, their interest in the lands of Castlenugent Co Longford,[3] and also purchased the same from Annie Plunkett, one of John Nugent's sisters,[4] and from Elizabeth Conmee, another sister of John Nugent.[5] These deeds look for all the world like perfectly normal transactions with a relative of the deceased buying out the other relatives and so inheriting the estate they are all coheirs to, although even the casual observer would pause before assuming that the proud John Nugent of Coolamber, later of Castlenugent where tradition has it that O'Carolan entertained the guests and of course composed songs in his honour and that of his sister Grace, would not pass the estate to another Nugent. But in fact it transpires that:

"Immediately after the death of the said John Nugent the closet wherein he kept his family deeds and papers was sealed up by Philip Boyse, gentleman and attorney at law, and by Patrick McDonagh who was agent and manager to the said John Nugent, to prevent any suppression or embezzlement of any of the Deeds or Papers, but Colonel Hugh Maguire, who was only a younger son of one the sisters of the said John Nugent, having early notice of the said John Nugent's death [and with the reputation Maguire had this might have been a loaded comment], came immediately to the said John Nugent's house, and though the said John's widow was then in the house he took upon him[self] to act as master of it, broke the seal, which had been put on the said closet door, took out such papers as he thought proper, and sealed up the closet again and when the said closet was publicly opened before the relations of the family the said Hugh Maguire attended and directed all that was done and as he then pretended possessed himself on behalf of the said John Nugent's sisters and their children, who were his coheirs at law, of all the family deeds and papers and among the rest of the said articles and settlement and afterwards purchased the said estate, which is worth £1,600 sterling a year, for seven thousand five hundred pounds, which estate would then and now sell for thirty thousand pounds sterling and upwards, and only passed bonds for the purchase money to the said John Nugent's sisters and coheirs." [6]

It is even speculated, by the Countess of Westmeath, that his elder brother Cuchonnacht was poisoned in 1739 which again might cast a shadow on Hugh:

"There's no proof but bare suspicion that Cohany [Cuchonnacht] Maguire was poisoned. Cousin Jack Nugent and Brother Jemmy went there, he was much encumbered but by his death most of his debts are paid, I hear the[y] don't effect the estate, if so tis better for Bob." [7]

Kedagh MacGeoghegan

Kedagh, who is unique among these three in always remaining Catholic, really comes across as a lovable rogue but a rogue nonetheless in his treatment of the Malone family who did so much to help their Catholic neighbours to get around the Penal Laws. This is quite an authentic history although it comes down to us as folklore and incidentally his colourful lifestyle that is here described was to be matched by his equally famous brother Jack, the 'Buck' Geoghegan.

A picture of Kedagh Geoghegan which used to hang in Jamestown Court. My thanks to the Geoghegan family of that townland, relatives of Kedagh who originate in Carne townland nearby, for all assistance in this history.

"From the traditions of the period we gather that Kedagh MacGeoghegan was a practical joker and palmed off some jokes on his neighbours which in those days would earn penal servitude for the unlucky wight who would play them. He was eternally at some scheme, whether as a matter of fun and frolic or with the intention of over-reaching those with whom he had any dealings it is difficult to say. With the latter disposition, however, we are inclined to agree, as he always derived a pecuniary benefit as the result of his jokes. He is also reported to have been a most litigious character, frequently getting into scrapes and always extricating himself by no matter what means. He believed and inculcated that no man could lead a happy life with his neighbours unless they brought each other into courts of law, for real or imaginary offences, at least twice a year. Kedagh was a strange compound of what is called in Ireland "the virtues and vices of a rale ould Irish gentleman." Kedagh held a large and valuable farm from the Prime Sergeant [Anthony Malone], subject to which lease probably that part of the Malone property may have been purchased. So far they were in the relation of landlord and tenant, Kedagh's property and rank in life, the scion of an old family who for centuries were lords of large tracts of land in Westmeath and King's County, and bade defiance to England and her rulers from the Anglo-Norman Invasion down to the glorious defence of Dunboy were such as to create an intimacy between the families; so that whenever he got into a scrape with his neighbours and that law proceedings were threatening or commenced he flew to his landlord and friend, the justly-celebrated Anthony, though on other occasions he was in the habit of saying that "he was a b____y old rogue of a lawyer that would lave a poor man bare and busy that would have any dealings with him," and Malone would express no higher opinion of Kedagh but that he was a d____d old cheat. Certain it is that he frequently had recourse to Malone for advice, and the lawyer appeared as his advocate either to affect a compromise or to plead his case. In either instance he was successful, but, as he said with regret, he never seen the colour of Kedagh's gold, silver, or bronze. This may have induced Anthony Malone to consider his client not over honest, and he resolved to withdraw from such unprofitable practice. The lease which Kedagh held under Malone had nearly expired and he well knew that before Malone renewed it that he should stump up some money for back rent, his professional services, and the cost of executing the legal parchment.

The rent had been partly agreed on, and the lease prepared under Anthony's eye, leaving the usual blanks for the terms to be inserted. A day was also appointed for Anthony to proceed to Jamestown to perfect the leases as Kedagh made up a plan not to attend at Baronston [Malone's residence] for that purpose. If he had he would not be able to carry out his intended scheme. On the morning of the day of the intended visit Kedagh at an early hour dispatched two of his herds with twenty-five fat bullocks as a present to the great man. The instructions were to block up the road over which Anthony's carriage was to pass so as to attract his attention, and after getting clear of the bullocks the herds were to drive them home again by another road to Jamestown. A short distance from Baronston the carriage and four horses of Malone's were sorely inconvenienced by coming in contact with a lot of twenty-live large, prime, well-fed bullocks, driven by the surly-looking men, who took care they should not pass the carriage without attracting the attention of its occupant, who, however, they affected not to know. For the purpose, the road being narrow, the cattle were driven against the horses and carriage and nearly succeeded in upsetting the whole concern into the ditch. Mr. Malone looked out in great wrath and asked how they dared to act in such an outrageous manner, and ran the risk of injuring his property and endangering his life. The herd said drily:

"The road was med for us jist as well as you, ould boy; a man wid a wheelbarrow has jist as much call to the road as you. A travelling tinker or a lord on horseback are all the same, so drive on wid yerself ould boy, and don't be delaying us. We're late enough already, and bedad it will be night before we get to our journey's end."

Mr. Malone asked them whose the cattle were and where they were driving them to.

"Driving them to is it ye mane? Well, pon me conshins we're goin to Baronston; they're a present from our master, Misther Kedagh Geoghegan, poor foolish man, to that rascally ould rogue of a lawyer that would talk the shirt off your back be all accounts," exclaimed the herd.

Mr. Malone, without further parley told the herd that he was the ould rogue of a lawyer he was going to with the cattle. Off went the caubeens and down on their knees went the herds. With well acted dismay and fright they begged his honour's pardon, and blessing themselves invoked the aid of all the saints in the calendar to help them out of the dilemma.

"Oh, mother of Moses," exclaimed the chief herd, "it's all over wid us. Mr. Geoghegan will shoot us like rats; bedad he'll flog us as thin as a Galway herring when he hears this."

The Prime Sergeant told them that he was on his way to Jamestown to see their master. The herds begged hard with tears in their eyes that, his honour would not mention what had occurred, all owing to their ignorance and stupidity.

"For sure if yer honour wud be after telling him of our conduct he'd lave ourselves and our childher on the high road."

They played their part of contrition and regret so well that they not only obtained Mr. Malone's pardon and promise and secrecy but also the gift of five guineas which they valued more than either. They were desired to drive on the cattle and to tell the herd to put them into the Church field, being the best pasture. Mr. Malone proceeded to Jamestown and signed the lease on advantageous terms to Kedagh. The next day the lawyer walked out to see the bullocks, and made inquiry of his herd where he had put them, as he sent him word to leave them in the Church field.

"Arrah, what bullocks does yer honour mane?"

"Why the twenty-five bullocks Mr. Geoghegan's herds left here yesterday."

"Oh the devil a foot Mr. Geoghegan's herds put here yesterday, and sarra bullock they left her at all, at all, yer honour."

"Done again," said Anthony, and true enough he was. At the first cross-roads the herds came to after leaving the Prime Sergeant they pocketed his five guineas and drove the cattle back to their own pasture. After this practical joke Kedagh was called "Kedagh an Muloge" (Keady the bullock).

When the herds returned to Jamestown with the twenty-five bullocks and showed Kedagh the five guineas they swindled Malone out of he laughed heartily and clapped them on the shoulders.

"Well done," he exclaimed, in a fit of boisterous merriment, "ye will be shortly as well up in humbugging ould thievish old lawyers as I am, and for your clever dodge I owe ye a treat, so drink boys, Kedagh MacGeoghegan's health, and that he may be always able to outwit a lawyer."

The incident, which was considered by his friends if not honest at least very clever, did not cause Anthony to alter his opinion of the honesty of his tenant and client, and for some time the intercourse between them was on the decline. Kedagh for some time after the occurrence abstained from playing practical jokes on his neighbours practical jokes that would bring him within the meshes of the law, as he had no counsel to defend him, and he was sorely perplexed to be idle. Kedagh got into some new trouble which his restless and litigious spirit would not suffer him to avoid, and it was necessary to have recourse to advice and talents of his landlord and old advocate to get rid of an action with which he was threatened. Kedagh was in a dilemma as how he would face the great lawyer and ask him to plead for him after all the tricks he played on him, particularly the last one which he declared was nothing but an innocent joke to get up a laugh against Malone. Necessity, we are told, is the mother of invention, and Kedagh was fertile in that branch. After mature deliberation he came to the conclusion that he would feign to be dangerously ill and past all medical aid, and send for the Prime Sergeant and make restitution to him for all the wrong he had done him, and draw up his last will and testament. Accordingly he became very unwell, taking good care his state should be reported at Baronston. Malone, as may be supposed, cared very little about the matter owing to how he tricked him in the past. But hearing daily how much worse Kedagh was getting he expected every moment to hear of his death. In this state of affairs a messenger arrived in great haste at Baronston requesting to see Mr. Malone, who, accordingly, directed his immediate admission to his study. In breathless haste the messenger informed the lawyer that poor old Mr. MacGeoghegan was just off. He was as weak as a straw upon water. He was at death's door and would get in without knocking, and that he'd hardly live to see the priest and his honor, and that he could not die easy barring Mr. Malone came to see him. And he was greatly afraid that his conscience was troubled on account of some wrong he done his honor, and that he wanted to make restitution to him before he died. Malone considered awhile and resolved to go to Jamestown, whether in the hopes of seeing a repentant sinner anxious to pay him all the money he owed and tricked him of, or of easing the last moments of Kedagh's life by forgiveness of the wrongs he considered he had done him. He went with as little delay as possible, and was ushered into a dark room in which poor Kedagh lay patiently awaiting the awful moment of dissolution. He looked ill, worn out by pain and disease and completely exhausted, pale and unshaved, and his servant the picture of silent despair. Mr. Malone went over to the bed, and said in as cold a manner as he could,

"Mr. Geoghegan, I have been informed you wished to see me, but the manner you have always treated me, I cannot conceive why you have requested my attendance, as I am determined never to be concerned for you again in any manner."

"Arrah, counsellor, asthore, sure that's the very reason I sent for you. Sure I know that I treated you bad, but I hope to make up for all the wrong I done you. Do you think I would leave this world in peace without settling with you. No, Mr. Malone, jewel, I would not. I am about making my will, and I will pay you to the last farthing every penny I owe you, and what I cheated you out of. I always intended to pay you before I would die. I just want you to draw up my will because if I left it to my children to get it done they might cheat you out of your own. I don't want to have any disputes after my death, and I cannot die easy unless you are paid."

Malone called for pen and paper and wrote out the will disposing of the property as Kedagh directed, and read it over to him. He then asked for the pen himself, and was raised in the bed, scarcely able to breathe from pain and exhaustion. He wrote "I bequeath to my dear friend, Anthony Malone, the sum of 500 for all the trouble he had with me." The will thus made was handed over to the village schoolmaster to make a copy of, which was done in the sick man's room, and when finished and compared, both were regularly signed, sealed, and witnessed, and the instrument conveying to Anthony Malone 500 made as perfect as legal talent could accomplish it. The will was handed to Mr. Malone to keep by the sick man, dear Kedagh, who said to him when going that he hoped he drew it up, so that he could not be done out of his money for he knew well there would be dissatisfaction about it when he was dead and gone with his children. The copy Mr. Malone locked up in Kedagh's old desk and gave him the key, which he safely put under his head. After receiving and carefully depositing the key of his desk containing the precious document, he mentioned to Malone that he would die easy and the lawsuit that blackguard attorney was going to bring against him did not signify, as he had not long to live, but it would be an ease to his mind leaving the world if it was settled. Mr.

Malone had never been informed of it, and inquired the particulars, which, when he heard Kedagh's version, he at once undertook, and as usual was successful for his client. The Prime Sergeant went home well satisfied with his day's work, and having considerably changed his opinion about Kedagh. Not so with Kedagh. His day's work was not yet over. As soon as Mr. Malone was gone he got up, copied the will verbatim, leaving out however, the bequest of five hundred pounds to his dear friend, Anthony Malone. He signed the will, had it regularly witnessed, and deposited it in the oak desk, having burned the copy. Kedagh got better, and in a short time was quite well and carried on for some years his practical jokes on his neighbours. He used to boast that he did not care a fig about anyone as long as he had the roguish old Prime Sergeant to back him up. He was able to take him out of any scrape from pitch-and-toss to manslaughter. After playing many practical jokes on his neighbours he at last paid the debt of nature. His dear friend, Anthony Malone, attended the funeral obsequies as one of his mourners, and good reason he had to mourn, and took the management of the funeral arrangements on himself, paying off all debts incurred. Having deposited his client, Kedagh, in his last resting-place, Mr. Malone notified to the relatives that he had MacGeoghegan's will which he had himself handed to him to keep, and invited them all to return and meet for the purpose of having it read. They all met and Mr. Malone's clerk was in attendance, when it was mentioned by the heir that they had found the will. He asked where it was found, and was informed it was in the oak desk.

He replied, "It's all the same; it is all right. There were two copies made. He kept one and I kept the other. Therefore, proceed and read the will you have."

The clerk proceeded to read the document, word by word, from the copy which he held in his hand. At last the Clerk read, "Signed, sealed, and delivered."

"Pray finish the will," said Mr. Malone, "and I will bequeath to my dear friend, Anthony Malone, £500."

"I have finished it, sir," said the clerk. "and read every word of it."

"Impossible, sir," said Malone, who stood up to look at it,

when to his dismay and disappointment he saw a will dated one day later than the document he held in his hand, and leaving out to him the most important bequest. True were the words of Kedagh, when he said, he knew there would be dissatisfaction about it when he was dead and gone. Mr. Malone said, "Kedagh, you lived on practical jokes; and you died a practical joker.""" [8]

Robert Nugent

Robert Nugent (1702-1788), who was known as Viscount Clare from 1766-1776 and Earl Nugent thereafter, was born into an aristocratic family in Carlanstown Co. Westmeath, entered British politics and rose to be President of the Board of Trade 1766-68 – usually a cabinet level position – and Vice Treasurer of Ireland 1759-65 and 1768-82 among other positions.

He was quite famous for his skill in marrying rich widows!, but also for a poem he wrote on his conversion from the Catholic to the Protestant faith, which starts:

"Remote from Liberty and Truth,
By Fortune's Crime, my early Youth
Drank Error's poison'd Springs.
Taught by dark Creeds and Mystic Law,
Wrapt up in reverential Awe,
I bow'd to Priests and Kings.

Soon Reason dawn'd, with troubled Sight
I caught the Glimpse of painful Light." [9]

He was in fact a leading member of the Freemasons all this time and which may have coloured these religious opinions:

"Mr. Dillon Pollard Hampson of Castlepollard, County Westmeath, was also another notable officer in the Grand Lodge of Ireland, being appointed Junior Grand Warden in 1731. Robert Nugent, of Carlanstown, County Westmeath, was appointed to the same office in 1732 and both men worked relentlessly for the advancement of the Masonic Order." [10]

You can read about Pollard also in what follows in the footnote and we can form from that quite a dark impression of what both really got up to in their land and legal dealings in Ireland.

Nonetheless it would unfair I think to completely right off this interesting politician's career or his contribution to public life. He was a genuine and knowledgeable patron of the arts for example, including figures like Gainsborough and Goldsmith, and also a talented poet and quite witty and erudite writer. He is well known to historians of the period for his opposition to unfair trade laws vis a vis Ireland and always spoke out in favour of Irish interests in the House of Commons. Furthermore he possibly regretted later the kind of practices that occupied his youth, even converting back to Catholicism before he died.

But nevertheless I think the conscientious historian, even of such a nondescript subject as a guidebook to the ROD, should I think attempt to strip off the layers of the period and really see how life was like for the 'little guy' trying to enforce his/her land rights in the Irish court system of the period. And unfortunately at that level, looking up at this 'great man' from the low perspective of his unfavoured relations, we get quite an insight into how the legal system really worked during that period and what he was really like when pursuing his legal interests.

This text that follows is the 1757 autobiographical account of Robert's illegitimate son, also Robert, by his cousin from Donore Co. Westmeath. This is a lively and factual account (although the writer sometimes uses Latin names to very thinly disguise his characters, in order to cheat libel laws no doubt) which begins here with the first meeting he had with his father as an adult fresh from Ireland:

"I was kept in suspense, two or three days before I heard anything in return; when late one evening, a post chaise drove violently into the inn-yard, a lusty tall gentleman, wrapp'd up in a horseman's coat, immediately stepped out, and coming into the house, in a voice the tone of which, not being modulated in the mildest strain, conveyed no very favourable opinion of the speaker to the ideas of the standers by, thus addressed himself to the lord of the Castle,

'Have you got, friend, in your custody a white-headed boy from Ireland?'

'Yes.'

'Why then do you not bring him?'

'You never implied so much before,' was returned.

'If you was not stupid, friend, there could have been no necessity to explain myself any farther.'

'You might speak a little civiler howsomever,' replied the landlord, 'but a horse as never eat oats, one cannot expect to' he was proceeding, when the gentleman's wide coat turning aside accidentally discovered the blaze of a broad gold lace, which had hitherto been concealed, the sight of which had such an effect upon the Publican as to make him forget the remaining part of his coarse proverb, and elevating his voice a degree higher,

'Why, Tim, do you not light his honour upstairs, as you see he is in such a haste; what would your honour please to have brought up?'

'Bring a bottle of wine.'

'A bottle of wine to the rose this moment. Please your honour permit me to light you up.'

Such was the dialogue, which with an aching heart I listened attentively to on the stair-head.

Upon entering the room,

'Set down the wine, friend, and retire.'

Which being complied with, he drew a chair, and calling me from the corner of the room where I was retired, and biting the ends of my fingers through fear

'Well, my boy,' says he, 'you come from Ireland I suppose?'

'Yes sir,' I replied, 'some days ago.'

'Ah, ah, your tongue betrays that sufficiently. Who is your father?'

'Tiberius Nugenius of Gosfield Sir.'

'Who told you that, boy? you must be mistaken, that gentleman informs me otherwise.'

'I was always esteemed as such in Ireland both by his relations and my mother's.'

'All lies, all lies,' said he with a smile, and pouring out a glass of wine, 'come drink, I suppose you can drink; if Tiberius is your father you can drink.' – after I had drank, 'if you are the person you say, and that I came to enquire after, you have the mark of a deep scar, occasion'd by a burn, on the left side your belly'; which was no sooner said, than pulling me to him, he took out my shirt, and having seen the distinguishing characteristic, 'it is all right,' said he, and after a considerable pause, ordered me to ring the bell.

The landlord coming up,

'Do you know me,' was asked?

'No, Sir.'

'What,' says he, 'don't you know esquire Forbes of Doverstreet?'

'Though I know the street very well, I cannot say I have knowledge of any such gentleman.'

'Well,' says he, calling him aside, in a whisper loud enough for me to hear, 'my name is Nugenius but for some private reasons do not chose the youth should be made acquainted with it as just yet,' then raising his voice, and at the same time drawing out his purse, 'here, landlord,' said he, 'is some money, do you procure the youth some cloths, more suitable to appear in, than what are on his back; I shall call again in a few days, and satisfy you for your trouble, in the meantime as I have no further occasion for you, you are at liberty to go down stairs.'

When left to ourselves, addressing himself to me,

'Have you brought along with you no letters from your mother and friends in Ireland?'

'None. Sir,' I replied, 'excepting a certificate of my birth, wrote by my mother,' which I no sooner produced, than he snatched it from me, and with an air of seeming indifference, not without symptoms of anger, tore it to pieces, saying,

'As this idle paper will be of no use but to exasperate Nugenius against you, think me your friend in destroying it; be cautious what you say, and expect to hear more in a little time', which was no sooner said, than he went away, and left me to reflect upon my melancholy situation.

Some days after this, one Mr. Bristow a periwig maker in St. Albans-Street, came to the Inn, with orders from my father to discharge the small arrears due to the landlord, and take me along with him to his own house: I soon found that it had been determined that this Bristow should take me as an apprentice; and was to receive as a premium at my being bound, fifty pounds, for initiating me in the profound art, and mysteries, of which he was a professor.

Conscious my own abilities would never let me attain to the degree of an adept, in this noble science, and after some days spent at the powder tub, I with great difficulty prevail'd upon my father, to extricate me out of the suds, and rather than compel me to depend upon so mean a business for my future subsistence, a business so much inferior to the rank and character of both my parents, as well as my education; to give me the liberty of serving his majesty on board one of his ships of war, tho' it were in the meanest capacity, I was the more emboldened to ask this favour, as such a proposal had been made me some time before.

This request of mine with seeming reluctance, at length was

granted: the station procur'd me, though no greater than that of captain's servant, as it was the gift of my generous father, I cheerfully accepted of. In which capacity, I sometime afterwards embarked on board his majesty's ship the Windsor of sixty guns, capt. Thomas Hannaway commander, not in the least doubting from my father's affluent fortune I should in every respect be suitably equip'd for the service I was now engaged in.

With this persuasion I took leave of my father, who as a fresh proof of his affection, sent me by the hands of his valet, one Christopher Cannon a present of five shillings, no doubt to bear my expenses down to Plymouth, in the same proportion he extended his liberality to my sea-chest, which not being stored with one half the compliment usual on such occasions, would have proved quite insufficient, had it not been for the generosity and kindness of the captain, who, out of compassion, ordered his own tailor to furnish me with what was wanting.

During the short time I was on the watery element, I had twice the pleasure of seeing my country triumph in her native ocean, being present at the destruction of two French fleets in the same year, the first by those experienced commanders Lord Johnson and Sir Peter Warren and the second, by the never too much esteemed and gallant admiral Hawke.

As the defeat of those fleets, and the capture of so many fine ships, the distress of the Gallich [French] and the glory of the British flag, in that remarkable year, cannot be unknown to any of my readers, I shall set aside giving any account of those glorious actions, and proceed to myself.

On my return to England at the conclusion of the late general peace, being discharged from my ship, and desirous of giving the most early testimonies of my duty and obedience, I waited upon my father, and presented him with my letter of attorney, to receive my prize money, which amounted to a considerable sum, and frequently on my future visits, humbly entreated him to make some other provision for me.

Some time after, my father informed me, he had procured me a berth, in the honourable East-India company, which he called a lieutenant of an India craft, and upon which station I was immediately to enter, but several circumstances which had lately occurred, giving me no small room to suspect the integrity of my father's intentions, and strongly pointing out to me, the necessity of the greatest circumspection: I had recourse to the advice of friends, who recommended it to me, to enquire into the nature of such a station, and the reality of my father's having procured it for me.

According I made application to some gentleman in the India House and quickly found the prudence of such precaution; being informed, I was to be enrolled by the fictitious name of Thomas Plunkett and in no other station, than that of Captain's servant as before, the astonishment of so dark a design in my own father, I may justly say, needs no description; for what had I not to apprehend, from so suspicious a circumstance: but, alas! this was only the prologue to such scenes of inhumanity, as no christian ear can hear without amazement, or story parallel. The strange name of Plunkett occasion'd the greatest confusion in my breast, a name I had never assumed, but on the contrary was an utter stranger to, except so far as knowing it to be the maiden name of my father's first lady. However, I resolved to conceal my apprehensions as much as possible, and only express my aversion to the voyage, and in the most humble manner entreated, he would be pleased to make some other provision for me, but finding my father inflexible in his resolution, and that I could promise myself but small success from my entreaties, I plainly acquainted him with the discovery I had made at the India-House and the information I had from thence received. Stung at the discovery, and looking upon his designs, at least for that time frustrated, he burst out into the extremist rage, denounced vengeance against me, for my disobedience as he termed it, banished me his presence, and charged me to approach him, or his house no more at my peril!

As soon as I was recover'd from the confusion this hard sentence plunged me in, I besought him to let me have part of my prize money, for my subsistence, but that, this inexorable parent also denied, alleging it was insufficient to repay the expenses, he had been at, in bringing me up; thus in a moment surrounded with penury and distress, without parent, without friend, exposed to the wide world, beset with ills, covered with misfortunes, and drove by a torrent of despair; what could I do? I had heard that his late royal highness the Prince of Wales tho' placed in too exalted a sphere to be acquainted with the common calamities and distresses of human nature, was possessed of a heart susceptible of every tender impression, and a ready hand always stretch'd out to raise up affliction from the dust, or succour with liberal bounty the pangs of unmerited distress; to him, my father being then steward of his household, I determined most humbly to address myself, and lay the detail of my sorrows at his feet, which I accordingly did, when his most royal highness, upon enquiry into the truth of my case, was most graciously pleased to order me an immediate supply, and also condescended to lay his commands on my father, to provide for me as in duty he ought. But my father was so greatly incensed at this application, that regardless of his royal injunctions, he was now resolved to set no bounds to his persecution.

I lodged at the George Inn in the Hay-Market when early one morning, who should pay me a visit but my quondam friend the perriwig-maker; a man dedicated to my father's purposes, and made use of by him, as an instrument to execute his unnatural designs upon his own child. This humane gentleman, covering his fraudulent intent under the cloak of friendship, after passing the common salutation, told me the purpose of his coming was to acquaint me, that Tiberius in person intended to call upon me at eleven, and that he certainly had something in view, very advantageous to my interest, which would then be communicated, so desired me not to be absent at the time appointed. Highly animated with so uncommon a mark of my father's kindness, my bosom glowed with gratitude, and I ardently wished for the hour that would permit me at his feet to implore his pity, and ask his benediction; the long expected hour at length arrived, and every moment increased my anxiety; the rapturous tumult which agitated my mind, at the hopes of meeting, so unexpectedly meeting, a kind relenting parent, far exceeds the description of the most fervent pen, and nothing but the indelible characters which nature hath stamped upon the human soul, can possibly give a true idea of. As I sat in my window, with a soul full of expectation, my heart rebounded at the sound of every coach, and my eyes were attentively fix'd upon the remotest chair in view; the sound of a person enquiring for Nugenius at length struck my ears. I hurried down stairs, and the sight of a great bluff fellow, with an iron countenance, struck an immediate damp all over me.

'Where is the gentleman that is Nugenius?' was answered from the bar, 'then. Sir, I have some business with you, a letter, Sir' and calling me into the entry,

'A gentleman whom you claim a near relation to,' says he, with a ghastly smile, 'sends you this letter,' which drawing forth from a greasy pocket book, he added, 'is without farther ceremony neither more nor less than a warrant; you must go along with me this instant before Justice Fielding.'

Incapable of answering, I was dragged through the public streets in an inhuman manner, to the magistrates house in Bow-street, Covent Garden; the justice was no sooner informed of my being there, than a messenger was sent to acquaint my father, who immediately attended; on his arrival, I was directly ordered in, which order was countermanded till a conference was ended, which my father had desired; at length being ordered admittance, I was thus addressed by his worship:–

'How come you. Sir, to be troublesome to this gentleman?'

In the midst of my confusion I replied, 'he was my father, and hope he will be kind enough to do something for me, so far as to relieve me from my present distress.'

Whereupon my father turning short to the justice, he said, 'Sir, 'twill be better to send the fellow to Bridewell, than be troubled with his impertinence.'

Terrified with the dread of a prison, I fell on my knees and offered to comply with anything that should be proposed; my father then applying himself to Mr. Fielding, said,

'I am eternally teased both in public and in private about him; and never shall be at ease, till he is locked up,' adding in the most unbecoming language, 'those B — ch's of Quality, either feel for him, or pretend to do so, to such a degree that the perpetual alaram now sounds in my ear'

The justice casting his eyes upon me, seeming to be mov'd, expressed some signs of lenity and compassion; and the whole tenor of my father's actions towards me, which encouraged by him, I gave a full account of, appearing perfectly cruel and inhuman, not only he, but several other gentlemen then present, generously became intercessors with my father in my behalf, whereupon he proposed giving me ten pounds, upon condition I should go instantly to Ireland, where he agreed to remit me the same sum annually, for four years to come, but that I should in their presence execute a bond for the whole fifty pounds. To this I agreed, received the ten pounds, and executed the bond in the penalty of one hundred pounds, with a special covenant for my immediate departure, which when I signed Nugenius he struck out, and obliged me to sign by the feigned name of Thomas Plunkett though the justice was kind enough to remonstrate with him upon that head, by reason that the warrant had been filled up with Nugenius, but in vain.

Being by this means delivered from the warrant; pursuant to the engagement in a few days I embarked for Ireland, comforting myself with the hopes of a better fortune, and that by my industry and application in some business or other, I might be able to secure a decent support, the aforesaid allowance had it been paid me, being barely sufficient to keep me from starving.

On my arrival in Ireland I immediately addressed myself to all those, from whose generosity or compassion I could hope the least favour or assistance, informed them of my earnest desire of entering into some business, and it was no small consolation to me, to find my intentions approved, and amongst others, the honourable colonel MacGuire, a relation of my mother's, assisted me in a particular manner, to get the better of my misfortunes, by procuring me a handsome largess from my mother; which out of his own bounty he increased to a sum of thirty pounds.

I had likewise about this time, the happiness of meeting with my old friend, Mr. Bond, at the Globe Coffee-House in Essex-street, Dublin, whose humane regards to me I can never sufficiently acknowledge, to whom I related the barbarous treatment I had met with in London which he heard not without amazement. By his advice, I made it my business to look for a shop, properly situated for the sale of groceries in Dame-street.

I soon found one fit for the purpose. I acquainted Mr. Bond

therewith, who was so kind as to recommend me to the notice of Mr. Brennan, a merchant in Aungier-street; the money I now was possessed of amounting through the bounty of Mr. Bond, to almost forty pounds, was laid out in repairing the shop, and the remaining part was expended in purchasing my stock, Mr. Brennan generously giving me credit for as much more.

Being thus placed behind my compter, my thoughts began to stream in a different current: I flattered myself, by an assiduous application to my business, I might acquire a comfortable support, not doubting but absence, and the insignificant charge I should now be to my father, was he to perform his engagements in the annual allowance, might rid me of all apprehensions for the future, of farther cruelties from his hands; and who would not have entertained the same opinion? But how insatiable is a persecuting spirit: no testimonies of an industrious disposition, nor the laudable desire of endeavouring, by assiduously prosecuting the business of my little shop, to be capable of supporting myself, could protect me from my father's restless malice, which now began its rapid progress.

About three weeks after I was settled in business, two ill looking men came into my shop, and asking for some brandy, were no sooner served, than one of them said,

'I suppose, Sir, your name is Nugenius.'

I answered in the affirmative.

'I shall make bold to chance it then by virtue of a writ,' which being immediately produced, struck me with such amazement that I lost the use of speech for some time.

'You don't know one Tiberius Magnus,' continued he, at the same time pointing to where the name was wrote, 'nor you don't remember the fifty pounds you borrowed and then ran away with. No, no, you don't remember all this, to be sure?'

I answered, 'I hope, gentlemen, my father did not order you to abuse me in the execution of your office.'

'Arrah by my shoul, but you are not your father's son,' wisely returned the other, 'for your name is Plunkett, but what matters all this jaw, come along, come along to your new lodging.'

I entreated earnestly for a few minutes to secure my books and shut up my shop, but was in most abusive language denied, one of the inhumane catchpoles seizing me by the collar, would not permit me even to take what little money I had in my till, but dragged me without ceremony, to that mansion of wretchedness, the Black Dog Prison; the bond which I executed before the justice in London being the instrument made use of to lodge me in this dismal place, it having been in Dublin as long as myself.

Resolved to act with the utmost honour I directly sent an account to Mr. Brennan the merchant, of the sad reverse in my affairs, desiring he would sell all my effects, pay himself the sum he had so kindly gave me credit for, and return the balance to me; all which he performed, and justly accounted with me, nor did his favours stop here, for I daily experienced them during my confinement.

Eight months did I pass away in this gaol, liberty appearing in the same point of view as at first, abandoned by my relations, I had almost said by hope itself, the last resource of wretchedness, and in the most destitute and abject condition; when it pleased Almighty Goodness to look down upon my distress, and to take away from the weight of my oppression, by inspiring the hearts of a noble earl, and an honourable lady, to compassionate my sufferings, and extricate me from this abyss of misery; in short.

They most generously enabled me to give bail for the action, of which intention, I no sooner gave notice of, according to the due course of the law, to Mr. Brady the attorney, culled out by my father as most proper to conduct these proceedings. O might the gain of such honour be the only reward of such pains: but he the more effectually to recommend himself to his employer, by further oppressing the oppressed, charged me with a second action, of one hundred pounds, being the penalty of the said bond, wickedly imagining though I might find bail for fifty, I could not for a hundred and fifty; but this was too flagrant an instance of cruelty to deter my generous friends from their charitable design, who persisting in their compassionate resolutions, I was at length by their means, once more restored to liberty.

About two days after my release from confinement, I accidentally met my father's agent at the Globe Coffee-House in Dublin, with whom I remonstrated on my father's proceedings against me, the unparalell'd cruelty of barbarously and unjustly throwing me into a gaol, when I was in a capacity genteely to have supported myself, without any further application to him; and by being then, though out of prison, still destitute of every means of support.

This gentleman, seeing me at liberty, and sensible should I contest that bond, on which I had been detained, I should certainly succeed, and imagining he could not more easily gain my father's esteem (being no stranger to his cruel disposition) than by displaying his art in contriving some further means of oppressing me, hit upon the following method: he affected a great concern at my sufferings, and made a voluntary offset of his utmost services, confessed the treatment I had met with was really very hard, and expressed an inclination to assist me with a sum of money, could he but form to himself a probability of being repaid, and at length said he would venture to advance me ten pounds, and run the risque. But I replied, that sum would be of no service to me; that I owed some small matters which I was desirous of paying, and intended to embark for Bristol, in order to entreat the advice and assistance of my brother Tiberinus Nugenius [Col. Edmund Nugent, Robert Nugent's son by Emilia, daughter of the Earl of Fingal.] who I heard was then there. I was likewise in great want of apparel, therefore less than twenty pounds would not answer my ends; with little persuasion, this generous and humane gentleman complied, instigated by the father of hypocrisy and lies, artfully to conceal under the cloak of humanity, designs of the blackest nature; not suspecting his diabolical intentions, and labouring under the greatest anxiety of mind, as well as the most pinching necessity, I was induced to accept this pernicious offer, and executed a bond for the same, in which was inserted a penalty of one thousand pounds. This bond he immediately transmitted to my father in England to be ready for the intended purpose of immuring me again in prison at his pleasure.

Having received this money, paid my few debts, and provided myself with some necessaries, I embarked for the city of Bristol and on my arrival there, I waited on my brother, to whom I related my sufferings, and entreated his good offices with my father, for obtaining me a restoration to his favour, not being conscious of having forfeited it any otherwise, than by declining his proposal to go to the East Indies and by petitioning his royal highness, the Prince of Wales in my great distress, and if these were crimes, they were such only as real distress had occasioned, though I had been persecuted for them with relentless fury; therefore earnestly hoped a brother's sufferings would meet pity, – but alas! How greatly was I disappointed. Pity and compassion were banished his breast, and his behaviour proved him an entire stranger to the common principles of humanity.

Our first meeting was attended with pretty high words; however, he at length condescended so far as to bid me call on him the next day; accordingly in the morning I waited upon him.

He sent for me up stairs, being yet in bed, though the sun had already gained his highest ascent; he threw open the curtains, and I was immediately complimented with

'How come you, Sir, to be troublesome so early?'

'I thought, Sir, you ordered me to wait upon you this morning.'

'What if I did,' says he, 'is that a reason why you should hunt me before I am out of bed, what do you want, what do you plague me for?'

'Sir,' I replied, 'setting aside the ties of affinity, which you are pleased to deny, though all the rhetoric you are master of will never be able to overpower truth, or persuade the world one man is not our father; let the force of humanity plead for me, stand betwixt me and my father's anger, mitigate his wrath, and let me not be tossed about the world destitute of support, and have no place to lay my head. If not to me, be just at least to your father and yourself; prevent the world from censuring.'

I was proceeding in this manner, but was interrupted with,

'No Methodist sermon, no preaching: Oon's, what would the man have?'

'What is not, Sir, in your power to give, humane usage.'

'I think I am overstocked both with humanity and patience, to hear a detail of such stuff; but I suppose the truth is you come upon the old errand you have so often seized my father with; money, friend, money: now for a modest request, how much want you?'

'Sir, it is too true, I have no money to carry me up to London, what you think proper for that purpose, will do me at present the greatest service.'

'Tom, give him pen and ink; write a receipt, friend.'

'For what sum. Sir?'

'Stay now, I think better of it, I will do it myself, give me the paper,' he wrote upon the pillow, and delivered it to me to sign.

I read as follows, 'I promise to pay to Tiberinus Nugenius or order, on demand, the sum of one guinea for value received.'

I took no notice of this amazing sum, but cooly taking up the pen, set my name to the paper, then taking up the piece betwixt my finger and thumb, I said,

'This, sir, I shall take care to preserve as a perpetual memorandum of paternal affection, and to what an excess of liberality the force of humanity is capable of urging such a tender hearted man as my brother Tiberinus.'

I said no more, but turning short, left the room without any further ceremony.

He wrote an account to my father in London by the next post, of my being in Bristol and the usage he had met with from me. The bond he had received from Ireland was immediately transmitted to Tiberinus with a writ thereupon against me in the penalty of one thousand pounds, on non payment; and the cup of my afflictions not being by him thought full enough, another gaol was now to be my portion. But as if by being conducted to prison in the ordinary manner was not enough to satisfy the most implacable malice, my good brother, willing to recommend himself to my father by some distinguishing act of inhumanity, condescended to perform the office of a bailiff's setter, in the following manner: a few mornings after our aforesaid conference; as I was walking solitarily towards the Hot-Wells musing upon my melancholy situation, I unexpectedly met in the road my evil genius; he checked his reins upon sight of me, and called me to him.

'Hark you. Sir,' says he, 'meet me at the breakfasting room, about ten o'clock to-morrow, and you shall hear something to your advantage; be sure you fail not being there at the time, because I am obliged to attend business in another place before eleven.'

I promised to be punctual, and he spurred on.

The next morning I failed not my appointment, where I met him according to promise; he retired along with me into a private room, and called for two dishes of coffee; the discourse at length settling upon the old affair, his base innuendoes, and indecent reflections on my mother, compelled some warm words from me. Seeming stung with the smartness of one of my answers, he took the opportunity of rising up, and striking the table with great violence, in an elevated voice, said,

'Then, you rascal, if nothing can tame you, but confinement, you shall have sufficient of it,' at which instant the door opening, Mr. Rhodes the bailiff attended by one of his followers came in, and laid hold of me. Several gentlemen who were in the adjacent rooms, upon hearing the bustle we now made, entered our apartment, and enquiring into the cause of the disturbance, my brother replied,

'An insolent rascal I have laid by the heels for a small action of a thousand pounds, is become obstreperous; take the fellow away, officer, take him away.'

'Fve fve,' said a gentleman, which if I rightly remember, was Mr. Crosby addressing himself to my brother, 'if you won't relieve the poor young fellow, don't use him in this barbarous manner.'

'Tell me not, Sir, of barbarity, the villain ought to be gibbeted alive, for imposing himself upon the public as my brother.'

'Brother or not brother, he is your very picture by G — d,' returned Mr. Crosby 'and I would at least have so much regard for a glass that represented me in such perfection, as not to destroy it.' 'You are at will to jest, Mr. Crosby, as much as you please, but I have my father's express commands for what I do, and sink me, but to gaol he shall go, should all the world intercede for him.'

'But in what light must the public look upon you, Nugenius, if you descend so low as to personate the vile character of a bailiff's follower?' said one Mr. Lynch who was now one of the crowd, 'retrieve this false step, and let the young man go about his business. Let him go, officer.'

'That. Sir, I cannot do,' said Mr. Rhodes who had hold of me still, 'but if Nugenius says the word, in presence of all these worthy gentlemen, I will with the greatest pleasure release him, and ask nothing for my trouble, for by G — d the writ would have laid dormant in my pocket these seven years had not he compelled me to do my office, by setting the man himself.'

'You are an insolent rascal,' replied my brother, 'and deserve to be well caned.' –

'The rascal you may take to yourself, and as to the caning part, I wish you had courage to attempt it.'

During this altercation, I sat drowned in tears, confused, and even stupefied at the sudden stroke, when one of the gentlemen coming to me, kindly asked me if I had any money, which I answering in the negative, he applied himself to my compassionate kinsman, in this manner

'Nugenius, the unhappy young fellow is destitute of cash, I hope you intend not to add to your inhumanity, by sending him penniless to so dismal a place. Mr. Rhodes be so good as to inform the young gentleman, what money will be wanted to keep the poor man from starving.'

'Let him starve and be damn'd,' was returned, –

'And without money,' replies the officer, 'starve he must, and worse damn'd he cannot be than when he finds himself at his entrance into prison, surrounded by a group of meagre wretches, demanding the tribute of five shillings for what they call garnish, it being customary to make a deposit of that directly, part of which is applied to the purchase of coals, and the remainder to allay the drought of throats seldom gratified with any thing superior to simple element. If the money is not paid, he certainly undergoes the ceremony of stripping, and is left to starve without pity, and without redress; neither is there in this place any allowance of bread, so usual in other prisons.'

The standers by were all affected with a sense of the miseries I was doomed to suffer: no entreaties were wanting, but all in vain; for the boisterous sea in the rage of hurricanes might sooner be supplicated to listen to the prayers of sinking navigators than this inhuman composition of pride, cruelty and malice be persuaded to turn an ear, to the dictates of pity and compassion. The gentlemen, to crown all their favours, generously made a collection for me, to which this humane officer, who had me in his charge, contributed half a guinea. I mention this with more pleasure, as there are but few instances of such humanity to be found in people of his station. We set out soon after for Gloucester, where I was resigned up the following evening to the care of Mr. Benjamin Hemmings, keeper of the castle.

Thus the reader finds me once more plunged in the horrors of a gaol, and surrounded with circumstances of the deepest distress; for after the consumption of the small sum I had received from the benevolence of the gentleman at the Hot-Wells I must inevitably have perished for want, had not the report of such unprecedented cruelties spread itself abroad, and excited the compassion of the benevolent and humane, for whose benign regards, I here must humbly beg leave to return my most grateful acknowledgements. Impelled by a sense of the greatest duty, in silent respect, I forbear to mention here, whose elevated rank and dignity strikes with awe, and whose innumerable virtues attract at once the love and respect of all mankind. Not under the same embarrassment to the rest of my generous benefactors Rowland Pitt, Esq; of the city of Gloucester, for his frequent favours, and likewise to Mrs. Owen, a lady of fortune in the same city, who not only clothed me, when I was almost naked, and preserved me from the fangs of pinching necessity, but became a generous intercessor with my father, in my behalf, though to little purpose.

The eight months of melancholy wretchedness I spent in this place, would have been equal in distress, to what I experienced during my confinement in the Black-Dog prison in Dublin had not an accident happened, which ingratiated me to Mr. Hemmings the keeper. The felons in this prison, by some remissness in the legislature, too frequent in most of the country gaols in this kingdom, are permitted the same liberty with the unhappy people confined for debt, and the benefit of the same yard is promiscuously enjoyed by both in the day-time, and not till nine in the evening are they locked up in their distinct ward. At which time a great brindled mastiff, a constant attendant of the turnkey, marches in a stately manner before him, with the massy keys, that command the entrance of those infernal mansions held in his fatal jaws, which his master, armed with a great oak sapling, when arrived at the ponderous door, demands the suppliant minister to deliver up; the necessary duty being performed, Cerberus immediately retires to his den, and his master to rest.

It happened one evening, the felons under sentence of transportation, having concerted a scheme to make their escape, were then about to put it in execution, to which purpose several had freed themselves from their fetters: their intent was when Bedal the turnkey came at the lock-up hour to secure them, to knock him down with the billets, (made use of for firing) and seize upon the keys. A dispute arising amongst them, just at the critical moment, and increasing to high words, was luckily overheard by some of the debtors, who on the instant came and acquainted Mr. Bedal of the same. He called immediately three or four of us to his assistance, and armed with cutlasses and bludgeons, Cerberus alias Lion leading the van, we soon quelled the desperate villains, though not till several wounds were distributed amongst them, and the dog seizing one, had very nigh tore out his throat.

My behaviour in this action recommended me to the favour of Mr. Hemmings who industriously applied himself to do me all the service in his power, would frequently indulge me with a walk in his bowling-green, gained me the notice of several people of quality, and whenever greatly distressed, would freely advance me small sums of money.

The general election of the city of Bristol now approaching, my father, who intended to appear a candidate, apprehending such a scene of continued tyranny to his own son, would by no means be favourable to him, in so critical a juncture; and not caring to have his unnatural proceedings laid open to the world, thought it necessary to change his plan, and instead of starving me in a prison, designed now to transport me.

This black design, through the merciful interposition of providence, was rendered abortive by my timely escape at the very juncture, when all things were in readiness to put it into execution.

A bond with a warrant of attorney, to confess a judgment in the penalty of six hundred and twenty pounds payable to my father, with a special covenant to indent myself to go abroad for several years, was transmitted by Mr Cox, my father's London solicitor, to Gloucester and forwarded to me in that castle of famine, with a generous offer of my liberty once more, provided I would execute the same, by the favourite fictitious name of Thomas Plunkett.

This was but cold comfort, being still uncertain as to my destined fate, but conscious of my inabilities to cope with so powerful an adversary, and wearied of being thus immured in gaols, I determined to get my liberty at any rate, and as soon as possible embrace the first opportunity of making my escape to France where I was in hopes of getting introduced to a near relation of my mother's, Ignatius Nugenius who at that time commanded in the French king's service, as a general of horse, to whom I proposed relating my sufferings, and doubted not finding a kind reception, or at least an asylum from the persecuting hand of a barbarous parent.

Accordingly, I acquiesced with the proposal, and was promised to be fitted out with apparel to the amount of £25, though the only articles I received was a coat and a pair of breeches, but as it was judged proper to have an attorney present on my part, in order to render their proceedings the more effectual in law, one Mr. Driver, a gentleman of fair character in that profession, was pitched upon, to act for me in this affair, which he at first strenuously opposed, declaring, from his knowledge, it was a transaction of the basest kind.

But the agent on behalf of my father, urging my consent, and putting the best face on this bad cause, at length found means to prevail upon him to do it, though Mr. Benjamin Hemmings the gaoler could by no means be prevailed upon to witness what he called so iniquitous a proceeding.

By this means, I once more turned my back on a prison, though with a mind totally confused, from the information I had received, of the plot laid for me, from which I earnestly besought the merciful disposer of all events to deliver me.

My design of going to Ignatius Nugenius, I had inadvertently communicated to my brother, who from the malignity of his heart, had carefully sent word of it to my father, and he, sensible how greatly all my mother's family resented the dishonour he had brought upon her and them, which had expelled him [from]

Ireland, could by no means relish that thought, and therefore Irenius Arrus, of Bristol, being then a superior magistrate of the county, was commissioned to prevent my intentions, by conducting the new-scheme as follows.

After I had signed the indenture, in which I bound myself for several years to serve one Capt. MacKenzie who was only master of a little Maryland trader, and being possessed of no property in America could not have any other view of making me turn out to his profit, than by exposing me to public sale; conscious of this, I made it my study to elude the wicked design.

As soon as I was discharged, three men were employed to escort me to Bristol where the moment I arrived, I was to be put on board, and without farther delay conveyed abroad; these ruffians were, a servant belonging to Irenius Arrus, one of Mr. Wades', my father's attorney in Bristol, and to complete the triumvirate, a bailiff's follower. Attended by these my honourable guardians, I set out from Gloucester.

I took particular care that my behaviour on the road might be such as to give no suspicion, that the villains might not entertain any apprehensions whatever. When arrived near our journey's end, I thought it proper to execute my design: strict orders, as I had been informed by some friends in Gloucester, had been given to this diabolical crew, to encourage me in drinking as much as possible. Aware of this design, I made it my endeavours to turn the scales upon them, which with a little art I affected.

At our entrance into Bristol, feigning myself very sick, this served me as an excuse for calling at the Edinburgh Castle, a house I had formerly been acquainted with. As soon as I alighted, I made it my care to complete their dose; my sickness increasing, I desired the favour of laying down for an hour or two, which they, having no suspicion of my design, readily granted. When retired to my chamber, I called up the landlord, and related to him my unfortunate situation; he was so honest, though employ'd at this time in keeping open house for my father, on account of the ensuing election, as to say,

'Sir, I have no charge over you, so consequently it would be illegal in me to offer to detain you, my doors are open.' – I took the hint, and slipping down stairs, left my guard in the lurch, and with the utmost expedition, made the best of my way to Mr. Charles Gordon at the Golden Ball in Wine-Street, where I had been directed.

Here I was inform'd, that at a certain attorney's house in Wine-Street where it had been concerted my trusty overseers should conduct me, a party of sea lambs, belonging to one Green a purveyor of transports, whose vessel was prepared to give me due reception, that very evening were lying in wait.

Overjoy'd at this eminent escape, I looked upon my present situation as an asylum, to secure me from surrounding dangers, and retired with great satisfaction to repose. Irenius Arrus, to reward his servant for his over abundant care and circumspection, discharged him the following day, and the fellow lives now at Bath.

How far this magistrate, or any of his friends, can reconcile these proceedings to the character of a good man, I leave the world to judge. But it is certain, by these means he thought the more effectually to gain the affection of my oppressor, for whose interest he was a great stickler. Here I would advise this gentleman, if he has any regard for his future welfare, in the most conspicuous part of his house, to have wrote in large Capitals the saying of a truly wise man, viz. 'Innocence though connected with misery is infinitely preferable to guilt and grandeur'. – This being perpetually in his eye, might one time or other strike his attention, when the parallel, so obvious betwixt him and me in that golden sentence, would perhaps be a means to point out his errors, and reclaim a lost sheep to its native fold.

But to proceed, the better to secure myself from any future attempts, and induced with the hopes of raising some friend, who might be able to protect me against their iniquitous schemes, I determined immediately publishing the hardships of my case; being urged the more to this last resource, upon account of writs having been absolutely issued out, and dispatched to all the sea port towns to prevent my getting away.

Here, methinks, I see the reader in amazement lift up his hands: was ever implacable anger carried before to such industrious lengths! is this the anger of a father to his child? – no, it seems rather relentless justice persecuting with iron hands, in the severest manner, rapes, murders, felony, and treason. It is not, it cannot be that ever parental ire, should be carried to such extremes against the issue of his own bowels – compelled by famine to commit the few errors he is charged with. But say, generous reader, how great the error? How weighty the crime? To look up to the authors of our being for subsistence, how aggravating the guilt, to ask support, from a parent whose innumerable servants sit round tables of plenty, the crumbs of which are denied to his own child? And yet, that this is the sole fault for which I have hitherto suffered, bewitness persecution, and malice in spite of thyself give evidence to.

My mother's family at this time were so highly incensed at my father's most ungenerous treatment of her, they would by no means permit her to countenance, what they looked upon as a living monument of their disgrace; and indeed, she being now connected to the interest of another family by marriage, it was not to be expected she should much more concern herself about me; knowing at the same time, how far my father's abilities were capable of advancing me, without either prejudice to himself, or any one else of his family; thus I fell a sacrifice to the carelessness of the one, and the tyranny of the other.

In short, I make no doubt, it will appear to the public, as well as myself, my father's sole intention was, and is nothing less than my destruction. Otherwise, as he knew my design to go over to France what reason can be assigned for his taking so much pains to obstruct me; but hitherto by the signal interposition of providence, I have escaped the fatal snare, preserved as yet from the secret perils of salt-water, the ravenous hunger of destroying sharks, and worse than these the shackles of endless slavery.

I was obliged during my stay at Bristol to confine myself to my room, officers of all denominations being employ'd to watch the door day and night, and all the avenues round, were kept secretly, though strictly guarded, as I found any attempt towards an escape was impracticable, I never endeavoured it, but made myself as easy as my present melancholy circumstances would permit.

As I had no other choice now, I set about writing an abstract of my case, with a fixed resolution to publish it without delay: my father being informed of my intentions, and not choosing the world should at this critical time, when every art is made use of, and the complicated force of bribes and flattery are thought insufficient to gain the unsteady multitude, be acquainted with his unnatural proceedings, and conscious it would give the opposite party the greatest satisfaction to expose his barbarity, and open the eyes of the public, in regard to a man they had fixed upon, as the most proper to execute an office of the highest trust, which likewise at the same time is one of the greatest honours capable of being conferred upon a subject. Being conscious, I say, of the difficulties he must lie under, should this dreaded case be published, he contrived every artifice, that subtlety and invention could put in practice to prevent it. Menaces and flattery were alternately made use of: to-day his emissaries breathed out the language of persecution, and nothing less than Newgate was to be my perpetual doom; to-morrow the scene was changed, and mountains were promised, which the successive day saw dwindle into molehills.

One day a certain gentleman of the broad-brim fraternity, vulgarly called quakers, was ushered into my chamber, and being seated:

'Friend,' says he, 'humanity and a desire to bring into the path of life a stray sheep, induceth me to call upon thee, that if possible I might open the ears of thy understanding, to the end that the light of the spirit might be admitted to operate upon thee, and thou shouldest become a new man.' – admiring so uncommon an introduction, with great civility I desired him to proceed, –

'Rebellion and disobedience to our superiors, will be punished in the regions of darkness. In the regions of darkness will they be chastised, where is weeping and wailing, and gnashing of teeth, and though thou deckest thy face in smiles, such as the prophane smileth, yet it behoveth me, to say unto thee, as Nathan said unto David, thou art the man' – after a sigh was continued,

'Friend, thou hast abused the ears of this city, moved thereunto by the father of lies, the ears of this city hast thou abused; thou hast sounded the trumpet of sedition, and division is scattered abroad, be no more as one of the wicked, take not thee part with the sons of Belial, but let the spirit hatch the seeds of truth, and thou shalt flourish, as flourisheth the godly.'

'I am afraid, Sir,' said I, 'it is the spirit of gold, not the spirit of godliness, to which I am indebted for this charitable visit.'

'Friend, friend, be not thou as the prophane one is, who stoppeth his ears to council, and sitteth in the chair of folly; for verily it is said, thou hast rebelled against thy father, who begot thee, yea, thou hast set thyself up against thy own flesh and blood, and evil, I say unto thee, evil must proceed there-from.'

Here a considerable pause ensuing,

'Sir,' said I, 'if compelled by hunger, my asking for bread may be termed rebellion, then have I rebelled, if endeavouring to fly from an implacable parent, to avoid the efforts of relentless tyranny, by seeking an asylum in a foreign country is disobedience, then I have disobeyed, but without farther prolixity, pray what have I to expect from a visit introduced in so uncommon a manner?'

To which was answered,

'I visit thee as Noah's dove visited the ark, verily I bring an olive branch as an overture of peace,' – here drawing a green purse from his pocket, he seemed to eye it attentively, though his looks denoted at the same time no great propensity to part with it.

'I will not say, friend, but I have orders,' continued he, 'to offer thee some pieces, wouldest thou hearken to proposals intended solely for thy benefit; four guineas will carry thee to the great city, and thou wilt have sufficient thereof remaining to answer all thy purposes until time shall come, when thou shalt be amply provided for; yea, and I say unto thee, that time is nearer at hand than thou devisest.'

'Sir,' said I, 'I am not willing to be an instrument employed to prejudice my father in any scheme he is bent to execute, but what security have I to depend upon, should I accept of your offer, which you may be certain I will not, or for your performance of what you promise, nay, what is it you promise or how shall I be provided for?'

To which, after some time spent in rectifying his starch band, Aminadab answered,

'Friend, thou art as one of the unthinking ones are, thou

shuttest thine ears to reason: O! may the thick darkness thou art involved in be dispersed, and the light internal shine upon thy understanding, and direct thee to walk in the right way. Haddest thou been attentive to what I said, thy intellects must have told thee, the rod of chastisement is withdrawn, and rebuke shall no more frown upon thee; here is three times more than sufficient to defray thy road expences, a great deal of money, friend, verily a great deal, if thou makest proper use of it,' telling out at the same time five guineas very deliberately upon the table, –

'What remaineth in thy pocket, will keep thee handsomely till thy father cometh up, who will without delay, he promises by me, procure thee some profitable employment under the government; yea verily, and something within whispereth me thou shalt in a little time become a great man.'

In short, not to fatigue the reader any more with a dull recital of what passed betwixt the sanctified surgeon and myself, the following day he agreed to make me a present of six guineas, to discharge whatever I owed to the landlord of the house, to give me security I should not be molested in any shape whatever, provided I would depart the city of Bristol the next day, and leave an instrument along with him, testifying my resolution to prosecute the author or authors of any pamphlet, bold enough to prefix my name thereto.

I blush to record my weakness, flattering myself with the hopes that my father would be pleased, at my entering so readily into his proposals, and fulfil the promise made by his agent, I accepted the terms, and once more fell into the snare prepared for me some time before: the next morning; early, I set out for London on foot, being determined to spin out my money to the greatest length, where in four days I arrived, nothing remarkable interv'ening during my journey.

In this manner having regained my liberty, and reflecting upon the danger I had escaped, my father's restless cruelty, and my brother's base behaviour; I found there was still no little reason to suspect the promises lately made, of procuring me a place in some of the public offices, so I resolved to keep myself as secure as possible, from any plot which now might be hatching against me. Till I had determined how to proceed, I procured lodgings in the most secret manner, at an Irish house in Princess-street, Leicester-Fields, the master of which I had formerly known, and knew I could confide in.

What little money I had to spare, was expended in purchasing upon some decent apparel, which I now greatly wanted, intending my father's arrival in town, to address him in the most dutiful and submissive manner, my design being to remind him of his promise made by the quaker –, and by testifying with the utmost humility my filial duty and respect, endeavour, if not to gain his esteem, at least to soften his resentment. If I should fail in that, my resolution was to retire without loss of time to France, being assisted in that design by a gentleman, whose sincere regard, and tender affection, will always be imprinted within my breast; gratitude for the kind reception, and generous assistance, I met with from his hands, compels me to cast a veil over that dear name, the beloved owner of which might tyrannically be persecuted upon my account.

I was not only furnished by him with ten guineas, and cloths to appear before the great man I now intended to seek relief from, but also provided with letters of recommendation, necessary for my introduction. To be brief, I looked upon the eve of my happiness to be as now arrived, a seat in the Dover coach was already took, and I scarcely imagined myself upon English ground; but alas! how soon were all my golden hopes blasted.

The morning before my intended departure, I was dodged from a friend's house in Leicester Fields to the George-Inn in the Haymarket by a couple of hell-hounds, attended by the clerk of an honest lawyer in Pater-noster-row, together with a servant of my humane father's, and was now apprehended by virtue of the last bond of six hundred and twenty pounds, with an execution tacked to the back of it; and being thrust immediately into a hackney coach, away jumble I and the fiends to the catch-pole's den in the Strand.

O reader, if ever thou was't unhappy enough to be involved in misfortunes, no doubt thou must have heard of this insatiable harpy, who had me now in his clutches, but to give thee at once a just idea of him, his name will be sufficient, and that is Randal.

The vicissitudes of human life, and the sudden transitions from wealth to poverty, from plenty to penury, make it not unreasonable in this place to entertain the public with a brief description of that infernal mansion, called a sponging house.

Whoever thou art that runs over these pages, may peace, plenty and happiness still wait upon thy steps, may'st thou enjoy a perpetual elysium in the arms of a faithful consort, and thy blooming off-spring live upon thy smiles, O may never a reverse of fortune snatch thee from every domestic joy, to this den of woe, whose fatal threshold pass'd. O! for a draught of Lethe to sink past scenes in oblivion, and deprive thee of all sensation; here, here, is the touchstone of friendship; ye time-serving crew, who feasted at my table, whose wine it was that nightly deprived you of your cares, when the festal bowl went gayly round, how lavish were ye, your fortunes and yourselves were freely offered, why suddenly so parsimonious; thou possessed of twice ten thousand, who hast experienced my liberal purse, more than once in time of almost need; my substance is abroad, till that returns, be my bail for this three hundred? Grant me patience! am I refused, monstrous villain! – be not amazed, try others, – deceived again! – The circle which but just now appeared crowded with friends, by applying the magnet of adversity is suddenly vanished.

The coach in which the unhappy wretch is carried to this house of slaughter, being ordered to draw up, he is pushed headlong out into a room, the doors and windows of which are trebly guarded with iron bars, here in all probability he is received by three or four brothers of misfortune, and after having for a while stupidly gazed at each other, he is perhaps invited to sit down, silence and sorrow swell up the short interval betwixt this and dinner, which though none of the most delicate, is introduced by the great bashaw himself, who, big with his own superior worth, in great dignity seats himself at the head; the wife, as next in authority, places herself at his right hand, and a couple of hawk-ey'd setters take their decrees at his left.

And now if the unhappy sufferer hath any appetite, let him sit down and partake of the unsanctified meal, if not, expect the she tyrant to growl:

'Marry come up, some folks are hard to please, though may be such a table of their own never called them master; and though I say it, as should not say it, the best lord in the land does not provide better, for I carries the ready to market, and no one can say as I owe them a single farthing, no no, I'm not the body that runs in debt, and gives honest folk the trouble to come at their own.' –

'But my dear,' answers old dignity from his elbow chair, 'what signifies being so hard on the gentleman, when his gall is broke he will be more cheerful. Come, Mary, fill him up a glass of wine.'

Which if refused, as most likely it may, is immediately swallowed up, by some of this unfeeling crew, who seldom leave the table till four or five bottles are added to the reckoning, which when night arrives must be discharged. At which time all credit expires, and if the bill comes within the limits of eight, nine, or ten shillings, think it completely moderate.

The gaoler now waits to see each to his separate apartment, where scarcely time is permitted to undress, before the light is rudely took away, and the harmonious clangor of massy bolts and bars conclude the scene.

Left thus to meditate on the dismal change, grief and anxiety banish sleep, which otherwise might seal the drowsy eyelids in spight of bugs and a flock bed. The painful hours at length bring on the opening day, that with much difficulty penetrates through the numberless bars, which endeavour to obstruct it's grateful entrance. Starting from the couch of misery, tattered curtains, dusty hangings, half a table, and a broken chair, greet the eye; the damp walls here and there adorned with an old ballad, the babes in the wood, or perhaps a quaker sermon; the ten foot room with unwearied step is now from side to side alternately measured; day advances, and the attentive ears listen to every noise, whilst the eye reckons up the iron studs, which chequer in geometrical squares the impenetrable door.

An hour short of noon, liberty is permitted to descend, when the morose tyrant, the muscles of his face contracted in the sternest manner, thus at the stair foot salutes you:

'Well. Sir, the twenty four hours allowed by act of parliament is expired, I am told there is no prospect of making your affair up, the debt is large, and for my own security, I must call a coach and conduct you to Newgate.'

Be not astonished at the terrifying sound, but cross the monster's venal palm with half a piece, instantly the features relax, and the tone of his voice is soften'd:

'Why, sir,' says he, 'I am a gentleman as scorns to use a man ill; so be as you think to make matters up, stay here in god's name, and let me tell you, many a great man whose name's shall be hush, has spent a merry hour in my house; for though I say it a bottle of better wine is not to be found in London.'

With this item he leaves you assiduously to follow his daily destructive occupation, and now if neither bail or money can't be procured, nor the relentless creditors give an ear to composition, take without delay the benefit of the Habeas Corpus act, which at the expence of about four pounds, will remove you from this den of perdition, to whatever commodious prison you think proper to choose, the Fleet, and the King's Bench, being in such cases the sad alternative.

Give no ear to the catch-pole, or any of his emissaries, who as long as you spend profusely will use all their art to detain you, will daily flatter you with hopes of compromising your affairs, and invent a thousand lies to deceive you; but when your money is gone, the cloven hoof discovers itself, most base and injurious language is made use of, and the very first bill of extortion you are incapable to pay, sends you indeed to Newgate.

This was my unhappy case, the artful villain soon found I had money, which he resolved should in a little time revert to him; in consequence of which, I was kept in perpetual suspense. Hopes were given me to-day, which alas! the following day proved false. Three or four shillings were added every night to my bill, for porters that were never employ'd, and as much for liquor I never drank. In the space of ten or twelve days my pocket began to ebb, and I found myself reduced to a single guinea, with which when the subtle demon was acquainted,

'Ay,' says he, 'tomorrow I will carry you to Mr. Cox your father's attorney in Paternoster-row and make no doubt but we shall complete your business.'

The next morning a coach was called, which big with the sanguine thoughts of liberty, I immediately entered. When the coach stopped, this inhumane monster, who had by various artifices received near ten guineas from me, stepped out, and giving me his hand,

'Now Sir,' says he, 'let me congratulate you upon your arrival to this famous and celebrated castle, where you will receive more strict attendance than my poor hut was capable of giving you.' – Newgate with all it's horrors presented itself to my eyes, and I was now for a third time plunged into the inhospitable mansions of a gaol, and surrounded with anguish and despair.

A subscription was open'd for me, by means of which, I not only bade adieu to the horrors of Newgate and was preserved from perishing, but for my future support, was enabled to lay before the public a full account of all my sufferings, the publication of which, my father, and his subtle agents strenuously endeavoured to prevent. Threats, menaces, and all the vengeance of future law, was employed to deter the printers, publishers, &c., from daring to print or publish a single sheet in my favour, yet all in vain. The unfinished pamphlet found its way to the press, and though composed in the utmost hurry, and favourably received by the nobility and gentry, to whom for their generous reception of such a trifle, I return my sincerest acknowledgments, and my bosom glowing with gratitude, daily supplicates almighty goodness ten thousand fold, to reward those my generous benefactors, without whose humane assistance, the grave before now, must have put a period to my miseries.

By the advice of several friends I was now brought up to Guildhall to take the benefit of the late act of insolvency, but my father's inhumanity was now arrived at so great a pitch, nothing could deter him from appearing against me in the face of the whole court. As the day was uncertain, he had the displeasure of attending three or four different times, being determined not to miss his opportunity, yet in case the court should grant me liberty, which was unhappily for me, not in their power, and to put a finishing stroke to his barbarities, a gang of sailors were planted at the doors of the Hall to seize me as I should come out, and with the utmost expedition carry me on board a tender.

My schedule when called for being produced contained nothing but a list of two hundred books and pamphlets, intitled the unnatural father, and which indeed was the sum total of all my effects. The court now fixed their eyes upon this persecuting parent, whose blood mounted in his cheek, and for once his assurance failed him. Several knotty points were now discussed, but the bond which I had been so artfully induced to execute in Gloucester-Castle exceeding the sum mentioned by act of parliament, it was with the greatest reluctance, that the court remanded me back to prison, giving me the full allowance permitted by the act, which is seven shillings and six pence per week.

To the recorder and lord mayor, I am under the greatest obligations for the pity and compassion they were pleased to shew my hard case, and think it no less than my duty to return my sincerest thanks in this place for such their benign regards.

(Note: This clause in the act of Insolvency, which detains me now in prison, may not be disagreeable to the reader. –

"Provided always that this act shall not extend to discharge any persons out of prison, taking his or her discharge under this act, with respect to any debt which he or she shall stand charged at the suit of the crown, or shall be indebted to any body politic or corporate, or to any one person, in any sum exceeding the sum of £500, besides interest and cost, unless such body politic or corporate, or creditor, shall consent thereto. And if any such body politic or corporate, or creditor, to whom a sum exceeding £500 shall be owing, shall oppose the discharge of such prisoner and shall insist that such prisoner be continued in gaol and that then in such case, such body politic, or corporate, or creditor, opposing the said prisoner's discharge as aforesaid, shall at his, her or their proper cost and charges, allow, and pay such a weekly maintenance, to the said prisoner, not exceeding three shillings and six-pence per week, in such manner, as the justices in their general or quarter sessions shall order, and upon non payment of the same, for the space of six weeks, the said prisoner, upon application to the said justices in their general or quarter sessions as aforesaid, shall be discharged pursuant to the meaning and intent of this act.")

How I found myself for life fixed in a prison, and shut out from the most distant hopes of ever attaining future liberty, as my injust action will for life detain me in durance and my misery only be increased, should my fellow sufferers, by the intervening mercy of any future act be admitted to partake of those blessings, which through the means of parental tyranny, are alas! for ever denied to me.

My father having thus compleated my misery, things remained for a while in a state of inaction until some months ago, proposals were again made for sending me abroad. The first mover of which, like a snake in the grass artfully kept himself concealed, to the end, he might the more effectually seize his prey.

A certain gentleman, a namesake, and as he says a relation of my mother's, who has had the honour of bearing a militia colonel's commission in some part of the West Indies where I am informed he is possessed of a considerable estate, came in person to the Fleet and applying himself to a gentleman conversant in the law, who had some small acquaintance with me; under the sanction of humanity and goodwill introduced himself in the following manner,

'Sir, I am informed an unhappy young fellow, the son of a near relation of mine, whose name is Nugenius, has been for sometime confined in this place. As I have the greatest regard for his mother, my endeavours shall not be wanting to get him out, my proposals I shall leave with you, to whom I have been particularly recommended, which you at leisure may communicate to him; tell him if he agrees thereto, I will out of my own pocket discharge his debt of six hundred and twenty pounds, together with costs, and according to his behaviour he may expect future favours.'

After he was gone the counsellor sent for me into the Coffee-room the uncommon news gave me no small transports, but how was that chilled, when I was acquainted with the heads of the proposals, and the unartful mask fell at my feet. I was in the first plan to indent myself for four years, to serve him upon a plantation of his, in the island of Santa Cruz; which by the by is a

Danish settlement, my salary to be twenty pounds per annum. I was to enter into a bond with a thousands [sic] penalty, never to use the name, which by the laws of my country I am entitled to, nor to return during the space of four years to England, nor ever be any more troublesome to Tiberius or his family. I was not to have either money or clothes till they had got me on board.

In consideration of agreeing to these articles, I was to receive fifty pounds when arrived in the West Indies, he, the colonel, was to pay my debts in the prison which might amount to about fifteen or twenty pounds, and likewise to provide me with all the suitable apparel. But observe the money which he laid out to pay my debts contracted in prison, and to furnish me with clothes, was to be deducted from the fifty pounds; and I was only to receive the balance, if any, in Santa Cruz. My passage etc. he would also pay, but I was still to be his debtor, and pay that when I should be rich. I make use of the express words as they stood in the proposals.

Such were the conditions proposed by this gentleman, to which the world will suppose I made several objections, a respectful and humble remonstrance he received from me a day or two after was productive of the following concise answer wrote upon a small scrap of paper:

'I find you begin to rebel before your enlargement, if you do not think proper to accept the terms, I wash my hands of you.'

In short this negotiation held off and on near three months, but hard as the conditions were I accepted of all even to the taking upon me the name of Plunkett, or Farrell another name which the colonel advised me to assume rather than that of Plunkett for what reason he only knows, yet as I would not be bound publicly to deny my real name, it dropt, and no more have since been heard from that quarter." [11]

Footnotes
1. Betty Rizzo, *Companions Without Vows: Relationships Among Eighteenth Century British Women* (Athens, Georgia, 1994), p.178-179.

2. See *Eighteenth Century Ireland*, vol 11 (1996), p.146.

3. 1750 146-195-97261 and 1752 157-202-104487.

4. 1749 133-453-92456.

5. 1749 137-43-92363.

6. "A state of the case of Colonel Count Thomas Nugent of Valdesotto...High Court of Chancery in Ireland..against Lieutenant Colonel Hugh Maguire", PRONI D3835/B/4/4/8. Unfortunately Count Valdesotto couldn't persist with the case due to lack of funds.

7. Tulchan April 29th 1739, PRONI D552/A/2/42.

8. James Woods, *Annals of Westmeath, ancient and modern* (Dublin, 1907), p.296-301.

9. *An Ode on Mr Pulteney* (London, 1739), p.3-4.

10. http://www.irishmasonicjewels.ie/Freemasonry in Meath and Westmeath By Larry Conlon.pdf, p.13.

11. First published in Caius Silius Nugenius [Robert Nugent], *The Oppressed Captive* (Fleet Prison, London, 1757), and reprinted in Claud Nugent, *Memoir of Robert, Earl Nugent* (Chicago and New York, 1898), p.318-344.

It appears that this Robert might have left jail eventually and settled in New York. That is if he is, as seems likely, the Robert Smith Nugent who married Phebe Pearson in that city in the late 18th century (for which see Mary Louisa Beatrice Olcott, The Olcotts and their kindred (1954), p.259).

It might also be of interest to read the experiences of some other members of Robert Nugent's family, both to get again a flavour of what life was like for the 'little people' in Ireland trying to enforce their land rights against powerful people, and also to corroborate the kind of person he was, and hence if the long account by his son is believable.

Firstly this is a letter written by his wife Elizabeth Berkely writing to the Earl of Temple, a friend of her estranged husband, from Spring [G]arden, 8th Nov 1761:

"My Lord

I must beg the favour of you to tell Mr Nugent, that if he has not common humanity to stay till I am brought to bed and in a fit condition to give a proper answer – or that he will not allow time for my uncle Colleton's coming to town whose advise and assistance I stand in need of – I must give my final answer – which is – that I am above fifteen hundred pounds out of pocket by my

marriage with him – and that I never will consent to the tying up any part of that allowance I receive from the Berkeley family – and that I shall not relinquish any part of the jointure I may expect from Mr Nugent as I have sacrificed my health to him. And after this if He chooses to make an attack on my character I must make the best defence I can – and return the obligation as far as lies in my power – I am told I can prove a marriage with him and Lady Munjoy at the time he married Mrs Nugent –, I shall release that son of his out of Newgate who has been unjustly kept there – I will expose that son of his who is now in Germany [Col Edmond] and who has behaved to me in a most ungrateful manner and who with Mr Nugent's sister [Peggy] has been the reason of this separation –. But I think it more advisable in Mr Nugent not to oblige me in my own defence to expose that character religion and fortune of his to the world which supports him in it at present – and necessitate me by that means to expose a man who I so unfortunately did the honour to make choice of as a second husband – besides in my humble opinion this cannot be the amicable separation I proposed and therefore I am not at all determined with myself if when I am recovered of my lying in [giving birth] I shall not come and live with him again and he may then get rid of me as he can –
and am you Lordship's most
Obedient Servant
E. B."

She added to this a further part dated to 'Saturday' and written at the same place:

"When I reflect upon all the misery which I have undergone since my last marriage, as well upon all the cruel aspersions with which my character has been attacked, you will not wonder that I should determine to procure a separation from Mr Nugent at any rate. Nor can you blame me if conscious of my own innocence I resolve not to receive from him or his family any pecuniary advantage whatever. In that light therefore I mean to return to him the only benefit I ever had from him that of my jointure of a thousand a year which I am very little likely to live to enjoy under the oppression of the grievous misfortunes with which I have now for some years been persecuted – I ask nothing of him but to be restored to a situation from which I wish to God I never had been taken – I flatter myself your Lordship will out of regard to me and my family see Deeds of Separation properly and effectually executed, that I may have a chance of being once again restored to some degree of tranquility and the sooner the better.

P S with regard to the child with which I am now pregnant, I have such an effection for all my children that I shall wish to keep it – and if you can procure Mr Nugent's consent to my having likewise my daughter that is now at Gosfield I shall be very happy."

What follows are some letters from Viscount Clare's aunt, Mary Anne Nugent, who was entitled to a part of his estate under his father's will. We know she was a Catholic from one of her letters ("...wanting a horse I footed to mass, whereby I have got a great cut in my foot...[and refers to Fr Delamere]...I am resolved not to be from door to door any longer, but settle in a town") but probably she was treated in this way simply to deny her the money that was due to her.

It makes very sad reading, initially he and his lawyer followed a simple policy of incurring enormous and clearly extortionate legal fees which they then claimed she owed, and sent court officials to arrest her on the strength of, and after that her abject poverty – she was actually in rags, as we also know from other sources – probably prevented her from realistically ever hoping to get justice.

What's even more remarkable is that when she died Viscount Clare proceeded to sue all the people associated with her, in particular those who could otherwise claim a part of her fortune, which again was a claim on his estate, by alleging that they maltreated her. This was true enough but it was doubtless intended to intimate them out of asserting any rights over her monies and hence Clare was left with his estate intact. It was obviously a completely cynical exercise because nobody maltreated her as much as he.

He sued them in 1753 via a Bill in Exchequer, as administrator of the effects of the late Mary Anne Nugent, against "all relations to and claimed rights of distribution, of the said Mary Anne's assets and effects." The Bill sought to interrogate all these relatives as regards any payments made to Mary Anne "in her lifetime in discharge of her fortune of 4 hundred pounds which was a charge on the said Robert's real estate and interest thereof."

Our first letter – and all are from her to Viscount Clare – begins with the simple point that she was frozen out of her family circle, doubtless deliberately to isolate her before cheating her out of her fortune:

30th Aug 1739
"Nothing would give me greater concern after our late fatal stroke, than to find that you sent for sisters Palles, Plunkett and Nugent to come to your [house in] town and forgot me quite;..."

28th May 1740
"I had not gone to law with you were it not you filed a Bill against me and served me with a subpoena. Councillor [illegible] advised me that I would be ruined if I did not answer your Bill.
...
I have several credible witnesses to prove I assure you. No martyr suffered by

hunger and cold more than I not getting one shilling out your estate to relieve me. Pollard [Robert Nugent's attorney] had me taken by a pursuivant though my attorney begod time for me to give in my answer. I delayed giving my answer fearing least it should commence a law suit betwixt you and I, for which I am told I am under half a crown a day expence ever since and do beg you will write to Mr Pollard to take off that expence as I am willing to come to your terms and if you will be so charitable as to order me some thing to get clothes for I am almost naked, for what little rags I had I was robbed of in Dublin and is [sic] now in a worse condition that a common...[presumably 'woman of'] the street.

I beg Dear sir in compassion to my deplorable condition, being destitute of all friends in the world excepting you and has not one friend in the world to give me a meal's meat or a night's lodging. Consider had this twelve month a pennies interest coming to me and begs you will set that money at interest for me and I'll strive to live on it.

I went five times to sister Nugent's [house] to get a shilling from her to keep me from starving but did not get [any] but James Fagan and his wife at each of the five times dragged me out to the watch at two o'clock in the frost which had like to cost me my life.

Pollard tells me that you wrote to him not to pay me that money until he would deduct your costs which I would not believe you would be guilty of, I not entering into a law suit with you and being told by the best lawyers in town I had a right to £1,200 and submitted to take 6 but now I have myself to your mercy.
...
[Pollard sent her a bill of costs of £51-15- and] he swelled up that long bill...and charged in his bill every term.
...
You oppress me in charging me with these costs when yourself began a lawsuit with me and I having no thought of going to law until you pressed me into it for fear to proceed against you. I would not even take out the copy of your Bill even though I am under 2 shillings and six pence a day ...[paying costs] every term."

Dublin 4th Oct 1740
"I have been these 9 months in a west [should be 'wet'?] cellar and Cousin Clare would not even suffer me to lye in the garret nor give me a pallet or blanket in the greatest hardship of weather. Though my dear brother desired I should have the furniture of my little room, as Fr Bartly can tell you, which I beg you will order for me though it is not 40 shillings.
...
But as you are the only alive I can depend upon, [I] shall expect your good

natured compliance in settling me otherwise and ordering me some kind of decency and write to Robert Nugent [of Farrenconnell] your agent to supply me with mourning for my dear sister since I got none for my dear brother.

You are very sensible you first commenced the lawsuit before I even in the least thought of it nor would to this day though my lawyers told me I should answer your bill which I never did 'till I was dragged and pulled about the streets by pursuivants whom I was obliged to satisfy with the little pence I had.

The week you went for England my agent made an offer to your agent that I was satisfied to take the five hundred and fifty pounds and not put either you or [any]one to further cost and let it lye till I could put [it] to Interest which Mr Bonnum, brewer in James St, can inform you and my attorney will make oath of it. I beg sir you will look into the affair, and have it settled of[f]hand. Counsellor Malone tells me [that] he will settle the cost, when heard, to about £10 and am sure you have too much honour to dispute with me in the poor condition I am now in.

As you are made sensible, I dropped the Cause as soon as you left the Kingdom. I declare [that I have] Counsellor Blake [and] French ... and others opinion that I could recover a thousand pound had I pursued the lawsuit, but ... am willing to make an amicable and ... shall be content with the five hundred and fifty pounds as you offered, for I would not have your displeasure for double the sum having no friend now alive to rely upon but you.

Nugent the tailor having taken the horse when I lodged turned me out and leaving the few clothes I had behind me have been robbed of every stitch and am now quite naked. Dear and worthy Sir take my miserable case into your consideration and relieve me by putting my fortune at interest and you'll oblige yours affectionately
M: Nugent

Dear Sir
I beg you'll write to Father Bartley to pay me the remainder of my Robery [sic] money which was left in his hands and is odds of thirty pounds. I beg once more that you may consider my poor condition and put my fortune to Interest. Consider I have not received a farthing since my brother died and am in a starving condition for Nugent the tailor has broke open my door and robbed me of every stitch of clothes I was worth, which I hope and expect you will resent for after he robbed he beat me in a most barbarous manner."

6th Dec 1740
"My miserable and deplorable condition is such that I am sure this will be the last letter I ever will write you wherefore I most earnestly entreat you to commiserate my perishing and starving condition
....[again talks about giving up the lawsuit and will settle for £550 to be set at

interest]...

if I be not speedily relieved and taken out of the melancholy condition I am now in it will be my death and hope by your speedy compliance you'll prevent that being an imputation upon you or your child. Mr Malone has fixed the cost of £26 pounds which is not worth your while to dispute with me in my present poor condition.

In fine I shall expect with impatience your favourable and compliance [sic] which will for ever relieve me and deserve you a perpetual blessing being all from

a most affectionate Aunt
Mary Anne Nugent"

"February the second day 1743/4 [sic, meaning that the date is written exactly like that]

Dear Sir

I find you have no though after so many melancholy letters as I have wrote to you. I am this twelvemonth very willing to take your six hundred pounds but your agent coming to town so often as he did would not see me because I happened to be destitute and had no friends to stand by me.

Dear Sir I beg you will be so good as to write to him and to Councellor Malone and to Kennedy to set it at interest. Sir you know the interest of my fortune this five years past comes to one hundred pounds and pray consider my hunger and thirst and my nakedness for upon my word I am worse than any beggar. I hope you will be so good as to allow some money to be close [hoping to get some money in hand] till the interest of my fortune will be due to support me.

I beg sir you will write to Father Bartly for my robbery of money brother ordered to be paid to me when he was on his death bed it is the family[?]. Feagan has pledged and sold all my clothes for the carriage [meaning that Fagan must have claimed that he was due money for transporting belongings and took the clothes in lieu of it?]. Pray send me speedy answer or I shall be obliged to go to England and die at your door for I owe above fifty pounds about the town to attorney and Mr Pollard would not give me one farthing out of my fifty pounds but twenty pounds so that no person on earth is in a poorer condition than I am. Now I beg you will be charitable to whom is your poor afflicted

Mary Anne Nugent

Sir be pleased to order your agent whatever you order me to get it at present to clothe me for the very mourning [monies given to family members in the event of a death to buy mourning cloathes] your honour ordered me he never gave me one stitch of it though it was ordered by your honour for my brother and sister and he has been in town three times this fortnight past and he would not speak one word to me. And [I] waited at his lodging door three days one after another till at last he ordered his maid to throw me down into the kennel.

Pollard took fifty pounds out of Court which he has five years in his hands and when I would go to his door to beg one shilling he would order his servant man and his servant maid to rack [sic, ?] me and drag me and beat me from his door. As for your agent when I threatened to complain to your honour the answer he makes me he does not regard my nephew nor myself one farthing."

[No date here and not all the letter, part is missing from the edge and from the beginning:]
"...the small pittance left me by my father which, if you consider rightly, I have as good title to in equity and conscience as you have to the plentiful estate left you by the same predecessor. Had you left me as you found me I should have some certainty of bread and not to be reduced to beg my bread as I am and what is much more deplorable is that my constitution is so broke that even this shift[?] ... had you but the charity as to pay me ... for my money it would be some relief to me.

I wrote to you several times and others in pity to me on this account but no answer. Councellor Malone in the presence of your agent ordered the ...

I beg you will consider my sufferance, believe me I must take some desperate course which must be to beg my way to you and die at your door.

I am Dear Sir

Your Afflicted Injured
Mary Anne Nugent

James Fagan sold me clothes on having no money to pay the carriage."

"Honoured Sir

Dublin Feb 25th 1743/4 [sic]

As this is the last letter I intend to trouble you with so begs you answer may be peremptory and to the purpose –
I am waiting for these two years of your agent who has been several times in this city and would not at all permit me to see him but at all times received

unbecoming usage from him.

As I have been willing to take your tender its hard I should be in the misery I am without it, as no object[?] can be greater, your agent to be sure has a view in keeping me out if it as he turns it to use in his way of stockjobbing.

In short worthy sir if you do not suddenly order me payment I must be under the necessity of begging my way to your house and there continue an object before your door.

You should for your interest as well as in compassion of my condition give me some bread while I live for if any thing should happen me you are the only living that shall have the benefit of it after my death. For if I had a million though cruel you have been to me I would not leave it from you.

Your good butler Fagan and Plunkett has sold all my clothes and left me quite naked and this done by the countenance and permission of your good sisters.

I leave the usage I received from all to God and am your most distressed and afflicted servant.

Mary Anne Nugent

P.S. I beg you will consider my sufferings, hunger and thirst for five years past and send me speedy succour and some small charity to buy my clothes. Besides your tender there is 41 pound I was robbed of which my brother your father got and ordered Father Bartly to pay it me but I never got it. I beg you will order it for me.

Its cruel I should be kept out of the interest all this time when its no benefit to me and order Mr Malone to lay it out and procure[?] it me."
(All references are from the Nugent section of the Stowe deeds and correspondence, Huntington Library, California but note also from the catalogues in the National Archives in Dublin, M 3268 a-r, dated 1739:
Mary Anne Nugent of Dublin, spinster, v. Robert Nugent, and others, relative to estate of her father Edmond Nugent Carlanstown, ...Bill, Answer, Petition, Briefs.)

APPENDIX H
ROD Note taking Template

What follows in the next few pages is a suggested template that you can photocopy out and use to mark in your notes when viewing the deeds in the Registry. The next two pages are what you can photocopy and the following three pages contain explanatory notes.

- -

Book-Page-Number   date of registry:_____ 17__

                                        date:_____ 17__

with another ☐, others ☐   with another ☐, others ☐

_____to_____

1)_____
2)_____
3)_____
4)_____

Lands:_____
_____
_____
_____
_____

Lives:
1)_____
2)_____
3)_____

Witnesses:

_____| to memorial only ☐

_____
_____
_____

Book-Page-Number   date of registry:_____   17__

date:_____   17__

with another ☐, others ☐   with another ☐, others ☐

_____ to _____

1)_____
2)_____
3)_____
4)_____

Lands:_____
_____
_____
_____
_____

Lives:
1)_____
2)_____
3)_____

Witnesses:

to memorial only ☐

_____
_____
_____

-D -

Book-Page-Number   date of registry:_____ **A** 17__

date:_____ 17__

with another ☐, others ☐   with another ☐, others ☐
_____**C** to_____**B**_____

1)_____**E**_____
2)_____
3)_____
4)_____

Lands:_____
_____**F**_____
_____
_____

Lives:
1)_____**G**_____
2)_____
3)_____

Witnesses:

H		
		to memorial only ☐

_____
_____**I**
_____

514

Note the two different dates here, the date of registry and the main date. The date of registry – obviously the date the deed was registered – is listed usually on the margin of the page beside the deed, and at the very end of the deed, while the main date – the date the deed was transacted – is listed in writing at the beginning of the deed. You should take down both dates although if you are in a hurry remember that the main date – not the date of registry – is the important one. It really only becomes an issue if there is a big gap between these dates, usually it should be just a few months or a year or so but it does vary.

These boxes make it easier to transcribe the details from the indexes, because frequently these indexes will mention that either the grantee or grantor of the lands was acting "with another" or "with others" or in Latin "et alios" which means the same thing. It obviously means that there are other parties to the deed, not just two, which will be obvious then when you see the deed itself.

Here you can list the simple details that you get from the indexes, either the lands or names index. There you will be told that the given deed transfers land, somehow, from the "Earl of Darnley to Plunkett", or whatever, and this you can write down here. Then when you get to see the deed itself you can write the person's address under the line beside the name, and also add in the Christian names that you don't have.

This, the extreme left hand corner, is obviously where you write down the book-page-number of the deed, which you will get from either of the indexes. The indexes might look something like: "lib:34 p:67 No.:56783" and you would then just write down 34-67-56783 in the blanks at this part of the template. "lib." is just short for "liber", the latin for "book", and "No." is short for "Number". These numbers are all you need to reference the deed in your notes and also to order copies of the memorial from the Registry.

The lines, underneath the "to", are numbered in case there are multiple parties to the deed whom you might like to take down and number accordingly. (In general always take down names, and their occupations and addresses, since this can be surprisingly difficult to find out otherwise for 18th century Ireland, depending on the rank of those parties obviously.) Otherwise you can just use these lines to write down anything that seems of interest in the deed, such as whether it is a marriage settlement and the basic facts of that settlement if so.

F These are the lands transacted in the deed, and not to be confused with the addresses of the parties. Obviously if you used the lands index you will be able to fill out one land name in this area before you see the deed itself. Unfortunately many deeds will list a vast number of townlands which you might not be able then to take down in full, but whatever you do don't forget to take down the exact acerage corresponding to each townland name that you do decide to transcribe. Also don't neglect to take down the parish and barony where the lands are, if specified.

G Although these three lives leases are only about, very roughly, a fifth of the overall total of leases in the ROD nonetheless they are so interesting that they deserve a seperate section here. Just write down the names that are stated in the deed as belonging to these lives, their relationship to each other, and their ages. Again when these three named people are dead the lease is up, or when 31 years have passed, usually, whichever is longer.

H No matter how long the deed is don't forget to take down the witnesses at the end. This list of names, addresses and occupations – which you can list underneath each other in the three lines provided – can be extremely interesting. Although sometimes they can be just lawyers and their clerks nonetheless they are very often friends and close relatives of the parties to the deed. Remember one party or witness to the deed itself will then witness the memorial, and swear that the memorial corresponds to the original deed. Of course if there are more witnesses to the deed then you can write them down in the lines at the bottom.

In general too it might be helpful if you left the other side of the page of the template blank and used it to write in any other details of interest that you don't have space for on the template itself. It should be borne in mind that these deeds come in all shapes and sizes and you really don't know what they look like until you see it, some are many pages long and some just a short paragraph.

I Also it is usual for one person to only witness the memorial, and not the original deed, so for that person it is convenient to tick the box provided (i.e. that person is a "witness to the memorial only"). The reason why it is useful to specify that is because if there happened to be a long gap in time between the date of the deed and the date of registry then it would confuse matters if you named a person as a witness to the deed who wasn't actually there.

APPENDIX I
Images of the Registry

These are obviously a few photographs of the Registry to give you an insight into what it looks like, and many thanks again to the staff there for all their assistance and permission to publish this here.

The Registry has asked me to point out that photography is normally forbidden but that, on a case by case basis for the purpose of historic research, permission may be granted by the Property Registration Authority. The Registry has also asked me to state that they normally retain copyright, and they state that the photographs would be the property of and reproduced with the permission of the Property Registration Authority.

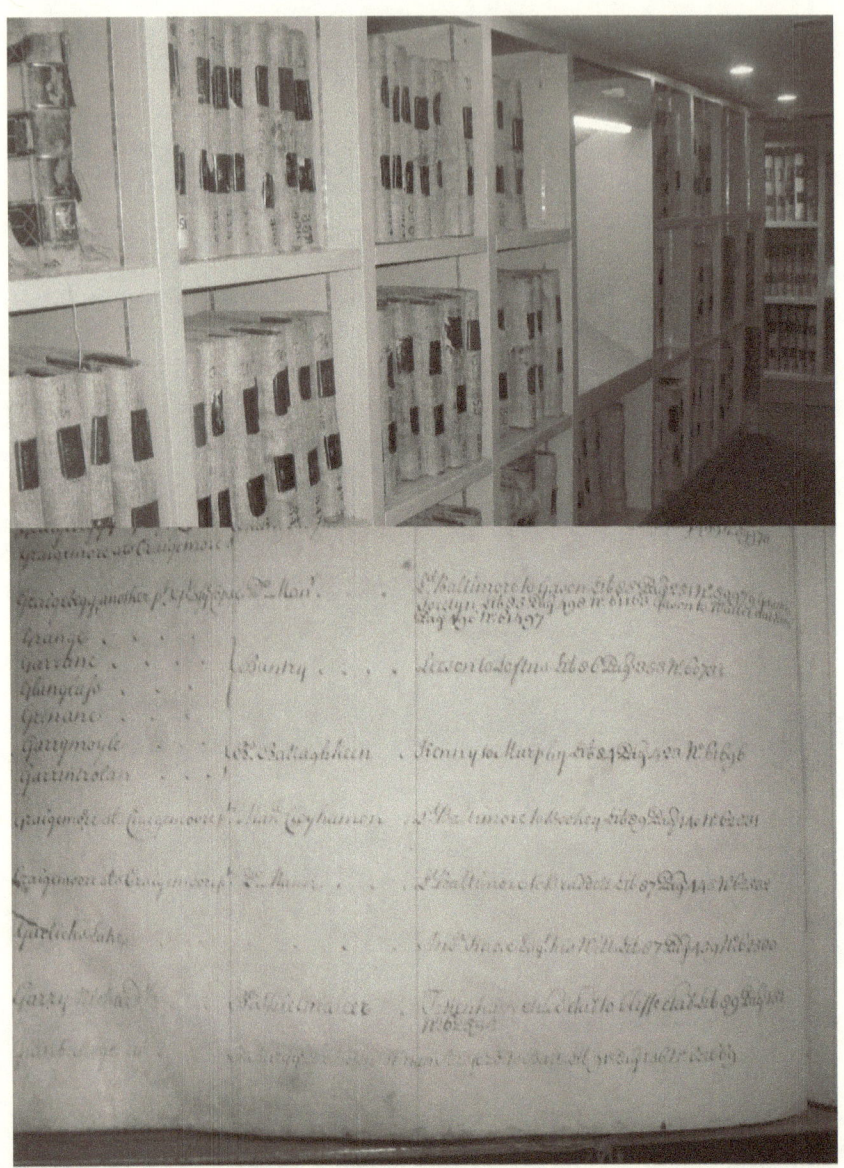

Some of the volumes of the Lands Index and this is what these indexes look like inside. Hopefully you can read that easily enough so that you can see what it is you need to take down on the template provided. Hence if you were taking down the second entry in this index you would write down the lands: Grange, Garrane, Glanglass, and Grenane, all in the town of Bantry, and in the top line: "Leeson to Loftus", and for the numbers: 86-353-60731, in the spaces provided. Then you go to the transcript room and look up volume number 86, page 353, and number 60731 and fill out the template with the more detailed information you get from looking at the actual memorial.

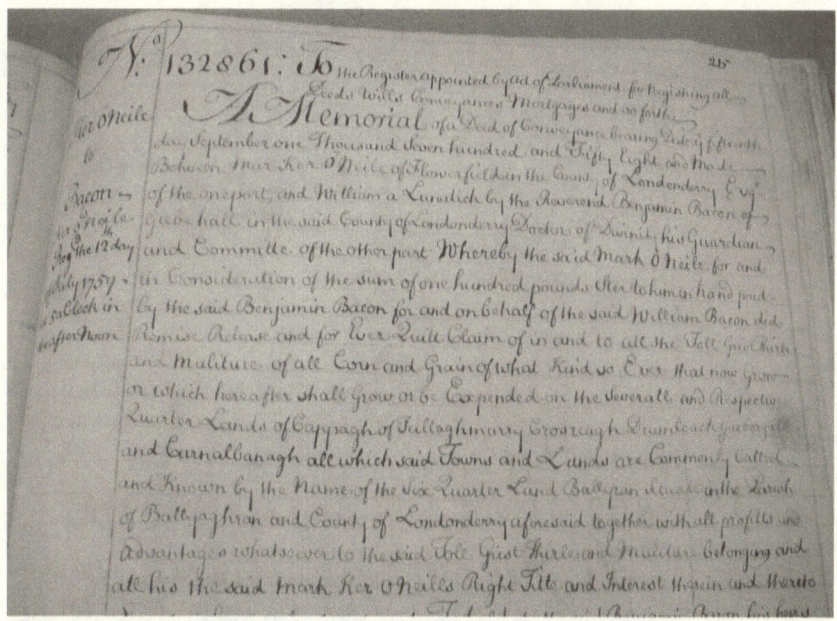

This then is an example of a transcript of a memorial, the kind of document you will be reading after you have taken down interesting references from the indexes. Again hopefully you can make out the text here, this is the beginning of it:

"N:132861: To the Register appointed by Act of Parliament for Registering all Deeds Wills Conveyances Mortgages and so Forth -
A Memorial of a Deed of Conveyance bearing Date the ["ye" here should be taken down as "the", the "y" stands for an old English letter called "thorn" and means "th"] fifteenth day September one Thousand Seven hundred and Fifty Eight and Made Between Mar[k] Ker O'Neile of Flowerfield in the County of Londonderry Esquire of the one part, and William [Bacon] a Lunatick by the Reverend Benjamin Bacon of Glebe hall in the said County of Londonderry Doctor of Divinity his Guardian and Committe of the other part[.] Whereby the said Mark O'Neile for and in Consideration of the sum of one hundred pounds ster[ling] to him in hand paid by the said Benjamin Bacon for and on behalf of the said William Bacon did Remise Release and for Ever Quitt Claim of in and to all the Toll Grist Thirle ["In Scots' law, thirlage is the servitude by which lands are restricted to a particular mill, being bound to have their corn ground there on certain terms."] and Muliture of all Corn and Grain of what Kind so Ever that now Grow or which hereafter shall Grow or be Expended on the Severall and Respective Quarter Lands of Cappagh..."

As you can see its quite interesting, Revd Bacon is acting as the representative of a "lunatick" who may be a relative of his? The "quarter" of course is the old Irish land unit that crops up quite frequently in these old deeds.

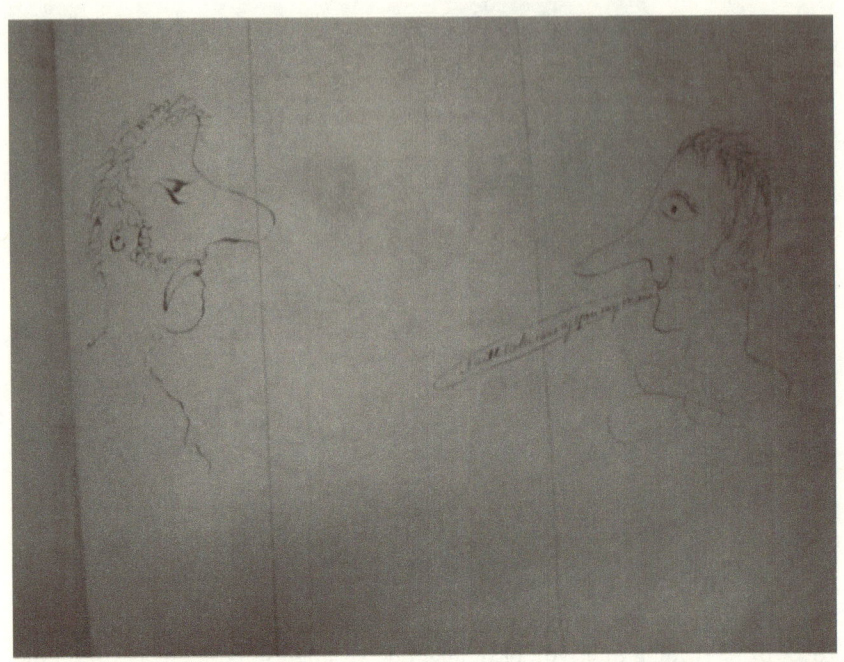

Above, and on the next page, are old doodles on the indexes and below is the public search room, where many people working for solicitors offices or banks (or even the Revenue Commissioners!) come to peruse the modern deeds.

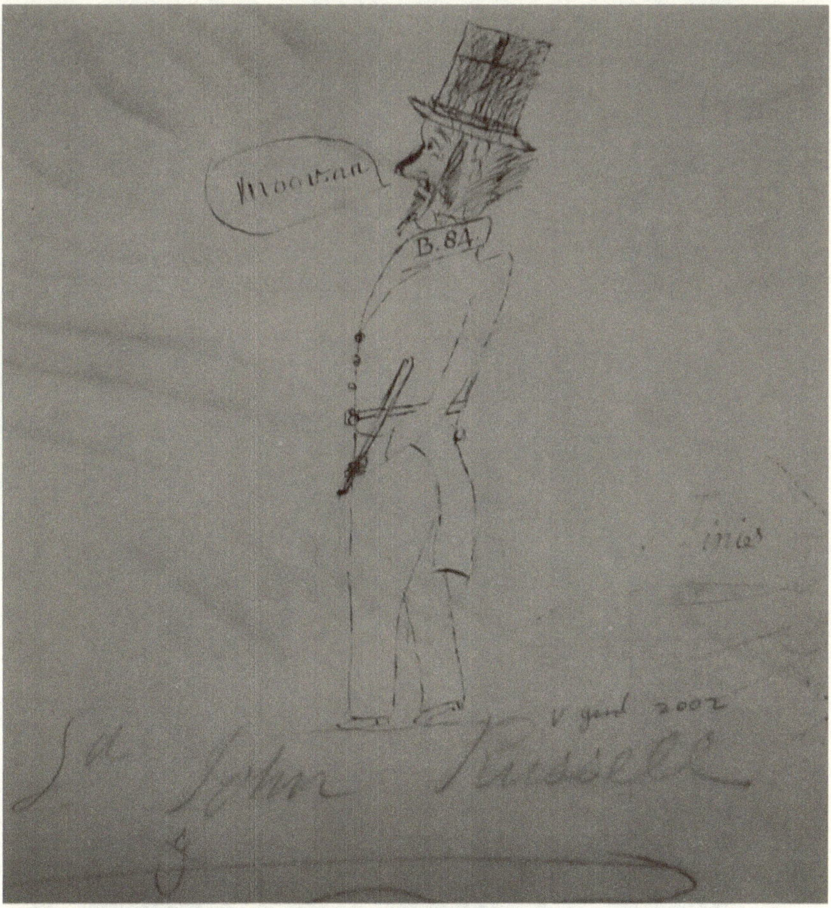
B.84
Sir John Russell

I've a pain in my belly
Sir

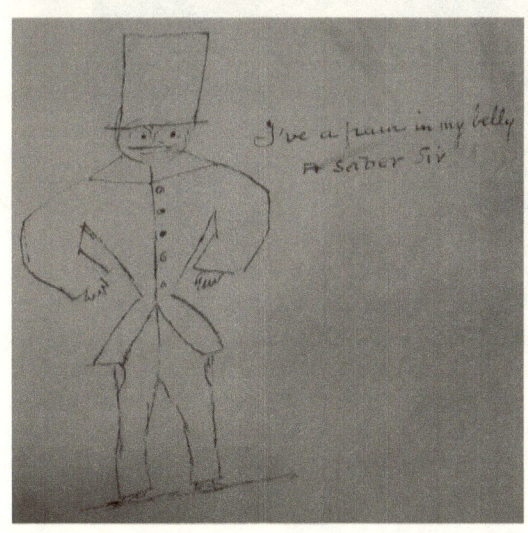

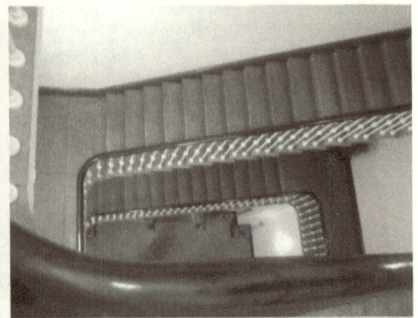

Of course the Registry is located in a beautiful Gandon custom designed neo classical type building. I say "custom" built because Gandon designed it specifically to hold the Registry. That's why there are no side windows in the Transcript room, because post 1798 the government, nervous about the deeds, was afraid of mobs throwing incendiaries through windows etc.

A sample of the abstract books that come into use in the Registry from the 1830s on. The idea was that a member of the staff would read over the memorial and decide what category of document it was (hence you see in the above picture the right hand column which reads: Assignment, Conveyance, etc ...and ends in Mortgage) and prepare these short abstracts to speed up the work of the legal searchers.

A sample of the names indexes, for the dates you can see, and for grantors with surnames beginning with letters "L" and "K". Below that is what the above books look like opened, in this case for the name LaTouche. Obviously this is a French Hugenot family that founded the Bank of Ireland who, as you can expect, tended to possess a lot of mortgages.

This is what the 19th century memorials look like and as you can see it is very easy and simple to look them up, there is really no difference between that quality of writing and a printed sheet, as the Registrar, Michael Dwyer, hotly asserted in his successful attempts to ward off the dreaded "progress" in the 1870s! But he was right, the ROD worked extremely efficiently before the advent of machines and the later computerisation.

This is the room where you read the actual transcripts of the memorials, one of which a researcher, Patrick Melvin, is pictured reading. If he seems a little Mona Lisaesque its because he was hard pressed to finish some research for his forthcoming book on Landed Estates in Galway and it was not made any easier by a certain person pestering him about photographs as the clock ran down! The thin volumes you see on top are some of the 19th century abstract books.

INDEX

The many personal and place names in Chapter 8, the case study, are not indexed here.

A

Abstracts (of memorials).................16
Acres, Cunningham........................24
Acres, Irish....................................23
Acres, Statute................................23
Acton, Thomas...............................58
Adams, Samuel..............................51
Adare (Co. Limerick)....................150
Aherne family (of Ross Co. Meath) 351
Ahmuty, Revd James......................67
Annals of Westmeath....................503
Antrim...............29, 35, 74, 78, 82, 83
Arbitration Agreements...................66
Ardnegross (Co. Westmeath)..........51
Armagh........30, 36, 59, 74, 78, 82, 83
Armstrong, R. O...........................407
Arran Quay (Dublin)......................69
Auburn Cottage (Co. Cavan) 352, 353
Augsburg Gazette.........................180
Australia..................................8, 453
Avena (ship).................................431

B

Balcarrow (Co. Westmeath)..........128
Balfe, Robert........................319, 328
Ballimore (Co. Westmeath)............60
Ballina (Co. Meath).....176, 183, 184, 186, 197, 198, 202, 204, 208, 215, 216, 218-221, 223, 244, 245, 248, 251, 256, 259, 263, 264, 266
Ballinderry (Co. Westmeath)........137
Ballindura (Co. Westmeath)...........60
Ballinlough (Co. Westmeath)........316
Ballinlough Big (Co. Meath)........137
Ballinrink (Co. Meath)..........105, 201
Ballneclunagh (Co. Westmeath)...126
Ballybetagh (land unit, townland). 25, 28-30, 37
Ballyboe (land unit)......25, 29, 30, 36
Ballycalrow (Co. Westmeath)........98
Ballycanvan (Co. Waterford) 153, 154
Ballycar (Co. Meath)....................164
Ballyeighter (Co. Tipperary)..67, 187, 189, 230, 231
Ballyhist (Co. Meath)...................333
Ballymoney (Co. Antrim)...............35
Ballymore (Co. Westmeath)...........64
Ballyragget (Co. Kilkenny)...........143
Baltrasna (Co. Meath)......21, 65, 220, 225, 255, 256, 320
Bank of Ireland.....33, 34, 84, 85, 524
Banknotes......................................33
Barcony (Co. Cavan).......21, 51, 113, 201, 220-222, 234, 237, 240, 241, 265, 268, 271
Bargain and sale..................44-46, 51
Baronston (Co. Westmeath). 463, 464, 466
Barony..22
Bartly, Fr.....................................506
Bayly, Thomas........104-106, 242, 243
Bedford Level..................................6
Belfast.............37, 112, 144, 453, 454
Berkely, Elizabeth........................503
Bermingham, Francis...................126
Betham, Sir William..................7, 116
Bethell, Richard (Lord Westbury)357, 361, 365, 380, 386
Bishop's Leases.............................40
Bismarck, Otto von.......................180
Black Baron (2nd Earl of Westmeath) 333, 334, 339, 343, 349, 350, 352-354
Black Castle (Co. Westmeath).........59
Black Dog Prison (Dublin)...480, 486
Blake, Ignatius.............................124
Blake, Margaret...........................124
Bobsgrove (Co. Cavan)....21, 51, 177, 201, 202, 263, 267, 268
Books of Survey and Distribution. 22, 24, 39, 73, 75, 77, 81, 82, 217
Boyse, Philip................................460

527

Bracken, Pat...................................58
Bracklyn (Co. Westmeath)...128, 136, 180, 219, 227, 245
Bradsheet, Dudley............................60
Brewery..............................35, 69, 507
Briody, James..................................334
Bristol (England)..301, 408, 481, 483, 487, 489, 491, 494
Brocas, Godwin................................58
Broderick, John................................23
Brogan, Hugh...................................58
Browne, Anne........................176, 204
Browne, Wogan................................51
Buckland, John..................................74
Buckley, Henry..........................106, 243
Buntin, Arthur.................................144
Burchell, Thomas..............................58
Burgess, Revd J B.............................57
Burke, Edmund................................120
Burke, John.......................................69
Butler, Theobald....................303, 328
Byrne, Joseph..................................126

C

Callaghan, Cornelius.......................137
Cannon, Christopher......................474
Carewe (land unit).......................28-30
Carlanstown (Co. Westmeath).....104, 107, 136, 173, 211, 235, 245, 246, 262, 263, 266, 469, 470, 510
Carlingford (Co. Louth).....43, 84, 85, 136
Carlow.31, 78, 82, 144, 153, 329, 361
Carpenterstown (Co. Westmeath)..63, 125, 136, 202, 204, 208, 215
Carrick, Manor of............................22
Carrow (land unit).....................25, 26
Cartron (land unit)..............26, 30, 31
Carucate (land unit)......28, 30, 31, 37
Castlenugent (Co. Longford)........460
Castlepollard (Co. Westmeath) 69, 77, 125, 202, 230, 232, 470
Catholic middlemen......113, 126, 136
Catholic Relief Act..........................89
Cavan 5, 21, 22, 26, 27, 29, 30, 35-38, 51, 61, 63, 74, 76, 83, 104-107, 109, 110, 125, 130, 137, 169, 177, 182-184, 186, 187, 197, 198, 200, 201, 205, 208, 209, 211, 215-218, 220-223, 229, 234, 235, 238, 239, 241-244, 248, 250-262, 264-266, 268, 312, 329, 330, 334, 339, 353
Chief Rent.......................................40
Civil Parish................................22, 23
Civil Survey.........................22, 72-74
Clanmahon Barony (Co. Cavan)...37, 74, 104, 105
Clare..170
Clogh Oughter (Co. Cavan)..........334
Clogheran (Co. Dublin)................100
Clonalis (Co. Roscommon)...........145
Clonbockoge (Co. Cavan).............113
Cloncullen (Co. Longford).............67
Clonin (Co. Westmeath)..60, 249, 259
Clonkieffy (Co. Cavan).................113
Clonlost (Co. Westmeath) 43, 98, 165, 172, 173, 190, 248, 250, 259, 264
Clonmel (Co. Tipperary).......150, 151
Clontiduffy (Co. Cavan)......169, 215, 218-221, 234, 235, 245, 262-264
Coates, James..................................58
Coddington, Henry.........................65
Coffee, Patrick...............................52
Coffy, Nicholas.............................165
Coins...33-35
Common Recovery 41-43, 47-51, 110, 124, 283
Compass improvements................429
Conmee, Elizabeth........................460
Connell, Phillip.....................333, 335
Conory, John.................................151
Constantinople (Turkey)...............176
Cooke, Ambrose.............................65
Cooke, Bryan.........................104, 105
Cooke, Connor......................104, 105
Cooke, Easter..........................65, 236
Cooke, James..........................65, 236
Cooke, Matthew....................104, 105
Coolamber (Co. Longford) 63, 70, 71, 460
Coolatore (Co. Westmeath).............52
Coolavin (Co. Sligo)......................145
Cooney family (Carpenterstown, Co.

528

Westmeath)....................................125
Cork.......25, 31, 79-83, 146-148, 152, 351, 361
Corstown (Co. Meath). 1, 2, 265, 266, 328, 333
Cortown (Co. Meath).....................328
Court of Claims..............129, 248, 259
Crimean War.................................179
Cromwell, Oliver.....39, 72, 246, 313, 334, 337, 342, 351, 354
Crover (Co. Cavan)......241, 338, 350, 352
Cullen, Louis..................................138
Cunlin (Co. Cavan)......106, 125, 202, 234, 243, 244, 260, 263
Cunningham, John..........................64
Curly, James...................................57
Curly, Patrick..................................61
Curraghmore (Co. Offaly)..............67
Cussenstown (Co. Westmeath).....165

D

Daly, Dan..58
Dancing..................................155, 163
Darcy, Christopher.......................165
Dates (in the 18th century)..............31
Dease family (Co. Cavan).............130
Deed poll...45
Derbyshire (England).......................19
Derrymadin (Co. Cavan).......104, 105
Devon (England).....................86, 239
Devoy, 'the'.............................316, 319
Dillon, Luke...................................166
Dillon, Thomas Arthur (inventor)....3, 396-399, 401, 402, 408-411, 413, 414, 416-418, 426, 429-432, 470
Discoverer, Protestant....42, 122, 124, 125, 132, 134, 137, 298, 299, 301, 302
District Electoral Divisions.............23
Dix, Henry T..369, 378-383, 389-391, 395
Dogstown (Co. Meath)..................105
Donegal...........29, 74, 78, 82, 83, 156
Donore (Co. Westmeath) 93, 126, 471
Dower.......................47, 96, 133, 134
Down Survey....59, 72-74, 76, 77, 81, 82, 267
Dowry....41, 47, 65, 95, 96, 192, 220, 236
Druganstown (Co. Westmeath).......60
Drumrora (Co. Cavan)..........239, 352
Dublin Castle...12, 20, 107, 221, 252, 397
Dungan, James..............................316
Dungimmon (Co. Cavan).....176, 184, 187, 188, 205, 230-232, 235, 265
DuNoyer, George..........174, 245, 335
Dunsany (Co. Meath)...104, 130, 204, 245, 329
Durham (England)................128, 166
Dwyer, Michael F..........408, 415, 429
Dysert (Co. Westmeath)..66, 245, 250

E

East India Company......................474
Economic History...........................67
Edgeworth, Maria.........................459
Edinburgh Castle (hotel in Bristol) 489
Edinburgh, Duke of......................430
Egan, Daniel....................................67
Egan, John.......................................67
Emmett, Robert...............................59
Enagh (Co. Cavan).......176, 177, 185, 190, 191, 197, 204, 205, 218, 220, 232, 245, 248, 250, 251
Encumbered Estates Court.....76, 361, 386, 415, 428, 446
English, Michael.............................58
Enniskillen (Co. Fermanagh).......212, 238, 310
Eustace, Catherine........................133

F

Fagan, James.................173, 506, 509
Fagan, Matthew.....................103, 114
Fairs (right to hold).........................63
Falley, Margaret.........................4, 16
Farnham, Earls of (Maxwell).51, 182, 183, 198, 220, 223, 237, 265, 268, 335, 353
Farrenconnell (or Bobsgrove, Co. Cavan)....21, 137, 176, 177, 184, 185,

190, 193, 196, 197, 200-202, 205, 230, 233-235, 248, 251, 256, 265, 301, 507
Farthing....33, 304, 467, 497, 507-509
Fax machine (invention of)...........431
Fee simple..40, 42, 99, 101, 299, 308, 393, 424
Fee tail......................................40, 308
Feoff (type of trust)............................9
Fermanagh. 27, 28, 35, 36, 74, 79, 83, 128, 198, 238, 240, 457
Ffolliott, Rosemary........................113
Fieri facias...47
Fine (for breaching the terms of a lease...39
Finea (Co. Westmeath)......63, 77, 107, 209, 252, 254, 256, 257
Fingall (branch of the Plunkett family)..130
Fishing rights....................................61
Fitzgerald, William........................299
Fitzpatrick, John...............................59
Flax.......................140, 144, 154, 169
Fleming, Robert.....................106, 243
Folklore....3, 5, 74, 81, 174, 183, 216, 217, 219, 221, 224, 225, 227, 229, 257, 266, 312, 332-335, 351, 461
Fore (Co. Westmeath)....27, 174, 176, 191, 197, 201, 202, 204, 213, 214, 296, 297, 299, 333, 334, 350, 351, 353
Forster, John...........................100-102
Forty shilling freehold.....................90
Fox, Matthew.................................137
Foyran (Co. Westmeath)........103, 220
Frankfort (Co. Offaly).......................67

G
Gallagher, James...............................58
Gallon (land unit)..............................26
Gallonbane (Co. Cavan)................105
Games, John....................................137
Gavelkind.......................129, 191, 309
Gaynor, James..................................57
Gaynor, Nicholas..............................59
Gaynor, Peter....................................93
Gaynor, William...............................58

George-Inn (Hay-market, London) 495
Gibbons, John....................................99
Gibson, John......................................57
Glascock, James................................43
Glencoe (Scotland)........................313
Globe Coffee-House (Dublin)......478, 480
Gloucester (England)...178, 486, 488, 489, 500
Gneeve (Co. Cavan).25, 31, 176, 197, 200-202, 208, 215, 218, 234, 235, 237, 264, 266, 274
Gordon, Charles.............................490
Gorges, Richard................................61
Gortnysillagh (Co. Galway)............69
Gosfield (England)................472, 504
Granard (Co. Longford)..........60, 211
Grattan, Henry...59, 87, 92, 127, 136, 268, 314
Gregorian Calendar..........................31
Gregory, Mr....................................433
Griffith's Valuation...........................75
Gt Britain St (Dublin)....................125
Guinea................33, 34, 483, 486, 498
Gurken (Co. Offaly).........................67
Gurwyn, Samuel.............................301

H
Habeas Corpus Act.........................498
Hale, Sir Matthew........................7, 19
Halifax (Canada)............................177
Hall, Edward....................................58
Hall, Richard..................................125
Hall, William.................298, 300, 301
Hampson, Dillon Pollard.....232, 470, 506
Handwriting (in the 18th century). 16, 18, 296, 300, 372
Hannaway, Capt. Thomas..............474
Hawke, Adm. Edward....................474
Healy, Thomas.................................58
Hemmings, Benjamin............486, 488
Hyde, Douglas...............................332

I
Indented deed (Indenture)....9, 44, 45,

530

259, 296, 489
Index, Lands....12, 13, 18, 21, 22, 54-56, 400, 401, 405, 407, 409-411, 418, 428, 518
Index, Names. 12, 13, 53, 55, 56, 400, 405, 409-411, 414
Industrial Revolution..............91, 130
Insolvency............................499, 500
Irish cottages................................353
Irish Land Commission...................11
Irish Record Commission.........7, 116
Irvine, George..............................177
Irvine, Georges.............................128
Irvine, Sophia...............................128

J

James St (Dublin)...................69, 507
Jamestown Court (Co. Westmeath) 323
John Freeman-Mitford (Lord Redesdale).....................................112
Johnson, William..........................474
Johnstone, Harcourt.....................433
Jordan, William..............................58
Joyce, Patrick Weston....................25

K

Keating, Patrick.............................52
Keatinge, M..................................408
Keeley, Dan...................................58
Kells (Co. Meath)...........................69
Kernan, Miles................................63
Kerry.......25, 31, 78, 80-82, 148, 149, 152, 156
Kidd, Saquill..................................58
Kilbride (Co. Cavan).............104, 105
Kilcormack (Co. Offaly).................67
Kildare..........30, 51, 78, 82, 207, 246
Kilgolagh (Co. Cavan).............63, 71
Kilkenny.......31, 79, 80, 82, 142, 143, 152, 205, 351
Killinebeg (Co. Westmeath)............64
Killiney (Co. Dublin)....................318
Killisheel (Co. Offaly)....................67
Killminin (Co. Waterford)..............61
Kilnacrott (Co. Cavan).106, 237, 239, 265, 352, 353

Kiltomb (Co. Westmeath)....136, 184, 190, 191

L

Lalla Rookh (poem by Thomas Moore)..336
Land Registry (or Registry of Title) 3, 4, 51, 355-364, 366, 368-372, 374-378, 380, 381, 383-394, 406, 414, 423, 426, 429, 442, 443, 445, 446, 453
Landed Estates Court.....76, 359, 363, 370, 376, 377, 384-386, 388, 407, 415, 425, 428, 434, 443
Laois..............22, 78, 82, 83, 329, 361
Larcom, Capt Thomas...............24, 25
Leach, Colonel..............................433
Lease and release...39, 44, 46, 51, 52, 298, 300, 301
Lefevre, Shaw........433, 444, 453, 454
Leitrim..63, 79, 82, 83, 183, 198, 211, 231, 245, 368
Levellers......................................142
Leycester, John..............................67
Leycester, Mary.............................67
Lickblea (Co. Westmeath).............173
Limerick (Co. Limerick)...............145
Limerick, Treaty of.......119, 120, 262
Lisnetinnure (Co. Cavan)...............61
Litton, Emily................................180
Livery of seisin..............................51
Loghgare begg (Co. Westmeath)...74, 76, 77
Longford 5, 26, 30, 63, 67, 79, 80, 82, 83, 140, 190, 193, 211, 212, 245, 263, 266, 460
Loughcrew (Co. Meath)........208, 333
Lougherry, Matthew.......................93
Louth............5, 30, 34, 43, 78, 83, 254
Lowther, George...........................104
Lurgan (Co. Armagh).............59, 410
Lynch, Joe....................................178
Lynch, S. J...................................407

M

Mac Cully, John.............................35
MacGeoghegan, Kedagh..3, 135, 245,

323, 324, 326, 457, 461-469
MacMahon, Collo...........................352
MacMahon, Orwin.......334, 336, 337, 341, 342, 344, 345, 347-352, 354
Madden, John (Dean of Kilmore)...38
Madder, Wyndam........................125
Magna Carta...................................311
Maguire, Cuchonnacht.................461
Maguire, Col. Hugh. 3, 115, 194, 457, 458, 460, 478, 503
Maguire, Joseph......18, 116, 135, 394
Mahoney, Pierce...........................452
Makaney, Edward.........................165
Malone, Anthony. 125, 299, 301, 462, 463, 467, 468, 507-509
Malone, Richard...125, 132, 134, 299, 300
Malpas, John.................................318
Malta..177
Malyn, Elizabeth (Lady Cathcart) 459
Manchester (England). 177, 335, 351-353
Manor of Carrick............................22
Manor of Munterconnaught............22
Manors....22, 275-278, 281, 283, 284, 287, 293, 307
Markham, Henry...........................351
Marriage Settlements...16, 41, 47, 56, 64-66, 95-97, 236, 241, 242, 259, 263, 380, 454
Martin, James.......................183, 354
Martin, John...........................297, 300
Martin, Patrick...............433, 448-453
Martland (land unit)..................28, 37
Masetowne (Co. Westmeath)..........74
Mass Lane (Dublin)........................93
Maugher, Daniel.............................61
Maxwell, John James.....................51
McCleland, Michael.......................58
McDonagh, Henry..........................57
McDonagh, Patrick.......................460
Mechanical Index (invention of)......3, 396, 397, 408, 416, 417, 422, 427, 429, 440
Memorials (summaries of deeds)...10, 12, 14, 15, 417, 419

Merrrion Square (Dublin)...............69
Microfilm machine (invention of) 433
Middlesex (London)........6, 8, 19, 355
Might, Robert.......................165, 503
Millbrook (Co. Meath)..........183, 354
Mineral rights.................................63
Moidore (Portuguese coin).......34, 70
Monaghan 27, 28, 35, 74, 78, 83, 113, 268, 352
Monaghan, Christopher................165
Money (in the 18th century)...........33
Monks, Michael..............................58
Moore, Beryl................................351
Moore, Sir Francis.........................52
Moore, Thomas............................336
Moortown (Co. Westmeath)...........60
Moran, Fr Nicholas.......................165
Morgan, George Osborne.............433
Mortgages....42, 84, 85, 94, 109, 110, 187, 189, 218, 220, 239, 260, 261, 268, 285, 289-292, 304, 360, 366, 372, 376, 379, 380, 382, 393, 434, 440, 446, 450, 453, 455, 523
Mount Leinster, Lord of (Cheevers) 316, 319
Mountnugent (Co. Cavan)...130, 184, 197, 217, 235, 351
Mulkearan, Bryan.........................166
Mullaghmast (Co. Kildare)...........313
Mullahoran (Co. Cavan).................61
Mullingar (Co. Westmeath)..113, 141, 226-229, 245, 247, 263, 324, 326
Multyfarnham (Co. Westmeath)....59, 60
Munterconnaught, Manor of..........22
Murray, Henry................................58
Murray, Herbert....................407, 434
N
Nangle, Francis..............................59
Napoleonic Wars..........................139
Newfoundland (Canada)..............152
Norris, Francis...............................52
Norris, Henry.................................52
Northumberland (England).............19
Nugent (Earl of Westmeath)....38, 43, 166, 233, 259, 262, 263, 326, 334,

Nugent, Christopher......................176
Nugent, Christopher Edward John 177
Nugent, Christopher James...178, 180
Nugent, Col Edmund....................481
Nugent, Edmond (Carlanstown Co. Westmeath)..........................296, 298
Nugent, Edmond (Clonlost)..........165
Nugent, Elizabeth..........128, 211, 352
Nugent, Elizabeth (Sabina)...........352
Nugent, George Frederick...............43
Nugent, Ignatius..............................488
Nugent, James..93, 99, 164, 188, 189, 191, 203, 205, 215-218, 220, 234-236, 240, 243-245, 250, 251, 259-263
Nugent, James (Clonlost)................98
Nugent, John..................................132
Nugent, John (Clontiduffy)............169
Nugent, John (Coolamber)...............63
Nugent, Lavallin....................128, 252
Nugent, Luke...................................67
Nugent, Mary Anne.....504, 505, 508-510
Nugent, Michael...111, 113, 221, 263, 299, 300, 302
Nugent, Moll.........................326, 327
Nugent, Oliver.....176, 183, 184, 188, 190, 197, 200-203, 218, 219, 248, 262, 264
Nugent, Pierce (father)....................67
Nugent, Pierce (son).......................67
Nugent, Richard...128, 136, 176, 183, 188, 202, 246, 248, 262, 263, 265, 351
Nugent, Ridgely.....................100, 101
Nugent, Robert........59, 104, 136, 169, 173, 245, 469, 504, 505
Nugent, Robert (Farrenconnell)....137
Nugent, Robert (son of Viscount Clare)...504
Nugent, Sabina (Elizabeth)..334, 351, 354
Nugent, St George Mervyn...........177
Nugent, Thomas (Count of Valdesotto).............................115, 503
Nugent, Thomas Herbert.................67

Nugent, Walter.......63, 113, 136, 166, 235, 250, 263
Nugent, William...189, 204, 208, 245, 334, 546

O

Ó Raghallaigh, Eóghan.................333
O'Brien, Denis..............................170
O'Brien, John..................................67
O'Carolan, Turlough......................460
O'Conor Don, The 433, 434, 436, 439, 442-445
O'Reilly, Edmond..........................350
O'Reilly, Edward...................329, 330
O'Reilly, Henrietta...65, 66, 177, 364, 365
O'Reilly, John.......9, 10, 106, 245, 268
O'Reilly, Myles McEdmond ('the Slasher')........198, 201, 208, 209, 252, 254-257, 313
Offaly...22, 31, 66, 67, 79, 80, 82, 83, 190, 246, 247, 254
Oldcastle (Co. Meath).......2, 106, 135, 197, 202, 226, 232, 234, 235, 241-243, 264
Ordnance Survey (Irish maps). 21, 24, 28, 59, 72, 75, 78, 79, 81, 188, 267, 271, 406, 407, 422, 423, 425, 426, 434, 443, 444, 448
Osborne, William..........................150

P

Pakenham, Edward Michael.........140
Palatines (German).......................150
Pallas (Co. Galway).......................61
Palles, Christopher (Chief Baron). 107
Palles, Ignatius......................107, 111
Palles, Mr......................................103
Paris (France).......132, 312, 323, 329, 330, 432
Parsons, John..................................58
Parvin, John.............................98, 99
Parvin, William..............................98
Patrickstown (Co. Meath).............333
Pells, Clerk of the.........................107
Penal Laws.......3, 6, 42, 93, 106, 108, 110, 111, 116, 117, 119, 121, 124-

126, 128-132, 134-137, 191, 195, 219, 223, 236, 237, 298, 303, 312, 315, 322, 324, 328, 458, 461
Penn, William..................................59
Peppercorn......................69, 139, 234
Phillips, Fabian...............................52
Pitt, Rowland................................486
Ploughland (land unit)........25, 28, 30
Plunkett, Alexander.......................301
Plunkett, Annie.............................460
Plunkett, Emilia............................136
Plunkett, George...........................105
Plymouth (England)......................474
Poll (land unit)................................26
Poole, Richard..............................125
Poor Law Union..............................23
Portaferry (Co. Down)..134, 249, 316
Portloman (Co. Westmeath)..........113
Pottle (land unit)...........26, 27, 36, 37
Potts, James....................................58
Power, Francis................................65
Prentinstown (Co. Westmeath).......60
Prices (in Ireland in the 18th century) 164
Probate Office..............................451

Q
Quakers...492
Quit Rent....................39, 73, 86, 221

R
Rabbits (rights to hunt for).....61, 146, 155
Radford, Newton...................296-302
Rashane (Co. Westmeath)....296, 299, 300
Rathaspick (Co. Westmeath)...22, 125
Reaghan (Co. Galway).....................69
Red Lyon (house in Trim, Co. Meath) 165
Reddan, Nick....................................5
Reeves, Dr William (Bishop of Down and Connor).........................27, 28, 38
Register of Saisines..........................6
Registry of Deeds Act...............3, 275
Reilly, Bryan........................105, 106
Reilly, Hugh..........113, 114, 169, 170

Reilly, Michael......106, 240, 242, 243
Reilly, Miles..........................105, 125
Reilly, Thomas......................105, 176
Remainder......................................41
Reul (Irish for 'real', a coin)............34
Robinson, William..........................57
Robinstown (Co. Westmeath)......125, 128, 136
Roscommon. 57, 79, 80, 83, 145, 148, 183, 233, 329, 332
Ross Castle (Co. Meath)......209, 333, 335
Rowley, Hercules Langford..........140
Russagh (Co. Westmeath).........24, 61
Rutledge, Andrew...........................58
Ryan, Pat..57

S
Safety Lamp.................................430
Santa Cruz (island in Caribbean). 501, 502
Savage, Andrew............................134
Scally, Edmund.............................103
Scire facias....................................47
Scotland.194, 195, 197, 310, 311, 452
Scully, Vincent..............................361
Seale, Thomas................................60
Seals....................14-16, 45, 261, 297
Seanachie.....................................334
Sebastopol (Crimea).....................179
Sessiagh (land unit).......25, 29, 30, 37
Sheelin, Lough (Co. Cavan) 220, 244, 256, 264, 333-335, 337, 341, 348-350, 352
Sheereny, Bryan.............................64
Sheridan, John................................57
Ship raising invention...................431
Signatures............14-16, 45, 370, 419
Singleton, Henry.............................65
Sligo.....................79, 83, 96, 145, 156
Smith, Constant...........................166
Smith, John...56, 58, 68, 84, 139, 300
Smith, Michael.............................166
Smith, William.............................101
Smyth, John..................297, 301, 302
Snells, Hannah.............................326
Sobraon (Battle of, India)............177

534

Sonnagh (Co. Westmeath)............136
Sponging House...........................496
Sproule, William..............................58
Stapleton, Bryan...................299, 300
Statutes Staple.........40, 290, 299, 300
Stepney, George............................324
Stuart, James (II).............................74
Summerhill (Co. Meath)................140
Surrey (England).............................19
Sweeney, Edward............................69
Sweeney, John.................................57
Sweeney, Judith..............................96
Swift, Godwin.................................44
Swift, Jonathan..........................34, 59
Swiney, Dugal...............................124

T

Taafe, Stephen..............................110
Taltarum's Case.........................48-50
Tarbert (Co. Kerry).......................149
Tate (land unit).........25, 27-29, 35, 36
Taylor and Skinner's maps..............78
Taylor, Thomas.............................321
Television (invention of)...............433
The Times (newspaper).................312
Thomas Street (Dublin)........316, 319
Thomas, Edwin................................58
Thompson, Joseph.................301, 302
Three lives lease......11, 39, 46, 85, 90, 98, 100, 139, 238
Tighe, James...................................57
Tihilly (Co. Offaly).........................67
Times newspaper..................132, 312
Tipperary 31, 67, 80, 82, 83, 142, 144, 234
Tithe Applotment Books.................75
Tithes...27, 38, 75, 142, 144, 159, 353
Title deeds..7, 11, 106, 110, 355, 395, 424, 452
Tonagh (Co. Cavan).......................334
Tone, Wolfe.....................................59
Tonemegeragh (Co. Cavan)...........125
Torrens, Sir Robert...8, 357, 361, 365, 423, 446, 453
Toties quoties (type of lease)..........40
Townlands.......................................21
Train inventions............................429

Transcript Books (containing copies of memorials)...12-16, 54, 55, 78, 406
Trevor, Arthur Hill........................128
Trim (Co. Meath)..........................165
Tuite, James..................................220
Tuite, Nicholas................................59
Tullyboy (Co. Cavan)............104, 105
Tullygraham (Co. Monaghan).......113
Tullystown (Co. Westmeath) 107, 220
Turbary rights (turf)........................60
Turin (Co. Westmeath).....63, 71, 125, 192
Twiss, Richard.....................33-35, 38
Tyrellspass (Co. Westmeath).........141
Tyrone......27, 30, 74, 79, 82, 83, 212, 213

U

Ulster Plantation........26, 74, 187, 267

V

Vanguard (ship)............................430
Vicars, William.............................137
Voltaire.................................316, 317
Voting Register...............................88

W

Walker, James.......................100, 101
Walker, Robert..........................37, 57
Walsh, Patrick.................................57
Walshestown (Co. Westmeath).....125
Walter, James..................................57
Warder Newspaper........................353
Warren, Peter.................................474
Waterford.......31, 61, 79, 81, 82, 148, 152-155, 261, 431
Waterlow, Sydney.........................433
Westmeath....5, 24, 26, 27, 30, 38, 43, 51, 52, 59, 60, 63, 64, 66, 73, 77, 79, 80, 82, 83, 98, 103, 113, 125-128, 132, 136, 137, 165, 166, 173-175, 178, 184, 186, 188, 190, 191, 201-204, 208, 212-216, 219, 220, 230, 232-238, 245, 248-250, 252, 254, 259, 262-264, 268, 296, 297, 299, 312, 316, 323, 324, 326, 333, 334, 350, 351, 353, 457, 461, 463, 469-471, 503

Wexford..........................31, 79, 82, 83
Whelan, Kevin.................94, 113, 136
Whiteboys..............................142, 159
Wicklow. 30, 78, 80, 82, 83, 236, 263, 313, 430
Wild Geese.....34, 128, 130, 190, 193, 459
Wild, Charles................................137
Wilkinson, Berdoe A......................407
Williams, Joshua...........................443

Wills...66
Windmill..69
Witherell, Henry....................100, 101
Woolen drapers................................69

Y

Yorkshire (England). 6, 8, 18, 19, 124, 156, 355
Young, Arthur................126, 140, 172
Young, Revd Edward....................459
Young, Sir William........................353

If you liked this book you might like to read some of the author's other works, including:

Shakespeare was Irish!
As more and more scholars come to realise that the accepted story of William Shakespeare is untenable, this book tries to unmask the covert Irish influence on his work and the remarkable career of William Nugent, the only Irish candidate ever put forward for Shakespeare. It includes the full text of many original documents on Irish history, from the Reformation to the 1641 Rebellion.
978-0-9556812-1-9

An Creideaṁ
This book seeks to illustrate the type of literature that shaped and influenced the Irish people's faith over the centuries. It is intended as a cornucopia of Catholic writing, a skirl around the kind of books and journals that graced Irish priest's libraries over the years. Outlined in chronological order it gives the full text of the Confession of St. Patrick, the Life of St. Columbanus, an ancient Irish tract on the mass; extracts from the Confessions of St. Augustine, the Irish Annals, and the fiction of Canon Sheehan; some theology from St. Thomas Aquinas, from 'A Handbook of Moral Theology', and the doctrine of Purgatory from an old Maynooth theologian; historical or contemporary accounts from all centuries, all the way from Tertullian, through Lough Derg in the 15th century, the Cromwellian Wars of the 17th century, to the social and economic teachings of the Church in the 19th and early 20th centuries.
978-0-9556812-3-3

Slí na Fírinne
This English language book puts the traditional Catholic proofs of God's existence into a modern context. It covers most of the arguments raging in the theism v atheism debate and also includes quotes on the nature of God and his existence from c.80 philosophers and scientists.
978-0-9556812-8-8

The Irish Invented Chess!
For over three centuries a controversy has raged as to the exact origins of 'fidchell' – in modern Irish 'ficheall' – or Irish chess, a game played in Ireland from biblical times. This book argues that that game of fidchell, or brannaimh, was recognisably our modern chess. It also raises disturbing questions about the real history surrounding the Lewis Chess find.
978-0-9556812-6-4

www.ingramcontent.com/pod-product-compliance
Lightning Source LLC
Chambersburg PA
CBHW021752230426
43669CB00006B/53